THE ESSENTIAL HBO READER

ESSENTIAL READERS IN CONTEMPORARY MEDIA AND CULTURE

This series is designed to collect and publish the best scholarly writing on various aspects of television, film, the Internet, and other media of today. Along with providing original insights and explorations of critical themes, the series is intended to provide readers with the best available resources for an in-depth understanding of the fundamental issues in contemporary media and cultural studies. Topics in the series may include, but are not limited to, critical-cultural examinations of creators, content, institutions, and audiences associated with the media industry. Written in a clear and accessible style, books in the series include both single-author works and edited collections.

SERIES EDITOR

Gary R. Edgerton, Old Dominion University

THE ESSENTIAL

HBO®

READER

Edited by
Gary R. Edgerton
and Jeffrey P. Jones

THE UNIVERSITY PRESS OF KENTUCKY

Publication of this volume was made possible in part by
a grant from the National Endowment for the Humanities.

The University Press of Kentucky

Scholarly publisher for the Commonwealth,
serving Bellarmine University, Berea College, Centre
College of Kentucky, Eastern Kentucky University,
The Filson Historical Society, Georgetown College,
Kentucky Historical Society, Kentucky State University,
Morehead State University, Murray State University,
Northern Kentucky University, Transylvania University,
University of Kentucky, University of Louisville,
and Western Kentucky University.
All rights reserved.

Editorial and Sales Offices: The University Press of Kentucky
663 South Limestone Street, Lexington, Kentucky 40508–4008
www.kentuckypress.com

12 11 10 09 08   5 4 3 2 1

Library of Congress Cataloging-in-Publication Data
The essential HBO reader / edited by Gary R. Edgerton and Jeffrey P.
Jones.
     p. cm. — (Essential television reader series)
  Includes bibliographical references and index.
  ISBN 978-0-8131-2452-0 (hardcover : alk. paper)
  1. Home Box Office (Firm) I. Edgerton, Gary R. (Gary Richard), 1952-
II. Jones, Jeffrey P., 1963-
  PN1992.92.H66E87 2008
  384.55'523—dc22
                                        2007037996

This book is printed on acid-free recycled paper meeting
the requirements of the American National Standard
for Permanence in Paper for Printed Library Materials.

Manufactured in the United States of America.

Member of the Association of
American University Presses

CONTENTS

ACKNOWLEDGMENTS

This book is the first in the University Press of Kentucky's Essential Readers in Contemporary Media and Culture series, which is designed to examine and analyze contemporary subjects in television, film, and popular culture. The main purpose of this series is to provide an in-depth, scholarly overview of each topic, along with explorations of critical themes.

The idea for this book was conceived on a plane ride between Norfolk and San Diego that I (GE) shared with my oldest daughter, Katherine, in March 2005. We were talking and joking about a variety of things when she observed that someone really should do a book on HBO. I immediately fell in love with her suggestion, and I have never looked back. Kate has also contributed to this project as a research assistant and in digitizing a number of the images that appear. Needless to say, we've enjoyed innumerable hours together watching and discussing HBO programming, along with my wife, Nan, and younger daughter, Mary Ellen.

Jeff Jones, too, has been involved as my partner on this project from almost the beginning. Together, we designed the format and organizational scheme and recruited the various contributors, co-editing the chapters as they came in. We owe an enormous debt of gratitude to the other authors who contributed their work to this collection. Each one added an indispensable dimension from his or her own special perspective. Jeff and I learned a great deal from all of our colleagues on this project, and we fully enjoyed working with each and every one of them. Most of all, though, I'd like to thank Jeff for making the collaborative process of completing this book a pleasure from start to finish.

Neither this book nor this series would ever have seen the light of day without the unflagging encouragement and enthusiasm of Leila Salisbury. She first sparked my interest in developing the series by sending me a copy of *The Essential Agrarian Reader,* a 2003 publication from the University Press of Kentucky, and suggesting that the kind of approach taken in this collection might work with a wide assortment of media and culture subjects. I agreed immediately and let that initial prompt percolate in the back of my mind for a while until everything took shape with this HBO project. This is the third book that I've done with Leila, and as always, working with her has been a delightful and rewarding experience. I also want to thank her assistant Will McKay, production manager Richard Farkas, publicity manager Mack McCormick, and the rest of their always helpful colleagues at the University Press of Kentucky who helped Jeff and me see this book from proposal to publication. Thanks too to Dean Chandra de Silva of the College of Arts and Letters at Old Dominion University for his generous support in funding the index, and to Dr. Marty Norden for creating a superb one. Finally, I express my deepest thanks and appreciation to my family and friends for their continuing love and support.

G.E.

I (JJ) wish to thank Horace Newcomb, to whom I dedicate this book, for insisting that once I had a bona fide job after leaving graduate school, it was my duty as a television studies scholar to subscribe to HBO. The narratives I found there (fiction and nonfiction) have led me to believe that television is not just America's "most popular art," but also one of America's most important and provocative art forms at this moment in time. I also wish to thank my wife, Shana, for the thought-provoking and enjoyable discussions that always accompany our watching HBO together. Although she declared war on the network for canceling *Deadwood,* the network redeemed itself in our household by offering *The Wire* as a substitute. Producers and writers David Simon and Ed Burns deserve thanks for bringing the tragedy that is Baltimore to the attention of the American public. Having lived in Baltimore, I am embarrassed and ashamed that our nation finds such poverty, injustice, and the breakdown of civil society acceptable, especially four decades after the publication of Michael Harrington's *The Other America.* But I appreciate daring writers and programming executives who are willing to produce what amounts to real-life stories and make them both compelling and heartbreaking.

I also wish to thank the newest addition to my family—Andrew Campbell Jones—for reminding me of the unbridled joy life can be and of the human need for uproarious bouts of belly laughter. Finally, I am indebted to my friend and mentor Gary Edgerton for including me in this project, for his continual support, guidance, and patience, and for his winning spirit and always pleasant disposition. Working hard is so much more enjoyable when people like Gary are along for the ride.

J.J.

INTRODUCTION

A Brief History of HBO

Gary R. Edgerton

The founding of Home Box Office Inc. (HBO) was a harbinger of something new and innovative that was happening to television as an industry and a technology during the early to mid-1970s. Cable entrepreneur Charles Dolan first conceived of the network in 1971 as the Green Channel. He was the owner of Sterling Communications, a growing cable concern in the New York metropolitan area that was largely subsidized by Time Inc. Dolan began work on the Green Channel with seed money from Time, hiring the thirty-three-year-old Wall Street lawyer Gerald Levin as part of his start-up team. Dolan and his associates renamed their channel Home Box Office, reflecting their theaterlike conception of a subscription television (STV) service that would primarily offer first-run movies and sporting events to its paying customers. HBO was based on an entirely different economic model than the one followed by the three major broadcast networks (CBS, NBC, and ABC), their affiliates, and the country's independent stations, which all sold specific audiences (most recently targeting young urban professional viewers above all others) to sponsors. Unlike this advertiser-supported system, HBO's subscriber format focused all of the channel's attention on pleasing and retaining its viewing audience. HBO and the other forty-five aspiring local and regional pay cable channels then trying to survive in America's media marketplace were shifting the center of gravity in this sector of the television industry away from advertisers and more toward serving the needs and desires of their monthly customers.[1]

The Federal Communications Commission (FCC), ABC (as the one-time perennial third network), local television stations, and especially movie theater owners long resisted STV. Much of this opposition subsided once the FCC "adopted a 'hands off' approach" with its "1968 *Fourth Report and Order* that opened the door to the creation of permanent subscription TV services."[2] The biggest concern of these recently created STV companies was simply providing programming that was attractive enough for viewers to sign up, pay a monthly fee, and stay connected to the service on a long-term basis. For its part, HBO debuted on November 8, 1972, telecasting *Sometimes a Great Notion* (1971), starring Paul Newman, and a National Hockey League game to a mere 365 cable-subscriber households in Wilkes-Barre, Pennsylvania. Three months and $1 million in losses later, Time Inc. fired Dolan and instated Gerald Levin as the new president of HBO. Levin kept HBO afloat for two more years before betting the network's future on signing a six-year, $7.5 million contract that allowed the channel access to RCA's newly launched communication satellite, Satcom 1, during the fall of 1975. On October 1, 1975, HBO inaugurated its satellite-cable service with the much-ballyhooed "Thrilla in Manila" heavyweight boxing match between Muhammad Ali and Joe Frazier. This brutal fourteen-round bout, won by Ali, was a hugely popular success for all concerned, especially the struggling three-year-old pay-TV company that carried the fight live from overseas. In one fell swoop, HBO became a national network, ushering in television's cable era (1976–94) with its first full year of regularly scheduled satellite-delivered programming.

Like America itself, television has always existed in a state of transformation, being continually reshaped and occasionally reinvented by a wide assortment of technological, commercial, and social factors. TV in the United States grew from a local to a regional medium during the 1940s and 1950s, finally becoming the centerpiece of national culture at the start of the 1960s. The three-network oligopoly that ruled the television industry in the United States during the network era (1948–75) was slowly withering away by the 1980s, as were the annual $100 million-plus profit margins that the top-down mass-market structure regularly provided for CBS, NBC, and ABC. These broadcast networks had achieved a kind of parity following ABC's rise to number one in the ratings during the mid- to late 1970s. Together, they survived the profound technological and economic conversion that remodeled TV into a multi-network niche-market industry after 1976. Along with this structural changeover, however, the three major networks started to lose

HBO inaugurated its satellite-cable service on October 1, 1975, with the much-ballyhooed "Thrilla in Manila" heavyweight boxing match between Muhammad Ali (right) and Joe Frazier (left).

"their near total dominance of the television market," as well as much of "their swagger, their corporate identities and perhaps also their hallowed traditions."[3] An estimated 70.5 million households, or 96.4 percent of the nation, owned TV sets in 1976; by 1994, these figures had grown to 94.2 million, or 98.3 percent of all residences (five percentage points higher than the number of American homes that had telephones).[4] More significantly, the typical TV household in the United States received on average only 7.2 channels in 1970; this climbed slightly to 10.2 in 1980, before rising dramatically to 27.2 in 1990.[5]

An increasing number of viewing options was an essential part of television's second age during the cable era, as the three-network bottleneck was broken beyond repair with the rise of cable and satellite TV. Although the first TV satellite, Telstar 1, was launched in July 1962, American television never fully realized its international promise until satellites and cable once again reinvented the medium after 1975. In the case of HBO, subscriptions grew rapidly from 15,000 to 287,199 in

3

1976 alone. By the end of 1977, HBO had 600,000 customers, enabling this pay-TV network to turn a profit for the first time. "HBO quickly became an incredible cash cow," reports George Mair in *Inside HBO*, "eventually outstripping" in profitability "the all-important magazine division" at Time Inc.[6] As a result, other basic and premium cable networks followed HBO's example of choosing satellite over terrestrial microwave delivery. Ted Turner took WTBS national via Satcom 1 in December 1976, while the Chicago-based Tribune Company similarly converted WGN into a superstation in October 1978. Another movie channel, Showtime, was created by Viacom in July 1976 and began satellite transmission in 1978. Niche channels of all sorts emerged during the late 1970s and early 1980s, including CBN (the Christian Broadcasting Network) and the USA Network (a broad-based entertainment channel) in 1977; ESPN (Entertainment and Sports Programming Network), Nickelodeon (children's programming), and C-SPAN (Cable-Satellite Public Affairs Network) in 1979; CNN (Cable News Network), BET (Black Entertainment Television), and TLC (The Learning Channel) in 1980; MTV (Music Television) and FNN (Financial News Network) in 1981; and CNN Headline News and The Weather Channel in 1982.

"In stimulating the creation of a wide variety of new satellite networks," HBO became, according to Les Brown, "the engine that was pulling cable."[7] The network's own subscriber base skyrocketed to 13 million by 1983; cable adoption throughout the United States spread from 15.3 percent of all TV households in 1976 to 21.7 percent in 1980 to 39.3 percent in 1983.[8] The addition of satellites was transforming the cable business beyond recognition. As early as 1948, community antenna television (CATV), or cable TV, was merely the means by which television signals were brought into hard-to-reach rural and mountainous regions. By the mid-1960s, the number of CATV systems had grown to more than 750 in nearly 40 states, so the FCC started regulating cable, for the most part to ensure that all local stations were being carried in their respective markets and were not being duplicated by any imported signals. In 1972, the FCC also lifted its restrictions on allowing CATV service into the nation's major metropolitan areas. Cable was no longer just the last resort for bringing television into the most out-of-the-way places in the country; instead, it had evolved into a fee-based TV alter-

Gerald Levin's plan for HBO to combine cable with satellite delivery was the final innovation needed to usher in the cable era. As a result, *Channels* magazine dubbed Levin "the man who started the revolution" in 1976.

native that offered urban, suburban, and rural viewers many more channels than ever before with much better reception. Gerald Levin's plan for HBO to combine cable with satellite delivery was the final innovation needed to usher in the cable era. A second television age was officially under way by 1976, when *Channels* magazine dubbed Levin "the man who started the revolution."[9] In turn, the rise of cable and satellite TV left CBS, NBC, and ABC in a kind of freefall; they shared just 67 percent of the available prime-time audience by the end of the 1980s (down from a high of 93.6 percent in 1975), with no end in sight to their spiraling downward.[10]

During the early 1990s, the ascent of cable television and the descent of the traditional broadcast networks was an unmistakable and irreversible foregone conclusion. Cable's penetration in the United States rose from 42.8 percent in 1985 to 63.4 percent in 1994.[11] At the beginning of the 1990s, basic cable attracted 20 percent of all prime-time viewers, and premium channels such as HBO added another 6 percent.[12] Both these figures would double again over the next decade. The whole TV viewing experience was changing for most Americans. The time-shifting capability of the videocassette recorder (VCR) was a welcome addition for most television viewers in the 1980s. Only 1.1 percent of TV households in the United States had VCRs in 1980; this number climbed to 20.8 percent in 1985 and reached 79 percent by 1994.[13] Along with the VCR came remote control keypads. These small hand-held devices were first introduced in the mid-1950s, but they did not become commonplace in American homes until the widespread adoption of cable and VCRs during the 1980s. "There's no doubt that the remote control switch revolutionized the way we watched TV in the '80s," announced *TV Guide* in January 1990. By 1991, 37 percent of domestic viewers admitted that they preferred channel surfing (or quickly flipping through the 33.2 channels they now received on average) to turning on their television sets to watch just one specific program.[14] Consumers at home were slowly becoming more proactive in their TV viewing behavior; their adoption of these new television accessories aided in the industry's wholesale transition from broadcasting to narrowcasting (targeting a narrower, more defined audience), as consumers searched out what they wanted to watch as never before.

Likewise, the cable sector of the television industry was already taking steps to supplement its licensing of older off-network programs and Hollywood movies with original productions tailor-made to the individual specifications of each channel's target audience. HBO led the way in this regard by producing its first original series, *Not Necessarily the News,* and its first made-for-pay-TV movie, *The Terry Fox Story,* in 1983, followed by its first miniseries, *All the Rivers Run,* in 1984. The cable sector "eclipsed broadcasting's assets and revenue values by the late 1980s." In its "short history," cable television had already "redefined television," argues Sharon Strover. "It spawned a huge variety of 'narrowcast' programming services."[15] A niche-market model supplanted the old way of doing business throughout the American economy beginning in the mid-1970s. For television in particular, made-to-order series by a new generation of creative writer–producers replaced the two-decade-long dominance of Hollywood's cookie-cutter mode of telefilm production. The best and most-influential new programs on both the broadcast networks (such as NBC's *Hill Street Blues* [1981–87]) and cable (such as Showtime's *It's Garry Shandling's Show* [1986–90], which later was revamped as *The Larry Sanders Show* [1992–98] on HBO) defied easy classification while attracting a preponderance of young urban professional viewers. The broader economic benefits of consumer segmentation also rendered the increasingly outdated mass-market model of the network era obsolete. In turn, branding became the standard way in which networks and production companies differentiated their programming from the competition.

The executive team that directed HBO in the late 1970s—Gerald Levin, Frank Biondi, and Michael Fuchs—realized even then that restricting their activities to being merely the wholesaler or intermediary between the movie studios and the nation's growing cable companies was a dead-end arrangement for HBO. Levin decided in tandem with Biondi and Fuchs that HBO needed to situate itself squarely in the content-development, not the transmission, business. They understood that average American viewers didn't care whether they saw their movies in theaters, broadcast over the air, by cable, or, beginning in the late 1970s, on videotape. Consumers just wanted convenient entertainment at affordable prices. Being both between and a part of the television, motion picture, and home video industries, HBO was perfectly positioned to diversify into original TV and movie production, home video, and international distribution, even as these once-separate entertainment sectors were beginning to converge into one globally expanding entertainment industry by the mid-1980s. Long before the term became fashionable, HBO was a brand that became indistinguishable from the notion of subscription television during the 1970s. More specifically, HBO's original image or utility brand was linked primarily to its function of providing Hollywood motion pictures to cable viewers in the comfort of their own homes, despite the fact that it also produced and telecast occasional stand-up comedy, sports, and music specials.

The major problem with basing a company's brand loyalty on the most prominent product that it provided was that there invariably appeared competitors who were willing and able to supply the public with the same service as the original seller. Viacom's Showtime was created soon after HBO in 1976 and began satellite transmission in 1978; Warner Amex launched The Movie Channel in 1979; Time/HBO countered by creating Cinemax in 1980; and Times-Mirror began Spotlight in 1981. That same year, moreover, the Justice Department prevented Twentieth Century-Fox, Universal, Paramount, Columbia, and Getty Oil from producing their own pay movie channel, Premiere, on the ground that it was monopolistic. HBO asserted its dominance as the channel that viewers most associated with movies; but by the 1990s, it also greatly expanded its output of original series, miniseries, made-for-pay-TV movies, documentaries, stand-up comedy, and sports in order to compete. When former HBO chairman and CEO Chris Albrecht was first promoted to programming chief in 1995, he called his executive staff together for a two-day meeting with the blessing of his boss, Jeffrey Bewkes, and asked them, "Do we really believe that we are who we say we are? This distinctive, high-quality, edgy, worth-paying-for service?" Albrecht remembered that the silence in the room was deafening. The executive team at HBO, headed by Bewkes, then began the slow and deliberate process of building "an outstanding one-of-a-kind programming service," because being an "occasional use" cable channel was "no longer sustainable" in the survival-of-the-fittest world that was then materializing with the emergence of digital television and the widespread adoption of the Internet.[16]

The pivotal innovation that shifted consumer interest beyond cable TV into the wondrous new world of cyberspace was the introduction of the first commercially available graphical browser, Netscape Navigator 1.0, on December 15, 1994, which made web travel relatively easy for the vast majority of Americans outside of the exclusive domain of computer scientists and other high-tech specialists. HBO transformed the creative landscape of television during the first decade (1995–2004) of TV's current digital era. It pursued the unusual and atypical strategy for television of investing more money in program development (from $2 million to $4 million per prime-time hour), limiting output (thirteen episodes per series each year instead of the usual twenty-two to twenty-six), and producing only the highest-quality series, miniseries, made-for-pay-TV movies, documentaries, and specials that it could. Along with a handful of other channels, such as MTV, ESPN, CNN, and Fox News, HBO established as strong an identity brand as there was on television. This spilled over into its overseas expansion (beginning with Latin America, Europe, and Asia), its DVD sales, its theatrical releases, its syndication of its own series on other channels (starting with *The Larry Sanders Show* on Bravo in 2002 and *Sex and the City* on TBS in 2004), and its production of original programs for other networks (such as *Everybody Loves Raymond* for CBS between 1996 and 2005). In

1997, Time Warner's then-chairman Gerald Levin remembered, "Twenty-five years ago, HBO invented a new form of television." Reflecting on the current state of the entertainment industry, he added, "HBO, the brand, is so powerful and HBO, the concept, is so dynamic that it's entering the digital future with the creative edge qualitatively superior to our competition."[17]

In this way, HBO is also an idea or identity brand. Ever since 1996, the network has been marketed with the tag line, "It's Not TV, It's HBO." What this branding slogan implies is that the series and specials produced by and presented on HBO are a qualitative cut above your usual run-of-the-mill television programming. By the late 1990s, HBO had emerged as the TV equivalent of a designer label. When Michael Fuchs assumed the top job at the network in 1985, his dual emphases were to increase the amount of HBO's original programming and to establish a growing presence for the network overseas. To his credit, he succeeded on both counts. Levin, Biondi, and Fuchs hired Sheila Nevins in 1979 to develop the network's documentary unit. She gradually built up the division and began executive producing a series of brash and gritty reality-based programs throughout the mid- to late 1980s, including the network's first Oscar winner (*Down and Out in America*) in 1986 and first Emmy winner (*Dear America: Letters Home from Vietnam*) in 1987, under the auspices of HBO's ongoing signature nonfiction series, *America Undercover,* which debuted in 1983. Michael Fuchs also enjoyed a good working relationship with his talented finance vice president and manager, Jeffrey Bewkes, and together they brought Chris Albrecht to HBO in 1985. Albrecht immediately proved his value to the network by producing the first *Comic Relief* special the next year. Fuchs supported a significant increase in made-for-pay-TV movie productions under the banner of HBO Films, as well as Robert Altman and Garry Trudeau's campaign mockumentary *Tanner '88* (1988), a miniseries that won wide acclaim and another Emmy for the network.

Michael Fuchs additionally invested heavily in more original comedy programs, including a wide array of cutting-edge stand-up specials through HBO Downtown Productions and a handful of 30-minute series such as the one-of-a-kind talk show parody *The Larry Sanders Show,* which debuted in 1992 and lasted six years, eventually winning a prestigious Peabody Award. Of note, Fuchs made a concerted effort to enhance HBO's brand awareness by launching the company's first-ever national image advertising campaign, "Simply the Best," in 1989. This initiative started the lengthy and expensive process of changing the overall impression of HBO from that of a first-run movie service to that of a premium network that produces and presents the most innovative original programming on television along with its usual lineup of feature films. As media technologies converged in the 1980s and 1990s, HBO expanded its repertoire to take full advantage of this transformation. HBO was the first pay cable channel to scramble its signal to combat piracy, in 1986; to offer its service on direct broadcast satellite, in 1994; and to adopt digital compression transmission, enabling it to "multiplex" (split its signal into two or more channels, thus expanding its service), in 1994. In 1998, HBO developed multiplexing further by creating the megabrand HBO the Works, a collection of channels that includes HBO2, HBO Signature, HBO Family, HBO Comedy and HBO Zone (added in 1999), and HBO Latino (added in 2000); and the network introduced the video-on-demand service HBO on Demand in 2001. With HBO's array of technological and programming innovations growing, Jeffrey Bewkes enlisted his executive vice president for marketing, Eric Kessler, to create an identity brand to complement the network's renewed focus.

HBO thus set out to intensify its connection with its subscriber base like never before. Bewkes allocated "$25 million a year just to advertise the HBO brand," and Kessler and his team kicked off a new ad campaign on October 20, 1996, which was the beginning of "one of TV's all-time great tag lines—It's Not TV, It's HBO."[18] Five years later, HBO had become the hottest destination on television. From 1996 to 2001, it increased its original programming from 25 to 40 percent of its entire schedule.[19] In that way, the branding line "It's Not TV, It's HBO" marked a transitional moment in the industry, when cable and satellite channels rather than the traditional broadcast networks became the first place to look for breakout programming. HBO had already established Sunday night as its own must-see-TV evening of viewing with such innovative original series as *Sex and the City* in 1998 and *The Sopranos* in 1999. Those two series were simply the tip of an iceberg that in hindsight included such dramatic series as *Oz* (1997–2003), *Six Feet Under* (2001–5), *The Wire* (2002–), and *Deadwood* (2004–);

made-for-pay-TV movies such as *And the Band Played On* (1993), *Gia* (1998), and *Lackawanna Blues* (2005); miniseries such as *From the Earth to the Moon* (1998), *Band of Brothers* (2001), and *Angels in America* (2003); comedies such as *Curb Your Enthusiasm* (2000–) and *Real Time with Bill Maher* (2003–); sports shows such as *Real Sports with Bryant Gumbel* (1995–) and *On the Record with Bob Costas* (2001–); six Oscar-winning documentaries between 1999 and 2004 alone; and theatrical releases such as *Spellbound* (2002), *American Splendor* (2003), and *Maria Full of Grace* (2004), which eventually were telecast on HBO after their initial runs in movie theaters.

HBO epitomized "appointment TV" (programming that viewers build into their daily schedules) for its 28.2 million subscriber households in the first quarter of 2006 (a figure that marked a slow but steady 2.6 percent increase in two years).[20] During the first decade of TV's digital era, American audiences were watching more television than ever before. According to Nielsen Media Research, the typical TV household in the United States had its set turned on for 7 hours and 15 minutes a day in 1995; for 7 hours and 26 minutes a day in 2000; and for a whopping 8 hours and 11 minutes a day by 2005.[21] Moreover, the average number of available channels shot up from 43.0 in 1997 to 96.4 in 2005. Of these, individual viewers spent the vast majority of their time watching just 10.3 networks of choice in 1997, increasing this total to 16.3 in 2005.[22] HBO was one of those networks of choice for more than 26 percent of the 110.2 million TV households in the United States. HBO subscribers were also more than just viewers; they were paying customers who shelled out approximately $15 a month to obtain the service. No longer were they settling for the least objectionable programming they could find: they were looking for something different, challenging, and more original on HBO, particularly since they were paying a monthly fee just to tune in. Most importantly, HBO posted nearly $1.1 billion in profits during both 2004 and 2005 for its parent conglomerate, Time Warner—up from its previous record-setting marks of $725 million in 2002 and $960 million in 2003.[23] These were the highest annual yields earned by any network in the history of television.

In addition, HBO's dramatic influence became evident on other cable and broadcast networks with the debuts of such series as FX's *The Shield* in 2002, *Nip/Tuck* in 2003, and *Rescue Me* in 2004—all nurtured by then–network chief and former HBO executive Peter Liguori—as well as Fox's *24* in 2001 and *Arrested Development* in 2003. HBO was occasionally attracting audiences comparable to the broadcast networks, even though its subscriber base was only slightly more than one-quarter of all the TV households in the United States. For instance, the most-popular programs on television in 2001–2 were NBC's *Friends*, averaging 24.5 million viewers each week; CBS's *CSI*, with 23.7 million; and NBC's *ER*, with 22.1 million. For its part, *The Sopranos* attracted 14 million people per episode that season, which gave it an audience size equivalent to a top-10-to-15 show in the broadcast universe, not just the cable and satellite sector.[24] HBO was redefining what was possible in terms of both quality innovations on the small screen and how much money could be made by pursuing alternative business models for TV. Unlike HBO, the traditional broadcast networks were still captives to their old economic formula of relying on "a single revenue stream based entirely on advertising."[25] After 1995, breakout programming was far more likely to originate in the cable and satellite sector of the industry. The fight among so many TV services not only to survive but to distinguish themselves in such an increasingly competitive environment had resulted in an unprecedented proliferation of original programming, with HBO setting the standard as the most innovative and lucrative bright spot inside the Time Warner conglomerate.

At the time, "HBO's achievements had a dramatic impact on the entire media culture; creatively it put its rivals to shame," proclaimed Peter Bart, editor of *Variety*, in 2002. This pay-television channel owed its success "to a potent mix: stable management; savvy blanket promotion of its shows; and a business model that relies on subscriptions rather than advertising."[26] Overall, "the traditional business model of television production [was] being rewritten," and the network that initially set this whole transitional process into motion with its distinctive breakthrough programming during the mid- to late 1990s was HBO.[27] For the first time in television history, the quality alternative was not CBS (as it was in the early 1970s), NBC (in the early to mid-1980s), ABC (in the late 1980s), or even PBS. "HBO is perhaps the greatest single producer of quality television drama and comedy in the English-speaking world," admitted British TV critic David Herman in 2004. "American television is on a roll," he continued, "[and] most of these programs, especially the most recent ones [*The Larry Sanders Show, Sex and the City, The Sopranos, Curb Your Enthusiasm, Six Feet Under,* and *Deadwood*], have been made by one company, Home Box Office."[28] Freed from direct ratings pressure, HBO invested its considerable cache of subscription dollars into hiring the best available talent, reaching deeply into the creative community. Its talent pool included writer-producers such as Tom Fontana (*St. Elsewhere* [NBC, 1982–88], *Homicide: Life on the Street* [NBC, 1993–99], and *Oz*), Darren Star (*Beverly Hills 90210* [Fox, 1990–2000], *Melrose Place* [Fox, 1992–99], and *Sex and the City*), David Chase (*Northern Exposure* [CBS, 1990–95], *I'll Fly Away* [NBC, 1991–3], and *The Sopranos*), Alan Ball (*Cybill* [CBS, 1995–98], *American Beauty* [1999], and *Six Feet Under*), and David Milch (*Hill Street Blues, NYPD Blue* [ABC, 1993–2005], and *Deadwood*), to name just a few.

HBO's ability to attract the entertainment industry's top creative people was unmatched by any other broadcast, cable, or pay-television network. For example, *Seinfeld*'s creator, Larry David, the producer and star of *Curb Your Enthusiasm,* "brought the project to HBO." All told, "the network's tendency to permit creative freedom made it a magnet for experienced producers, directors and writers looking for an outlet for projects to which they [were] deeply committed."[29] By the mid-2000s, HBO engendered a certain backlash from its competitors and some television critics for not being able to produce more breakout hits fast enough, but the aftereffects of the network's shows were clearly evident in the programming and branding strategies of not only FX and Fox, but also Showtime (with *Weeds* [2005–], to mention just one), the USA Network (with *Monk* [2002–]), TNT (with *The Closer* [2005–]), and even ABC. When Marc Cherry created ABC's *Desperate Housewives* (2004–), for instance, "he decided to 'write an HBO show'— something like the ones [he] himself loved, maybe 'a *Sex and the City* meets *Six Feet Under.*'"[30] *Desperate Housewives* at its best was the kind of custom-tailored program that defied easy categorization. Audiences at first weren't sure whether it was a darkly dramatic sitcom or a hip, ironic soap opera. From a business point of view, *Desperate Housewives* was more edgy and idiosyncratic than the standard-grade product that usually succeeded in the advertiser-supported environment of the broadcast sector. The series became an immediate buzz-worthy hit for

ABC during the fall of 2004, which both elevated the profile of the network and prepared the general public for the program's eventual release across a variety of subsequent platforms, including syndication, DVD, and the fast-growing on-demand window.

"The mass digital conversion of the past ten years" placed consumers "at the very heart" of an increasingly personalized TV business environment.[31] According to a 2005 tracking study conducted by the Cable and Telecommunications Association for Marketing, "more than three-quarters (77%)" still tuned into programs at "their scheduled date and time."[32] A growing segment (23 percent) of the national audience, however, was already time-shifting and place-shifting, watching programs when and where they wanted to, "liberated from the constraints of the old analog world."[33] The key to thinking about television in the digital era is to reenvision it in terms of screens (of all shapes and sizes) rather than merely households, which no longer offer a complete and accurate picture of TV penetration. At HBO, thirty minutes of originally scripted prime-time programming currently costs between $1 million and $2 million. HBO's parent, Time Warner, therefore looks "to spread the cost of programming across as wide a footprint as possible."[34] "Repurposing"—referring to the process by which TV content is adapted across as many platforms as possible (including traditional TV sets, DVD players, the Internet, MP3Video players, stand-alone and portable digital video recorders [DVRs], and even mobile phones)—has emerged as the watchword of the television industry during the 2000s. The United States is on the threshold of being converted into an "on-demand nation," where one-on-one distribution of TV programming via cable or the Internet provides yet another alternative to the advertiser-supported model. The new digital era of "on-demand entertainment" is signaling the beginning of "the end of TV" as most people knew it before 1995.[35]

As the one-time sacrosanct business model of television splinters into multiple options beyond advertiser-supported programming—including subscription services (ranging from 24-hour networks such as HBO to on-the-go broadband content providers such as HBO Mobile and HBO Family Mobile), product placement, domestic and international syndication, DVD sales, and program downloads—breakout signature shows are the most essential ingredient enabling this newly emerging multidimensional personal-usage market structure to flourish.[36] Viewers are not going to pay to download mediocre, run-of-the-mill programs. Hit series such as *Sex and the City, The Sopranos,* and *Six Feet Under,* however, help to brand networks such as HBO, generate word of mouth, and ultimately create multiple revenue streams. Broadcast, cable, satellite, and now online networks in the digital era are content providers first and foremost, launching programs and thus priming the public to watch them in their initial runs. Afterwards, consumers pay directly for these shows as they migrate to other distribution windows within and outside the conglomerate. In fact, consolidation without content innovation has proved to be a limited business strategy in the digital era. A case in point is the 1999 Viacom-CBS marriage that ended in a kind of divorce on January 3, 2006, despite the fact that Sumner Redstone remains the executive chairman of both conglomerates.

The promise of synergy between Viacom and CBS, with its supposed "cradle-to-grave one-stop shopping for advertisers," was never fully realized.[37] Instead, a new Viacom was created to shelter the younger, higher-growth subsidiaries (such as the MTV network division including MTV, Comedy Central, Nickelodeon, Spike TV, and VH1) and the movie studios (Paramount Pictures and DreamWorks), while the CBS Corporation maintained control over the older, slower-growing properties such as CBS-TV, UPN (now 50 percent of The CW), the Showtime Networks, CBS Radio, Simon & Schuster, and CBS Outdoor Advertising.[38] In a similar vein, the 1989 merger of Time Inc. and Warner Communication that created Time Warner, and the 2001 alliance between Time Warner and AOL, also experienced early growing pains, although both unions eventually held together (with Time Warner even dropping the "AOL" from its corporate title in early 2003, when the value of this Internet service provider plummeted $35 billion after the dot-com bubble burst during 2001–2).[39] The long-range hope for the AOL–Time Warner merger was to create "the Wal-Mart of the information age, a one-stop-shopping company," including the highly profitable boutique network HBO.[40] CBS has adopted similar aspirations for Showtime since 2004. "As Showtime continues to add high-quality programs" (such as *The L Word* [2004–], *Huff* [2004–], *Weeds, Sleeper Cell* [2005–], and *Brotherhood* [2006–]), reasoned CBS president and CEO Leslie Moonves, "there is no reason it won't become for CBS what HBO is for

"We showed what was possible to do on television," asserts former HBO chairman and CEO Chris Albrecht. "It's good for everybody when the bar gets raised."

Time Warner."[41] Showtime, FX, Fox, the USA Network, TNT, ABC, and other TV networks have subsequently upped the ante for HBO. "We showed what was possible to do on television," asserted Chris Albrecht. "I think what that did was to bring more people into the category and to spend more money on original scripted programming. It's good for everybody when the bar gets raised."[42]

After more than three and a half decades, HBO has grown from being mainly a domestic movie channel to being an international cable and satellite network with a presence in more than seventy countries, as well as a full-service content provider known for its own distinctive brand of programming.[43] HBO's widespread influence on its fellow broadcast and cable networks is widely acknowledged. In a "now famous letter" written in the summer of 2001, for example, "NBC chairman Robert Wright challenged his colleagues to consider what they might learn from HBO's extraordinary success."[44] In response, NBC produced *Kingpin*, a tepid clone of *The Sopranos* set within an international drug cartel à la *Traffic* (2000), which lasted for just six episodes as a midseason replacement in February 2003. At about the same time, the real *Sopranos* was busy "recoup[ing] the entire production costs" of its first three seasons "from DVD sales alone." So too was *Sex and the City*.[45] By 2004, HBO had earned another $350 million from the domestic sale of *Sex and the City* during its first syndication cycle to TBS and local broadcast stations.[46] In early 2006, HBO collected an additional "$190 million or a record $2.5 million an episode for *The Sopranos*" from A&E.[47] Next up was an exclusive arrangement with Bravo for *Six Feet Under,* which prompted FX to test the waters by leasing *The Shield* to Spike TV. HBO was again leading other cable and satellite channels into an area of the television business once dominated exclusively by the major broadcast networks along with a few select first-run syndicators.

From an industrial perspective, therefore, HBO is like a cat living out its nine lives, nimbly landing on its feet time and again in an atmosphere of unparalleled change. HBO still features first-run Hollywood movies and sporting events. Moreover, it originates some of its own programming; finances, coproduces, and telecasts many other independently created series and one-time shows; and syndicates most of this work worldwide as well as distributing much of it on DVD, while making its entire catalogue available day and night to its on-demand subscribers. In addition, HBO has distinguished itself over four widely different programming areas—drama, comedy, sports, and documentary. It has significantly altered the ongoing relationship between programming executives and creative staff, with executives such as Carolyn Strause (of HBO Entertainment), Colin Callender (of HBO Films), and Sheila Nevins carefully nurturing and supporting creative personnel to a degree that is unusual in the industry. Most importantly, HBO has been a change agent for nearly four decades, by jump-starting the cable era with its satellite service and by pioneering an alternative economic model for the television business. Similarly, it has been on the forefront of technological innovation since the mid-1970s, beginning with satellite distribution and eventually adding a wide assortment of digital TV advances, including multiplexing in the mid-1990s and on-demand reception in the early 2000s. Finally, the network suddenly emerged as television's gold standard for its breakout series and specials during the late 1990s and early 2000s, generating an HBO aftereffect that remains readily apparent in the signature programming choices on many other cable and broadcast networks. Above all, HBO has parlayed its position among, between, and inside the various mass media to develop into the prototypical entertainment corporation of the twenty-first century.

Notes

1. Janet Wasko, *Hollywood in the Information Age: Beyond the Silver Screen* (Austin, Tex.: University of Texas Press, 1994), 75.

2. David Gunzerath, "'Darn That Pay TV!': STV's Challenge to American Television's Dominant Economic Model," *Journal of Broadcasting and Electronic Media* 44:4 (2000): 670.

3. Les Brown, "Looking Back: Five Tumultuous Years," *Channels: '87 Field Guide to the Electronic Environment* 6:11 (December 1986): 9.

4. Christopher H. Sterling and John M. Kittross, *Stay Tuned: A History of American Broadcasting*, 3rd ed. (Mahwah, N.J.: Lawrence Erlbaum, 2002), 864–65; George Gilder, *Life after Television: The Coming Transformation of Media and American Life* (New York: W. W. Norton, 1990), 22.

5. Ed Papazian, *TV Dimensions '97* (New York: Media Dynamics, 1991), 21.

6. George Mair, *Inside HBO: The Billion Dollar War between HBO, Hollywood, and the Home Video Revolution* (New York: Dodd, Mead & Company, 1988), 26, 30–31, 53.

7. Les Brown, *Les Brown's Encyclopedia of Television*, 3rd ed. (Detroit, Mich.: Gale Research, 1992), 316.

8. Craig Leddy, "Cable TV: The Tough Get Going," *Channels of Communications: The Essential 1985 Field Guide to the Electronic Media* 4:11 (December 1984): 35.

9. Brown, *Les Brown's Encyclopedia of Television*, 316.

10. J. Max Robins, "The Four Networks: Bang the Drum Slowly," *Channels: 1990 Field Guide to the Electronic Environment* 9:11 (December 1989): 73; Leonard Sloane, "ABC on Its Way Out of the Cellar," *New York Times*, 9 November 1975, F1.

11. Sterling and Kittross, *Stay Tuned*, 871.

12. "2000 Report on Television: The First 50 Years" (New York: Nielsen Media Research, 2000), 17.

13. Sterling and Kittross, *Stay Tuned*, 866.

14. David Lachenbruch, "Television in the '90s: The Shape of Things to Come," *TV Guide*, 20 January 1990, 13.

15. Sharon Strover, "United States: Cable Television," in Horace Newcomb, ed., *Encyclopedia of Television*, vol. 3 (Chicago: Fitzroy Dearborn, 1997), 1721.

16. Bill Carter, "He Lit Up HBO. Now He Must Run It," *New York Times*, 29 December 2002, sec. 3, 1; Carla Power, "Art of the Tube; Market This: HBO

Has Put America ahead of Britain as the Leader in Quality TV, and It's Rolling in Profits to Boot," *Newsweek International,* 1 December 2004, 77.

17. Cynthia Littleton, "Net Still Growing Strong," *Variety,* 3 November 1997, 35.

18. Elizabeth Lesly Stevens, "Call It Home Buzz Office: HBO's Challenge—To Keep the High-Profile Programs Coming," *BusinessWeek,* 8 December 1997, 77; Verne Gay, "What Makes HBO Tick?" *Cable World,* 4 November 2002, 2.

19. "Jeffrey L. Bewkes: Home Box Office," *BusinessWeek,* 14 January 2002, 62.

20. R. Thomas Umstead, "HBO Looks for Missing Link," *Multichannel News,* 10 July 2006, at http://www.multichannel.com/index.asp?layout=articlePrint&articleid=CA6350486.

21. "2000 Report on Television: The First 50 Years," 14; Sterling and Kittross, *Stay Tuned,* 867; Mavis Scanlon, "2006 Industry Overview" (Washington, D.C.: National Cable & Telecommunications Association, 2006), 15.

22. Papazian, *TV Dimensions '97,* 21; "Nielsen Report: Americans Have More TV Channels, Watch Less of Them," *Media Buyer Planner,* 14 March 2006, at http://www.mediabuyerplanner.com/2006/03/14/nielsen_report_americans_have/.

23. Umstead, "HBO Looks for Missing Link"; Joe Flint, "As Critics Carp, HBO Confronts Ratings Decline," *Wall Street Journal,* 8 June 2005, B1; John Dempsey, "Billion Dollar Baby: Cable Fees, DVDs Drive HBO's Profits," *Daily Variety,* 23 December 2004, 1; Thane Peterson, "The Secrets of HBO's Success," *BusinessWeek,* 20 August 2002, at http://www.businessweek.com/bwdaily/dnflash/aug2002/nf20020820_2495.htm.

24. Polly LaBarre, "Hit Man: Chris Albrecht (Part 1)," *Fast Company,* September 2002, 90.

25. Bill Carter, *Desperate Networks* (New York: Doubleday, 2006), 1.

26. "Up the Tube," *Economist,* 11 April 2002, at http://www.economist.com/printedition/displayStory.cfm?Story_ID=1066319.

27. Jacques Steinberg, "Digital Media Brings Profits (and Tensions) to TV Studios," *New York Times,* 14 May 2006, sec. 3, 1.

28. David Herman, "Thank God for HBO," *Prospect,* November 2004, at http://www.prospect-magazine.co.uk/article_details.php?id=6510.

29. "The Way of Success: A Bent Toward Counterprogramming Informs Much of the Original Programming on HBO," *Multichannel News,* 4 November 2002, 6.

30. Carter, *Desperate Networks,* 162.

31. Peter Chernin, "Golden Oldies," *Wall Street Journal,* 9 February 2006, A12.

32. Linda Haugsted, "Making Sense of New Tech," *Multichannel News,* 15 May 2006, at http://www.multichannel.com/index.asp?layout=articlePrint&articleid=CA6334322.

33. Chernin, "Golden Oldies," A12.

34. "All in the Family: In Television, It's Best to Be Big," *Economist*, 11 April 2002, at http://www.economist.com/printedition/displayStory.cfm?Story_ID= 1066632.

35. David Kiley and Tom Lowry, "The End of TV (As You Know It)," *BusinessWeek*, 21 November 2005, 40.

36. Karen Brown, "Sharpening the Moving Picture," *Multichannel News*, 3 April 2006, at http://www.multichannel.com/index.asp?layout=articlePrint&articleid=CA6321230; Anne Becker, "HBO Goes Cellular with Cingular," *Broadcasting & Cable*, 15 December 2005, at http://www.broadcastingcable .com/article/CA6291907.html?title=Article&spacedesc=news.

37. Karl Taro Greenfeld, "A Media Giant," *Time*, 20 September 1999, 53.

38. "Viacom Completes Split into 2 Companies," *New York Times*, 2 January 2006, C2.

39. David D. Kirkpatrick and Jim Rutenberg, "AOL Reporting Further Losses; Turner Resigns," *New York Times*, 30 January 2003, A1.

40. Ken Auletta, "Leviathan: How Much Bigger Can AOL Time Warner Get?" *New Yorker*, 29 October 2001, at http://www.kenauletta.com/leviathan .html.

41. George Vernadakis, "No Time Like Showtime: Putting a Premium on Originals," *Multichannel News*, 26 June 2006, at http://www.multichannel .com/index.asp?layout=articlePrint&articleid=CA6346382.

42. Umstead, "HBO Looks for Missing Link."

43. Power, "Art of the Tube; Market This," 77.

44. Kathy Haley, "Rocking the Industry: HBO Has Redefined Excellence in TV Entertainment. What's Next?" *Multichannel News*, 4 November 2002, 3A.

45. John M. Higgins, "Angels, Emmys and DVD; Award Haul Promises to Lift HBO Miniseries' Home-Video Sales," *Broadcasting & Cable*, 27 September 2004, 12.

46. Bill Carter, "HBO Moves to Develop and Show New Situation Comedies," *New York Times*, 3 June 2004, C6.

47. Linda Moss, "Original Shows Add Fuel to Cable's Syndie Fire," *Multichannel News*, 29 May 2006, at http://www.multichannel.com/index.asp? layout=articlePrint&articleid=CA6338676.

PART ONE

DRAMA

Producing an Aristocracy of Culture in American Television

Christopher Anderson

What makes a urinal or a wine rack that is exhibited in a museum a work of art? Is it the fact that they are signed by Duchamp (recognized first and foremost as an artist) and not by a wine merchant or a plumber?
—Pierre Bourdieu

The work of art is an object which exists as such only by virtue of the (collective) belief which knows and acknowledges it as a work of art.
—Pierre Bourdieu

The Sopranos sustains its hyper-realism with an eye and ear so perfectly attuned to geographic details and cultural and social nuances that it just may be the greatest work of American popular culture of the last quarter century.
—Stephen Holden, *The New York Times*

It's Not TV

When did it become permissible to view a drama series produced for American television and think of it as a work of art? We're used to thinking of television programs as seductive attractions designed to coax viewers into the grasp of advertisers. With the rise of academic television and cultural studies, we've learned that television programs can be interpreted as cultural symptoms, expressions of profound, if often obscure, social meanings. We've seen television programs serve as the fetish object of worshipful fans, the illicit thrill of guilty-pleasure seekers, and the target of irony-wielding wiseacres. We have even watched television and felt the glow of nostalgia for lazy childhood afternoons sprawled before the TV set. There are many ways to find

In 1999, the *New York Times* hailed *The Sopranos* as possibly "the greatest work of American popular culture of the last quarter century." (Left to right) Joe Pantoliano as Ralph Cifaretto, Steve Van Zandt as Silvio Dante, James Gandolfini as Tony Soprano, and Tony Sirico as Paulie "Walnuts" Gaultiere.

value in a television program, and still more to feel indifferent or appalled, but at some point in the past decade, cultural critics, including those in the employ of the venerable *New York Times,* have grown comfortable with the notion that a television series may be judged, first and foremost, as a work of art.[1]

In some respects, we have HBO to thank for this turn of events. Since the premiere of *The Sopranos* in 1999, HBO has invited viewers to approach American television series with a peculiar sensibility—a mode of experience that sociologist Pierre Bourdieu has labeled an "aesthetic disposition."[2] In the case of HBO dramas, the aesthetic disposition brings to television the cultivated expectation that watching certain television series requires and rewards the temperament, knowledge, and protocols normally considered appropriate for encounters with museum-worthy works of art. HBO signals this shift in expectations with the slogan, "It's Not TV, It's HBO." As one business reporter has noted, "this single statement contains a critique of the entire system of American commercial television."[3] Against the profane flow of everyday television, in which the run-of-the-mill runs with the metronomic precision of commercial necessity, HBO stands alone. Safely quarantined from the distractions and interruptions of commercial television, the viewers of HBO dramas are permitted to detach themselves from typical modes of television viewing, to approach the state of disinterested contemplation idealized in Kantian aesthetics, a disposition instantly adopted by patrons in a museum gallery or a symphony concert hall, but one seldom achieved in the family room.

For those who have acquired the cultural competence needed to adopt an aesthetic disposition, it is possible to look differently upon a television series: to perceive the artistic vision of an individual creator where once one may have seen stories with no discernible author; to reflect on the meaning of form even as one feels drawn into the pleasure of a gradually unfolding narrative; to recognize the threads of cultural and historical references woven into the fabric of a story; to appreciate the subtle subversion of genre conventions and audience expectations; and, most importantly, to celebrate the transcendence of the artwork over everyday experience and more mundane forms of popular culture. Television series have provoked many responses over the years, but only recently have they invited cultural consecration as works of art.

In the past, critics have claimed artistic merit on behalf of individual television series that appeared to transcend the constraints of the medium or to make a dramatic leap forward in the development of a particular genre. At irregular intervals since at least the 1970s, one critic or another has asserted that television drama series demonstrate the narrative complexity and subtle delineation of character normally associated with the novel (in fact, this has become a tiresome critical cliché). But among intellectuals there hasn't been a consensus that television series ought to be treated as legitimate works of art, or that it would be appropriate—except as camp—to adopt an aesthetic disposition toward commercial television.

Critic Gilbert Seldes brought a fully developed aesthetic sensibility to the criticism of popular broadcast series beginning as early as the radio era, but fellow intellectuals saw bread and circuses where Seldes saw an emergent art form; he was largely without peer and, ultimately, without followers.[4] With the television landscape engraved as a vast wasteland on maps of American culture by the early 1960s, the ability to conceive of a television series as a work of art was beyond the realm of permissible thought until the 1970s, when the press began to notice iconoclastic new producers, such as Norman Lear and Larry Gelbart, and a generation of lapsed literary scholars somehow avoided the more characteristic move into film criticism and began to apply their critical acumen to television. Horace Newcomb published the groundbreaking *TV: The Most Popular Art* in 1974, and a small but steady stream of enthusiasts—professional scholars and critics in the popular press—followed in the 1980s, making artistic claims for *Hill Street Blues* (NBC, 1981–87), *St. Elsewhere* (NBC, 1982–88), *Miami Vice* (NBC, 1984–89), *thirtysomething* (ABC, 1987–91), *Cagney & Lacey* (CBS, 1982–88), or *Magnum, P.I.* (CBS, 1980–88), or any number of individual dramas.[5] Still, one should not overestimate their cultural influence; commercial television, when not an object of derision, was at best a guilty pleasure for intellectuals. Even the short-lived phenomenon of *Twin Peaks*, which attracted otherwise TV-phobic intellectuals to the television set when it debuted in 1990, failed to elevate the status of the medium in the eyes of any but those already converted.

For much of the medium's history, television was simply not an "artworld," in the sense that Pierre Bourdieu has used the term to describe a "restricted" field of cultural production in which independent participants share a set of collective beliefs and practices necessary for recognizing certain objects as works of art. Bourdieu begins his discussion of the artworld with a paradox familiar to the philosophy of art: "the question of what enables one to distinguish between works of art and simple, ordinary things." The answer, he asserts, will be found not in the characteristics of the artifact, but in the social field that creates and sustains a *belief* in the exalted value of the artwork. "The art object," he explains, "is an artifact whose foundation can only be found in an artworld, that is, in a social universe that confers upon it the status of a candidate for aesthetic appreciation."[6]

Of course, it is not possible to believe that certain artifacts are legitimate works of art unless one also believes that others are illegitimate and should be excluded from consideration. In identifying this difference—by selecting legitimate candidates for aesthetic appreciation and ignoring or dismissing the illegitimate—artists and intellectuals mark the boundaries between "high" and "low" culture and participate in ongoing "struggles for the monopoly of artistic legitimacy" within a society.[7] Bourdieu claims that cultural institutions, such as museums, galleries, and awards, supported by networks of critics, scholars, and other independent cultural intermediaries, provide the validation that transfigures artifacts, converting them into works of art. The routine practices of the artworld serve as acts of cultural consecration that create and sustain a belief in the distinctive value of art.[8]

For much of its history, television has lacked these institutions, this network of critics and independent cultural intermediaries who have sufficient cultural authority and independence from the television industry to claim convincingly that commercial television series are candidates for aesthetic appreciation. Television awards, for instance, tend not to bestow cultural prestige that is recognized beyond the industry. The Emmy Awards have never transcended their origins as a self-congratulatory exercise in industry public relations. The Peabody Awards, although independent of the broadcasting industry, are largely unknown outside the business and tend to be noticed only when someone in the industry appropriates their reputation to burnish the public image of a program or a network in a short-lived public relations campaign. Museums devoted to radio and television may resemble art museums, but they have not fostered an aesthetic disposition toward television. As Bourdieu writes, "[art] museums could bear the inscription: Entry for art lovers only. But there is clearly no need for such a sign, it all goes without saying. . . . The artistic field, by its very functioning, creates the aesthetic disposition without which it could not function."[9] Unlike art museums, which serve as quasi-sacred sites of reverence and contemplation for works of art, museums devoted to radio and television are more like P. T. Barnum's dime museum in the nineteenth century. Filled with strange and wondrous artifacts from the lost continent of history, they amaze and amuse, but rarely leave a patron with a particular reverence for the art of television. At best, the public perceives the television programs on display as historical documents rather than artworks. In this setting, programs offer a glimpse into the strange popular tastes of earlier generations or bear witness to past events. For a variety of reasons,

cultural institutions that exist to recognize and promote artistic achievement in television have not produced the collective belief required to
transform an ordinary television program into a work of art.

The aesthetic disposition toward American television—the collective
belief that television series deserve to be perceived as legitimate works of
art—is a phenomenon that has come into focus gradually over the past
decade, almost in spite of the established institutions that one might
expect to be responsible for promoting television as an art form. Instead,
several technological, industrial, and social changes have combined to
alter the experience of a television series, making possible contemplative
modes of viewing and fanatical attention to detail that contribute to the
growing belief that television series are worthy of aesthetic appreciation. As evidence, one might point to the technological enhancement of
the viewing experience offered by high-definition TV sets and digital
sound, the emergence of do-it-yourself archives made possible by the
digital video recorder and the sale of DVD box sets, and new means of
social communication permitted by the Internet and wireless technologies, which lead to new formations of knowledge and pleasure centered
on television series. Consider the heightened awareness of television's
creative process now that viewers have grown accustomed to authorial
commentary on DVDs and the various podcasts and video weblogs that
studios have made available on the Internet. Viewers of the television
series *Battlestar Galactica* (2003–) don't even have to wait for the DVD
to hear authorial commentary; they now have the ability to download
podcasts with commentary by writers and producers to accompany each
new episode aired by the Sci Fi Channel.

Of course, it isn't as though these changes have transformed the
entire medium of television, giving every program a claim to artistic
legitimacy. The rise of the HBO drama as an object of critical esteem
coincides almost perfectly with the emergence on American television of
its guilty-pleasure antithesis, the reality-based series. *Survivor* (CBS,
2000–), after all, debuted little more than a year after *The Sopranos,*
and its success in the ratings, along with that of *American Idol* (Fox,
2002–) and other unscripted series, has made reality formats the
decade's major program innovation. While HBO viewers were measur-
ing *The Sopranos* for a pedestal in the pantheon of modern culture,
millions of Americans (including more than a few *Sopranos* fans)

watched contentedly while contestants on NBC's *Fear Factor* (2001–6) munched insect larvae in a competition whose stakes and outcome have been lost to the passage of time. Such are the dialectics of television in the new century. The ability to think of one television series as a work of art exists alongside a belief that others are nothing more than noisy diversions clattering along the conveyor belt of commercial culture. Since the rise of cable TV, American television has become organized around such extreme disparities in emerging hierarchies of taste. HBO hasn't caused these changes in the landscape of American television, but it has responded by cultivating an aura of aesthetic distinction and by positioning itself at the top of these hierarchies. Such decisions make sense given the business model of a subscription cable network, which must continually prove its value to subscribers.

An Aristocracy of Culture

Popular wisdom would have us believe that there is no accounting for taste. In fact, HBO's strategies for acquiring and securing the loyalty of viewers reveal a precise accounting: it is known in the cable television business as "churn," and it is measured by the number of subscribers who disconnect from a premium service like HBO as they calculate whether its program offerings warrant the cost of each month's subscription payment. As current HBO chairman and CEO Chris Albrecht has said, "the products that the broadcast networks sell are the ones that appear on the commercials in between the shows. The product that we sell is HBO the network. You can't buy a piece of it. You have to buy it all."[10]

HBO does not report the rate of churn among its customers, but industry analysts estimate that each year 50–60 percent of HBO subscribers cancel their subscriptions with the cable operators or satellite systems that provide access to the network.[11] Some move from homes or apartments and later re-subscribe; others simply decide that the service is not worth the cost of subscription—particularly those who take advantage of promotional deals that invite consumers to subscribe initially at a discount rate. The cost of holding onto subscribers is a daunting expense in the HBO business model, trailing only the cost of programming. In the late 1990s, analysts estimated that HBO spent more than $200 million a year (10 percent of its annual revenue) in marketing and promotions aimed largely at winning back fickle former subscribers—and these costs have only grown in the current decade, as the competition for viewers has intensified.[12]

Broadcasters have always designed their programming services with an eye toward earning and rewarding viewer loyalty (the better to deliver predictable audiences to advertisers), but the direct subscription model leaves premium cable networks like HBO particularly vulnerable to the least manageable element in the economy of cultural production: the mercurial tastes of audiences. The promiscuity of the viewer in the multichannel, multiscreen video universe poses a challenge for any program service that must prove itself worthy of a subscription payment each and every month. In order to ensure HBO's continuing *economic* value for subscribers, the network must establish a unique *cultural* value among television networks.

This process has occurred in two stages that essentially trace the history of HBO's evolving programming strategies. The first stage, which lasted until the mid-1990s, involved creating a consistent and identifiable HBO brand, a luxury brand in a populist medium. In this stage, HBO programming began with feature films and special events, before branching out to made-for-TV movies. Once the HBO brand had been established, the second stage involved building a deeper and more durable *relationship* between subscribers and the brand. In this stage, HBO turned increasingly to the production of original series that had the potential to engender loyalty among viewers by insinuating the network into their weekly viewing habits. This pattern in the history of the HBO brand—the shift from the brand as a corporate trademark to the brand as an integral experience in the lives of consumers—follows the larger patterns in the marketing of consumer goods. For HBO, as for Nike or Starbucks or any of the leaders in the marketing innovations of recent decades (including such profitable cable networks as MTV, Nickelodeon, and ESPN), the object is to build an ongoing relationship with particular groups of consumers, so that the brand conveys meanings that circulate through the culture independently of the company's products and serve as a key resource in the consumer's repertoire for creating a social identity.[13]

HBO has changed its programming strategies and redefined its brand in response to changing conditions that have affected all media companies. As a cable network, however, HBO is positioned to pursue innovations in a way that the broadcast networks are not. The broadcast networks are obligated by government regulations and by contractual relations with affiliate stations and advertisers to deliver an extensive program service that accumulates groups of viewers from across a range of social and demographic categories. Faced with changes in society or in media technologies, broadcasters typically fight a rearguard battle to protect their existing business model, which uses programming to deliver large numbers of consumers to advertisers. HBO has never used this model. HBO's parent company, initially Time Inc. and currently Time Warner, operates one of the largest distribution companies in the cable TV industry. As a result of these origins in the cable business, HBO's remarkably durable team of executives (in particular, successive CEOs Jeff Bewkes and Chris Albrecht) have tended to look for new opportunities in the social and technological changes that broadcasters face with apprehension.

First, HBO distinguished itself from commercial television by identifying itself as a source of commercial-free, uncut feature films and special events. This programming strategy gave the network a clear brand identity, which survived until the widespread adoption of the VCR in the mid-1980s, when HBO lost its claim to being the preeminent choice for watching feature films at home. Michael Fuchs, who was HBO's CEO at the time, has said, "if there had been a debate at HBO about how much we had to spend on original programming, that debate ended with the VCR."[14] The next major step in the evolution of the HBO brand involved the decision to produce original programming, beginning with feature films. Fuchs carved out a niche for HBO as a source for the sorts of topical films about social and political issues that had nearly disappeared from movie screens and commercial television. After establishing its film unit, HBO branched out again with occasional long-form dramas and miniseries that would never have appeared in theaters or on any network except HBO—including *And the Band Played On* (1993), an adaptation of Randy Shilts's panoramic narrative of the early years of the AIDS epidemic, and *The Corner* (2000), an adaptation of a book by David Simon and Ed Burns that tells the stories of people whose lives are otherwise ignored in the media, those who live in one devastatingly poor African American neighborhood in Baltimore.

During this period, HBO earned awards and critical praise, building its reputation for quality. But these original productions did very little to redefine the relationship between HBO and its subscribers, who thought of HBO as a luxury brand, a network to watch occasionally.

In 1995, Jeff Bewkes succeeded Michael Fuchs as president and CEO of HBO and introduced a different conception of branding, one more in line with changes taking place throughout the marketing world. Bewkes's goal was to create a more intense relationship between HBO subscribers and the HBO brand by producing original series. He increased the budget for original programming from $50 million per year to more than $300 million and promoted Chris Albrecht to the position of president of original programming.[15] After years in which HBO's brand identity represented a distinct alternative to the commercial networks, Bewkes and Albrecht made a major concession to the commercial model when they chose to add episodic series available weekly.

Beginning with radio, the commercial networks recognized that the key to cultivating loyalty among viewers depended upon a fixed, reliable schedule: the goal was to integrate network programming into the temporal rhythms of modern social life, particularly those of a "typical" American family. This meant scheduling programs in accordance with the rhythms of the modern workweek and, on an even more intimate level, with the temporal flow of everyday life in a family—hence the development of weekly and daily series that favored familiarity over novelty. HBO, on the other hand, began its existence as a monthly service; the subscription fee was due when each month's cable bill arrived in the mail, carrying with it a brochure laying out HBO's schedule for the month ahead and highlighting the new movies to be introduced. The monthly program schedule serves the administrative schedule of corporate billing cycles, but as a means of organizing time it coincides with few other social activities. With its movies scattered throughout the month, HBO's schedule bore no meaningful relationship to the experience of time in the lives of most Americans.

Chris Albrecht, who eventually succeeded Jeff Bewkes as president and CEO, has explained the decision to develop ongoing series in terms that recognize how different scheduling practices affect a network's relationship with viewers:

Under Michael Fuchs we looked at ourselves as a monthly subscription service. We didn't really believe that we could compete on a weekly basis in the series area, which is the programming currency of the broadcast networks. We knew that we had to become more valuable, so we made a conscious effort to explore the series area. Then we said, "Look, we need to anchor these things because it's too hard to find them." So we transformed ourselves into a regular-use network, a habitual-use network, rather than an occasional-use network . . . that was a huge transformation but one that was necessary.[16]

Albrecht also has described this decision as a response to the changing media landscape of the mid-1990s, in which cable systems began to offer more channels, and potential viewers also explored the temptations of video games and the Internet. "With so many choices," he explained, HBO could not "afford to be an occasional-use medium. We need people on a regular basis. . . . Series bring stability and regularity to HBO's schedule."[17]

Having witnessed Albrecht's thoughtful discussion of HBO's programming strategies, it comes as a surprise to read the many interviews in which he then claims not to know who actually subscribes to HBO or whether the original series have been successful in attracting and retaining subscribers. When asked to characterize the HBO audience, Albrecht pleads ignorance: "We have a very broad subscriber base that is slightly more upscale than a broadcast network audience. But without knowing exactly who our subscribers are—and we don't, because we're not exactly provided that information by the cable companies—it's very hard for us to actually make a statement one way or another."[18] In discussing the apparent success of HBO's breakthrough series, *Sex and the City* (1998–2004) and *The Sopranos*, Albrecht claims to be unable to link the programming with an obvious increase in the number of subscribers: "Did people get HBO just to watch *The Sopranos?* The answer is probably not, but we'll never know."[19] In another interview he seems entirely to discount the shift in programming. "HBO grew at the same rate before those shows were on the air as it did after those shows were on the air," he has said.[20]

In this age of intense market research, when media executives run focus groups on any decision more important than today's lunch order, it's difficult to believe that HBO—the most profitable company in the Time Warner empire—would risk its billion dollar annual profits without knowing everything it is possible for contemporary market researchers to know about current and potential subscribers. One may suspect a bit of self-mythologizing in Albrecht's denial: like showmen of an earlier era, he often seems to suggest, HBO executives make decisions based on innate taste and gut instincts, not on market research, nor on ratings.[21] It is also possible that after many bruising contract negotiations with performers and producers, Albrecht may not want to sacrifice bargaining leverage by giving any individual series too much of the credit for HBO's undeniable financial success.

Even if an observer can only make inferences about HBO's audience based upon its program choices and public relations campaigns, it isn't difficult to conceive of HBO as an exclusive cultural domain, appealing to a restricted taste culture and to viewers of privileged economic circumstances. For all its faults, commercial broadcasting is a truly populist medium; for the price of a television set and the willingness to tolerate commercials, programs are available to anyone within range of the signal. Premium cable networks offer a form of television for the age of the gated community, in which a homeowner's association and restrictive covenants provide an exclusive experience but also enforce particular standards of taste. By producing original programming, HBO has transformed itself from a movie channel that simply exhibited Hollywood features into a cultural phenomenon, one designed almost perfectly to solicit the attention and affections of an educated upper-middle class. In a series of clever promotional spots, HBO has depicted its drama series as "watercooler" TV—the sort of programs that people feel compelled to discuss with coworkers the following day. It is a knowing, ironic image of television as a collective cultural phenomenon, a joke for those who understand how much television has changed in the age of audience segmentation—when every taste is a minority taste. *The Sopranos* and *Six Feet Under* (2001–5) certainly have been the topic of conversation around the watercoolers of suburban office parks, downtown law firms, and university English departments, but it's fair to wonder about the muffler shop and the lumberyard.

Of one fact we can be certain: even at the height of its cultural impact and critical acclaim, HBO has never surpassed 29 million subscribers in a country with nearly 110 million TV households.[22] This in spite of the fact that the HBO service is nearly universally distributed on cable and direct broadcast satellite systems—in other words, available to anyone who already pays a monthly subscription fee for a program service. Think about it in slightly different terms: While HBO has racked up every award in sight, and while Tony Soprano's family and the women of *Sex and the City* have appeared on magazine covers across the land, more than two-thirds of the TV households in the United States have resisted the temptation to subscribe.

Once HBO executives chose to compete directly with the commercial networks by introducing original series, they had erased one of the key points of distinction that separated HBO from its commercial competitors. The answer was to translate the reputation for quality earned by its award-winning movies into the realm of series television, while making this distinction salient for the upper-middle-class viewers who were its most likely subscribers. HBO has earned its reputation for quality in part by lavishing more money on the production of its drama series than any of the broadcast networks can possibly afford, given their business models. These extraordinary investments are meaningless, however, unless viewers recognize and value the signs of quality in HBO series. With this in mind, HBO also spends more on marketing and promotions than any other network. The budget for each episode of *Deadwood* (2004–) has been roughly $4.5 million, twice the average of even the most expensive network series. The first season of the period drama *Rome* (2005–7) cost even more—nearly $100 million for ten episodes. The annual budget for marketing and promotions is also generally twice what the broadcast networks spend.[23] At the same time that HBO has created the programs, its public relations department has promoted a television culture in which it is possible to think of a television series as a work of art. This is a crucial step in the creation of HBO's distinctive cultural value.

The publicists at HBO deserve every Time Warner stock option that plumps their investment portfolios (with apologies for the disappointing performance of shares since the disastrous AOL merger). The HBO publicity machine, led by Eric Kessler, has created the impression that HBO's original programming—in spite of its relatively small audience—has played a disproportionately major role in American culture

The heart of the lavish HBO-BBC coproduction *Rome* is the on-again off-again relationship between the friendly, slower-witted Titus Pullo (Ray Stevenson, left) and the stoic, honorable Lucius Vorenus (Kevin McKidd, right).

over the past decade. "We treat the launch of every single piece of programming like an event," Kessler has explained. "We believe in investing in the marketing to generate the awareness. We know we need to be part of the popular culture."[24] To achieve this impact, they cite an Everest of Emmy Awards and the occasional Peabody, the adoration of critics, steady audience growth, staggering profits, and the unmistakable influence of HBO series on the programming decisions of their oft-bewildered competitors in basic cable and the broadcast networks.

More importantly, HBO promotes the creators of the drama series and encourages reporters to flesh out their biographies so that the public learns to identify the artistic vision of a single creator behind each series, no matter the scale and complexity of the production or the number of people involved in bringing it to the screen. David Chase has been a writer and producer in the television business for decades, but it is only with *The Sopranos* that we have grown accustomed to reading statements such as this from a writer on the series who is quoted in a cover article in *Vanity Fair*: "Every shot, every word, of *The Sopranos* is David in some way or another."[25] For all that anyone outside the television industry knows, David Chase might not have existed before he arrived at HBO. Although his name has appeared in television credits countless times since the 1970s, he toiled in lucrative anonymity. Now he is acclaimed as an artist capable of placing his signature on every shot of a television series. Pierre Bourdieu is certainly not alone in making the claim that the "charismatic ideology" of authorship—the belief in the artistic vision of a sole creator—"is the ultimate basis of belief in the value of a work of art."[26] In its avid promotion of those who have created its drama series, HBO has enhanced the value of its brand while also contributing to a more widespread discourse of authorship in television. In doing so, the network has played a part in making it possible to believe that a television series can be thought of as a work of art.

In Bourdieu's account of cultural production, the value of an artwork is created through a process of "social alchemy," a term that accurately describes the miraculous elevation of David Chase to the status of creative genius following decades of anonymous labor in the television industry. Bourdieu describes a production of collective belief that one may behold in the marketing of any cultural good, but it is particularly evident in the case of HBO, which distinguishes its brand by cultivating an aura of artistic achievement: "It is both true and untrue to say that the commercial value of a work of art is incommensurate with its cost of production. It is true if one only takes account of the manufacture of the material object; it is not true if one is referring to the production of the work of art as a sacred, consecrated object, the product of a vast operation of social alchemy jointly conducted, with equal conviction and very unequal profits, by all the agents involved in the field of production."[27] In this passage, Bourdieu shifts attention from the artist to the independent cultural intermediaries who may not profit directly from the work of art, but who are nevertheless eager to participate in its consecration: "the producers of the meaning and value of the work—critics, publishers, gallery directors and the whole set of agents whose combined efforts produce consumers capable of knowing and recognizing the work of art as such."[28]

In the case of HBO drama, one sees an ideal example of this process of social alchemy at work. The public relations juggernaut at HBO has masterfully pulled the strings of a credulous press to stoke the fires for each successive series, but this isn't a case of brainwashing. Each of the agents involved in producing the value of the work has an independent interest in contributing to an artworld that allows for the belief that certain television series are candidates for aesthetic appreciation. Newspapers and magazines are eager to upgrade coverage of pop culture, and television in particular, in their desperation to engage a dwindling audience of young readers. Of course, HBO benefits from the corporate synergies provided by its sibling publications at Time Warner, including the weekly magazines *Time* and *Entertainment Weekly,* but it isn't just corporate logrolling that accounts for the attention lavished on HBO dramas. Pursuing the same demographic group as those who subscribe to premium cable, the *New York Times* alone has devoted so many column inches to *The Sopranos* that it sometimes reads like a virtual house organ for HBO.[29] In the echo chamber of cultural production, HBO then feeds the press coverage of its programs back through the public relations machinery, so that people begin to speak about the positive press coverage. "We also did something that changed the way a lot of people looked at an aspect of television, which is what the TV critics say," Albrecht has explained. "We took the praise and used that as a way to draw attention to the shows, to show the pedigree of the shows, to help define the shows—and later on, when people started to talk about the network, to help define the network."[30]

As with HBO's promotion of authorship, its active promotion of TV criticism has helped to elevate the status of television criticism in general. By drawing attention to the aesthetic claims of TV critics, HBO has contributed a measure of legitimacy and cultural authority to those who would speak about television series as works of art. Coincidentally, this helps to make critics more effective agents in the production of cultural value. As the present volume attests, academic critics have filed into line, playing a small part in the most solemn rite of contemporary television culture—the cultural consecration of HBO. Our interests are a bit more obscure than those of writers in the popular press, but, collectively, we contribute to the value of the HBO brand by producing consumers capable of recognizing the HBO series as a work of art.

Notes

The epigraphs to this section are drawn from Pierre Bourdieu, *The Field of Cultural Production* (New York: Columbia University Press, 1993), 258, 35; and Stephen Holden, "Sympathetic Brutes in a Pop Master-piece," *New York Times*, June 6, 1999, sec. 2, 23.

1. Through the entire history of American television, there has been an oddly dialectical relationship between modern art and commercial television. In part, this has involved questions about the aesthetic status of commercial television, particularly in negotiating the boundaries of taste along the line that divides high and low culture. For insight into the history of this relationship, see Lynn Spigel, "High Culture in Low Places: Television and Modern Art, 1950–1970," in her book *Welcome to the Dreamhouse: Popular Media and Postwar Suburbs* (Durham, N.C.: Duke University Press, 2001), 265–309. See also Lynn Spigel, *TV By Design: Modern Art and the Rise of Network Television* (Chicago: University of Chicago Press, forthcoming). For the purposes of this essay, I am speaking specifically about the aesthetic status of the fictional television *series*, and not of individual programs or commercials, nor of television conceived as a more general cultural phenomenon.

2. For an introduction to this concept, which appears throughout Bourdieu's work, see Pierre Bourdieu, *Distinction: A Social Critique of the Judgment of Taste* (Cambridge: Harvard University Press, 1984), 28–32, 53–58.

3. Verne Gay, "What Makes HBO Tick?," *Cable World*, November 4, 2002, 41.

4. See, for example, Gilbert Seldes, *The Great Audience* (New York: Viking Press, 1950). See also Michael G. Kammen, *The Lively Arts: Gilbert Seldes and the Transformation of Cultural Criticism in the United States* (New York: Oxford University Press, 1996).

5. Horace Newcomb, *TV: The Most Popular Art* (Garden City, N.Y.: Anchor Books, 1974). Among the books and articles to appear in the 1980s, the most valuable sustained discussion of the television series as an aesthetic form is Jane Feuer, Paul Kerr, and Tise Vahmigi, eds., *MTM: "Quality Television"* (London: BFI Publishing, 1984).

6. Bourdieu, *The Field of Cultural Production*, 254.

7. Bourdieu, *Distinction*, 57.

8. For an exemplary study based on Bourdieu's insights into the production of value in cultural fields, see James F. English, *The Economy of Prestige: Prizes, Awards, and the Circulation of Cultural Value* (Cambridge, Mass.: Harvard University Press, 2005).

9. Bourdieu, *The Field of Cultural Production*, 257. There is now a large body of scholarly literature on the history and politics of the museum and its relation to other "cultural institutions of display." For excellent introductions to the issues involved, see Tony Bennett, *The Birth of the Museum: History, Theory*

and Politics (London: Routledge, 1995), and Barbara Kirshenblatt-Gimblett, *Destination Culture: Tourism, Museums, and Heritage* (Berkeley: University of California Press, 1998).

10. A. J. Frutkin, "Enemy of the Safe," *Mediaweek,* June 16, 2003, 1.

11. John M. Higgins, "Premium Networks Take a Hit," *Broadcasting & Cable*, February 9, 2004, at http://www.broadcastingcable.com/index.asp?layout=articlePrint&articleID=CA380315.

12. John M. Higgins and Donna Petrozello, "HBO Reaching for the Stars," *Broadcasting & Cable,* March 23, 1998, 28.

13. There are dozens of books on strategic brand management that advocate particular practices of branding, usually through case studies of actual brands. This literature is useful to critics for the insights it provides into the knowledge and assumptions of the corporate managers and marketing professionals involved in developing brand strategies. See, for instance, David A. Aaker, *Building Strong Brands* (New York: Simon & Schuster, 2002). Business historian Nancy F. Koehn describes the history of branding from the corporate perspective in *Brand New: How Entrepreneurs Earned Consumers' Trust from Wedgwood to Dell* (Cambridge, Mass.: Harvard Business School Press, 2001). Celia Lury discusses the social implications of recent branding practices in *Brands: The Logos of the Global Economy* (London: Routledge, 2004).

14. Ann Hornaday, "Programming for Reputation and Profits," *New York Times,* November 7, 1993, sec. 2, 37.

15. Wayne Walley, "Originals Now a Must for Cable," *Electronic Media,* August 28, 1995, 3.

16. "Albrecht Likes New 'Problems' HBO is Facing," *Hollywood Reporter,* March 1, 2002, 1.

17. Jim McConville, "Competition Driving HBO," *Electronic Media,* October 25, 1999, 1.

18. "A Highly Original Interview with HBO's Albrecht," *Multichannel News,* June 11, 2001, 124.

19. Peter Thal Larsen, "Never Mind the Quality, Feel Those Margins," *Financial Times,* April 1, 2003, 2.

20. Frutkin, "Enemy of the Safe," 1.

21. "All our programming decisions are judgment calls," Albrecht has claimed. "I have no idea if *The Sopranos* makes money for HBO, because we don't sell directly to anybody. . . . We sell to the cable operators." See Lynn Hirschberg, "Thinking Inside the Box," *New York Times Magazine,* November 3, 2002, 67.

22. R. Thomas Umstead, "HBO Looks for Missing Link," *Multichannel News,* July 10, 2006, 20.

23. Joe Flint, "HBO's Next Business Model," *Wall Street Journal,* January 5, 2004, B1; Jesse McKinley, "'Deadwood' Gets a New Lease on Life," *New York*

Times, June 11, 2006, B1; Randall Tierney, "Brand of Brothers," *Hollywood Reporter,* November 2, 2002, 32.

24. Tierney, "Brand of Brothers," 32.

25. Peter Biskind, "An American Family," *Vanity Fair,* April 2007, 241.

26. Bourdieu, *The Field of Cultural Production,* 76.

27. Bourdieu, *The Field of Cultural Production,* 81.

28. Bourdieu, *The Field of Cultural Production,* 37.

29. This generous coverage has been compiled in a book, *The* New York Times *Guide to* The Sopranos, revised edition (New York: I Books, 2002).

30. Robert J. Dowling, "From the Top," *Hollywood Reporter,* November 2, 2002, 7.

ONE

Films

Dana Heller

Perhaps more than any other recent filmmaking venture in the United States, HBO Films has granted a sense of authenticity to the dwindling aura of the movies. Or to put it another way, HBO Films is a rebuff to Walter Benjamin's argument that film technology can offer no more than a cheap imitation of the singular and unique presence of the work of art.[1] By exhibiting a restless fascination with the meaning of "originality," HBO has strategically distanced its films from the formulaic excesses of made-for-TV movies and Hollywood's obsession with box office receipts. The result is that HBO has redefined originality in filmmaking: rather than signaling the original quality of discrete objects, HBO takes originality as a freestanding quality in and of itself. And although part of this redefinition is merely the effect of HBO's promotional branding, there is clearly more at play in the company's success story than creative marketing tactics.

HBO began making feature films in 1983 when it presented *The Terry Fox Story*, the first made-for-pay-TV movie. The film was based on the "true" experiences of the legendary Canadian whose bout with bone cancer at the age of seventeen left him with one leg, and whose determination to run coast-to-coast across Canada to raise money for medical research led to the annual international charity run in his name. In choosing to lead with a biopic, HBO Pictures anticipated the central role this subgenre would come to occupy in its evolution. But at the same time, director Ralph L. Thomas demonstrated certain iconoclastic tendencies that placed the picture at odds with the typical pieties of made-for-TV biographical films. *The Terry Fox Story* did not embrace its subject with calculated reverence; it was widely noted (not least of all by members of the Fox family) for its portrayal of Fox as an ambiguous hero with a difficult personality and fiery temper. Yet the film remains to this day a revealing register of HBO's early ambitions and emerging sense of itself as a maverick filmmaking force. Even from the beginning, HBO sought to break with the conventions of made-for-TV biopics that had been established as early as 1971 with the immensely popular sentimental melodrama *Brian's Song*.

This sense was confirmed in 1986 when HBO began making films under a second banner, HBO Showcase, the explicit goal of which was to push the "boundaries of contemporary drama."[2] This venture earned HBO its first prime-time Emmy Awards for *Age Old Friends* (1989), starring Hume Cronyn and Vincent Gardenia as elderly nursing home residents who help each other maintain humor and dignity in the face of their declining physical and mental capacities. Ten years later, HBO Showcase expanded and was renamed HBO NYC Productions. The move aimed to strengthen HBO's investment in producing "edgier and more diverse" projects,[3] and it led to the presentation of *If These Walls Could Talk* (1996), a film that examined the personal lives of three American women confronting the controversial public and private politics of abortion in three different time periods and social climates. Four years later, HBO followed up with *If These Walls Could Talk II* (2000), a film that traces the conflicts and desires of three different sets of lesbian occupants in a single California bungalow over a forty-year span that witnesses the intolerance of the early 1960s, the second-wave lesbian feminism of the 1970s, and the contemporary movement toward the creation of gay families.

At the same time, the cable company continued making "safer" dramatic fare under the banner of HBO Pictures, producing a total of 115 features and securing HBO's dominant position at the annual Emmy Awards. Like *The Terry Fox Story*, the last of these features, *RKO 281* (1999), was a celebrity biopic; it told the story of Orson Welles's battle with William Randolph Hearst over the making of *Citizen Kane*. The film captured the 1999 Golden Globe Award for Best Movie Made for Television, a triumph that *RKO 281*'s subject matter seemed to prophesize, as the premier pay cable channel had now clearly established itself as a substantial match for the network giants.

In 1999, HBO merged HBO Pictures and HBO NYC to form a single movie division, HBO Films. The consolidation marked HBO's strategic diversification of projects—large and small, innovative and mainstream—under one banner that would produce original feature films and miniseries for the television market as well as feature films for theatrical distribution. This includes small-budget independent films such as *American Splendor* (2003), *Maria Full of Grace* (2004), and *The Notorious Bettie Page* (2005), along with big-budget miniseries such as *Band of Brothers* (2001), *Angels in America* (2003), and *Empire Falls* (2005). HBO Films remains a division of the HBO cable television network; however, its theatrical releases are usually handled by Picturehouse, a joint venture between Time Warner subsidiaries New Line Cinema and HBO Films, whose role in the production of HBO theatricals is discussed in detail in chapter 17 of this volume.

Over the years, HBO has established itself as an undisputed pioneer in feature filmmaking. Given its unique background, it could be argued that in the age of media convergence, as the lines separating systems of production and channels of distribution have become increasingly permeable, HBO Films constitutes a significant chapter in the history of the ongoing merger between the film and television industries, as the very notion of film has shifted from a box office medium to a home-based medium. Having garnered numerous Golden Globe and Emmy Awards, as well as the 2003 Sundance Film Festival's Grand Jury Award for *American Splendor* and the prestigious Palm d'Or at the 2003 Cannes Festival for *Elephant* (2003), HBO has proved that successful dramatic filmmaking has less to do with the screening venue than with commitment to "quality" and "originality." The irony is that HBO's success in distinguishing its films is partly the result of its promotional insistence on the very distinctions that its history denies. By contending that its films are categorically groundbreaking—a stand-alone breed—HBO has rendered all but irrelevant the difference between movies made for television and movies made for theatrical distribution.

In other words, HBO films are marked above all by their unwavering emphasis on unconventionality and by their tendency to fixate on the HBO signature as the sine qua non of originality, even when working with the familiar genres and typically uplifting narrative structures of Hollywood and made-for-TV movies. The result is a recognizable brand of cinematic work that exploits the freedoms granted to subscription television (adult language, nudity, sexual content, excessive violence); capitalizes on the talents of writers, directors, and performers whose names are associated with the big screen; and benefits from the well-tested melodramatic conventions of popular network TV movies without the burden of frequent commercial interruptions.

Perhaps nowhere else do these elements come together more effectively than in *Gia* (1998), the story of the rise and tragic fall of the 1970s supermodel Gia Carrangi. The film is upfront in its uncensored portrayal of lesbian sexuality, drug addiction, and the brutal mindset of an industry that cannibalizes female youth and beauty. It features an all-star cast with a young, fiercely seductive Angelina Jolie (who plays Gia) and a stately Lauren Bacall. Yet the film plays upon the maudlin conventions of typical melodrama, with Gia's terminal illness from AIDS providing the tear-jerking framework for a morality tale that ultimately cautions against the destructive cultural excesses of the 1970s.

The film is broadly representative in another way. In the opening scenes, Gia knowingly yet tauntingly asks: "Do I make you nervous? Good." In a sense, HBO films retain the provocative trace of this question in their signature "edgy" productions, as the company continuously touts its fearlessness in taking on subject matter that most network television producers would consider too hot to handle: abortion (*A Private Matter* [1992], *If These Walls Could Talk*); homosexuality (*Tidy Endings* [1988], *If These Walls Could Talk II*); prison life (*Prison Stories: Women on the Inside* [1991], *Stranger Inside* [2001]); transgender identity (*Normal* [2003]); hate crimes (*The Laramie Project* [2002]); U.S. government corruption (*Conspiracy: The Trial of the Chicago 8* [1987], *Doublecrossed* [1991], *The Pentagon Wars* [1998]); genocide (*Conspiracy* [2001], *Sometimes in April* [2005]); AIDS (*And the Band Played On* [1993], *Angels in America, Yesterday* [2005]); global terrorism (*Investigation: Inside a Terrorist Bombing* [1990], *Path to Paradise* [1997], *Dirty War* [2005]); sexual abuse by the clergy (*Judgment* [1990]); U.S. racism and social inequality (*Into the Homeland* [1987], *The Tuskegee Airmen* [1995], *Miss Evers' Boys* [1997], *Boycott* [2001], *Walkout* [2006]); and environmentalism (*The Burning Season* [1994]), to name just a few.

HBO's eagerness to take such risks prompted one critic to dub it "the auteur studio of the nineties."[4] In other words, HBO has effectively seized the mantle of "quality television" that was attributed to MTM Enterprises in the 1970s. And just as MTM cased its "quality" productions in the popular formats of the sitcom and hour-long ensemble drama, HBO's "groundbreaking" material is more often than not shrewdly narrativized within the familiar, prevailing genres and sub-genres of mainstream dramatic television entertainment, such as the thriller, espionage, historical romance, and—above all—the biopic.

As with both Hollywood and network films, HBO's heavy reliance on the biopic champions the cultural value of celebrity, notoriety, and individual heroism in the cinematic representation of history, both distant and more recent. Working from Oscar Wilde's assumption that "it is personalities, not principles, that move the age," HBO's most notable dramatic features are those that negotiate the past and interrogate cultural memory through the depiction of individual lives that are positioned at the center of national struggles, community conflicts, social movements, and scandals. Traditionally, biopics have served as propaganda and pedagogy in the shape of popular entertainment: they offer model lives for the purposes of admiration and emulation, and they communicate to us the vitally uplifting message that the times we live in are better—or are getting better—thanks to the triumphs or failures of individual agents "embedded in a larger history that is always progressive."[5]

However, as one of the stalwart "genres that HBO Films has made its own,"[6] the biopic has had its customary practices and principles effectively slanted by the network. For example, in *Warm Springs* (2005), Kenneth Branagh chronicles Franklin Delano Roosevelt's early physical and spiritual struggle with the paralysis resulting from his bout with polio. Hoping for a miracle cure, Roosevelt seeks treatment at a rural spa in Warm Springs, Georgia, where his sense of social privilege and rank is challenged by his encounters with poverty and racism and by the humbling realities of learning to live with disability. Kathy Bates plays Roosevelt's pragmatic therapist, and Cynthia Nixon portrays Eleanor Roosevelt, who reluctantly assumes her husband's public functions as he wrestles with the possibility that his political career has reached an end. The film presents Roosevelt's crisis as a formidable part of his making as a leader, caring politician, and man of the people. The film humanizes presidential history and power by identifying weakness and vulnerability as the locus of personal and—by extension—national courage; it relies on the appeal of the "true but little-known" chapter of a well-known life, a behind-the-scenes look at what made the man. Although the film could have easily resorted to tabloid history, or the reduction of the past to "organized gossip," it seeks rather to demystify American history and political power by demonstrating that dedicated national leadership is not always born of personal strength.[7]

HBO biopics that portray the lives of shadier historical figures have tended to be less critically successful, although it's reasonably fair to say that the network deserves kudos for even attempting to render in plausible human terms the disreputable lead characters depicted in *Citizen Cohn* (1992), *Stalin* (1992), *Rasputin* (1996), *Gotti* (1996), and *Don King: Only in America* (1997). In these instances, despite some excellent performances, quality too often succumbs to one-dimensional tabloid history. Such is the case in *Citizen Cohn*, the film based on Nicholas von Hoffman's biography of Roy Cohn, the lawyer whose prominent role in the prosecution and eventual conviction of Ethel and Julius Rosenberg led to his appointment at the age of twenty-four as Senator Joseph McCarthy's chief counsel. Although Cohn's pugnacity, arrogance, and penchant for professional misconduct have become legend, the HBO film does little to suggest the complexities of history and of experience that might have produced the extraordinary schism between his private life and the powerful public persona that he laboriously sought to micromanage until his death from complications resulting from AIDS in 1986. Lacking a balanced script, James Woods delivers a scenery-chewing performance of lusty villainy, with more than a hint of obligatory self-loathing to account summarily for Cohn's persecution of alleged Jewish communists and malevolence toward gays. As a historical film, *Citizen Cohn* proves that if mawkish piety is the risk of the overly flattering biopic, disfiguring caricature is the risk of the chastising one. Such lopsidedness can only undercut quality, especially when a film promotes itself as "The True Story," as this one does.[8]

Time and again, HBO turns to American social history for its raw material. A number of interesting films set in America's past draw on the history of civil rights struggles and the achievements of marginalized groups: women, African Americans, gays and lesbians, and Latinos. Arguably, the best HBO films in this vein are those that tacitly acknowledge the difficulties of truthful representation in historical film. *Boycott, The Laramie Project,* and *Iron-Jawed Angels* (2004) are examples of films that interrogate traditional structures of historical representation through genre-splicing, combining elements of the biopic with those of the documentary, romance, and drama. In other ways, these films employ strategies identified by Robert Rosenstone as postmodern, in the sense that they challenge conventional cinematic realism and attempt to expand the possibilities for historical narrative.[9] Multiple perspective and interpretation, as most overtly demonstrated in *The Laramie Project*'s piecing together of the collective voice of a quiet western town suddenly thrust into the national spotlight by a brutal hate crime, is one such strategy.

Anachronism, as evident in *Boycott* and *Iron-Jawed Angels,* is another strategy aimed at rendering history in multiple and complex ways that defy easy access to the so-called True Story. *Iron-Jawed Angels* focuses on a group of lesser-known twentieth-century suffragettes who were instrumental in taking the women's suffrage movement out of the Victorian era and influencing passage of the Nineteenth Amendment. They achieved this by abandoning ladylike lobbying tactics and by taking their demands to the streets of the nation's capital, where they had the audacity to stage parades, distribute fliers, picket the White House, and raise their voices in public. The film's musical score includes contemporary pop songs by female vocalists such as Michele Branch and Avril Lavigne, thus providing a girl-power backdrop to some of the narrative's more triumphal highpoints. Noticeably at odds with corsets and high button shoes, the new age score is further accompanied by rapid editing techniques synched with the music in a style that mimes music video production.

In this way, the film uses anachronism to link the spirit of U.S. feminism's rebellious foremothers with the self-empowerment ethos and nonconformist styles of contemporary girl culture. The connection is reinforced not only by the casting of Hilary Swank (an actress recognized for taking on gutsy, independent female characters) as the fearless activist Alice Paul, but by the opening scenes, in which Paul and Lucy Burns (played by Frances O'Connor) compete tenaciously for the purchase of an extravagant hat in a shop window. The effect of these anachronisms can be read two ways: on the one hand, they amount to an assimilation of feminism's past victories into an illusory present where victory remains secure and the buoyant beat of gender equality and consumerism goes on. On the other hand, they communicate a refusal to dismiss women's suffrage as part of the distant past. Much like *Boycott* and the recent *Walkout* (2006), *Iron-Jawed Angels* suggests that history lives in the *now* and is relevant to the ongoing struggle for social justice.

If viewers detect some ambiguity in HBO Films' championing of progressive values it may be because entertainment value is compromised by excessive preaching, no matter how original or cutting edge. *Boycott*, for example, is a film that clearly serves a pedagogical function in that it aims to teach viewers something about the less-celebrated heroes of the American civil rights movement and the early, ambivalent rise to leadership of the Reverend Martin Luther King Jr. At the same time, the film must walk a fine line in linking those lessons emphatically to a vision of continued social change. The film's affecting conclusion is a case in point. Following the success of the bus boycott, a young King (played by Jeffrey Wright) declines to board a local bus with fellow organizers and chooses instead to walk home. "We who believe in freedom cannot rest," King's voice-over eulogizes, as the streets he strolls along are suddenly projected into the future, an anachronistic shift marked by modernized architecture, mixed-race couples walking hand-in-hand, and a patrol car genially staffed by a Latina and an African American male police officer. King, taking casual note of the peculiar time warp, stops to converse with a group of black men on the street, a signal that his work continues—as does ours, as engaged citizens and students of history. Thus, although *Boycott* suggests a vision of historical progress typical of made-for-TV films, it does not allow for closure or complete resolution of the ongoing conversation about civil rights leadership in America.[10]

Another notable scene in *Boycott* occurs when Coretta King (Carmen Ejogo) encounters Bayard Rustin (Erik Dellums) when he arrives in Montgomery to write about the boycott. She recalls hearing him lecture on nonviolence when she was a student in college. "You said something about history," she says, "something that I've always remembered." She repeats to him the lesson he taught, that "history wasn't an accident . . . that history is a choice." Puzzled, Rustin asks her why those words made such an impression, and she replies that "it means we can do something about our lives and we're not stuck with the way things are." Here, the critical lesson of progressivism that shapes the narrative is indirectly "taught"—and carefully contained—within a remembered college lecture.

We witness something similar in *Walkout,* a film that chronicles the "true but little-known" story of Mexican American high school students who, fed up with widespread discrimination against Chicanos in the educational system, staged a 1968 walkout at five East Los Angeles high schools.[11] Their inspiration is shown to be their teacher, Sal Castro, who early in the film passionately instructs his Chicano students to take note of the fact that "we are not in the history books." As the students realize that they will have to take action if they wish to see their names written into history, the film's championing of progressive social change is packaged as a lesson from the classroom lectern.

Walkout, unlike *Boycott* and *Iron-Jawed Angels,* adheres more faithfully to the conventions of cinematic realism. However, all three films are representative of broader tendencies in HBO's understanding of cinematic originality. These tendencies are demonstrated in the films' focus on the underrepresented figures of history; their use of multiple-perspective, which allows for the narrative portrayal of collective rather than individual heroism; their experimentations with the conventions of cinematic realism, such as anachronism; and their unabashedly progressive vision of the "lessons" generated by the past. This, in combination with HBO's freedom from commercial intrusions and restrictions on adult content; its willingness to invest in challenging high-quality literary and theatrical adaptations, such as Margaret Edson's *Wit* (2001); the consistently high caliber of its writers, directors, and performers; and its ability to integrate quality production and complexity even into its intermittent and unapologetic forays into the outré, or topics gleefully "ripped from the headlines," such as *The Positively True Adventures of the Alleged Texas Cheerleader-Murdering Mom* (1993) and *Mrs. Harris* (2005), have all contributed to HBO's successful harnessing of the aura of cinematic originality in a non-risk television age of relentless *CSI* and *Law & Order* franchising and mind-numbing Hollywood remakes. In the end, analyses of the films themselves reveal that HBO's commitment to originality derives as much from everyday convention as from instructional provocation, or the contradictory packaging of edgy, socially relevant narratives of gender, race, ethnicity, and sexuality in well-worn TV-movie genres.

Notes

1. Walter Benjamin, "The Work of Art in the Age of Mechanical Reproduction," in Hannah Arendt, ed., *Illuminations: Essays and Reflections* (New York: Schocken Books, 1968), 217–52.

2. "About HBO Films," at http://www.hbo.com/films/about.

3. Ibid.

4. Al Auster, "HBO Movies: The Cable Giant as 'Auteur,'" *Television Quarterly* 31:1 (2000): 75–83.

5. Robert A. Rosenstone, *Visions of the Past: The Challenge of Film to Our Idea of History* (Cambridge, Mass.: Harvard University Press, 1995), 55–56.

6. "About HBO Films," at http://www.hbo.com/films/about.

7. George F. Custen, "Making History," in Robert A. Rosenstone, ed., *The Historical Film: History and Memory in Media* (New Brunswick, N.J.: Rutgers University Press, 2001), 67.

8. This phrase, as Steven J. Bottoms points out, is used as the subtitle for the Warner Home Video edition of *Citizen Cohn*. See Bottoms, "Re-staging Roy: *Citizen Cohn* and the Search for Xanadu," *Theatre Journal* 48:2 (1996): 157–84 (specifically, 184, note 6).

9. Robert A. Rosenstone, "*Walker*: The Dramatic Film as (Postmodern) History," in Robert A. Rosenstone, ed., *Revisioning History: Film and the Construction of a New Past* (Princeton, N.J.: Princeton University Press, 1995), 202–14.

10. For a fuller analysis of the film's conclusion, see Valerie Smith, "Meditation on Memory: Clark Johnson's *Boycott*," *American Literary History* 17:3 (2005): 530–41.

11. Here I am referencing HBO's promotional Web site for the film, http://www.hbo.com/events/walkout/index.html (accessed June 6, 2006). The film's tagline, "Reading, Writing, Revolution," is equally instructive.

TWO

Oz

Michele Malach

It is 1997. A man is strapped to a gurney, sedated, and locked in a small cell to restrain him. He is known as one of the most volatile and violent criminals in this prison. But the crime for which he is now being punished was a mercy killing. Having befriended a prisoner on the AIDS ward during a punitive work assignment, this man strangled the patient at his own request. But the authorities don't believe him, and nearly everyone in the Oswald Maximum Security Penitentiary (later Oswald Maximum Security Correctional Facility: Level Four), or Oz, hates him. The cell door opens, and another prisoner steps inside. After passing money to the guard who let him in, he pours a clear liquid over the restrained man, lights a match, and drops it.

Thus ends "The Routine," the first episode of HBO's first original weekly, hour-long drama series. Dino Ortolani (Prisoner #96C382, played by Jon Seda), the man on the gurney, is introduced as one of the main characters in Oz, only to be gruesomely dispatched at the end of the very first episode. Welcome to *Oz,* and welcome to HBO drama. With the help of Tom Fontana, best known for his work on *St. Elsewhere* (NBC, 1982–88) and *Homicide: Life on the Street* (NBC, 1993–99), HBO quickly established itself as pushing the boundaries of serial television. Although *Oz* never reached the levels of commercial success of later series such as *Sex and the City* (1998–2004) or *The Sopranos* (1999–2007), critical response was mostly positive. However, the graphic depictions of violence and sex, often in the same scene, were too much for some critics. According to Scott Tobias, "after years of self-censorship, both with *Homicide* and earlier as a writer for *St. Elsewhere,* Fontana finally allowed his id to run amok in the HBO series *Oz,* unburdened by the rigors of nervous executives, skittish advertisers, and, in many respects, good taste."[1] Nonetheless, over the course of six seasons, *Oz* managed to win the hearts and minds of most critics and a devoted group of fans with its intensity, strong acting, serious contemplation of difficult issues, and often over-the-top baroque melodrama. And of course, the male nudity and violence.

In brief, *Oz* is an ensemble-cast serial drama set in the state penitentiary of an unnamed state.[2] The characters include both inmates and prison staff, with a focus on the residents of an experimental unit within the prison. The wardens, prison psychologist (also a nun), doctor, chaplain, unit manager, and a couple of the corrections officers are major characters, and the governor appears whenever it suits his purposes to do so. The inmates are divided into fairly strict groupings, by ethnicity or ideology: Italians, Irish, Aryan Brotherhood (neo-Nazis), Homeboys, Muslims, Gays, Christians, Latinos, and a loose-knit group of unaffiliated prisoners known as "the Others." The story lines are myriad and often Byzantine, as individuals and groups vie for their share of the prison drug trade, exact revenge for insults both real and imagined, and simply try to stay alive. Characters are executed and paroled (and usually returned), fall into and out of love, run elaborate schemes, kill and are killed.

"There is no yelling, no fighting, no fucking. Follow the rules. Learn self-discipline. Because if you had any self-discipline, any control over yourself at all, you wouldn't be sitting here now." In "The Routine," Officer Diane Whittlesey (played by Edie Falco, who left her recurring role on *Oz* when *The Sopranos* became successful) introduces several new prisoners to an experimental unit in Oz known as Emerald (Em) City. The bulk of the narrative over the run of the series takes place here. It is a unit dedicated to regimentation and rehabilitation. The cells are made of clear plastic, the ratio of guards to prisoners is higher than in other units, and the inmates must have work assignments somewhere in the prison. Unit manager Tim McManus idealistically created Em City out of a belief in the power of rehabilitation through regulation and personal responsibility. The unit is composed of a limited number of inmates from each of the major groups or cliques within the prison population itself. Even aging prisoners, a growing subset of the prison population in general, are represented—by Bob Rebadow (Prisoner

#65R814; played by George Morfogen) and Agamemnon Busmalis (Prisoner #98B242, played by Tom Mardirosian). A microcosm of the prison—and American male—population, Em City functions as a kind of metaphor for the social and economic pressures of prison life.

Oz ran from 1997 to 2003, albeit not in traditional weekly series form. First of all, HBO did not follow the networks' usual September–April television season. *Oz* premiered on July 12, 1997, preempting the networks by two months. This is a pattern HBO has used successfully to compete with the broadcast networks, rolling out a rotating roster of series, with a new season (or new series) premiering nearly as soon as the previous one ends. Because of the large number of regular characters (not counting the recurring characters and guest stars) and the complexity of the narratives, Fontana also persuaded HBO to shorten the season for *Oz,* down to eight episodes per year.

One exception to this pattern was season four, which ran in two parts of eight episodes each (July 12 to August 20, 2000, and January 7 to February 25, 2001). When HBO learned that David Chase was going to need longer to produce the next season of *The Sopranos,* Fontana agreed to produce a second eight episodes of *Oz* to be called the second part of season four. Whereas the first four seasons premiered in mid-July, the second half of season four premiered in January, changing the rotation of the series for the last two seasons. The producers of *Oz*—as with other HBO series—didn't have the same time constraints as producers of broadcast network shows. Fontana and company had an actual hour a week to work with, without having to factor in regularly scheduled commercial breaks. The narrative flow, although still typically following a three-act structure, didn't always follow the timing of other networks' programs.

A man in a wheelchair sits in a glass cage, which rotates occasionally. He speaks: "Oz, the name on the street for the Oswald State Penitentiary." Structurally, the major innovation of *Oz* was its narrator (for the first five seasons), Augustus Hill (Prisoner #95H522, played by Harold Perrineau). One of the inmates of Em City, Hill functions as a kind of Greek chorus, usually appearing at the beginning and end (and sometimes in the middle) of each episode to set up the common themes running through the various story lines. A paraplegic former drug dealer serving life for killing a police officer, Hill is the moral and philosophical center of *Oz*. Although the character doesn't break the fourth wall during his regular story line, his commentary is often performed from a rotating glass cell or in costumes of various kinds, setting it apart from the rest of the happenings. Hill's commentaries are an articulate, philosophical break from the visceral horrors of Oz, but they also tend to be heavy-handed explanations of the complex themes of the program (just in case the viewers can't figure it out for themselves). Whatever issues are in play in any given episode—from the larger, more all-encompassing (e.g., drugs, racial politics, economic oppression) to the smaller and more specific (e.g., voting rights of prisoners, death penalty for the developmentally disabled)—Hill typically outlines the liberal position for the audience's edification, presumably voicing that of the show's creator and primary writer.

The use of Em City as the narrative focus gives *Oz* an unusual look and allows for a set of spatial arrangements uncommon in television. The series was shot in warehouses, first in New York and then in New Jersey. The warehouse setup allowed Tom Fontana to house the entire production, offices and all, in the same space. It also allowed the production crew to build sets that mimicked the labyrinthine nature of an actual prison. The cafeteria/performance space, gym, showers, and infirmary, and the offices of the warden, chaplain, and psychologist, are regular settings for the action; but the large, bright, open set that makes up Em City is the focus. Emerald City is set up as a kind of Benthamite Panopticon, with an open guards' station in the center of two tiers of cells. Nearly all the walls are clear, allowing constant monitoring of the prisoners, by both guards and other inmates. Although this creates a distinct sense of space for the viewer, it presented distinct difficulties in shooting a weekly television series. In Emerald City, there is no privacy. A lovers' quarrel is observed by a man on a toilet in the next cell. Inmates are constantly on display, often performing dual roles: for the corrections officers, they behave as model prisoners, except when the pressures are too much; for one another, they perform threats, insults, and masculine rituals of power (or lack thereof). The nature of Em City is that the audience sees both.

A man stands shirtless in a tiny storage room. Arms outstretched, his hands grip the shelves on either side of him so hard his well-developed muscles bulge. His industrial gray pants are open, and another man

Although *Oz* was notorious for its graphic depictions of sex and violence, creator Tom Fontana (right) regularly explored philosophical and religious themes with such characters as Reverend Jeremiah Cloutier (left), played by Luke Perry.

kneels in front of him, head bobbing. The standing man grimaces, postponing his climax as long as possible. As he gets close, he reaches down as if to caress the other man's head. His large hands wrap tightly around the head and, in a flash, snap the kneeling man's neck. The dead man falls to the concrete floor, eyes open, mouth agape. Such scenes are emblematic of the themes, style, and overall discourse of the series. Although *Oz* was widely known—and repeatedly spoofed—for its graphic violence, male nudity, and brutal sexuality, Fontana was largely interested in exploring specific political and philosophical (and in some cases, overtly religious) themes.[3]

Fontana created *Oz* as a commentary on the American penal system, but he also used the program to ponder issues of gender and sexuality, ethnicity and aging, and perhaps most significantly, guilt and redemption. Having worked primarily in network television, Fontana also saw creating a series for HBO as an opportunity to stretch the boundaries of acceptability. And stretch them he did. In an episode about the hypermasculinity and patriarchal/hierarchical nature of prison life, most of the extras walk around the set naked while Augustus Hill pontificates on the fairly obvious connections between the penal/"penis" system

Best known for his work on *St. Elsewhere* and *Homicide: Life on the Street*, creative producer Tom Fontana further challenged the boundaries of serial television with *Oz*.

and a culture almost entirely ruled by regressive and essentialist definitions of masculinity and power.

Not typically a subtle show, *Oz* nonetheless has episodes—and sometimes entire arcs—built around such complex issues as the voting rights of prisoners, the economic impact of prisons, the aging of the prison population, medical treatment (particularly AIDS care) in prison, rehabilitation and punishment, and of course, capital punishment (Are inmates sometimes set up for the death penalty? What happens when execution goes wrong? And, more recently topical, What about the execution of the mentally challenged?). Behind the more overtly political subjects addressed are the larger philosophical matters at stake. Although a culture based on single-sex incarceration for the purposes of punishment and segregation from society might raise a whole host of issues, Fontana chose to focus largely on the interconnection of good and evil (particularly within the individual), the possibility of redemption or lack thereof, the inherent humanity of the apparently inhumane, and the role of personal responsibility in an extreme environment.

On the one hand, *Oz* attempts to contextualize the penal system within the larger ideology of contemporary, mainstream American culture and to foreground economic and political issues most of us ignore in the same way that we ignore prisons themselves. On a less-obvious level, the series concerns itself with the role of the individual in the system and the system's impact on the individual. The liberal politics of the series regarding society's role in constructing both the individuals and the system are often seemingly at odds with the program's focus on individual responsibility. *Oz* draws attention to the ways in which prisons and their inmates are manipulated and used, both before and after the prisoners' incarceration. Much of the focus of the series, however, is on the individual's response to the restrictions and manipulations they undergo. In a prison setting, simply surviving is complicated, and much of what *Oz* shows is the nature of survival. But a goal of this system is also rehabilitation, which is shown as nearly impossible. In fact, in Oz, redemption more than rehabilitation is an ideal held up as perhaps the greatest, and least-obtainable, good. Guilt is a given in prison, at least from a sociological standpoint. What is not typically understood is the humanity of the guilty. We as a society have chosen to respond to particularly egregious violations of our social compacts by devoting ever-increasing resources to punishment by incarceration and segregation. *Oz* addresses what that choice does to those who are in the system, either voluntarily or by force.

It was an already well-established trope of the prison genre that prisoners are rarely entirely evil and staff members rarely entirely good. Nearly every character in *Oz*, whether staff or inmate, embodies the struggles of the individual in an extreme, inhumane environment. One major character, Tobias Beecher (Prisoner #97N909, played by Lee Tergesen), is an upper-middle-class lawyer from a patrician family, in prison for having killed a young girl while driving drunk. Literally branded almost immediately as the "prag" (also known as the punk, or bitch) of the inside leader of the Aryan Brotherhood, Beecher undergoes perhaps the most body- and soul-searing transformations. As over-the-top as it sounds (and often is), in the course of serving his sentence, Beecher falls in love with a serial killer, has his arms and legs broken, has his children kidnapped (and one of them killed), kills a neo-Nazi guard with his fingernails, divorces, bites off a man's penis, backslides into alcoholism and recovers, and receives parole but fairly quickly violates it and is returned to Oz. Apparently, recidivism rates are high among the middle class as well as the working class. Although Beecher is clearly meant to be the audience's point of identification for entry into the prison system, he does not remain static and is never wholly sympathetic. He navigates the system, learning as he goes. The restrictions of incarceration put heretofore-unknown stresses on Beecher, causing fractures in his previously unquestioned worldview.

For the most part, the prison staff comprises people who are struggling to reconcile the demands of their jobs with their own ideologies. Corrections officer Diane Whittlesey is a working-class single parent with a sick mother, working at Oswald because it is one of the only employers in the area with decent pay and benefits. She has compartmentalized her life and emotions in order to deal with the stresses of being a woman in a violent, masculine environment. The pressure increases when a former biker buddy of Whittlesey's ex-husband enters Oz, and when a riot breaks out at the end of season one, she cracks, committing an unauthorized—but understandable—act of violence.

The inclusion of not one but two Catholic clergy in the cast brings an unmistakable overlay of Catholicism to the series' ideology. Both the prison chaplain, Father Ray Mukada (played by B. D. Wong), and the prison psychologist, Sister Peter Marie Reimondo (played by multi-award winner Rita Moreno), have significant roles in the lives of the prisoners and the institution. Needless to say, their occupational requirements often come into conflict with their belief systems, allowing for ongoing investigation into the role of the individual in the system. A prisoner confesses to Father Mukada multiple murders for which he has not been convicted. Sister Peter Marie must counsel a developmentally disabled inmate to prepare him for his execution, despite her own opposition to the death penalty. At one point, she almost loses her job because of her anti–capital punishment activism; at another, she considers leaving the order. Both Sister Peter Marie and Father Mukada believe deeply in the possibility of redemption or they would not continue their work in Oz. Their powers are restricted, however, largely by a system focused more on punishment than on rehabilitation. They also face inmates bent more often on working that system than on taking personal responsibility and attempting redemption.

Oz was the audience's introduction to what would clearly be HBO's philosophy of original, serialized, dramatic programming. Equal parts melodramatic, political, and deeply philosophical, Tom Fontana's series showed that HBO would not fear censorship of any kind, and that it would push the envelope in terms of scheduling, format, and most especially content. *Oz* broke the necessary ground for all of the dramatic series that followed, from the graphic violence of *The Sopranos* (1999–2007) to the explicit language of *Deadwood* (2004–). At the end of the series, Augustus Hill returns from the dead to comment on the entire six seasons, and his final speech seems to encapsulate what *Oz* was about from the beginning:

> So, what've we learned? What's the lesson for today? For all the never-ending days and restless nights in Oz. . . . That morality is transient, that virtue cannot exist without violence, that to be honest is to be flawed, that the giving and taking of love both debases and elevates us? That God or Allah or Yahweh has answers to questions we dare not even ask? The story is simple: a man lives in prison and dies. How he dies, that's easy. The who and the why is the complex part. The human part. The only part worth knowing. Peace.

Notes

1. Scott Tobias, "*Oz*: The Complete First Season (DVD)," *A.V. Club*, April 17, 2002, at http://www.avclub.com/content/node/5888.

2. The state was widely believed to be New York, and in fact, New York state flags are sometimes visible in the background of scenes.

3. Among the series that have parodied *Oz* are *South Park* and *Saturday Night Live*, where even the opening notes of the bass-heavy theme song can evoke laughter.

THREE

The Sopranos

David Thorburn

The signature program of the post-broadcast era, *The Sopranos* debuted on HBO in January 1999 and became the first cable series to achieve larger audience ratings than its broadcast competition. The series also received unprecedented critical acclaim in both popular and elite circles. Even intellectuals who had previously disdained television hailed the show as a groundbreaking work of art. One measure of the program's unique status as a cultural icon was the screening of the entire run of its first two seasons at the Museum of Modern Art in New York City as the featured item in a retrospective of gangster movies chosen by David Chase, *The Sopranos'* creator and executive producer. The show's quality had been so widely acknowledged by the beginning of its sixth season that Nancy Franklin began her *New Yorker* review of another HBO series, *Big Love* (2006–), by expressing baffled sympathy for the makers of the new program, which had been scheduled to follow "What May Be The Greatest Television Show Ever."[1]

The popularity of *The Sopranos* was particularly demoralizing for the broadcast networks, in decline through the 1980s and 1990s as a result of competition from cable and satellite subscriber networks. The show's success in the ratings against "free" network programs was decisive evidence that the mass audiences and consensus programming of the broadcast era were now historical artifacts. Although HBO's subscribers constituted only one-third of the total TV audience, the series was watched by an estimated 14 million viewers in 7.3 million TV homes during its third and fourth seasons, by far the largest continuing audience ever assembled by cable television. As Bill Carter put it in the *New York Times:* "HBO now has the first television megahit ever to be unavailable to the majority of viewers."[2]

James Gandolfini (left), who plays mob boss and middle-aged family man Tony Soprano, sits with David Chase, *The Sopranos*' creator and executive producer.

The Sopranos marks a genuine watershed in American popular culture, although its full significance has been partly misunderstood as a result of its very success and, I suspect, the HBO advertising campaign proclaiming, "It's Not TV, It's HBO." The misunderstanding grows from the implication that traditional broadcast television is a totally different experience from HBO. In fact, the program's roots in traditional television are at least as deep and as nourishing as its filiations with the gangster movie.[3]

Something of the show's revisionist, post-heroic realism is captured in its brilliant title sequence. Quick images of the roof and wall tiles of the Lincoln Tunnel filmed through the windshield of Tony Soprano's speeding car yield to the tunnel's exit ramp, the New York skyline briefly visible across the Hudson River through the passenger window. (The twin towers of the World Trade Center were framed in a quick close shot of the car's side mirror during the first two seasons, but this image was removed after September 11, 2001.) Then, images of North Jersey's

If the *Godfather* movies give us the Mafia family for the decades before and after World War II, and *Goodfellas* the same family in the cocaine-addled suburbs of the 1970s and 1980s, the Sopranos are the crime family for our age of therapy and Prozac. Psychiatrist Jennifer Melfi (Lorraine Bracco, left) with patient Tony Soprano (James Gandolfini).

absurdly named Meadowlands, the state's ugliest industrial sprawl—noxious Secaucus, polluted waterways, smokestacks—rush past, followed by shots of highway exit signs, Tony steering, and the grimy downtowns of the dwindled cities in which Tony grew up and in which much of the series' action takes place. This quick tour of the terrain of *The Sopranos* concludes with shots of modest working-class, then middle-class city homes, and finally the forested road leading to the driveway of Tony's lavish suburban brick palace. The sequence is a social history of Italians in America and, specifically, a chronicle of the protagonist's life and work, distilling essential elements of the saga of Tony Soprano (James Gandolfini), his dual identity as a suburban husband and father and as angst-ridden godfather in meaner streets than those of the mythic city across the river.

The very first scene of the first episode of *The Sopranos* clarifies and extends the antiheroic import of the title sequence, introducing the viewer to this contemporary godfather in his reluctant first visit to a psychiatrist. If the *Godfather* movies (1972, 1974, 1990) give us the Mafia family for the decades before and after World War II, and *Goodfellas* (1990) the same family in the cocaine-addled suburbs of the 1970s and 1980s, the Sopranos are the crime family for our age of therapy and Prozac. "Things are trending downward," Tony complains to his shrink, Dr. Jennifer Melfi (Lorraine Bracco), displaying one strand of the show's comedy in his very diction. These days no one has the discipline for "the penal experience."

The movie gangsters are not merely implicit references in the series, but active presences. Tony's mob crew is fond of quoting *The Godfather* and other shaping ancestors, and such allusions often create complex ironies, suggesting how eagerly these "real" gangsters embrace the aggrandizing images of the movie culture. "The eye was just how Francis framed the shot—for shock value," says Tony's lieutenant Paulie Walnuts (Tony Sirico) in the third episode, explicating a famous close-up in the montage of assassinations at the climax of Coppola's film. In a later episode we see Tony tearfully watching *The Public Enemy* (1931) on the day of his mother's funeral; the famous James Cagney melodrama about a gangster killer whose mother's love never wavers implicitly judges Tony's reptilian mother (Nancy Marchand in her last and greatest role), who terrorized him as a child and colluded with his Uncle Junior (Dominic Chianese) to have him killed because she blamed him for moving her to a nursing home.

"*Goodfellas* is my Koran," David Chase tells his interviewer (the actor-director Peter Bogdanovich, who plays Dr. Melfi's psychiatrist in the series) in the voice-over commentary on the DVD of the first season.[4] And as even casual viewers know, *The Sopranos* is full of allusions and sometimes fawning references to Scorsese himself, as well as to his films. The best known of these homages is often mentioned to me by *Sopranos'* fans and has surely generated essays and mash-ups in the film schools. This is the scene in the eighth episode of the first season, in which Tony's henchman Christopher Moltisanti (Michael Imperioli) shoots a young bakery cashier in the foot, an eruption of violence as brutally narcissistic and gratuitous as its original in *Goodfellas,* where a much younger Imperioli is the victim of the shooting.

The Sopranos takes full advantage of its freedom from the constraints of broadcast television. Both male and female characters speak with the profane candor of real people; mayhem and murder are dramatized with pitiless, shocking directness; there is considerable (but not full frontal) nudity. But this license in what is seen and heard is never gratuitous or sensational, and the many eruptions of crippling or murderous violence have disturbing authority in part because they take place in such mundanely realistic spaces and are committed or endured by unpretty, ordinary characters the audience has come to know. The series breaks with broadcast conventions in other ways as well, notably in its readiness to dramatize its characters' dreams and fantasies, some of which achieve a macabre, disorienting intensity.

But its sense of the ordinary, the quotidian, the *not mythic* is the real key to *The Sopranos.* Tony Soprano is a stone killer and mob boss, but he is also a middle-aged father with a discontented spouse and a son and daughter no more deranged than most privileged teenagers in our high-tech, motorized, image-saturated suburbs. The juxtaposition—sometimes the intersection—of these apparently alternate worlds generates complexities undreamt of in most movies or earlier forms of television. The program mobilizes a sustained, ongoing experience of moral ambiguity, as Tony and some of his criminal cronies display a range of comic, sentimental, deeply ordinary traits in their dealings with aging parents, wives, children, and mistresses, and then in other moments perform acts of sickening disloyalty, brutality, and murder. One of the story's deepest revelations, repeated in astonishing variation in the main plot and subplots, is that Tony's two families are really one, that the corruption, violence, and hypocrisy that are the tools of his trade seep into and come to define his own family, as they did his father's before him.

These defining qualities of the series emerge decisively in the fifth episode of the first season, in which Tony takes his daughter Meadow (Jamie-Lynn Sigler) on a tour of colleges in New England and, in a stop at a gas station, recognizes an informer, once part of his crime family, now in hiding in the witness protection program. Scenes of intimate bonding between father and daughter are intercut with Tony's stalking of the informer, whom he ultimately attacks from behind and strangles with a wire. The murder is not quick: the victim struggles hard before he dies. Moments before, this killer had been a doting father, communing with his daughter in a common American parenting ritual. Then, in their final ride home in the car, Daddy driving, Meadow in the front seat beside him, he lies fluently, with quick, improvising intelligence about the lost watch, the bruises on his hand. She looks back at him warily. She's learning suspicion, and not to trust her father.

As this episode implies, *The Sopranos* does not, as many have claimed, repudiate or totally transcend traditional television. For all its cable-licensed profanity, sex, and violence, the series embraces and deeply exploits TV's unique hospitality to serial narrative as well as the central subject of television drama of the broadcast era, its ideological core—the American family.

The show has a specific ancestry in *The Rockford Files* (NBC, 1974–80), whose staff David Chase joined in 1976 as writer and producer. That private-eye series starring James Garner was also a hybrid of comedy, crime, and (sometimes) family drama, and it used the format of the weekly series to explore the ongoing, changing relations among its recurring characters. Several episodes of *Rockford* clearly anticipate *The Sopranos*. In one of these, a two-part story first broadcast in 1977, George Loros, who plays the mob capo Raymond Curto in the HBO series, portrays a Mafia hit man undone by his city-boy's ignorance in the wilds of nature. This episode hints at the bleak, murderous comedy of the memorable installment from the third season of *The Sopranos* in which Paulie Walnuts and young Christopher are trapped together without food or transport in the wintry Pine Barrens of southern New Jersey.

The series format, traditional television's essential feature, is *The Sopranos'* fundamental resource as well. It permits the program to dramatize the unsteady, troubled maturation of Tony's children, for example; the ebb and flow of his cankered intimacy with his wife Carmela (Edie Falco); and the murderous, shifting alliances and hostilities within his own crime family and among rival mobsters. As the series unfolds during its first five seasons, its account of the primary characters deepens; aspects of Tony's past emerge in fitful, accreting detail; and the experiences and inner lives of many secondary characters are explored more fully. The social and political reach of the story is enlarged in some of these secondary strands—for example, when Christopher and his girlfriend (Drea de Matteo) move the story into the world of contemporary hip-hop and the racial politics of the music business.

The performances are always vivid and memorable—those of secondary figures as well as the principals, especially a frequently blubbery (and, in later seasons, overweight) Gandolfini and the superbly nuanced Edie Falco. Moreover, as the show progressed, these performers aged visibly before the watching audience, and the viewers' knowledge of their histories and their interconnections informed every later scene. It is important to recognize that the movies cannot replicate this sort of accretive intimacy and understanding between characters and audience. *The Sopranos* is not a film. It is a television series. It uses the strategies perfected over decades in daytime soaps and prime-time series. It draws on a tradition of visual mastery developed equally in the interior spaces and tight, compelling close-ups of soaps, sitcoms, and family melodramas *and* in the fluid editing and skill at framing action and exterior spaces for TV's small screen of the cop and private-eye shows.

In its first five seasons, the damaged, unstable family order of the program becomes a compelling metaphor or distillation of the larger social order. In its enlarging power to explore personality as it evolves in time, and in its stringent, ramifying stories of crime, injustice, marriage, and family, the series had become a twenty-first-century equivalent of the great English and European novels of the nineteenth century.

Then came the sixth season. The show had faltered before, but mostly in minor ways. At times, for example, its knowing winks to movie buffs feel gratuitous, as in one sequence where the great Scorsese (actually a look-alike actor) is shown waving to his adoring fans as he enters a dance club. And the production was on occasion simply careless, as when the elegant sedan in which Tony and his daughter drive on their tour of colleges morphs unexplained into Tony's monster SUV when they return home. A more serious form of inattentiveness, slightly undermining our understanding of Tony's character, also surfaces more than once in the early seasons. In one episode, for example, he condescendingly corrects a subordinate who confuses Nostradamus with the hunchback of Notre Dame, yet in a later episode Tony himself confuses Martin Luther King with Rodney King. Different writers, of course, episodes apart, and perhaps an inattentive executive producer, David Chase, who had been a reluctant servant of TV since the 1970s and, not so secretly, wanted out.[5]

In its sixth season, however, the show begins to repeat itself in certain ways and to pursue subsidiary plots involving minor characters that are not as richly or decisively linked, as those of earlier seasons are, to the primary themes and characters. The season opens with Uncle Junior's addled accidental shooting of Tony and Tony's near-death adventure in a coma-dream that lasts through episodes two and three in counterpart with far more interesting "real" scenes, in which his actual family confronts his possible death and his Mafia family begins to disintegrate in rivalry and greed. The core of this material is a pallid replay, lacking the familial ferocity and cunning that incite Junior's botched hit on Tony in the penultimate episode of the first season. In the earlier case, the attempted assassination grows from a tangle of links and connections going back to Tony's childhood, his mother's relations with him, with his father, and with Uncle Junior. In the sixth season's replay, an old man with Alzheimer's disease shoots someone by mistake. (Although, to be fair, it is a mistake grounded in a generations-old murder-robbery, a criminal obsession and sense of having been cheated of money so tenacious it survives the decay of most of his other cognitive abilities.)

Tony's near-death experiences as dramatized over two full episodes feel stagy and pretentious. Shot in a strangely lit, almost lunar environment of featureless modern hotels and bars, the scenes seem fake, especially compared with the grainy, authentic realism of the show's usual location shots amid the traffic thunder of Lodi or Kearney or Bloomfield Avenue in East Orange. It's as if we've stumbled into a play or film by an imitator of Samuel Beckett or Jean-Luc Godard, not the North Jersey Tony knows. And the "plot" of this coma-dream seems equally factitious, like a student's thesis or a preacher's lesson. Tony is metamorphosed into his doppelgänger, a businessman named Finnerty, and struggles like a Franz Kafka character to recover his identity. Characters he's murdered appear as friendly guides and hosts, ushering him into some sort of Mansion of Eternity . . . when his daughter's voice, at his bed stand in the hospital, recalls him to real life. Good-bye Finnerty. Good riddance.

Even what many saw as the most notable subplot of this penultimate part of the sixth and final season represents a falling away from the high standards set in the first five seasons.[6] This is the sequence many called the "Brokeback" story for its resemblance to *Brokeback Mountain*, the 2005 film sympathetically depicting gay cowboys. In this gangster version, an obese, pretty-faced capo (Joseph Gannascoli), Tony's top wage earner, as we learn during this unfolding parable of mob homophobia, murders a friend to keep his gay identity secret, then flees for a gay idyll in Maine before meeting an end I leave undescribed. It's tough to be a gay mobster, but even so, this worthy point feels belabored after several episodes and at best simple, compared with the multiple ways the major subplots from earlier years link organically to the central characters and extend the moral and political implications of the series as a whole.

But many great stories have broken or disappointing endings. One of these is Homer's *Odyssey*. Damaged or weary endings are the norm for television series, even the greatest, such as *Gunsmoke* (CBS, 1955–75) or *All in the Family* (CBS, 1971–83). Whatever the final verdict on its twilight episodes, *The Sopranos* has secured its landmark status in American cultural history. It is a brilliant hybrid culmination of film and television, and an originating text as well, among the first complex expressions of the digital future now impending. It is probably the first great work of American art of the twenty-first century.

Notes

Thanks to Micky DuPree for ideas and research assistance and to Daniel Thorburn and Barbara Thorburn for acute criticism and help on this essay, which revises and enlarges my entry on *The Sopranos* in Horace Newcomb, ed., *The Television Encyclopedia*, 2nd ed. (New York: Fitzroy Dearborn, 2004).

1. Nancy Franklin, "On Television: Triple Threat," *New Yorker*, 17 March 2006, 78. *The Sopranos* almost surely received more critical praise across a range of publications than any program in TV history and also generated a lot of intelligent commentary. Among many thoughtful responses to the show, I found these especially helpful: Caryn James, "'Sopranos': Blood, Bullets and Proust," *New York Times*, 2 March 2001, B1, B30; Steven Johnson, *Everything Bad Is Good for You: How Today's Popular Culture Is Actually Making Us Smarter* (New York: Riverhead Books, 2005); David Lavery, ed., *This Thing of Ours: Investigating* The Sopranos (New York: Columbia University Press, 2002); Elaine Showalter, "Mob Scene," *American Prospect* 11:8 (February

2000): 28; Alessandra Stanley, "Bullies, Bears and Bullets: Its Round 5," *New York Times,* 5 March 2004, B1, B28.

2. Bill Carter, "Calibrating the Next Step for 'The Sopranos,'" *New York Times,* 7 October 2002, C1.

3. Horace Newcomb makes this argument as well. See "'This Is Not Al Dente': *The Sopranos* and the New Meaning of 'Television,'" in Newcomb, ed., *Television, The Critical View,* 7th ed. (New York: Oxford University Press, 2006), 561–88.

4. The Sopranos, *The Complete First Season* [DVD], interview with David Chase by Peter Bogdanovich (2004; New York: Home Box Office Home Video, 2005).

5. David Chase's ambivalent relation to his masterpiece will someday be the subject of dissertations. Let those students of the future get started with three articles—a *New Yorker* essay that incorporates comments from Chase, and two interviews, all three orchestrated by Chase, it would seem, in part to confer an auteur's aura on the expensive HBO enterprise and in part to let Chase make movies, finally (although he does permit himself one tip of the cap to his TV past in an early episode when Big Pussy cries, "What am I, Rockford?"). See David Remnick, "Is This the End of Rico?" *New Yorker,* 2 April 2001, 38–44; Virginia Heffernan, "The Real Boss of the 'Sopranos': Why David Chase Will Never Work in TV Again," *New York Times,* 29 February 2004, sec. 2, 1, 20; and Elizabeth Primamore, "This Thing of His," *New Jersey Monthly,* April 2002, 84–87, 116–17 (illuminating on Chase's Italian American childhood in northern New Jersey).

6. The sixth and last season was divided into two parts. The first twelve episodes were originally telecast between March 12 and June 4, 2006, while the final nine "bonus" episodes aired between March 8 and June 10, 2007.

FOUR

Six Feet Under

Kim Akass and Janet McCabe

> The importance of *Six Feet Under* is not that it is like anything else,
> but that it isn't.
> —*Mark Lawson*

Six Feet Under debuted on HBO at 10:00 P.M. on Sunday June 3, 2001.
It was the first drama series launched by the channel since *The Sopranos*
(1999–2007), and HBO anticipated success, commissioning a second
season before the first had even aired. This confidence appeared justified: the show received the highest ratings of any new HBO series, with
a reported 5 million weekly viewers (compared with *The Sopranos*' 3.3
million in its first season). Set in a Los Angeles family-owned funeral
parlor, *Six Feet Under* is another family saga—this time telling the idiosyncratic, darkly humorous, and profoundly moving story of the dysfunctional Fishers. In the opening moments patriarch Nathaniel (Richard
Jenkins) dies in a tragic road accident when a city bus ploughs into his
hearse. The family is left bereft, and the brothers—Nathaniel Jr., or
Nate (Peter Krause), and David (Michael C. Hall)—charged, along with
restorative artist and long-time employee Federico "Rico" Diaz (Freddy
Rodriguez) with continuing the family business. Winner of two Golden
Globe awards in 2001, including Best Television Series–Drama, *Six Feet
Under* broke new ground. Never in the history of American television
has a show contemplated the frailty of our lives in quite such a quirky
yet deeply introspective way.

Practitioners and Personnel

Central to HBO's definition of original programming is its promotion of
the TV auteur. Any survey of original publicity for *Six Feet Under*

Set in a Los Angeles family-owned funeral parlor, *Six Feet Under* is the family saga of the Fishers, who cope with death, old age, sickness, adolescent angst, homosexuality, interracial relations, mental illness, and drug addiction. (Left to right) Long-time employee and restorative artist Federico "Rico" Diaz (Freddy Rodriguez), with David Fisher (Michael C. Hall), and Ruth Fisher (Frances Conroy).

reveals the emphasis placed on the creative genius behind the show, Alan Ball: creator, writer, director, and executive producer. Ball started out in theater, helping to set up the General Nonsense Theatre Company in Florida (1980–86) before moving to New York, where he formed the Alarm Dog Repertory Company (1986–94) with friends. Writing and producing off-off-Broadway black comedies, he eventually came to the attention of prominent television producers Tom Werner and Marcy Carsey, for whom he became writer-producer first for *Grace Under Fire* (ABC, 1993–98) and then *Cybill* (CBS, 1995–98). In 1999, he signed a three-year television development deal with the Greenblatt Janollari Studio—the production company responsible for *Six Feet Under*—and together they made the short-lived *Oh, Grow Up* (ABC, 1999). But Ball's experiences in network television proved dispiriting, and he wrote a screenplay as an exit strategy. He has said, "it's no mistake that *Amer-*

ican Beauty [directed by Sam Mendes, 1999] was about a man who was beaten down and lost interest in his life rediscovering his passion for living."[1]

This detour into film would change Ball's profile when, in 2000, he won the Academy Award for Best Original Screenplay. The enormous critical and commercial success of *American Beauty*—nominated for eight Oscars and winning five—meant that Ball was much in demand, but like David Chase (*The Sopranos*) and Darren Star (*Sex and the City* [1998–2004]) before him, he chose HBO and a return to television rather than another film or theater project. A strange choice maybe, but according to Ball, he "didn't want to become a hired gun" or "to be hired to write other people's ideas."[2] Ball was initially approached by Carolyn Strauss, senior vice president for original programming at HBO, about the possibility of writing a series for the network. After she told him that her favorite films were *The Loved One* (Tony Richardson, 1965) and *Harold and Maude* (Hal Ashby, 1971)—"black comedies that take decidedly irreverent attitudes toward death"—Ball wrote the pilot. HBO bought the concept and gave him a thirteen-episode commitment—and *Six Feet Under* was born. Or so the story goes. Ball admits that had *American Beauty* not been a hit, "HBO would not have come along and offered [him] almost total freedom on *Six Feet Under*."[3] Conversely, however, he also admits that without the success of *The Sopranos,* he would not have been "so excited about the possibilities of television."[4]

Ball cites his own life as inspiration for the series. When he was thirteen years old his older sister, Mary Ann, was killed in a car accident while driving him to a piano lesson. He says of the tragedy: "That separated my life into a life before and a life after. It was really my first experience of losing someone close to me in the worst possible way—out of the blue and in front of my eyes . . . nothing else in my life has affected me quite as profoundly as that."[5] Six years later, his father passed away from lung cancer. Both bereavements had an impact on the story lines in terms of plot and character. Other influences listed included Jessica Mitford's *The American Way of Death* (1963) and Thomas Lynch's award-winning books *Bodies in Motion and at Rest* (2000) and *The Undertaking* (1997), which Ball asked the writers and cast members to read before filming started.

Intelligent writing is key to HBO's original programming, and *Six Feet Under* is no exception. Each of the seven main writers—Bruce Eric Kaplan (former creative consultant on *Seinfeld* [NBC, 1990–98]), Laurence Andries, Scott Buck, Rick Cleveland (best known as the writer who shared an Emmy with Aaron Sorkin for cowriting *The West Wing* [NBC, 1999–2006]), Jill Soloway, Christian Taylor, and Kate Robins—were hired for their unconventional writing styles and eclectic experiences. The group met under the guidance of Ball, discussed ideas for episodes, and plotted out narrative trajectories and character development. Differing from usual television writing practice, where the writer develops a script from scratch, here one writer was assigned an episode after initial script suggestions had been discussed among the team.

Ball may have both written and directed the pilot, but he enlisted such directors as Ted Demme (*Blow* [2001]), Rose Troche (*Go Fish* [1994]), Nicole Holofcener (*Lovely & Amazing* [2001]), Lisa Cholodenko (*High Art* [1998]) and Miguel Arteta (*Chuck & Buck* [2000], *The Good Girl* [2002]) to take the helm for later episodes. Besides those with established reputations in independent filmmaking are those who built careers directing television, like Michael Engler, Daniel Attias, and Allen Coutler. Added to this roster are Kathy Bates, Oscar-winning actress and sometime *Six Feet Under* guest star, and Rodrigo García, son of Nobel Laureate in Literature and magic realist patriarch Gabriel García Márquez. Such an eclectic mix of directing talent has contributed to the distinctive and highly original visual style.

Of the original cast, Peter Krause, who made his name in the 1990s with shows like *Cybill* (where he met Ball) and *Sports Night* (1998–2000), and antipodean actress Rachel Griffiths, well regarded for her films *Muriel's Wedding* (1994), *My Best Friend's Wedding* (1997), and *Hilary and Jackie* (1998; for which she was Oscar-nominated) were the best known. Alongside them were acclaimed stage actors Frances Conroy and Michael C. Hall, whose reputations had been made on Broadway. Lili Taylor, darling of independent filmmakers, features heavily in season three as Nate's granola-crunching wife, Lisa, to cover Rachel Griffiths's maternity leave; and veterans of film, theater, and television Kathy Bates, Joanna Cassidy, Harriet Sansom Harris, Patricia Clarkson, and James Cromwell bring further dramatic weight to the cast.

Thomas Newman was an obvious choice for Alan Ball when he was deciding on a composer for the new TV series. Ball had worked with Newman on *American Beauty,* for which Newman had picked up various accolades including an Oscar nomination and a BAFTA (British Academy of Film and Television Arts) Award. The practice of turning to well-known composers to score music for main title sequences of television programs has fallen out of favor due to the high expense involved, but Ball obviously felt that Newman, with his filmic pedigree and reputation for "bringing an emotional strength and accuracy to [his] scores,"[6] would provide the perfect main title theme to his series. Richard Marvin provided the rest of the score, while Thomas Golubiç and Gary Calamar supervised the acquisition of copyrighted material. As with the writing, however, Ball retained overall control, partly because of his "incredible knowledge of bands and music,"[7] and partly because of the integral role music plays in setting the emotional tone of the drama.

Sociocultural Context

Six Feet Under, premiering only months before the terrorist attacks of September 11, 2001, chimed in with an elegiac cultural zeitgeist obsessed with mortality. Arguably, American culture has long been obsessed with death—with guns, violence, and killing. But September 11 ushered in a period of national introspection, a questioning of the fragility of our lives and how well we live them. Such contemplation is evident in literature (Alice Sebold's *The Lovely Bones* [2002]) and films (*The Sixth Sense* [M. Night Shyamalan, 1999], *The Others* [Alejandro Amenábar, 2001], *American Beauty*) when the dead narrate, and in television (*Dead Like Me* [Showtime, 2003–4], *Providence* [NBC, 1999–2003], *Desperate Housewives* [ABC, 2004–]) where the dead never seem to die. No television series better captured this cultural mournfulness than *Six Feet Under*—the finality of death and what it means for the living. Peter Krause mused that "after Sept. 11, a lot of people who do TV went back to work and thought, 'Oh, jeez. This is meaningless' but our show is now as meaningful as ever. The basic theme of our show is, you've got one singular life and that's it. . . . It makes people think about themselves and their place in the world."[8]

Six Feet Under may start with a dead patriarch, but the series tapped into a broader unease with patriarchal authority permeating modern cultural politics. "With the loss of this paterfamilias," Robert Tobin argues, "the Fisher family becomes a symbol of the society in which it lives: the post-patriarchal West, in which all the rules have to be remade." *Six Feet Under*'s characters are indeed drawn from the post-Vietnam, postfeminist, post–civil rights, post-Watergate eras of social upheaval, in which patriarchal authority became suspect; the aftermath of September 11 led to a further questioning of American patriarchy—its foreign policy, the Bush administration and the Republican agenda, and the rise of Christian fundamentalism. Many episodes struggle with the attempt to "provide a positive answer to the question of how society should develop without patriarchal guidance."[9]

Strict gender binary categories are made suspicious; heterosexual privilege is similarly doomed. In the post-patriarchal world of *Six Feet Under,* sexual politics and relationships are viewed from a decidedly queer perspective, offering an affirmative but alternative image of non-traditional families and couples. David and Keith Charles (Mathew St. Patrick), signaled as the right match from the start, work through various traumas and conflicts before emerging as the ideal couple at the end. Initially separating because David refuses to be open about his homosexuality (and indeed David struggles with his internalized homophobia until the last episode), theirs is the relationship that matures, is full of sexual passion and selfless support, leading to their eventual adoption of Anthony and Durrell and their setting up home in the Fisher house.

In a twist, the other "right" couple—Nate and Brenda—do not fare so well. Passionate maybe, but their relationship is full of secrets, infidelities, and frustrations. Marriage and the desire for a child only intensify their troubles, and the more the couple pushes for domestic contentment the more it contains them, leading finally to Nate's death from a brain disorder, arteriovenous malformation, brought on by stress. Unlike Keith and David, the heterosexual couple has nothing but expectations. Heterosexual relationships in fact inevitably seem hopeless because of what Merri Lisa Johnson calls "the inevitably disappointing expectations of romantic mythology or the disciplinary force of the traditional marriage contract."[10] Women, in particular, experience immense disillusionment and letdown with respect to the heterosexual script of romance, sex, marriage, and family. Widowed matriarch Ruth slips easily back into old relationship patterns; and daughter Claire shares similar suffocating tendencies when it comes to her relations with

The tempestuous relation-
ship between Nate (Peter
Krause, left) and Brenda
(Rachel Griffiths, right) is
passionate, but full of
secrets, infidelities, and
frustrations. Their even-
tual marriage and desire
for a child only intensify
their troubles.

men. She may possess an erotic attachment to the romance of the tor-
mented, brooding male archetype, but the reality is a series of bad dates,
trouble with the authorities, and an unwanted pregnancy. Caught between
desiring the social sanction of the heterosexual script and the ambivalence in living it, these women eventually settle for unconventionality.

Undoubtedly, the show is less about death than about the art of living well, or as Christopher Moore puts it, *Six Feet Under* "makes emotional connections between characters based on the fragility of life."[11]
Each episode starts with a death that brings the Fishers some trade;
these deaths vary from the absurd to the achingly poignant, from an
insurance salesman diving into his pool and sustaining a fatal head
injury while Dean Martin croons "Ain't life a kick in the head?" ("The
Will," 1:2) to the final shot when Claire's cataract-filled eyes close for

the last time ("Everyone's Waiting," 5:13). However, as Thomas Lynch eloquently states, by putting a dead body in the room you can say pretty much anything. "My sense is that Ball opens every show with a death mostly because every show needs a corpse—a dead body in the room—which will allow the free range of conversation on what would otherwise be 'difficult' subjects: gay love, love past middle age, young love, life in all its untidiness and grey tone. A dead body (like a naked one) ups the emotional ante so much that we can, indeed, talk about anything."[12] The finality of death, and often its tragic irony, structures each episode, leading characters to search for meaning in their lives. But what becomes unique about *Six Feet Under* is the ordinariness in which issues are tackled.

Visual Style

Visually, *Six Feet Under* strives for more than merely creating a look—picking up on narrative themes, the show develops them visually and uses the camera to convey additional information about the characters. Again drawing on his own memories and experiences of funeral homes, Ball recalls the muted colors, the soothing music, and a feeling of being trapped in time. With this in mind he searched for a cinematographer who could do more than just capture a feeling; specifically, he wanted someone who would bring "a cinematic sensibility to TV, and who would strive to create a visual palette that would not only tell the story of the Fisher and Sons funeral home but also comment on it." Enter director of photography Alan Caso, who worked with the writer to come up with what Ball calls "an anti-TV language." Caso describes it as "a combination of very painterly, motivated, natural lighting, desaturated colors and lots of depth."[13] Deliberately avoiding "the kinetic, almost chaotic movement style of network TV, the *NYPD Blue* thing," Caso says, "we don't move the camera a lot unless there is a reason to move it, motivated by the emotional intent of the scene. We do a lot of very formal shots where you let things play out in a proscenium, treating the frame almost like it's a stage."[14]

Season three saw the production team switch to a wide-screen format to give the series an even more cinematic sensibility. Caso made the lighting moodier: "I feel like we're always in a bat cave. We're in their environment and the rest of the world is always trying to invade, but never really gets into the dark corners of the Fisher house. Every character on the show is so messed up that the lighting really works with them—there are so many dark areas in their psyches."[15] Using a wide lens, a rarity on network television, "gives a much more in-your-face style than traditional television."[16] It also has an effect on the narrative in that it provides "proscenia for the actors to play in and make bold statements about the emptiness of someone's life by isolating him, creating a conflict with the composition of the frame, or show his misery by making him look small and insignificant in the frame."[17]

The effect of this can clearly be seen in the mise-en-scène of the kitchen, which according to Alan Ball "is the heart of the home, the source of nourishment and sustenance, the congregating place, the hearth." Despite the fact that the kitchen holds a central place in the lives of the Fisher family, and especially Ruth, Ball adds, "it's not a completely warm and rosy place, because the Fishers live in the constant presence of death."[18] The kitchen, in particular, becomes symbolic of family matriarch Ruth's inner journey as, locked in domestication, recently widowed with her children grown up, she gradually becomes lost in her attempt to find a place in the world. Although she is initially positioned as swathed in the kitchen's warmth, busily preparing the Christmas dinner and anticipating her family reunion in the pilot, she soon becomes trapped, and the kitchen threatens to overwhelm her. "The Room" (1:6) finds Ruth standing statuelike, gripping a saucepan with her children bustling about her. "The Invisible Woman" (2:5) sees her dreaming of the bare house—stripped of furniture and devoid of life, the domestic space cold, barren, and unforgiving. And it is ultimately a solitary dinner in a cavernous kitchen that signals the end of domestic bliss for Ruth ("Back to the Garden," 2:7). Low camera angles, wide lenses, and sinister lighting turn the hitherto cozy kitchen into an uncanny prison, emphasizing the emptiness of Ruth's life.

Surreal lives lurking beneath the mundane are central to the series. Part of the show's distinctive visual style, "startling tableaux" convey these interior states of being in which the ordinary is made strange.[19] Rodrigo García, in particular, has brought magic realism, as the dead mingle with the living, to the televisual mise-en-scène. A *Six Feet Under* regular, he directed season three opener "Full Circle." Featuring alternative realities hallucinated by Nate during his surgery, when blood vessels in his brain rupture, this episode has Nate catapulted into a *Six Feet Under* limbo. When Nate is joined by his dead father for a metaphysical journey of "life-revealing flashbacks and foreshadowings," the episode breaks every TV convention. According to Alan Poul, "there are many different parallel universes in which every permutation of every possible occurrence are taking place simultaneously. That's what is being illustrated in the opening scene, and I think that in the same way we are saying that that applies to storytelling as well. We are choosing to tell the story of Nate in that reality."[20] That Garcia's brand of magic realism is laid over Nate's existential hallucinatory state makes the episode stand out as one of the most remarkable in a television series, rivaling even Tony Soprano's extraordinary dream sequence in season five of *The Sopranos* ("The Test Dream," 5:11).

Conclusion

Searching for new subjectivity in particular has given rise to hitherto unseen representations of the middle-aged, postmenopausal widow; the teenage daughter discovering who she is; the feckless eldest son suffering an existential crisis and later coping with a life-threatening illness; and the youngest negotiating his way out of the closet. Never simple clichés, always defying stereotypes, the characters represent a subtle complexity rarely before seen on American television screens. The intimacy of the mise-en-scène accentuates the psychological introspection of these protagonists. With a small ensemble cast, *Six Feet Under* is able to devote substantial narrative time and space to characters—their dilemmas, their life choices, their relationships.

Six Feet Under was laid to rest in 2005, following each of the Fishers into the future and concluding their stories with their eventual deaths—leaving the audience in no doubt that this is truly the end for the series. Over its five seasons, it fulfilled the HBO agenda of challenging conventional television wisdom and representing that which had rarely before been seen on our screens. But even so, it pushed HBO to its limits: the series is difficult to place in institutional and generic terms; it walks a fine line between comedy and tragedy; it teeters on the edge of unbearable poignancy before tipping over into corny melodrama. Structurally, it deals with the space between death and burial; thematically, it focuses on cultural taboos—homosexuality, mental illness, old age, sickness, drug addiction, adolescence, race, and class—which in turn are used to revisit traditional cultural certainties like religion, marriage, and the family; and ultimately, it questions who we are.

Notes

The epigraph to this essay is drawn from Mark Lawson, "Foreword: Reading *Six Feet Under*," in Kim Akass and Janet McCabe, eds., *Reading* Six Feet Under: *TV To Die For* (London: I. B. Tauris, 2005), xxii.

1. Bernard Weinraub, "An Oscar Winner Returns to TV on New Terms," *New York Times*, 4 March 2001, 21.

2. Ibid.

3. Ibid., 21, 25.

4. Paula Hendrickson, "How Dare You!" *Emmy* 24:3 (2002): 114

5. Peter Ross, "Death Becomes Him," *Sunday Tribune*, 2 November 2003, 11.

6. Peter Kaye, "I'm Dead, Wow, Cool: The Music of *Six Feet Under*," in Akass and McCabe, eds., *Reading* Six Feet Under, 195.

7. Richard Marvin, quoted in ibid., 204.

8. Jeffrey Zaslow, "Quite an Undertaking," *Daily News*, USA Weekend, 15–17 March 2002, 10.

9. Robert Deam Tobin, "*Six Feet Under* and Post-Patriarchal Society," *Film and History* 32:1 (2002): 87–88.

10. Merri Lisa Johnson, "From Relationship Autopsy to Romantic Utopia: The Missing Discourse of Egalitarian Marriage on HBO's *Six Feet Under*," *Discourse* 26:3 (2004): 22.

11. Christopher Moore, "When *Six Feet Under* Strikes Close to Home," *WestSider*, 9–15 May 2002, 9.

12. Thomas Lynch, quoted in Ross, "Death Becomes Him," 12.

13. Ron Magid, "Family Plots," *American Cinematographer* 83:11 (November 2002): 71–72.

14. Joy Press, "Exquisite Corpses," *Village Voice*, 19–25 March 2003, 55.

15. Alan Caso, quoted in ibid.

16. Ibid.

17. Magid, "Family Plots," 72–73.

18. Ibid., 76.

19. Press, "Exquisite Corpses," 55.

20. Gary Montgomery, "Pouling Together," *Next*, 14 March 2003, 37.

FIVE

The Wire

Brian G. Rose

From the start, *The Wire* (2002–) was a departure for HBO, the network that had made its reputation departing from traditional television ways. Instead of offering a dramatic alternative to the program formats of its commercial broadcast rivals, *The Wire* was a direct assault against that most venerable of TV genres, the cop show, with the goal quite literally to explode the creaky, hidebound world of prime-time crime and law enforcement from within. Gone would be the stalwart cop, able to thwart, sometimes single-handedly, the continuous eruptions of violence and illegal activity from the bowels of the city. Banished also would be the one-hour solutions and easy, triumph-of-justice explanations carted out at the end of each episode to mollify viewers with the reassurance that their world was not spinning wildly out of control.

The Wire had different political intentions and strategies in mind. Creator David Simon and his cowriter Ed Burns were eager to throw out the moribund certainties of the cop genre and inject not just a measure of reality, but a potent and potentially combustible mix of urban sociology, fiercely argued politics, and, believe it or not, macroeconomics. Added to this was a firm conviction that a reconstituted police show could easily embrace all layers of society—not just the enforcers and the enforced—providing a sharp-edged tool to examine the pressures and policies that govern everyone's lives, from the dispossessed to those doing the dispossessing, from society's outcasts to the corporations and institutions indifferent to those cast out by their new economic realities.

The broad scope they hoped to portray would be matched by a similar sweep in storytelling and style. *The Wire* was conceived, according to Simon, specifically as "a visual novel"[1]—a phrase that quickly became

82

The Wire was conceived by creator David Simon and cowriter Ed Burns as "a visual novel" that each season offers twelve- or thirteen-part story arcs with some plot strands buried for weeks at a time. In the pilot episode, for example, Officer Jimmy McNulty (Dominic West, pictured) remarks that he would least like to be stationed on "the boat"; by season's end, however, his fears are realized as he is transferred to the harbor patrol. Photograph by David Lee.

the easiest way to explain the show's distinctive, and demanding, viewing experience. Instead of the individual episode, the basic structural unit would be the series as a whole, permitting vast twelve- or thirteen-part story arcs (with some plot strands buried for weeks at a time), kaleidoscopic character groupings (with a shifting cast of more than thirty players), and a quirky belief that viewers needed to work hard to keep up and make thematic connections that were rarely italicized or foregrounded.

HBO was initially reluctant to accept the series' challenge to the fifty-year legacy of the cop show, primarily because it was, at least on the surface, still a standard cop show, and thus part of the commercial TV universe the alternative network was designed to oppose. It took more than a year of script revisions and forceful argument before Simon (who would serve as the series' co-executive producer with Robert F.

Colesberry) could convince programming executives that it would be a "profound victory for HBO to take the essence of network fare and smartly turn it on its head."[2] Production for a thirteen-episode season finally began in November 2001.

For Simon, the difficult fight to get *The Wire* approved marked another achievement in an unusual television career. Starting out as a reporter at the *Baltimore Sun,* where he mostly worked the police beat, he wrote two well-received books based on intense immersions in the crime-ridden streets of the city. The first, *Homicide: A Year on the Killing Streets,* came out in 1991 and was turned into an NBC series by producer Barry Levinson two years later. (Simon ended up joining the show's writing staff, ultimately becoming one of its producers.) His second book, *The Corner,* marked his first collaboration with Ed Burns, a former Baltimore homicide detective. They had originally met back in 1985 while Simon was reporting on a famous wiretap investigation set up by Burns and his partner. Impressed by Burns's wayward intelligence and spirit, Simon convinced him in 1993 to delay his plans to become a public school teacher and instead work with Simon on a project examining the lives of the inhabitants of a typical West Baltimore street corner torn apart by the ravages of drugs. Their three-year effort, *The Corner,* appeared in 1997, and was made into an Emmy Award–winning miniseries for HBO in 2000 (Simon and Burns served as cowriters, with Simon acting as co-executive producer with Robert F. Colesberry).

The Corner's success convinced Simon that the time was right for him and Burns to tackle a new approach to the police genre, particularly as they surveyed the terrain around them. The prime-time cop show had evolved (or devolved) over the last decade into a series of sensationalism-laced, procedural investigations, led by the astonishing popularity of NBC's *Law & Order* (1990–) and its numerous progeny. CBS had just launched *CSI: Crime Scene Investigation* (2000–), which also would mutate, this time with a surprising collection of geographically themed spin-offs. The then-recent cancellation of *Homicide* (NBC, 1993–99) was, for Simon, conclusive proof of the format's creative dead-end on commercial television, particularly as he recalled the notes he and his fellow writers would receive from NBC demanding, "Where are the life-affirming moments? How can our viewers hope?"[3] They created *The Wire* in the belief that, by subverting the cop show's strategies of individual heroism and ideological uplift, they could more accurately reflect the multilayered realms of law and lawlessness they had witnessed in their previous roles as reporter and policeman.

The first episode of *The Wire* was a bold statement of their ambitious goals. In surveying the legal bureaucracies and illegal street life of Baltimore, Simon and Burns dispensed with the conventional pieties (both political and cultural) surrounding the judicial system, police enforcement, local government, and inner-city drug dealing and instead posed a sweeping view in which everyone—from top to bottom—is subject to similar kinds of institutional pressures and tensions. Parallels are drawn between the various worlds (a scene with a cop being chewed out by his superior is followed by a scene with a young drug dealer getting an equally humiliating reprimand from his boss) to connect the strains of organizational life and the price that individuals who work for them, in whatever capacity, must pay. With only a few scenes detailing domestic concerns, the focus remains firmly on the rigors of work and survival, whether for a regular paycheck, untaxed cash, or a dope vial. As David Simon observed, "you are ultimately compromised and must contend with whatever institutions you are committed to."[4]

During the next twelve episodes of this first season, the series graphically depicts the fury and futility of the city's drug war, a battle aptly characterized by one of the show's detectives when he remarks, "you can't call this shit a war . . . wars end." The various combatants engaged in this all-consuming armed conflict—whether police, judges, lawyers, politicians, drug dealers, or drug users—are not portrayed as selfless defenders of the good or brutal psychopaths or hopeless losers, but rather as complicated individuals ensnared in and driven by larger social forces. Given the often hellish challenges they face and the extremes of behavior this produces, *The Wire* nevertheless viewed its characters with affection and a healthy dose of profane humor, preferring to launch its ire against more impersonal targets. "*The Wire* is most certainly not about what has been salvaged or exalted in America," Simon noted. "It is, instead about what we have left behind in our cities, and at what cost we have done so. . . . It is a very angry show."[5]

This anger fueled the program's next three seasons as well, which engage in a broad range of social and political arguments. The futility of drug laws and their terrible toll on the inner city are expanded, both geographically and thematically, in season two to look at the dying piers of the Baltimore harbor and how the collapse of working-class life and dreams leads inevitably to the same conditions of despair and criminal activity that envelop the city's most hopeless neighborhoods. The black drug organizations of season one are here mirrored by white counterparts, extending from comically inept imitators of their speech and dress codes to international operators who use the ports to smuggle in drug-processing chemicals (and eastern European prostitutes). The season's finale finds the harbor an empty shell, its workforce scattered, its land ready to be used for upscale condo development, while the key criminal elements behind the drug trade once again elude prosecution.

Season three grapples with the almost insurmountable difficulties of reform—institutional, social, and personal. For twelve episodes, the series examines the efforts of various individuals and groups to change calcified power structures and rethink traditional solutions. Whether a former convict hoping to set up a free boxing program for inner-city kids, a frustrated police major establishing a no-arrest zone for dealers and users in a deserted part of Baltimore, an ambitious city councilman willing to confront the crime-fighting programs of an entrenched mayor, or the efforts of a top drug kingpin eager to become a legitimate real-estate tycoon, the results are usually the same—a few small victories but an overarching sense that change is rarely, if ever, possible in the context of entrenched bureaucracies and the interlocking economic and political forces that rely on them for survival. The montage sequence that concludes the season (like similar montages at the ends of seasons one and two) makes it clear that the narrative arc of *The Wire* is one that permits little in the way of growth or resolution, mirroring the intractable problems of so many real-life American cities. The majority of the characters are left struggling to endure or regroup, while the operations of the drug trade that fuel so much of urban life continue to flourish unabated.

In season four, *The Wire* continues its incisive portrait of Baltimore's governing and enforcement organizations while adding a new layer to its social landscape—the city's dysfunctional school system and its porous relationship to the troubled world outside its walls. As Ed Burns, whose experiences as a teacher inspired the season, observed: "I think it's neat to find out where these drug dealers and drug addicts are coming from. And where they're coming from is a failed education process."[6]

The political scope and social and economic questions posed by *The Wire*'s first four seasons were strikingly unconventional, particularly in series-based television, where certain governing rules and approaches (even at HBO) tend to prevail. *The Wire*, however, challenged these assumptions on numerous fronts, not only in terms of its iconoclastic themes, but also in the ways it handled the basic building blocks of character, narrative, and style.

In contrast to most prime-time series, where the focus rarely strays from the dilemmas faced by the lead personalities, *The Wire* is far more intent on serving the demands of its almost sociologically driven story arcs, which are planned several seasons in advance. Though there are several prominent characters in its large, and largely African American, cast (again, an uncommon feature even in contemporary dramatic television), they sometimes disappear from the action as a way to highlight other figures and concerns. In a similar fashion, the program refuses to showcase its stars in a predictable manner or repeat viewer-appealing situations and personality traits. Simon's reaction to fans outraged by the murder of one of the series' most compelling central characters was typical—"Holding on to a character and then twisting the story to serve the character? . . . There's no gratification in that for anyone. We're not doing a soap opera here."[7]

What *The Wire* is also not doing is making it easy for casual viewers to simply tune in and start watching the show. The narrative moves in distinctly un-television ways. There are no recaps at the beginning of each episode, nor are there self-contained climaxes to reward the single-episode viewer fifty-five minutes later. A plot detail might be mentioned early in the season and not reappear until eight weeks afterward (the most notorious example of this is in the pilot episode, when Officer Jimmy McNulty [Dominic West] is asked where he would least like to be stationed and replies "the boat," meaning harbor patrol; sure enough, at the conclusion of the first season, after twelve episodes, he's shown launching out to sea). Even the police wiretap aspect that gives the series its name and could serve as a central thematic anchor for viewers is treated as just one of many narrative threads, its activities usually not fully operational until the midpoint of each season. As *Variety* observed, the program "is so assiduous in its storytelling as to be almost impenetrable to the uninitiated."[8] Although this novelistic pacing and scope may have alienated the inattentive, it was a point of pride for David Simon, who went to great lengths to hire writers who were not only outside the standard Los Angeles/New York entertainment industry axis, but were also, in the case of George Pelecanos, Dennis Lehane, and Richard Price, well-regarded urban crime novelists who had never worked in television before. Each was drawn by Simon's reassuring, and rarely heard, promise to "not compromise story for the sake of a studio, a director, or a movie star."[9]

The Wire's densely layered story lines are complemented by an equally scrupulous attention to atmosphere and style. This was the direct result of the contributions of co-executive producer Robert F. Colesberry, who had previously produced films for innovative directors like Ang Lee, Martin Scorsese, and Robert Benton. During his two seasons with *The Wire* (he died as a result of complications from surgery in February 2004), Colesberry helped fashion a distinctive visual approach that was fully in keeping with the series' assault against the norms of the contemporary cop show. Many of the milestone police programs of the previous decade, such as *NYPD Blue* (ABC, 1993–2005) and *Homicide,* shared an edgy style that was partially influenced by handheld documentaries and even modern advertising techniques. Colesberry rejected this self-conscious flashiness and instead employed a more filmic strategy, emphasizing clarity, spatial depth, and the relationship of characters to their environments. The goal was a style mirroring the show's narrative pace. "We wanted," Simon explained, "more languid camera movements, we wanted the background to show great detail . . . we didn't want the camera to have any advance knowledge of the story, since we're asking viewers to follow the story very carefully and pick up facts as they go along and never pick up more facts than we're allowing."[10] Working closely with cinematographer Uta Briesewitz, Colesberry provided the series with an expressive approach to on-location shooting, perfectly capturing *The Wire*'s dark moods and evocative urban flavor, while avoiding the film noir clichés that littered so many modern "city at night" movies and TV cop shows.

Given all of the various challenges that *The Wire* presented to viewers, from its Byzantine storytelling to its large and shifting cast of characters to its unapologetic use of inner-city argot, it's little wonder that HBO was apprehensive about the fate of the series when it was first launched in the summer of 2002. To help set the stage, the network insisted that TV critics be sent not just the pilot, but the next four episodes as well, so they could better understand the program's broad scope and complicated plotting. The strategy worked, and the show was greeted with raves from all over the country (except for the New York City papers, which took a bit longer to come around).

Viewers were also somewhat slow in coming to terms with *The Wire*'s demands, but by the end of the first season, the series was earning respectable ratings and had been picked up for renewal by HBO. The second season, which premiered in June 2003, proved to be its most popular, even though it lost nearly 3 million viewers from *Sex and the City*'s (1998–2004) lead-in. But its critical stature was zooming—in July 2003, it won *Television Week*'s semiannual poll of TV critics for the best show on TV, and a few months later earned the prestigious Peabody Award. Troubles started, however, with the third season. The series, now moved from the summertime to September (and thus competing directly with the fall schedule of the commercial networks, including ABC's smash hit *Desperate Housewives* [2004–]), faced its biggest challenge when Nielsen changed the way it measured HBO's programming. As a result, the show's ratings dropped 33 percent. HBO's support also began to waiver, particularly since the season ended with the conclusion of its longest-running, and most dynamic, narrative arc. As HBO entertainment president Carolyn Strauss noted, "it's a high-prestige show for us," but "they'd tied up so much of the story so well, we wondered if we should go on."[11] Reaction was much quicker to the prospect of a fifth season—thanks to the tremendous critical reviews that greeted season four after its premiere, HBO announced a few weeks later that *The Wire* would be back for a "final" season (typical of the show's ambitions, it would examine, according to David Simon, "our own relationship as Americans to the culture of violence and how our media reflects that."[12])

Unlike HBO's far more prominent series, such as *The Sopranos* (1999–2007) and *Sex and the City*, *The Wire* has always tended to attract a small, but intensely devoted audience, composed of critics (who, when not comparing it to the work of Charles Dickens or James Joyce, or Greek tragedy, continually cite it as the best program on TV); actively engaged viewers willing to work hard to follow its intricate

Unlike HBO's far more prominent series, such as *The Sopranos* and *Sex and the City*, *The Wire* has always tended to attract a small, but intensely devoted audience, including critics who, when not comparing it to Dickens, Joyce, or Greek tragedy, often cite it as the best program on TV. (Left to right) Detective William "Bunk" Moreland (Wendell Pierce), Officer James "Jimmy" McNulty (Dominic West), Detective Shakima "Kima" Greggs (Sonja Sohn), and Detective Lester Freamon (Clarke Peters). Photograph by David Lee.

plotlines; and, as Simon fondly notes, a strong following among both cops and criminals, who admire the show's faithful recreation of their lives.[13] What that audience has discovered is that, throughout its five seasons, *The Wire* has, in many ways, helped to reinvent the wheel, transforming the police drama from its emphasis on investigative heroics into one of the few places in television willing to argue passionately about the world outside the boundaries of the small screen.

Notes

1. Ian Rothkerch, "'What Drugs Have Not Destroyed, the War on Them Has,'" *Salon.com*, 29 June 2002, at http://www.salon.com/ent/tv/int/2002/06/29/simon.

2. Rafael Alvarez, The Wire, *Truth Be Told* (New York: Pocket Books, 2004), 37.

3. Rothkerch, "'What Drugs Have Not Destroyed, the War on Them Has.'"

4. The Wire, *The Complete First Season* [DVD], Episode one commentary by David Simon (2002; New York: HBO Home Video, 2003).

5. Alvarez, The Wire, 8.

6. "A Teacher in Baltimore" [interview with Ed Burns], at http://www.hbo.com/thewire/interviews/ed_burns.shtml.

7. Lola Ogunnaike, "Whacked! Another HBO Main Player Meets His End," *New York Times,* 13 December 2004.

8. Brian Lowry, "The Wire," *Variety,* 13–19 September 2004, 53.

9. Alvarez, The Wire, 28.

10. David Simon, interview by David Bianculli, *Fresh Air,* National Public Radio, 23 September 2004.

11. Stu Miller, "The Accidental Success Story," *Broadcasting & Cable,* 9 May 2005, 12.

12. David Simon, personal interview, 15 February 2006.

13. Jesse Walker, "David Simon Says," *Reason,* October 2004, at http://www.reason.com/news/show/29273.html.

SIX

Deadwood

Horace Newcomb

It is perhaps indicative of the current state of television at large, and certainly indicative of television series produced for HBO, that *Deadwood* (2004–) is most often referred to as "David Milch's *Deadwood*." Just as *The Sopranos* (1999–2007) is often linked directly to creator and executive producer David Chase, and *The Wire* (2002–) to David Simon, *Deadwood* is all but inseparable from the authorial, or auteur, status of Milch.[1] Indeed, most of these series are said to grow from or to be otherwise related to the professional, at times intensely personal, biographical experiences of their creative "fathers." Certainly in the case of Milch the program is linked to his biography as well as to his television work prior to *Deadwood*.

Milch's credentials as author in various genres are well known: Yale degree in English, with distinction; master of fine arts degree from the Iowa Writer's Workshop; instructor at Yale; working with Cleanth Brooks, Robert Penn Warren, and R. W. B. Lewis; poetry and fiction published in appropriate literary journals and magazines. The story of his move to Hollywood is equally familiar: "Trial by Fury," his first *Hill Street Blues* (NBC, 1981–87) script for Steven Bochco, opened the third season of the series and received the Emmy for Writing for a Dramatic Series, the Writers Guild Award, and the Humanitas Prize. Work on various other Bochco projects followed, with the greatest success coming as executive producer on *NYPD Blue* (ABC, 1993–2005) and with the development of its remarkable central character, Andy Sipowicz (Dennis Franz).

Equally well known is the personal background that shadowed the professional glories. That history—of various addictions, some violence, smidgens of criminality—might be described as the "darker" side of Milch's experience, and although he might acknowledge the validity of the adjective, it is doubtful that he would accept the conventional implication that goes with it. Rather, as he has said of two of his principal characters in *Deadwood,* Al Swearengen and Seth Bullock, it is merely that his life has lived him more than he has lived his life. Would the strength of *Blue,* the eloquence of *Deadwood,* or the profound humanity and humility of either have been accomplished without it? Hard to say. But in those efforts all influences are blurred, and Milch's lived experiences have certainly become central to the attendant publicity that has driven wider recognition of his works. HBO has certainly not turned away from it.

Milch's auteur status exhibits all the qualities of the creative process in the television industries. In guides to the series he is, in fact, formally credited with authorship for only two of his own scripts. Perhaps the sparse output results from his unusual method for "writing" *Deadwood,* as described here in a *New Yorker* profile: "While others sat on a sofa or chairs, Milch reclined on the floor in the center of the room, a few feet from a microphone and a twenty-inch computer monitor, on the other side of which was a desk where an amanuensis, seated in front of a computer and another monitor, was poised to type whatever he dictated."[2]

Other writers for the series doubtless use their own methods of composition. At least one, Ted Mann, credited with three scripts, chooses not to be present for the dictation sessions and has allowed that he "wouldn't have wanted to watch William Faulkner write, either."[3] At least nine other writers have received credits for one or more scripts; among them, in addition to Mann, are Elizabeth Sarnoff and Jody Worth, with four each. Similarly, ten outstanding directors have guided episodes of the series. Ed Bianchi, with six, and Davis Guggenheim, with four, lead in numbers. As "creator and executive producer," however, Milch reviews every script; all go through his edit, alteration, and approval, dictated or otherwise formed. And it also remains part of the executive producer's role to oversee all other elements of the production process, from performance to final editing.

Milch first approached HBO in 2002 with this pitch: "St. Paul gets

As creator and executive producer of *Deadwood*, David
Milch oversees every element
of the program's production
process, from performance
to final editing.

collared."[4] The idea was for a series "about the lives of city cops in
ancient Rome during Nero's reign, before a system of justice had been
codified. 'I was interested in how people improvised the structures of a
society when there was no law to guide them. . . . How the law developed out of the social impulse to minimize the collateral damage of the
taking of revenge.'"[5] Elsewhere, Milch points out that this description
of the development of the law is from Oliver Wendell Holmes's discussion of the rise of common law.[6] Clearly, the concept can be applied in
a range of social and historical contexts. Thus, because the network was
at that time already developing *Rome* (2005–7), Milch was asked about
other settings for his thematic interests and replied that he could place
them in a western. HBO premiered *Deadwood* on March 21, 2004,
with Milch's pilot script, titled "Deadwood," directed by famed action
director Walter Hill.

At the beginning of the creative process, two years of research and writing established the factual underpinnings of *Deadwood*. The mining camp came into existence following the discovery of gold in Deadwood Gulch in 1875. The strike was part of the larger gold rush in the Black Hills that began a year earlier during an expedition led by George Custer. At the time, the entire region was protected and reserved for the Lakota Sioux under the Treaty of Fort Laramie, signed in 1868. The discovery of gold led to various actions, including an offer of $6 million made to the Native American groups in exchange for the land. The offer was refused, and in 1876 Congress repealed the Fort Laramie treaty and took the Black Hills and other lands from the Native Americans. In the same year, Custer was defeated and his troop destroyed in the Battle of the Little Big Horn, further "justifying" the flood of settlers who moved into the region.

Deadwood, the mining camp, was indeed an infamous slough. Not unlike other such settlements created in the "territories" that would become North and South Dakota, the camp was filled with characters of tarnished or at least ambiguous reputation. Most of the principal characters, as well as some secondary roles, are based on actual persons known to have lived and worked there. Some of these characters and central aspects of their lives are well known. The most familiar of these is Wild Bill Hickok, who was murdered there in Nutall's Saloon by Jack McCall.[7] And indeed, as in the series, Hickok had arrived in Deadwood with Charlie Utter's wagon train, accompanied by Calamity Jane. Personages such as Seth Bullock, Sol Star, Al Swearengen, and others were also "real" people. A few composite characters were constructed from "types" of Deadwood residents. And some, such as George Hearst, did take part in the development of the camp and the region, but at dates that might not have coincided so directly with the narrative of the television series.

Facts, however, go only so far in explaining the texture and power of *Deadwood,* and can account only in limited fashion for the praise and blame that have attended it. It is much more probable that Milch's attention to language is what attracts notice to the series. Two qualities of Milch's language have guided two major responses—intense notoriety and profound admiration. The notoriety results most frequently and obviously from the use of language conventionally defined as obscene and profane, with word choice often relying on dense application of the four-letter vernacular term for sexual intercourse, often in colorful, spectacular, and inventive grammatical constructions. Or, as it might be phrased in *Deadwoodese*, from the use of language conventionally fucking defined as fucking obscene and profane, often fucking relying on dense fucking application of the spectacular and inventive use of variations on "fuck," also known to some fuckers as fucking "sexual intercourse," and fucking often presented in compound and fucking complex sentences. Other terms, such as references to close oral attention to male sexual organs, to incestuous male-mater sexual relations, or to a fully developed lexicon describing both female and male sexual parts, are also used. So, too, are various conventional blasphemous calls upon a range of deities.

Admiration for the language of *Deadwood,* as extensive as the approbation, recognizes that even such socially censured words may be woven into poetry. As presented by an outstanding cast, the language is most often described as Shakespearian, and it is indeed important to note that the language is performed, not merely spoken. Subtle distinctions of diction and voice, vocabulary, and inflection serve to distinguish characters. Soliloquies and muttered musings offer insight into the psychology, the motivations and speculations, of individuals, but also into relationships among them. Confrontations, meetings, private or intimate conversations define the social fabric of the Deadwood community, imply values and dreams, and thereby exhibit a sense of personal and communal history.

As "author," in this sense, Milch's function, perhaps more so than with many other creators and executive producer–head writers, is all but transcendent, in the most theological significance of the term. *Deadwood* may be solidly based in factual history, but it is fully realized, created, from Milch's vision. As much as it is Shakespearian, then, the language of *Deadwood* also draws on that other great text of the period, the 1611 Authorized (King James) Version of holy scripture. The language is biblical. In *Deadwood* a world is molded from the materials of history and historical research, the muck of primal matter. It is as if the place is spoken into being, as if Milch's dictated pilot is a Genesis of sorts.

This, of course, points to yet another literary model, for this world is populated with beings already far fallen from paradise. In this regard,

Deadwood is Miltonic in that knowledge of good and evil is nothing new to the series, but already sharply developed. Likewise, Al Swearengen (Ian McShane) is a character worthy of comparison with the heroic Satan of *Paradise Lost*.

Deadwood is Miltonic as well as Shakespearian. Here, knowledge of good and evil is a thing not new, astonishing, and bewildering, but already sharply developed. Those who populate this place are enlivened with breath not divine, but divinizing. As they wade through perpetually mudded streets, their creator probes the soiled recesses of individual souls and the noblest attempts to "minimize the collateral damage of the taking of revenge."

Milch's version of Al Swearengen, developed from the far less complex historical person, is a character worthy of comparison with the heroic Satan of John Milton's 1667 *Paradise Lost*. It is a tribute to the series' writers that he can appear noble in acts of murder, pathetic for thinking it significant to serve peaches at his formal meetings, and genuinely sympathetic as he reveals his childhood abandonment and abuse while being fellated by one of his young prostitutes. Seth Bullock, in a more conventional narrative, would be pure light to Swearengen's shade. He is a study in anguish, attempting to atone for his sins, having "sacrificed" his own son and compromised his best impulses in the interest of expedient alliance with Swearengen. Calamity Jane wanders the alleys of the camp, lost in drunken reveries of Hickok, confused by her lesbian affections, outraged by almost any attempt by those who would offer sympathy. Trixie, the whore with the heart of brass, sees and knows more than most. It is no coincidence that "innocence" entered the camp in the person of Sophia Metz, nor is it coincidental that she entered mute. The fictional survivor of an actual massacre, Sophia has gained speech and, as an observer of her benefactor, Alma Garrett (another fictional character), has likely lost a good deal of that original innocence.

Garrett herself—sophisticated, educated, gentle misfit, drug addicted, complicit in adultery with Bullock, guardian of the lovely Sophia, wealthiest woman in the camp, founder and executive of the first bank—embodies one version of "civilization," the world still thriving to the east of Deadwood. Her antagonist, an equal representative of some form of the "outside" world, is George Hearst, a creation loosely based on the actual person. In *Deadwood,* Hearst is ruthless in his pursuit of Garrett's gold mine, but equally ruthless in his rejection of all normal social restrictions. He is a society unto himself, financially able to mount armies, if necessary, to do his bidding.

Taken together, these two point toward a central complication in *Deadwood* and in the cultural questions and problems it poses. The structure of the conventional western is the movement from savagery to civilization. Many versions of this transition occur on the literal cusp of the frontier, the site where the two concepts are in direct conflict. Resolution usually favors the coming of structured society, with its schools and towns and homes driving out saloons and brothels, its sheriffs and marshals surviving danger to overcome thugs and murderers. In some cases, there is elegant loss. Gallant gunfighters and noble natives must ride into the distance, no longer necessary or no longer tolerated by those who have come to settle down. So-called revisionist westerns undercut this narrative by showing how truly difficult the process can be, how the "winners" in this contest must often engage in corruption as deeply as those who lose.

From this perspective, Deadwood is not a western at all, neither conventional nor revisionist. The ease with which Milch transferred his thematic exploration from one setting to another confirms this. It is the "people" who interest him; it is improvisation in the absence of law. His intention to explore the development of the law is an abstract concept if ever there was one. But the abstraction is made concrete by context, by the social impulse. And that impulse is defined. It is the attempt "to minimize the collateral damage of the taking of revenge."

Many, if not most of the central characters in *Deadwood* are seeking to improvise in the absence of law, seeking to develop some social structure. Bullock searches for order in conventional enforcement of order, even when that order itself demands improvisation rooted in violence. His partner, Sol Star, searches through commerce and his affection for Trixie. Trixie seeks some sense of coherence and selects from every quarter the props for her improvised and unfinished persona. Albert Merrick, the newspaper editor, believes in communicating information, whether in print or through the electronic power of the telegraph. Jack Langrishe puts his faith in art, E. B. Farnum in the opportunities offered by civic graft, Doc Cochran in science and sheer grit, Joanie Stubbs in something like love, Cy Tolliver in avarice.

All of these, however, and all the other characters, no matter how much they strive for order, for the coming of "the law," are themselves examples of collateral damage. Some who have come to this place continue to exercise dreadful actions rising from the most venal motivations and impulses. Others seem to exist outside any conventional moral structure, constructing "systems" of honor and obligation, reward and punishment, as if such things had never before existed. Some seem to wish to forego or, more accurately, to overcome the drives of discrete, personal goals—or lusts—in order to survive. All have been deeply impaired.

The deep, driving questions in *Deadwood* concern the source of this damage. If, as Milch suggests, it is caused by the taking of revenge, on what, then, or on whom have these characters taken their revenge, and in that taking been so severely injured? One answer is that they have taken revenge on the very "civilization" that stands opposed to Deadwood and to places like it. But which version of civilization do we examine? Alma Garret's genteel yet decayed tradition, or George Hearst's rapacious, yawning maw of the new West? Which is most responsible for the broken treaty, the arrogance of Custer, the decimation of native societies? Could it be either? Or both?

But if "civilization" is thus historicized, it is no answer at all. Even when the "law" is developed and in place, it is often inadequate to halt the taking of revenge and thus to stop, or at least minimize, the collateral damage that results. Certainly this would seem to be the case in Milch's other work, as evidenced in his treatments of Frank Furillo in *Hill Street Blues* and Andy Sipowicz in *NYPD Blue*. For these, and the characters in *Deadwood,* taking revenge is the surest way to harm the self. Milch's first concern is with the potential universality of the problems he defines. Human beings hurt other human beings. Those who are hurt seek revenge. In carrying out revenge they damage themselves. Attempting to minimize this collateral damage they develop the law. Inevitably, laws—and the best of intentions—fail. Hurt begins again.

Deadwood is not a western because it tells its tale by digging out the root elements of the western. It neither revises those elements nor replays them. It exposes the western, the genre itself, as an attempt to provide "endings" that can never be true. History, as event or person, in this case is simply a near-perfect example of individuals and societies stripped bare. Al Swearengen, at the center of this narrative, manipulates, destroys, murders and mutilates, humiliates and abuses—stands on his balcony, observes, comments, and attempts to direct, or at least not drown in, the coming tide of change. George Hearst arrives as a version of that future, breaks open the walls of his hotel room in order to stand, like Swearengen, above the cluttered fray taking place among the damaged souls below. He, too, intends to direct the future. Bullock walks the sludge beneath and between them, attempting to minimize the collateral damage that falls almost randomly on the ragged citizens of Deadwood, himself among them. There is no winner. It is only the contest that matters.

Or, in Milch's words, "What I wanted to re-enact in this series was a form of original sin."[8] For some, such a pronouncement would project a dark and hopeless account of the human condition. But this view overlooks the "fortunate" aspects of the fall from grace and paradise, for it is only in recognizing the full weight of that first error that we can hope for redemption. In one way this is always the promise of the West and the western, the frontier as site, the cusp of new hope, new life. If, as seems likely, Milch has the strong sense that things may not get better, the dignity he provides for the Bullocks and the Swearengens, for even the Hearsts, and certainly for all the calamities, Jane and others that inhabit Deadwood, bespeaks a profound compassion. "My feeling about 'Deadwood' is it's a single organism," he says, "and I think human society is the body of God, and in a lot of ways it's about the different parts of the body having a somewhat more confident sense of their identity over the course of time."[9] The truly fortunate aspect of this vision is that it includes us, the viewers, as well.

Originally planned as a four-year project, designed to follow the four-year, unincorporated, and lawless existence of the historical Deadwood mining camp prior to its absorption into Dakota territory, the expensive series encountered problems typical to all television production. In 2006, at the beginning of the third season, HBO chose not to renew contracts with the large cast, indicating that there would be no fourth season. Following negotiations, however, it was later announced that the series would conclude with two two-hour movies set to air in 2008.

Although the unexpected and somewhat unsatisfactory "conclusion" of *Deadwood* led to "a bitter taste in the cup"[10] for Milch, his strong relationship with HBO continued. One rationalization for the *Deadwood* arrangement came in a somewhat backhanded expression of confidence. Milch had moved ahead with a new project, *John from Cincinnati* (2007–), and network executives seemed worried that, without his complete attention as show runner, *Deadwood* might drift. The new project, however, again offered Milch a chance to exercise his own creative impulses, to explore themes in which both biography and intense fictional characterizations would come together.

As described by David Carr in yet another profile of Milch's creative process, *John* presents "a dysfunctional family viewed through the twin prisms of surfing and heroin addiction, a space alien, and a lawyer named Dickstein. It should be mentioned that some characters occasionally levitate." Milch offers his own description: "Ostensibly it is about a family of surfers who seem to have become more and more disassociated from themselves and from good surfing. They were all champions, and they are in one way or another alienated, loaded and ascetic. . . . And then a strange guy comes into their life: John from Cincinnati." Carr also mentions that one part of the story conference he observes is a discussion of "where John is from—Cincinnati and/or outer space."[11]

The "theological" underpinnings of Milch's work also continue to appear as he develops the new series. "I am an instrument of purposes that I don't fully understand. . . . Time will tell whether I am a wing nut or a megalomaniac. . . . The difference between a cult and faith is time. I believe that we are a single organism, and that something is at stake in this particular moment."[12] Perhaps it is not a long step from the chaotic frontier in *Deadwood* to the beach, to the edge of a continent, to outer space, or to whatever weirdness defines Cincinnati and all other similar locales. Milch and his teams of supporters, writers, and actors are on a continuing quest. They need a new world, a perfect wave, a television network that will permit religious ecstasy and stoned frenzy, sometimes all in the same scene.

Notes

1. This may suggest that the term "auteur" could be replaced by "David"—that one must bear a particular given name in order to be truly successful with such dark-shading-to-grim series. David Janollari was perhaps recruited among other producers to secure this quality on the merely intermittently grim *Six Feet Under* (2001–5). Larry David, of course, with a name in reverse, is relegated to high comedy with *Curb Your Enthusiasm* (2000–).

2. Mark Singer, "The Misfit," *New Yorker,* February 23, 2005.

3. Ibid.

4. Ibid.

5. Ibid.

6. Heather Havrilesky, "The Man behind 'Deadwood,'" *Salon.com,* March 5, 2005, at http://dir.salon.com/story/ent/feature/2005/03/05/milch/index.html.

7. Details related to the "factual" basis and subsequent modifications of character and event can be found at http://www.legendsofamerica.com/WE-DeadwoodHBO.html.

8. Kate O'Hare, "HBO Goes in Search of 'Deadwood,'" *Zap2it,* March 17, 2004, at http://tv.zap2it.com.

9. Havrilesky, "The Man behind 'Deadwood.'"

10. David Carr, "A Producer Hangs 10 in a Risky HBO Pilot," *New York Times,* February 20, 2006.

11. Ibid.

12. Ibid.

SEVEN

Tanner '88

Joanne Morreale

Tanner '88 aired on the HBO network during the 1988 presidential primary campaign. At a time when cable was still a novelty, and few cable networks had original programming, *Tanner '88* was a mock documentary film that created the presidential campaign of a fictional Democratic candidate, Jack Tanner, whom it ostensibly followed as its subject. It starred Michael Murphy as Tanner; Cynthia Nixon as his college-age daughter, Alex; and Pamela Reed as his campaign manager, T.J. Cavanaugh. The idea for the series came from Bridget Potter, vice president of original programming at HBO. She contacted *Doonesbury* cartoonist Garry Trudeau, who agreed to write the project if filmmaker Robert Altman directed it.[1] The consequent series was a unique collaboration between the two, who were both credited as executive producers.

The one-hour pilot, entitled "The Dark Horse," aired on February 15, 1988, on the eve of the New Hampshire primary. On the basis of positive critical response, HBO agreed to produce further episodes, resulting in ten additional half-hour episodes broadcast throughout the primary campaign. Unlike traditional series, episodes aired intermittently, following the trajectory of the "real" campaign. To convey a sense of immediacy and to keep up with current events, shows were shot and edited up until the last possible moment. According to Trudeau, "there was no opportunity for HBO to review scripts or look at rushes, so to our everlasting gratitude, Bridget Potter and her boss, Michael Fuchs, mostly left us to our own devices. Few artists have ever been given such creative freedom and support in developing a new TV series. For Altman and me, it was as good as it gets."[2]

Although Trudeau and Altman wanted to continue the series through

Tanner '88 aired on HBO during the 1988 presidential primary campaign, starring Michael Murphy as Jack Tanner, a liberal Democrat who is idealistic in outlook and committed to social change.

the general election (Tanner would have become an independent candidate), HBO decided not to renew the series once Michael Dukakis won the Democratic nomination in July. But *Tanner '88* continued to receive critical acclaim. Altman won an Emmy for his direction of "The Boiler Room," the penultimate episode of the series, which captured the Tanner campaign's excitement, anxiety, and then angst on the final night of the Democratic National Convention. *Tanner '88* also won the prize for best television series at the Festival International de Programmes Audiovisuels at the Cannes Film Festival.

The impetus for *Tanner '88* came from HBO's desire to produce

Written by *Doonesbury* cartoonist Garry Trudeau and directed by Robert Altman, *Tanner '88* lasted through a one-hour pilot and ten additional half-hour episodes covering the trajectory of candidate Tanner's "real" campaign.

original programming, along with the fact that it promised to be an interesting election year. With President Ronald Reagan's second term coming to an end, both Democratic and Republican candidates were fighting for their party's nomination. There were indications that the Republican Party was vulnerable. The Democrats had won control of the House during the 1986 mid-year elections, the economy was in a downturn, and the Iran-Contra scandal dogged Vice President George Bush. There was no consensus that Bush could carry the party, and he had several rivals for the nomination, most significantly Bob Dole, Jack Kemp, and Pat Robertson. The Democratic field was wide open, with Bruce Babbitt, Paul Simon, Gary Hart, Al Gore, Joseph Biden, Richard Gephardt, Michael Dukakis, and Jesse Jackson all initially vying for the Democratic nomination. The party was split between moderate candidates who sought to win back Democrats who had voted for Reagan during the previous two elections, and more liberal candidates who wanted to reinvigorate the party's base on the left.

Trudeau and Altman positioned Jack Tanner on the left of the American political spectrum. Tanner is characterized as a divorced history professor from East Lansing, Michigan, a former congressman who relinquished his political career ten years previously when his daughter, Alex, was diagnosed with Hodgkin's disease. During the 1960s, Tanner was an antiwar and civil rights activist, and he remains idealistic and committed to social change. Despite having virtually no name recognition, he decides to enter the primary at the last minute because of what he describes as "the dearth of quality candidates." Tanner is anti-apartheid, against aid to the Nicaraguan contras, and pro-environment, and he advocates improving inner cities, tax benefits for companies with day-care facilities, and most radically, legalizing drugs. According to Trudeau, "he perceives himself to be what is known as a generational candidate, that he speaks for a certain group of people with whom he came of age as a radical history professor during the late-'60s."[3] It is worth noting that members of this generational group were also likely to subscribe to HBO.

Henry Allen comments on the deliberate irony of the choice of actor Michael Murphy to play Tanner: "Michael Murphy got famous as the fretful, well-bred sneak in 'An Unmarried Woman' and 'Manhattan'— as exactly the sort of educated, ambitious, weightless WASP stereotype that Trudeau has pilloried, blamed, then forgiven only to pillory again in 'Doonesbury.' That archetype is one of the many the Democratic party has worked so hard to shed."[4] But *Tanner '88*'s purpose was not simply to skewer left-wing holdouts from the sixties. *Doonesbury,* for which Trudeau won a Pulitzer Prize in 1975, was far more critical of the political right than the left. Robert Altman was also an outspoken political liberal. Both the form and the content of his films challenged conventions, whether those of classical narrative filmmaking practices or the social and political orders these helped naturalize. In fact, his 1975 film *Nashville* was a critical commentary on American politics and culture that shared structural and stylistic features with *Tanner '88*. Given their similar politics, Trudeau and Altman's collaboration on *Tanner '88* satirically explored the modern-day presidential campaign from the vantage point of a rather naïve candidate, his family, the campaign staff, and the press assigned to cover the campaign.

With *Tanner '88*, Trudeau and Altman delved into the spectacle of the modern-day presidential campaign, from small-state electioneering to the making of political films and commercials, to fundraisers, stump speeches, debates, rallies, and convention deal-brokering. Altman noted, "we broke into new form. We used a mix of drama and comedy and reality and satire, fiction and non-fiction."[5] They seamlessly combined fictional and real-life characters and events, so that as Jack Tanner experiences life on the campaign trail, "the effect is a production that calls attention to itself not as a fiction, but to the reality it mimics as fiction."[6] In doing so, it indicts the American political process, as well as political candidates who are literally the product of media representations.

Although Jack Tanner is a fictional candidate, his campaign is conducted as though it is real. The inclusion of different news genres—a television talk show interview, clips from evening news reports, televised debates, and the ever-present press coverage of the campaign—contributes to perceptions of its reality. He has a campaign headquarters (a rented storefront in the atrium of the CNN building), filled with actors who played his staff. His campaign begins in New Hampshire and ends at the Democratic National Convention in Atlanta, and throughout, he interacts with "real" candidates and voters, some of whom were given scripts and others of whom were not. Tanner encounters Bob Dole, Richard Gephardt, Gary Hart, Jesse Jackson, and Pat Robertson, all of whom willingly accept the free exposure. In "The Dark Horse," fictional *Globe* reporter Taggerty Hayes asks Pat Robertson if he is playing "Christian hardball," and Robertson provides a "real" answer that implies he takes the question seriously. On the Criterion *Tanner '88* DVD interview with Trudeau and Altman, Altman claims, "at that point, I knew we were on to something."

In "Moonwalker and Bookbag," Tanner meets with a real group of Washington political consultants and insiders who give him advice at a fictional fundraiser, and in "Bagels with Bruce," Bruce Babbitt, after dropping out of the race, shares what he learned with Tanner as they stroll around the reflecting pool at the Lincoln Memorial. According to Trudeau, Babbitt was only told to give the best advice he had. There was no scripting.[7] Throughout the series, celebrities, news reporters, politicians, political consultants, and ordinary Americans play themselves. Although Trudeau wrote scripts that loosely outlined scenes, as with many Altman films the dialogue was improvised and often overlapping. Thus, conversations appear spontaneous, unplanned, and certainly unscripted, and as in real life, words sometimes can't be heard.

Tanner '88 shares characteristics with two documentary subgenres:

the docudrama and the mock-documentary, both of which were innovative in the 1980s. It functions as a docudrama in its seamless interweaving of fact and fiction, and particularly in its "soap opera" narrative with multiple intersecting story lines that defy easy closure. Actors were filmed interacting with one another, seemingly unaware of the presence of the cameras, but their stories were invented in order to build suspense and interest. There are three main narrative threads: Tanner's relationship with his family (consisting of his father, daughter, and lover), interactions within the campaign staff, and the press who cover the campaign. Many of these narrative threads intertwine and provide story arcs that continue throughout the series. In one recurring story line, for example, Tanner has a secret affair with Democratic candidate Michael Dukakis's deputy campaign manager, Joanna. There is an awkward moment in "For Real" when Tanner's media manager, planning on defecting to the Dukakis campaign, comes face-to-face with Joanna, whom he recognizes as the woman Tanner has been seeing. Eventually, one of the members of the press catches on, and in "The Great Escape," the affair becomes public.

In "Something Borrowed, Something New," Tanner and Joanna plan a wedding at Tanner's aunt's house, but the ceremony is disrupted when an overzealous NBC reporter, Deke Connors, tries to get close-up shots from the ladder of a helicopter that flies into the backyard. In another soap opera twist, Deke had been the filmmaker on Tanner's campaign, but was fired when he made commercials based on material taken from Tanner's private journal. In "Reality Check," the final episode of the series, Kitty Dukakis plays herself in a scene where she forgives Joanna. She insists, "family is all that matters," then immediately undercuts her own remark when she asks Joanna for a political favor: to secure Tanner's support for Michael. According to Trudeau, this scene was largely improvised; Kitty was only asked to forgive Joanna for betraying her trust.[8]

The soap opera elements were designed as hooks to keep viewers coming back week after week, but they remain subordinate to *Tanner '88*'s generic status as a mock-documentary, which provides it with both humor and a political edge. Jane Roscoe and Craig Hight distinguish between "degree 1" mock-documentaries, which are less critical, and "degree 2" mock-documentaries, "characterized by a greater engagement with political commentary, an aspect of parody which would seem a natural subject for the mock-documentary form, but one which is rarely explored with any depth." According to Roscoe and Hight, "degree 2" mock-documentaries "demonstrate an ambivalence towards factual discourse, but they also arguably develop reflexivity through their engagement with issues related to the legitimacy of wider political processes, as much from the complexity of their use of the mock-documentary form."[9] *Tanner '88* is a "degree 2" mock-documentary that uses the codes and conventions of cinema verité to provide a sense of authenticity—at the same time that it mocks them.

Not coincidentally, Robert Drew's *Primary* (1960), an account of the Wisconsin Democratic primary that follows presidential hopefuls John F. Kennedy and Hubert Humphrey, is largely credited with introducing cinema verité to a nationwide television audience in the United States. Cinema verité aims for naturalistic storytelling, giving the impression of reality simply appearing rather than being ordered and arranged. The verité filmmaker tries not to manipulate or interfere with his or her subjects. As was the case with *Tanner '88*, verité films often use nonprofessional actors, live locations, natural sound and lighting, and no voice-over narration. *Tanner '88* was shot on videotape (to look like journalistic news footage); the handheld camera often lurches to follow an action, or characters walk in and out of frame. In the opening shot of the series, for example, the camera lingers in a close-up of coffee cups and fast-food containers, as if unsure where to settle next. One of *Tanner '88*'s running gags is that Deke, who considers himself an "experimental neorealist" filmmaker, is continually disrupting "reality," as in the case of the wedding, or when he rigs a "thrill cam" to swoop down from the ceiling to get a close-up of Tanner speaking and the flying camera almost kills the candidate.

Despite the fact that *Tanner '88* mimics verité-style filmmaking, it addresses viewers who know that what they are seeing is not "real." It uses documentary film conventions, but exaggerates them in order to indicate their arbitrary and constructed nature. In doing so, the film becomes a parody. Its nature as parody becomes apparent early on when Deke, hired to produce Tanner's campaign biography, shows the staff the first rushes. Here *Tanner '88* deconstructs the conventions of the biographical presidential campaign film. As in most films of this genre made about candidates who were World War II veterans, there is grainy, black-and-white, "authentic" war footage that is cut to portray the subject as a patriotic soldier. In biographical films, viewers are not meant to question the origins of the archival footage. But in this case, one of the staff observes that this is not footage of Tanner, and another notes that the scene looks familiar. Deke responds, "I lifted it from the Dole campaign film. I mean, hell, he lifted it from stock. You don't really think they sent a crew out to shoot a future president, do you?"

Another convention of the biographical campaign film is to show the candidate as high school athlete, again using old photographs or film clips. Even here, shots meant to show Tanner playing basketball in high school turn out to be shots of professional athlete Wilt Chamberlain. "Well, he's a team player," Deke explains when confronted by the staff. Further, in a dig at the practice of using focus groups to test campaign films, the film is shown to a "diverse" group of voters who are wired to electronic monitors. However, the dial plunges downward when Tanner explains on camera that he quit politics to spend more time with his daughter when she was diagnosed with cancer. "Too sappy," is the response. As parody, the conventions of the campaign "biography" are re-contextualized so that viewers see them as fabrications rather than representations of reality, just as *Tanner '88* re-contextualizes the conventions of the entire presidential campaign so that viewers see its arbitrary and constructed nature.

Throughout, *Tanner '88* uses the conventions of the mock-documentary to comment on American politics. In some ways, Jack Tanner is just as "real" as the other candidates who make brief appearances on screen. On the eve of the California primary, HBO ran six episodes in a row, in a special hosted by reporter Linda Ellerbee. Each episode was introduced with a clip of Tanner and other candidates making speeches, cleverly edited so that there were no clear markers to indicate that Tanner was a fictional candidate. Viewers were told that one of the candidates was fictional, and most were no doubt aware of the game. At the end of the evening, viewers were asked to call in their votes to HBO, and Tanner won. In "The Great Escape," Ellerbee also moderated a mock debate between Tanner and Jesse Jackson, again edited to make it appear as though the two men actually engaged in a face-to-face debate. Both the television special and the single episode further elided the lines between fiction and reality. According to Michael Agger, "the joke, which gained momentum, was that many spectators could not tell the difference between Tanner's simulated campaign events and the real ones. Altman and Trudeau had created a fake campaign with better production values (and, arguably, a more appealing message) than Michael Dukakis's."[10]

There are moments when the fictional world of Tanner is more "real" than the simplistic photo opportunities that mark typical presidential campaigns. One of the most powerful episodes in the series is "The Girlfriend Factor," when Tanner attends a rally in a Detroit ghetto sponsored by the group SoSad (Save Our Sons and Daughters). (According to Altman, the police refused to accompany them to the neighborhood.[11]) Despite (or perhaps because of) the episode's realism, the opening sequence makes no attempt to emulate verité filmmaking. At the rally, the group Prince Vine and the Hip Hop Force performed a rap song, which Altman recorded and used to begin the episode. The song's refrain, "We Need a Change," provides the sound for images of a robotics exhibition Tanner visits, with the machines' movements seemingly synchronized to the beat of the music. The tension between the two emphasizes the disjuncture between human needs and technological progress, a tension that is somewhat dissipated when a robot assails Tanner and his staff and asks them if they like to take drugs.

At the rally, parents who lost their children speak plaintively about the need for politicians to do something about kids and violence. A black father reads a poem about his young daughter who had been the victim of random gunfire. The fictional candidate and the television viewers hear the heart-wrenching stories of the victims of inner-city violence. It is rare for such marginalized voices to find their way into the media coverage of political candidates, but *Tanner '88* has provided these voices extended time, and in effect, introduced their concerns to a much wider audience. As the episode concludes, Tanner, en route to his car, happens to find the body of a young black boy lying in a vacant lot. The camera freezes on the boy's face, with the final words of the rap song, "brutally died," repeated in a loop. This last scene is obviously fiction, though like the opening sequence, it is interwoven with the real to make a powerful political point.

In addition to critiquing politics, *Tanner '88* assesses the construction of the presidential persona. Tanner is moral and idealistic, yet he is also a blank slate upon which the advice, opinions, and desires of others—his daughter, his campaign advisers, or the public—are projected. One critic observed, "for much of the first episode he seems like a walking definition of the phrase 'wimp factor,' weak, clumsily ingratiating and at the mercy of his own promotional team."[12] The character is, as Trudeau observed, "baffled," and thus he leaves the details, such as the shaping of his persona, to his more sophisticated and self-aware campaign manager, T.J. Even T.J. finds his lack of self-assertion frustrating. In "The Girlfriend Factor," she states in exasperation, "things just happen to this man. He is constantly being overtaken by events."

Tanner is constructed by an array of multiple, often inconsistent voices.[13] Structurally, the predominance of multiple characters and story lines makes it difficult to provide lengthy narrative explanations of Tanner's motives or inner life, and consequently he appears to lack depth and complexity. In "The Dark Horse," Tanner resents it when his handlers try to package him to deliver his message most efficiently. As he rebels, he (privately) gives an impromptu speech in which he extols the virtues of the American political process and the American people. Yet, even this attempt at authenticity becomes another campaign product. Deke, the cameraman, hides under a coffee table and secretly videotapes the speech through the glass. The distorted images of Tanner refracted through the glass become a series of campaign commercials, and the speech begets an ironic campaign slogan: "Tanner . . . For Real." The commercials jump-start his campaign and make him a viable candidate.

In "Child's Play," the actress Rebecca De Mornay asks him to speak to her honestly because "there's no TV screen here." The irony is of course that there is a TV screen, though one where the actor Michael Murphy is portraying a character. Tanner tries diligently, but then excuses himself and walks away. He is unable to assert a coherent sentence that is not a platitude or sound bite, and he no longer knows what he stands for. Later, the campaign hires an outside consultant to help Tanner sharpen his image. He gets voice and speech lessons, until he is able to stand at a podium and boom dynamically, "I am somebody!" His own smaller voice immediately follows, asking, "I am somebody?" He stares directly into the camera, and the episode concludes. Unlike Jesse Jackson, whose community litany Tanner is quoting here, Tanner is obviously not so sure.[14]

Tanner is not the only character subject to parody. Tanner's idealistic campaign staff becomes increasingly cynical as the campaign progresses. His media assistant Andrea grows from a naïve young woman in awe of Jack Tanner to one who can take charge and handle a crisis. "The difference between then and now," she says at the end of the campaign, "is that I am no longer a nice person." His campaign manager T.J. is shrewd, manipulative, and clearly should have been running her own campaign. Media reporters are incompetent and neurotic, as witnessed by the hapless Deke or NBC correspondent Molly Hart, who routinely misses stories and fears losing her job. Fictional *Boston Globe* reporter Taggerty Hayes is more interested in Tanner's personal life than the issues. The electorate is also shown in a less-than-flattering light, lacking intellectual curiosity and primarily relating to politics as media hype or entertainment. For example, farmers in New Hampshire (played by actors) collect pictures of candidates that they trade with their neighbors, but they don't know who the candidates are or what they represent.

Tanner '88 aired only once until the Sundance Channel bought the original rights in 2004, and both *Tanner '88* and its sequel, *Tanner on Tanner,* were released on DVD. *Tanner '88* was rerun on the Sundance Channel during the 2004 presidential primary, along with new introductions to each episode. The new segments were again directed by Altman and scripted by Trudeau, and feature Tanner, T.J., and Alex sixteen years later as they reminisce about losing the election to Dukakis. The Sundance Channel then decided to shoot a sequel, and in the four-episode *Tanner on Tanner* Alex, now a documentary filmmaker, makes a film that looks back on her father's presidential campaign. This latter series enabled Altman and Trudeau to critique the constant mediation that is now so endemic to our lives.

Bold and risky, *Tanner '88* helped brand HBO as "quality" television. Both Trudeau and Altman have said they are proud of their work on *Tanner '88,* and Altman claimed that it was the most creative work he ever did.[15] It is both a docudrama that interweaves reality and fiction to heighten dramatic interest, and a mock-documentary that parodies the conventions of the verité-style political campaign film that presents itself as a representation of reality. As with all parodies, part of its appeal comes from recognizing the conventions of the form that it imitates. Its visual style gives the impression of spontaneity, unpredictability, and unplanned observation, while it simultaneously calls into question those very processes of representation that, it was believed, simply allow reality to appear. It uses parody for satiric ends, targeting not simply the political campaign documentary, but the reality that the documentary appears to represent. Both its formal blending of reality and fiction, and its content—which ostensibly provides a behind-the-scenes peek at the modern-day presidential campaign—deliberately challenge the idea of authentic representation and any political candidate who is not a packaged product. And the character of Jack Tanner echoes this crisis of representation. He is entirely defined by the media, his campaign staff, and even his daughter, often in conflicting ways. His campaign slogan, "Tanner . . . For Real," is an ironic comment on his lack of authenticity and substance—a lack that became more pronounced as the campaign progresses. *Tanner '88* makes no distinction between Jack Tanner and the "real" candidates who occasionally appear on screen. All are equally complicit and, by implication, inauthentic. Many of its observations ring even truer today, and it can be enjoyed as much for its political insight as for its humor. It highlights the artifice of the modern-day presidential campaign and the public personas of those who run for office, calling attention to the media construction of political spectacle and the way that candidates' personas are designed and created for public consumption. The media, campaign workers, and even voters are indicted for their participation in this process.

In retrospect, *Tanner '88* was most important to HBO because of its innovations, merging the docudrama and mock-documentary to satirize the presidential campaign process. It exerted some influence on later political works, some fiction and some documentary, such as *Bob Roberts* (1992), *Wag the Dog* (1997), *The War Room* (1993), and even *The West Wing* (NBC, 1999–2006). Altman also (disapprovingly) suggested that *Tanner '88* smoothed the way for reality television.[16] But it is primarily its formal innovations, rather than subject matter, that have had a lasting influence on television. *Tanner '88* was a precursor to later television shows, many on HBO, that blur the boundaries between fact and fiction, comedy and drama, reality and representation. Programs such as *The Larry Sanders Show* (1992–98), *Curb Your Enthusiasm* (2000–), *Entourage* (2004–), *Extras* (2005–6), and *The Comeback*

(2005) use many of the same formal devices and strategies as *Tanner '88*. Yet these are critiques of the entertainment industry rather than of politics, and the one attempt at a televised political satire that merged reality and fiction, *K Street* (2003), failed in one season. Although the content of *Tanner '88* may be inimitable, its formal stylistics have become standard on HBO as well as other cable and broadcast networks. Overall, the continuing influence of *Tanner '88* is still widely felt and acknowledged throughout the industry.

Notes

1. Garry Trudeau, "'Now What?' Winging it with 'Tanner '88,'" *Crain Communications Inc,* 28 October 2002, 23.

2. Trudeau, "'Now What?'" 23.

3. Jon Burlingame, "Prime-Time Pick," *St. Petersburg Times,* 15 February 1988, 7D.

4. Henry Allen, "Art Imitating Politics: The 'Tanner '88' Set," *Washington Post,* 21 July 1998, B2.

5. Gavin Smith and Richard T. Jameson, "The Movie You Saw is the Movie We're Going to Make," *Film Comment* 28:3 (May–June 1992): 30.

6. Robert T. Self, *Robert Altman's Subliminal Reality* (Minneapolis: University of Minnesota Press, 2002), 122.

7. Trudeau, "'Now What?'" 23.

8. Trudeau, "'Now What?'" 23.

9. Jane Roscoe and Craig Hight, *Faking It: Mock-Documentary and the Subversion of Factuality* (Manchester, UK: Manchester University Press, 2001), 140.

10. Michael Agger, "Candidate," *New Yorker,* 2 August 2004, 25.

11. *Tanner '88* [DVD], Interview with Garry Trudeau and Robert Altman (Criterion, 2004).

12. Kevin Jackson, "The White House Pretender," *Independent,* 23 September 1988, 16.

13. Self, *Robert Altman's Subliminal Reality,* 125.

14. Ibid.

15. *Tanner '88* [DVD], Interview with Trudeau and Altman.

16. Vicky Hallett, "The Candidate to Watch," *US News and World Report,* 2 February 2004, 17.

EIGHT

From the Earth to the Moon

Michael Allen

Executive-produced by Hollywood A-list star Tom Hanks, *From the Earth to the Moon* premiered on HBO on Sunday April 5, 1998. This original twelve-part miniseries, screened in blocks of two episodes over six consecutive Sunday evenings, was HBO's most prestigious and expensive production to date. It had a dramatic impact, picking up an Emmy for the best miniseries of the year. *From the Earth to the Moon* chronicles the events of the Apollo program of moon explorations (1961–72) through the personal stories of the astronauts, their families, and the NASA engineers and technicians, set against the turbulent events of the decade. Documenting the most astonishing and awe-inspiring of modern American accomplishments, *From the Earth to the Moon* was itself impressive in the way it challenged the boundaries of its own industry. The question both projects asked of themselves was, in the words of the title of the first episode, "Can we do this?"

Personnel

Despite its providing some of the most enduringly iconic cultural images of the twentieth century, up to the end of the 1990s only one television movie (*Apollo 11* [Family Channel, 1996]) and two feature films (Philip Kaufman's *The Right Stuff* [1983] and Ron Howard's *Apollo 13* [1995]) had documented the 1960s space race. Howard's relatively big-budget feature film, starring Tom Hanks, describes NASA's efforts in April 1970 to rescue the crew of Apollo 13 after two fuel tanks exploded 200,000 miles from Earth. *Apollo 13* also whetted Hank's appetite for the history of the American space program. During the making of the film, Hanks read Andrew Chaikin's authoritative account of that his-

Executive produced by Tom Hanks, *From the Earth to the Moon* chronicles the Apollo program of moon explorations from 1961 through 1972 by telling the personal stories of the astronauts, their families, and the NASA engineers and technicians, set against the turbulent events of the era.

tory, *A Man on the Moon* (1994), as part of his research for his role as the mission's commander, Jim Lovell. Chaikin's accounts of the missions and the personal stories behind them fired Hanks's imagination, and he developed a desire to turn them into filmed reality. He realized, however, that the two-hours-plus duration of a feature film was just too short to cover the dramatic events involved. The scale of his ambition required a different format—the television miniseries.

At the same time, Hanks felt that the network miniseries format might also prove unsatisfactory, because the constant interruption of commercials would break up the narrative flow and tension: "It would have been very, very difficult to put this on a network in which we'd have to take a break every 20 minutes," he recalled. "We didn't know how long these stories would take to tell. HBO said, 'do whatever you want to.' And that kind of creative leeway we simply would not get from a commercial enterprise."[1] HBO was to prove the perfect home for such a project. Hanks's Clavius Base company, in partnership with Imagine Entertainment (a major Hollywood independent production company responsible for such films as *Apollo 13, The Nutty Professor* [1996], *Ransom* [1996], and *Liar Liar* [1997]), approached HBO chairman Jeff Bewkes with the project. Bewkes's reaction was that HBO had never done anything of that scale before. Nevertheless, the production was approved at a budget of $40 million, "ridiculously high by cable standards, but one that Bewkes instantly knew was unrealistically low."[2] By the end of the production, the final budget had escalated to $68 million—$6 million more than the cost of *Apollo 13*. Another $10 million was allocated for promotion.

Tom Hanks presented the introductions to each of the episodes, wrote one and cowrote three others, directed the first (which covers the Mercury and Gemini programs), and played a character role in the last episode. Further Hollywood talent included *Apollo 13*'s producers, Michael Bostick and Brian Grazer, and director, Ron Howard, who all acted as producers for *From the Earth to the Moon*. David Frankel directed three episodes, and nine different directors took the helm for each of the others. Most were experienced television directors, such as David Carson—who had worked on *Star Trek* (NBC, 1966–69), *Northern Exposure* (CBS, 1990–95), and *L.A. Law* (NBC, 1986–94)—or feature film directors such as Frank Marshall (*Arachnophobia* [1990], *Congo* [1995]) and Gary Fleder (*Things to Do in Denver When You're Dead* [1995]). The actress Sally Field had a part in one of the episodes and directed "The Original Wives Club," which concentrates on the emotional toll suffered by the astronauts' wives. Cinematographer throughout the production was Gale Tattersall, who had operated the camera on such films as *The Emerald Forest* (1985) and *The Addams Family* (1991), and had been cinematographer on *The Commitments* (1991) and *Virtuosity* (1995). These various notable names were all employed, as Tattersall phrased it, "to give this project a big-screen, feature film look."[3]

Production

The series was shot over 271 days in more than 100 locations, including the Kennedy Space Center at Cape Canaveral; Edwards Air Force Base in California; and Disney-MGM Studios in Orlando. Its average of 120 to 140 scenes in each one-hour episode—compared with the usual 40 in standard television drama—is an indication of the enormous concentration of information packed into each narrative; and its 468 visual effects, as many as in a blockbuster special-effects movie, were far in excess of the number normally used in cable channel productions. As Bewkes commented, "it has special effects that we haven't done before—and frankly no one in cable has—at a cost that was a bit daunting to contemplate."[4] Several leading Hollywood effects houses, such as Area 51 (*Millennium* [Fox 1996–99], *Buffy the Vampire Slayer* [WB, 1997–2001; UPN, 2001–3]), Hunter/Gratzner Industries (*Stargate* [1994], *Independence Day* [1996]), and Pacific Titles (*True Lies* [1994], *Eraser* [1996]), were hired to provide the special effects of rockets blasting off, spacecraft drifting in lunar orbit, and astronauts walking on the surface of the Moon. The experience and techniques each company brought to the miniseries from their big-budget Hollywood feature production work resulted in the high-quality images that mark *From the Earth to the Moon* as a television production with aspirations toward the cinematic. The dazzling effects and motion picture stylistics made the production look distinctively different on the small screen.

HBO was now regularly striving for this kind of visual quality by 1998, as it sought to establish its brand name in a competitive marketplace. Commentators noted that "the dramatic hike in HBO's original program budget—nearly double what was spent in 1995—is a function of the network's need to deliver programming that subscribers can't find elsewhere and its desire to attach top Hollywood talent to that fare."[5] HBO's new original programming initiative—which had begun in 1997 with *Oz* (1997–2003), a drama series set in a maximum security prison—ran with the slogan, "It's Not TV, It's HBO." *From the Earth to the Moon,* with its high production values and the involvement of Tom Hanks, who had become one of Hollywood's top stars after having won two Oscars (for *Philadelphia* [1993] and *Forrest Gump* [1994]), reaffirmed the claim that HBO's product was not like regular television, and was an explicit announcement of the network's presence as a major player in television as a whole during the late 1990s.

Narrative Structure

Although there have been very few enacted film or television accounts of the American space programs, the events and images of the missions into Earth's orbit and to the Moon have become part of the national and international cultural memory—both through endless reproduction of certain iconic images, such as Neil Armstrong first setting foot on the lunar surface, and in a wide range of documentary programs about the history of space explorations that are repeatedly shown on other broadcasting and cable channels. Part of the challenge for the makers of *From the Earth to the Moon*, therefore, was how to approach this overly familiar history so that the final work would attract subscribers to HBO.

The series as a whole negotiates a delicate balance between the public and the private, the large-scale and the intimate, detailing the major events of the American space programs in the context of the personal lives of those involved. As such, it follows very much in the vein of *Apollo 13*. Tackling a historic event that still had a place in popular memory, *From the Earth to the Moon* did much the same in exploring the hidden history behind the official story, even though the details of that event had faded with time. In this aspect, Chaikin's account of the missions was important: he had spent years interviewing all of the major and minor figures who had been involved in the space programs. "I really wanted to write the story of the Moon flights as if it were a historical novel," he recalled. "These guys were more than just *Life* magazine stereotypes. They were more than just *The Right Stuff*. Having this marvelous dialogue of astronauts' private conversations. . . . They were real human beings with thoughts and feelings."[6]

The episodes of *From the Earth to the Moon* are made up of pairings that are subtly developed in terms of common themes or opposing styles and tones. The first two episodes, "Can We Do This?" and "Apollo 1," discuss, respectively, the pre-Apollo period of the Mercury and Gemini programs, and the fire in Apollo 1's capsule that killed the three astronauts inside and halted the program during the eighteen-month investigation that followed. The triumphant tone of the first episode, as NASA grows to believe in its ability to fulfill President Kennedy's 1962 challenge of landing Americans on the Moon by the end of the decade, is bluntly countered by the solemn tone of the second. Episode three, "We Have Cleared the Tower," uses the making of a fictitious documentary as a device to explore the anxieties experienced by the crew of Apollo 7 following the resumption of the program, and episode four, "1968," intercuts staged color scenes of Apollo 8's flight to lunar orbit with real black-and-white documentary footage of the civil and political unrest that marked that year in America.

The crew of Apollo 8 flew to the moon to test procedures for entering the lunar orbit because the lunar module they were expecting to test in Earth's orbit was not ready in time. Episode five of the miniseries, "Spider," focuses on the story behind that delayed delivery, detailing the troubled development of the lunar landing craft that, as shown in episode six, "Mare Tranquillitatis," allowed the crew of Apollo 11 to make the first lunar landing. Episode seven, "Is That All There Is?," lightheartedly describes the camaraderie of the Apollo 12 crew while also giving a sense of anticlimax and waning public interest following the first moon landing. Its partner, episode eight, "We Interrupt This Program," concerns itself with the short-lived revival of public interest generated by the rescue of the crew of Apollo 13 following its onboard explosion, framed within the context of the shifting style of television journalism, from respectful scientific knowledge to tabloid-style sensationalism.

Episode nine, "For Miles and Miles," focuses on Alan Shepard, America's first man in space, as he returns to astronaut duties on Apollo 14 having been grounded for years with an inner-ear disorder. The following episode, however, "Galileo Was Right," undercuts the "right stuff" heroism represented by Shepard by concentrating on the unheroic "wrong stuff" of the geological training that the crews of the final three Apollo missions underwent. The penultimate episode, "The Original Wives Club," sensitively describes the emotional strain suffered by the wives of the astronauts; and the final episode, "Le Voyage Dans La Lune," inventively intercuts a recreation of the making of Georges Méliès's 1902 film *Le voyage dans la lune* with an account of the final lunar landing mission, Apollo 17.

To an extent, this variation was prescribed by the events of the

Apollo program itself, which developed a real-life alternating narrative across its missions: the tragedy of the Apollo 1 fire; the nervousness of Apollo 7; the awe and wonder of Apollo 8's courageous first flight to the moon; the unspectacular but essential testing of the lunar lander on Apollos 9 and 10; the triumph of Apollo 11; the anticlimax of Apollo 12's broken camera; and the drama of Apollo 13's rescue. The progression from mission to mission was in reality fraught with setbacks and unexpected reversals before new victories were achieved. The shifts in style across episodes of *From the Earth to the Moon* reflect the noncontinuous nature of the Apollo story. Furthermore, they significantly allow the miniseries to avoid what happened to the media coverage of the real events: a sense of sameness and lack of variety in the telecasts and television coverage of the moon walks. Audiences dwindled as each mission did more of the same things its predecessors had done, another rocket blasting off to take men to walk on the moon, with its attendant, repetitive preparations. *From the Earth to the Moon* could easily have fallen into the same trap if each episode had had the same visual and aural styles and concentrated on showing the events of each flight and lunar exploration. By varying the styles and approach with each episode, the series continually refreshed itself and remains engaging to watch.

Sociocultural Context

In this narrative strategy, it could be argued, we are witnessing the beginnings of HBO's interest in addressing great American cultural and mythical institutions by looking "behind the scenes" at their personal and domestic dimensions—a dynamic that would later be played out in the Mafia boss as husband-and-father-in-therapy in *The Sopranos* (1999–2007), the inscrutable funeral home run by the dysfunctional Fisher family in *Six Feet Under* (2001–5), and the domesticating of the Wild West in *Deadwood* (2004–). The familiar and clichéd are given an unexpectedly human dimension.

In light of this institutional self-determination, it is significant that several of the episodes are centrally concerned with the relationship between the Apollo program and the two media of film and television. Early fantasy film and documentary and television news reportage are all centrally referenced and used to structure episodes. Tom Hanks admitted that one of the major influences on the look and ambition of the series was the work of Ken Burns, specifically his 1990 multipart documentary series, *The Civil War*. Burns's pioneering use of montage to link together contemporary photographs and diary records was an exercise in the resurrection and re-assemblage of cultural memory that was to heavily influence the producers of *From the Earth to the Moon*. As Hanks acknowledged, he "knew from the start that in doing this, we would always have the burden of being the definitive piece about the Apollo program."[7] The decision to make the miniseries coincided with HBO's new ambitions within the post-1996 television marketplace. Chris Albrecht, HBO president of original programming and independent productions at that time, felt that a positive response to *From the Earth to Moon* would encourage Hollywood talent to consider bringing their projects to the network: "Once they see [*From the Earth to the Moon*], all kinds of artists will see what is [possible], what kind of work they'll have an opportunity to do here, and I think the result will be our best calling card for future relationships."[8] Attracting major creative talent and providing them with sufficiently high budgets to realize their projects, it was hoped, would propel HBO into the forefront of American television production. Although one can argue the extent to which the network met this goal, there have definitely been ambitious HBO productions involving Hollywood talent known for taking creative risks, including *Band of Brothers* (again involving Hanks, screened in 2001) and the multi-award-winning *Angels in America* (directed by Mike Nichols and starring Al Pacino and Meryl Streep, shown in 2003).

By foregrounding the growing importance of television running in parallel with the Apollo program as it progressed throughout the 1960s, HBO was essentially promoting *From the Earth to the Moon* as a self-reflexive gesture to position itself as a similarly important television phenomenon of the late 1990s. By working with top Hollywood talent and backing their efforts with budgets unheard of at the time, as well as relinquishing a great deal of creative control, HBO used *From the Earth to the Moon* to help establish a yardstick for future industrial practice—not just for itself, but eventually for the entire cable industry. The great achievement of the moon landing, therefore, mapped onto HBO's confirmation of its growing industrial weight and significance during the late 1990s and afterwards.

Notes

1. Tom Hanks, quoted in Donna Petrozzello, "HBO Sets Its Sights High with 'From the Earth to the Moon,'" *Broadcasting & Cable,* March 23, 1998, 30.

2. Donna Petrozzello and John M. Higgins, "HBO: Reaching for the Stars," *Broadcasting & Cable,* March 23, 1998, 28.

3. Gale Tattersall, quoted in Jean Oppenheimer, "A Trip to the Moon," *American Cinematographer,* April 1998, 77.

4. Jeff Bewkes, quoted in Petrozzello, "HBO Sets Its Sights High with 'From the Earth to the Moon,'" 30.

5. Petrozzello and Higgins, "HBO: Reaching for the Stars," 29.

6. Andrew Chaikin, quoted in Kathleen O'Steen, "Moonstruck: With the Help of HBO—and $65 million—Tom Hanks Re-creates Mankind's Giant Step," *Emmy,* April 1998, 25.

7. Tom Hanks, quoted in O'Steen, "Moonstruck," 22.

8. Chris Albrecht, quoted in Petrozzello, "HBO Sets Its Sights High with 'From the Earth to the Moon,'" 30.

NINE

Band of Brothers

Thomas Schatz

For more than a half-century, Hollywood has been steadily refining and recasting the "war film," a genre that coalesced during World War II and that has continued to evolve through successive U.S. military conflicts without ever losing sight of that generative historic event. The genre was born by federal mandate, quite literally, when President Franklin D. Roosevelt in December 1941 ordered Hollywood to document and valorize the war effort. The studios complied, producing hundreds of war-related films from 1942 through 1945—most of them combat films focusing on male initiation and camaraderie, on hyperviolent conflict and selfless sacrifice, and perhaps most fundamentally, on the pathology of soldiering. The WWII film underwent a brief postwar hiatus but then came roaring back in 1949 with huge hits like *Sands of Iwo Jima, Battleground,* and *Twelve O'Clock High.* Hollywood has been rolling out WWII films ever since. There have been other wars and other war-film cycles since then, of course, but still the WWII film persists. In fact, with each ensuing U.S. military episode, from Korea and Vietnam to the Persian Gulf and Iraq, the WWII film becomes an increasingly paradoxical subspecies—the veritable Ur-narrative within a steadily expanding genre, a template for all subsequent war-film variations, and a moral and thematic standard against which other war films (and other wars) would be gauged.[1]

WWII films have tended to come in cycles, geared to current geopolitical conditions—and conflicts—as well as the genre's odd admixture of history and mythology, and its distinctive appeal to the collective memory of those involved and the nation at large. The latter factor was of particular import to Stephen Ambrose, best-selling author and inveterate chronicler of WWII, who speculated that the advancing age of combat veterans was a crucial factor in the recent revival of WWII films. "Many are realizing that they don't have much time left in the world, and many, for the first time, are willing to talk about their experiences," said Ambrose. "If they don't tell them, they'll go to the grave with them."[2] Interviews with D-day veterans provided the primary research for Ambrose's 1992 book *Band of Brothers,* which HBO adapted as a ten-hour miniseries in 2001.

By then, the recent cycle of WWII films was cresting, thanks to hit films like 1998's *Saving Private Ryan* (on which Ambrose served as a consultant) and *The Thin Red Line.* HBO's *Band of Brothers* marked the culmination of that cycle in two very different ways. In terms of production values and sheer ambition, it was the consummate "war film" of that era—a distinct hybrid of cinema and television that brought a new dimension to HBO's remarkable run of original series programming. Budgeted at more than $120 million, *Band of Brothers* was the most ambitious project ever produced for television, and one that involved a major Hollywood force, DreamWorks, and major filmmaking talent like Steven Spielberg (as executive producer) and Tom Hanks (in multiple creative roles). Moreover, HBO was basking in the glow of recent Emmy Awards and critical accolades for its original series (including *Sex and the City* [1998–2004], *The Sopranos* [1999–2007], and *Six Feet Under* [2001–5]), and it heavily promoted *Band of Brothers* as a worthy successor to these programs and to the Hanks-produced, Emmy-winning 1998 HBO series *From the Earth to the Moon.*

Expectations were high, therefore, when the miniseries was launched on Sunday, September 9, 2001, and the impact of its debut episode was still being gauged when, some thirty-six hours after its premiere, the events of September 11 forever changed the course of world history and utterly redefined the American experience—and perception—of war. The series run of *Band of Brothers* directly coincided with the intense initial stages of America's "New War"—a war that was, in many ways, being dramatically constructed by the broadcast and cable news networks during the same weeks of HBO's lavish recreation (and reconstruction) of a now-ancient conflict. Thus the fall of 2001 saw two colossal media events depicting what may well be the two most significant military conflicts in modern American history. But under the extraordinary circumstances, and given not only the collective psyche of the American public but also the massive media resources used to depict (and formulate) the War on Terror, HBO's ambitious portrayal of the Second World War and the Greatest Generation now seemed oddly anachronistic.

One can only speculate how *Band of Brothers* might have fared with viewers and critics under different circumstances. The September 9 premiere drew a reasonably strong audience of some 10 million viewers—roughly one-third of HBO's subscriber base and certainly on a par with an excellent "opening weekend" for a theatrical movie release. But the viewership declined significantly in subsequent weeks, eventually leveling off by week four at about 6 million per week—substantially lower than HBO's *The Sopranos,* but on a par with its other hit series at the time, *Sex and the City* and *Six Feet Under.* Although the ratings were disappointing, HBO undoubtedly expected to realize some "prestige value" from the series. A limited series like *Band of Brothers* can scarcely be expected to attract new subscribers, so cultural cachet may well have been a prime motivation for HBO's massive investment. Critical response was solid if not spectacular, and its sizable haul of major awards included a half-dozen Emmys, a Golden Globe, and a Peabody Award. It did well in syndication and was a major hit on Britain's BBC2 (which licensed the series in a cofinancing deal with DreamWorks for $10 million and drew some 5 million viewers per week), and also enjoyed success on DVD. The stature of the series among the canonized WWII films remains to be seen, although it is certainly far stronger than most of its big-screen generic counterparts—most notably the global blockbuster *Pearl Harbor,* a summer 2001 hit—and stands alongside *Saving Private Ryan* as the best of the recent cycle.[3]

As a hybrid of cinema and limited-series television, *Band of Brothers* enjoys an odd and somewhat unique status among WWII films. The relationship with Spielberg, Hanks, and DreamWorks underscores HBO's obvious strategy to push more aggressively into the cinematic realm in order to both counter and complement its growing reliance on original long-form series—a trend that was increasingly at odds with its insistent tagline, "It's Not TV, It's HBO." *Band of Brothers* also tapped directly into the current WWII cycle, which included books and television programs but was primarily associated with studio-produced features. Its most obvious antecedent is Spielberg's *Saving Private Ryan,* and in fact the co-executive producer of *Band of Brothers,* Tony To (the hands-on producer and thus the closest thing to what's termed a "show runner" in the realm of regular series television), readily acknowledged that pedigree. "Steven has set such a template for us with 'Ryan' that we agreed to use the filmmaking language he created there—the handheld, subjective point of view, the image shaker, the grunt's view of battle."[4] Beyond the visual style of *Band of Brothers,* the influence exerted by *Saving Private Ryan* ranges from the story itself (i.e., the D-day invasion and its aftermath) and its narrative focus on a single combat unit, to the art direction and production design. The overall look and feel of *Band of Brothers* are remarkably similar to the Spielberg film. Much of the series was staged and shot in the same location, an airfield in Hertford-shire, outside London, which DreamWorks had converted into a movie lot for *Saving Private Ryan.* Almost all of *Band of Brothers* was shot at Hertfordshire, where empty airplane hangars were used for indoor sets and an exterior village set was redressed as eleven different locales.

Despite its cinematic lineage, however, *Band of Brothers* is very much a television series. Here, too, it is something of an anomaly—longer than most miniseries at ten hours, but with a set number of episodes that gives it tremendous advantages over the conventional, open-ended series. Back in 1995, Charles McGrath, editor of the *New York Times Book Review,* wrote a piece for the *New York Times Magazine* called "The Triumph of the Prime-Time Novel," in which he argued quite persuasively that hour-long TV dramas of that era like *ER* (NBC, 1994–), *NYPD Blue* (ABC, 1993–2005), *Law & Order* (1990–), and *Homicide* (NBC, 1993–99) were the real literature of our age and represented the most innovative and important achievements among all the arts.[5] We have witnessed the inevitable exhaustion of those series since then; as is so often the case with broadcast network television's strongest series, popularity necessitates narrative interminability and creative storytelling lapses into tired formula. But interestingly enough, this trend in television narrative was not only sustained but effectively enhanced via the rapid rise of original series programming on HBO, which in many crucial ways has liberated, if not revolutionized, American television.

Unrestrained by the vagaries of broadcast TV—network censors, ratings-driven executives, demographics-obsessed sponsors (and ad agencies), mind-numbing commercial interruptions, standardized production seasons, interminable open-ended series runs—HBO's series have reinforced McGrath's argument with a vengeance. Like *ER, The Sopranos,* and other quality hour-long drama series, *Band of Brothers* strives to blend serial and episodic narrative techniques, so that each series segment stands alone—something like a distinct chapter in a novel, in McGrath's view—while distinctly advancing the story, developing the principal characters, and intensifying the long-term dramatic stakes. Like most of the hour-long dramas that McGrath describes, this miniseries is an ensemble piece that, in a very real sense, is also a "workplace" drama. In fact, most of the quality cop shows and medical dramas in recent decades, dating back to *Hill Street Blues* (NBC, 1981–87) and *St. Elsewhere* (NBC, 1982–88), are set in modern urban "war zones" rife with what network executives call "jeopardy" (i.e., the threat of violence), and where the ensemble of working stiffs live by an unspoken code and provide one another with the only real family they can know, given the overwhelming demands of their profession. *Band of Brothers* operates along much the same lines, but with the stakes raised exponentially.

The perils in *Band of Brothers* involve survival more than anything else—certainly more than the outcome of the war, significantly enough, since by the time that the story really gets underway in June 1944, the eventual Allied victory was already a foregone conclusion. Other stakes apply, of course, most of which relate to the uncommon "brotherhood" and sense of family created by the soldiers' circumstances. In the series premiere, most of the brothers are introduced in the obligatory basic-training segment, in Georgia in 1942, when they volunteer for an elite paratrooper unit—Easy Company of the 101st Airborne. From that point onward (episodes two through ten), the story traces the fate of that unit through the final year of the war, from their landing in Normandy on D-day through their battles across Europe (peaking, in effect, with the Battle of the Bulge), and finally into Germany where, in the last two episodes, they liberate a Nazi concentration camp and capture Eagle's Nest, Hitler's mountain fortress.

The episode structure works extremely well in that each of the series segments involves a distinct dramatic event and thus stands as a narrative unto itself. This is mainly a function of the military incidents being portrayed in each segment, of course, and other key structural factors as well. Each episode opens with a prologue in which actual members of Easy Company—men now in their seventies and eighties—recollect events and incidents related to that particular episode. The effect is quite striking, at once personalizing the narrative and injecting a sense of documentary realism, while efficiently outlining both the dramatic stakes and the thematic subtext of the series segment. As the series wears on, both the aged veterans and their dramatic "characters" become increasingly familiar, and in an odd sense the older and younger versions of the Easy Company warriors gradually fuse. This clearly distinguishes *Band of Brothers* from other WWII films, successfully conveying the complex play of time and memory, love and loss, guilt and regret—the same effect that Spielberg had tried and utterly failed to realize in the cloying graveyard scene that opens and closes *Saving Private Ryan*.

Another factor that distinguishes the individual series segments involves a combination of setting, military situation, and mise-en-scène. Although the overall visual style of the series is consistent, particularly in terms of camerawork and editing strategies, the different environments and fighting conditions—village or field, day or night, rain or shine, summer or winter, pinned down or on the run, in the open or under cover, and so forth—give each episode a particular look and feel of its own. The half-dozen villages featured in various episodes take on individual personalities in the course of one or two segments. Perhaps the most memorable setting is the forest near Bastogne, Belgium, in the dead of winter, where Easy Company, short of ammunition and basic supplies, is pinned down by relentless German artillery fire. The horrible beauty of the constant barrage in the falling snow, as the treetops explode like surreal flowers, is offset by the stark reality of men—who by now (in episode six) we've come to know quite well—simply holed up, waiting for the next shell to fall, and hoping to survive.

The "Bastogne" episode is told primarily through the viewpoint of an experienced medic (Shane Taylor) who, under the circumstances, is on the verge not only of frostbite and starvation, but also nervous exhaustion, or "shell shock"—a malady that already has befallen other members of the unit. The medic hangs on and attends resolutely to his wounded and dying comrades. By the end of the episode, our understanding of his character and his role within the group has grown considerably. This narrative technique of following a particular character and privileging his viewpoint through an entire episode is used effectively in a number of series segments, steadily enriching the ensemble while fueling our emotional investment in both the individual characters and the unit at large.

This technique is employed democratically throughout *Band of Brothers,* to the point of seeming rather arbitrary at times and thus producing an effect that is reinforced by the casting. Unlike *Saving Private Ryan,* an unabashed star vehicle for both Hanks and Spielberg, *Band of Brothers* features a non-star cast. In fact, the only familiar actor is TV series star David Schwimmer (of NBC's *Friends* [1994 2004]), cast against type as an insecure, power-hungry junior officer who is initially feared and eventually reviled by his men. The series includes some five hundred speaking roles, with fifty actors featured as members of Easy Company. In the entire run of the series perhaps a dozen of the characters emerge as distinguishable, fleshed-out individuals. The ensemble is suitably large and variable, and the narrative approach sufficiently democratic, so that only a few of the actors really have a chance to distinguish themselves.

The most distinctive cast member is Damien Lewis in the role of Richard Winters, the officer who succeeds Schwimmer and gradually wins the respect and confidence of the men. Winters comes closest to being the main protagonist of the piece, and through the first several episodes it seems that *Band of Brothers* will follow the WWII film's tendency to maintain a significant and ongoing focus on the agonizing responsibility of leadership—a theme that has informed the genre from 1940s classics like *They Were Expendable* (1945) and *Twelve O'Clock High* to Spielberg's own *Saving Private Ryan.* But this is one area where the *Saving Private Ryan* template does not apply, in that all too soon (in episode five), Winters is promoted to battalion executive officer and thereafter is effectively demoted to a secondary dramatic role. This marginalization of Winters's character is an unfortunate development for several reasons. Not only is Lewis a talented actor whose dynamic screen presence is sorely missed during the second half of the series, but his Officer Richard Winters, much like Hanks's character in *Saving Pri-*

vate Ryan, emerges early on as the series' emotional, psychological, and professional center. By episode five, Winters has become the veritable heart and soul of the unit—and the narrative—the natural leader whose quiet confidence, grim resolve, and knack for warfare are tempered by sensitivity, vulnerability, and a barely subdued distaste for both the army bureaucracy and the military tasks at hand. Once he is displaced from that central position, much of the narrative and thematic focus of the series is lost.

This non-star casting and lack of a central, organizing sensibility within the narrative is evident offscreen as well. Although the commitment of Spielberg and Hanks as executive producers was crucial to the development of the series, neither played a hands-on role during every stage of the epic production. Spielberg brought DreamWorks to the table, adding significantly to his own inestimable clout, and he was actively involved in casting and rounding up the top talent for the series, including a good many of his collaborators on *Saving Private Ryan.* Spielberg apparently provided little to the actual series beyond that, however, other than his creative inspiration via the *Ryan* template. Hanks was far more engaged, coscripting the premiere episode and directing the fifth. Of the seven different writers and eight directors who worked on the series, Hanks was the only individual to both write and direct. Erik Bork, who coscripted two episodes, also received credit as supervising producer, but there is no indication that he or anyone else exercised creative control of the series.

In the vast majority of cases, quality hour-long drama series on television are "authored" by executive producers with a background in writing who are directly and intimately involved in every phase of production. These auteur producers supervise the writing, hire and fire the directors (sometimes on a regular basis, since directors are basically guns-for-hire in the television world), oversee the editing, and, crucially, monitor and shape the overall development of the narrative over the course of the series run. Spielberg himself is well aware of this fact, since his Amblin Productions tends to employ auteur producers on its hit series—Michael Crichton and John Wells on *ER,* for instance. HBO has followed a similar tack with David Chase on *The Sopranos,* Alan Ball on *Six Feet Under,* David Milch on *Deadwood,* and so forth. *Band of*

Brothers, however, seems to have been created more on the principles of a military campaign than those of a prime-time television drama, with Spielberg installed as chief of staff but no one taking creative command of the project itself.

McGrath underscores this view of the auteur producer in his piece on the prime-time novel, and he makes another critical point for our purposes as well. "TV, of late, has become much more of a writer's medium than either movies or Broadway," he writes, "which are more and more preoccupied with delivering spectacle of one kind or another." He goes on to suggest that this has happened "because of the very nature of the medium (spectacle doesn't show up well on the small screen, and it's too expensive anyway) and because of the almost accidental fact that the people who create and who produce most shows are also the people who write them, or else they're former writers."[6] Television screens are bigger today than when McGrath wrote that in 1995, but spectacle is still too big and too expensive for television—unless it's Spielberg and Tom Hanks and DreamWorks behind a $120 million project, and unless "it's not television, it's HBO." By the series' end, however, the narrative and dramatic imperatives seem to have been overwhelmed by the quest for cinematic spectacle and the sheer scope of the campaign. Without a firmer hand on the creative controls and a sense of proportion better suited to the television medium, and without a governing narrative sensibility overseeing the entire project, the whole of *Band of Brothers* is ultimately less than the sum of its parts.

This is not to denigrate the series, particularly since so many of its parts, from individual episodes to the inspired use of interviews throughout the series, are truly exceptional. The point, rather, is that *Band of Brothers* is at its best when it recognizes that it *is* television and realizes its full potential as television series narrative. The interviews are a case in point. In giving voice to the actual combatants (and "brothers"), and in gradually revealing, from episode to episode, the aged warriors' younger fictional selves, *Band of Brothers* is truest to its formal, aesthetic, and industrial nature, exploiting the cumulative effect of the series, bringing present and past, documentary and dramatic representation, into a creative symbiosis that is impossible in any other medium.

Notes

1. For an excellent comprehensive treatment of the WWII film, see Jeanine Basinger, *The World War II Combat Film: Anatomy of a Genre* (New York: Columbia University Press, 1986). Regarding the government mandate and regulation of war-film production, see Clayton R. Koppes and Gregory C. Black, *Hollywood Goes to War* (Berkeley: University of California Press, 1987).

2. Quoted in "Historian Stephen E. Ambrose, Author of 'Band of Brothers,' Discusses the Story of Easy Company," HBO press release, July 13, 2001.

3. Neil Smith, "The Channel That Transformed TV," *BBC News Online*, February 25, 2004, at http://news.bbc.co.uk/2/hi/entertainment/3485916.stm.

4. Quoted in "Executive Producers Tom Hanks and Steven Spielberg, along with Co-Executive Producer Tony To, Are the Driving Creative Force behind *Band of Brothers*," HBO press release, July 13, 2001.

5. Charles McGrath, "The Triumph of the Prime-Time Novel," *New York Times Magazine*, October 22, 1995, 52 et seq.

6. McGrath, "The Triumph of the Prime-Time Novel," 53.

TEN

Angels in America

Gary R. Edgerton

Angels in America (2003) is one of the most ambitious and celebrated productions in the history of HBO. The six-hour adaptation of Tony Kushner's sweeping seven-and-a-half hour, two-part play (*Angels in America: A Gay Fantasia on National Themes, Part One: Millennium Approaches* and *Part Two: Perestroika*) was shepherded from stage to screen after a thirteen-year gestation process by independent producer Cary Brokaw (whose portfolio includes *Nobody's Fool* [1986], *Drugstore Cowboy* [1989], and *The Player* [1992]). Brokaw "started a campaign to obtain the rights to adapt it as a film" after reading it in 1989 as a work in progress before the play was ever produced.[1] *Part One: Millennium Approaches* debuted on the Eureka Stage in San Francisco in May 1991, moving to the Royal National Theatre in London in January 1992. *Part One* and *Part Two* were fully staged together for the first time at the Mark Taper Forum in Los Angeles during November 1992, leading to the play being awarded the 1993 Pulitzer Prize for Drama. Breaking all box office records in Los Angeles, *Part One: Millennium Approaches* premiered on Broadway at the 945-seat Walter Kerr Theater on May 4, 1993. Its $2.2 million budget and $50 to $60 ticket price was unheard of for a nonmusical at the time.[2] *Angels in America* won four Tonys (including Best Play), the New York Drama Critics Circle Award, and five Drama Desk Awards in 1993. *Part Two: Perestroika* opened on November 23, 1993, and it, too, was awarded the Tony for Best Play in 1994.

The critical and popular reception for *Angels in America* was unprecedented. Jack Kroll of *Newsweek* echoed many reviewers when he called it "the broadest, deepest, most searching American play of our time." The Royal National Theatre eventually named it in 2000 as one of the

It took executive producer Cary Brokaw thirteen years to adapt *Angels in America* from stage to television screen. As early as 1993, Al Pacino was fully committed to playing Roy Cohn.

ten best plays of the twentieth century. Even before reaching the screen, *Angels in America* emerged as "the biggest event involving the gay movement in the history of American popular culture."[3] Although fully animated from a gay perspective, *Angels in America* addresses a much wider panorama of concerns than just sexual politics. It is additionally about love and betrayal, the possibility of spiritual redemption and renewal, and the struggle for individual and collective meaning in millennial America. The work is at once intimate and epic, presenting a story of subtle emotions and national scope. At its core, the plot follows the slow and inevitable dissolution of two couples—one gay and one straight—amidst the backdrop of Reagan-era politics and the nationwide AIDS epidemic. In 1981, there were only 199 reported cases of AIDS; eight years later, "more than 55,000 persons had died . . . , exceeding the total of U.S. combat deaths in either the Vietnam War or the Korean War."[4] The play brings history to bear on the action in the portrayals of Joseph R. McCarthy's one-time boy wonder Roy Cohn, a highly successful closeted gay New York lawyer and power broker at the beginning of *Part One* in 1985, as well as the ghost of Ethel Rosenberg, who was convicted of espionage in 1951 and later executed along with her husband Julius in 1953. Besides these historical figures, the play is populated with a wide panorama of ethnic, racial, and sexual types, including white Anglo-Saxon protestants, Jews, Mormons, blacks, whites, gays, straights, and even an angel from heaven.

Over the years, *Angels in America* retained its relevancy; its diverse cast of interconnected characters and themes remained as compelling and trenchant as ever, which encouraged a number of prominent directors to try their hands at adapting the play, first as a theatrical motion picture and eventually as a television miniseries. The initial filmmaker to sign on was Robert Altman. He had just completed *The Player* and *Short Cuts* (1993) for Cary Brokaw's Avenue Pictures production company, where these theatrical features were released through Fine Line, the arthouse division of New Line Cinema. For eighteen months during 1993 and 1994, Altman worked closely with Brokaw on preparation and with Kushner on scripting, before leaving the project for good when Fine Line balked at his asking price of $40 million to produce *Angels in America* as two successive 150-minute movies.[5] Even at this early date, Al Pacino was fully committed to play Roy Cohn (the role he later enacted in the HBO version). Other actors "close to inking deals" on the film pending Fine Line's budgetary approval were Julia Roberts, Tim Robbins, Daniel Day-Lewis, Jodie Foster, and Robert Downey Jr.[6]

As a result, Kushner "tried to collapse *Angels* into one three-hour movie and found that it was impossible" because it "literally has too much plot."[7] While rewriting, he and Brokaw collaborated with a series of filmmakers throughout the remainder of the 1990s, including Australian P. J. Hogan (*Muriel's Wedding* [1994]), Mormon Neil LaBute (*In the Company of Men* [1997]), Oscar-winner Jonathan Demme (*Silence of the Lambs* [1991], *Philadelphia* [1993]), and the openly gay Gus Van Sant (*Good Will Hunting* [1997]).[8] In the end, no movie studio would take a chance on funding and producing *Angels in America* because of its projected cost, its nontraditional length, and the prominence of its gay characters, perspective, and sensibility. Pay television turned out to be a much better fit for this wholly original project. By the late 1990s, HBO saw itself as "filling the role of supporting independent filmmaking in America," explained Cary Brokaw. The network offered "a safe haven, a protected environment, in which creative talent can

Director Mike Nichols hired Richard Edlund, winner of four Academy Awards for the original *Star Wars* trilogy and *Raiders of the Lost Ark,* to add more than four hundred special effects shots, most involving the two visitations of the Angel of America (Emma Thompson).

take risks and make movies that would otherwise not be made and released in theaters."[9] Brokaw first worked with HBO in 1997 as the executive producer of the controversial docudrama *Path to Paradise: The Untold Story of the World Trade Center Bombing.* Four years later he went back to the network with producer-director Mike Nichols and writer-actor Emma Thompson to adapt Margaret Edson's 1999 Pulitzer Prize–winning stage play, *Wit,* winning his first Emmy, for Best Miniseries or Motion Picture Made for Television, in the process.

Flush on the heels of this major success, Brokaw asked Nichols about collaborating again on *Angels in America* for HBO. The director "leapt" at the opportunity and immediately recruited Meryl Streep and Emma Thompson to join Al Pacino, which fulfilled "HBO's prime proviso" of assembling an all-star cast.[10] HBO Films president Colin Callender then committed the network's full financial support for *Angels in America,* budgeting it at $62 million—essentially five times more than what the network typically allocated for six hours of prime-time programming at the time.[11] The shooting schedule, too, which lasted 137 days spread

The climb to heaven by Prior Walter (Justin Kirk) was shot at Hadrian's villa, just outside of Rome.

over nine months (May 2002 to January 2003), was also twice as long as HBO's already high-end standards for television production.[12] Mike Nichols, moreover, hired Richard Edlund (who had won four Academy Awards for the original *Star Wars* trilogy [1977, 1980, 1983] and *Raiders of the Lost Ark* [1981]) to add more than four hundred effects shots, most involving the angel's two visitations to Prior Walter (Justin Kirk), shot over six weeks at New York's Astoria Studio, as well as Prior's later climb to heaven, which was filmed at Hadrian's villa, just outside of Rome.[13] On-location shooting also included the breathtaking opening sequence, where the perspective soars high above the clouds as though accompanying an angel on a transcontinental flight over the Golden Gate Bridge in San Francisco to the Gateway Arch in St. Louis to the Sears Tower in Chicago to the Empire State Building in New York before landing gently at the Bethesda Fountain in Central Park, where an eight-foot bronze angel miraculously turns its eyes upward, inviting the viewer into the action.

The narrative begins with one of Meryl Streep's four bravura performances, here an orthodox rabbi eulogizing the elderly grandmother of

Louis Ironson (Ben Shenkman), evoking images ("the melting pot where nothing melted") of a widely shared, intrinsically American immigrant experience. Louis sits quietly in the temple behind his immediate family with his lover Prior, who later that same day reveals a small sarcoma lesion that has just surfaced on his shoulder, a surefire sign that he has developed full-blown AIDS. A young Mormon couple, Joe (Patrick Wilson) and Harper Pitt (Mary-Louise Parker), are then presented in their Brooklyn apartment. Joe is a conservative Republican lawyer and protégé of Roy Cohn, who has just offered him an internal affairs job at the Reagan Justice Department in Washington, D.C. When Joe tells his agoraphobic and drug-addled wife the good news, Harper tells him in no uncertain terms that she doesn't want to move. Overall then, "Chapter One: Bad News," introduces two relationships that are rapidly coming apart at the seams.

"Chapter Two: In Vitro," follows these two couples as they completely unravel and separate. Unable to cope with "Prior's disease," Louis walks out on him "to find some way to save [him]self." Harper, too, retreats into her valium-induced hallucinations with an "imaginary friend" called Mr. Lies (Jeffrey Wright). She informs Joe that "I'm going to have a baby," which turns out to be another one of her home-cooked fantasies. For nearly five years, Joe has been a distant, unresponsive husband to Harper, and their marriage ostensibly ends when he finally admits to himself and confesses on the phone to his mother back in Salt Lake City (and later to his wife in their apartment) that "I am a homosexual." His mother Hannah (Meryl Streep) journeys all the way to New York City to rescue her son and, ironically, ends up saving Harper instead, as well as befriending Prior. Louis, a clerical worker, bumps into Joe at the Brooklyn Federal Court House and they quickly become friends and then romantically involved. Roy Cohn is admitted into intensive care for "liver cancer" (AIDS) at an area hospital, where he is cared for by black, gay registered nurse Belize (Jeffrey Wright) and periodically haunted by the ghost of Ethel Rosenberg (Meryl Streep). Also hospitalized in a different facility in "Chapter Three: The Messenger," Prior conjures up specters of two blue-blooded ancestors before an angel from heaven bursts through the ceiling of his hospital room at the end of *Part One,* calling out to him in a loud voice: "Greetings, prophet!

Meryl Streep's four bravura performances in *Angels in America* include Mormon mother Hannah Pitt, who journeys from Salt Lake City to New York to rescue her son. Ironically, she ends up saving his estranged wife, Harper, instead, as well as befriending AIDS patient Prior Walter.

The great work begins! The messenger has arrived!" Consequently, Prior is one confused and terrified "prophet" at the start of *Part Two*.

In "Chapter Four: Stop Moving!" Prior discloses to his longtime friend Belize that an angel has appeared to him and that she commanded that he "submit to the will of heaven" before physically mating with him in an indescribably transformative experience (referred to as "Plasma Orgasmata"). Surprisingly, it is Hannah Pitt who most helps Prior understand his special calling ("an angel is just a belief with wings and arms that can carry you"). After learning from Belize that Louis is involved with Joe, Prior accidentally meets Hannah in "Chapter Five: Beyond Nelly," while following her son to the Mormon Visitor's Center in New York City where she now volunteers. The gravely ill Prior collapses, and Hannah accompanies him in a taxi back to the hospital where they talk and, most improbably, become fast friends.

In the sixth and final chapter, entitled "Heaven, I'm in Heaven," the angel returns ("I, I, I, I am the bird of America, the bald eagle"), only

Roy Cohn (Al Pacino, left) is told by Ethel Rosenberg (Meryl Streep) that he has been disbarred just before he dies. Nevertheless, she later helps Louis Ironson to say the Kaddish over his dead body.

this time Hannah is in Prior's hospital room and sees her too. A shaft of amber light illuminates the angel as she has orgasmic relations with Hannah as well. Clearly, this heavenly being is a spiritual avatar of America, and she is there to mark the millennial changeover where the old ways of seeing, thinking, and believing are replaced by an entirely new order, because "the world only spins forward." Prior climbs a flaming ladder to heaven and learns that God has deserted the angels. He, too, decides to return to earth and asks for their angelic blessing ("I want more life. I can't help myself"). In a different hospital, Ethel Rosenberg tells Roy Cohn (described by Louis as "the polestar of evil") that he has been disbarred just before he dies. She, however, helps Louis say the Kaddish (a prayer and blessing for Cohn) over his dead body. Louis was originally summoned by Belize to smuggle out Cohn's cache of the experimental antiretroviral drug AZT after he died so they could distribute it to as many of their sick friends as possible.

In a moving coda, a recovering and beatific Harper is seen leaving Joe for good on a redeye flight to San Francisco; she addresses the camera directly, telling the audience that "nothing's lost forever. In this

Angels in America culminates with (left to right) Louis Ironson (Ben Shenkman), Hannah Pitt (Meryl Streep), Prior Walter (Justin Kirk), and Belize (Jeffrey Wright) meeting at the Bethesda Fountain in Central Park. Prior has lived with AIDS for five years and they come together to celebrate his birthday.

world there is a kind of painful progress. Longing for what we've left behind and dreaming ahead." The story culminates with Prior meeting Louis, Belize, and Hannah on his birthday at the Bethesda Fountain in Central Park. It is 1990, and he has now lived with AIDS for five years. "Prophet" Prior likewise turns to the camera at the very end and blesses all the viewers, wishing them "more life" and reminding them once more that the "great work begins."

From start to finish, *Angels in America* is a successful mixture of disparate styles. At times it is darkly realistic; at other times fanciful and surreal. It is often tragic, but filled throughout with black humor, even concluding on a note of hard-won optimism. "Nichols's lavish production" blends "the grandeur of film with the theatrics of the stage and the immediacy of television," as one critic pronounced.[14] In this way, special effects render believable the angel's visitations as well as Harper's psychotic trip to Antarctica and Ethel Rosenberg's ghostly ability to walk through Roy Cohn's apartment and hospital room walls. Similarly, *Angels in America* exhibits the bold theatricality of having Harper and Prior address the camera head-on as the miniseries comes to a close. Nichols even continues the long-standing stage convention of casting actors in multiple roles, with Justin Kirk as both Prior Walter and the man in leather cruising Central Park; Ben Shenkman as Louis Ironson and the Angel of Oceania; Jeffrey Wright as Belize, Mr. Lies, and the Angel of Europe; Meryl Streep as Rabbi Isidor Chemelwitz, Ethel Rosenberg, Hannah Pitt, and the Angel of Australia; and Emma Thompson as Nurse Emily, the homeless woman, and the Angel of America.

These highly self-reflexive techniques aptly reflect the theatrical roots of *Angels in America* without ever seeming overly "self-conscious or self-congratulatory" in their translation to TV.[15] "Cable has changed everything," asserted Tony Kushner.[16] "Television feels more like theater. The fact that it's on television preserves the kind of intimacy of the stage."[17] Kushner, moreover, believes that because of this "strong affinity between television and theater," plays "may adapt better into television than into theatrical release."[18] Ever since the cancellation of PBS's *American Playhouse,* which adapted 189 plays over eight seasons between 1982 and 1989, American TV has produced very few Broadway and off-Broadway plays for the small screen, with the sole exception of HBO Films (whose catalogue currently includes such works as *Wit* [2001], David Feldshuh's *Miss Evers' Boys* [1997], and Moises Kaufman's *The Laramie Project* [2002]). Colin Callender, who won an Emmy for producing David Edgar's *The Life and Adventures of Nicholas Nickleby* as a nine-hour PBS miniseries in 1982, assures playwrights that HBO will provide their work with a far greater "exposure to a larger audience than [they] would ever get on Broadway."[19] The premiere of *Angels in America, Part One: Millennium Approaches* on December 7, 2003, attracted 4.2 million viewers; a week later *Part Two: Perestroika* garnered 3 million for a 3.6 million average. During this second week, HBO also telecast *Angels in America* in two three-hour segments, six one-hour episodes, and one six-hour block, with a cumulative tally of 7.8 million unduplicated viewers, the equivalent of filling the Walter Kerr Theater to capacity day after day for 22 straight years.[20]

HBO's senior vice president for corporate communications, Quentin Shaffer, has acknowledged that the network measures success in three ways: it begins with critical reaction, followed by the overall number of viewers a program generates across all of its distribution platforms (including network telecasts, on-demand showings, domestic and international syndication, and DVD sales), before finally factoring in industry-wide awards and recognitions.[21] In the case of critical reception, *Angels in America* was overwhelmingly lauded both domestically and internationally. The *New York Times* called it "the most powerful screen adaptation of a major American play since Elia Kazan's *Streetcar Named Desire* a half-century ago"; the *Washington Post* "thought-provoking, mind-blowing and, at times, breathtaking"; the *Chicago Tribune* "a spiritual rebirth in the secular world of cable television"; *Time* "dazzling, poetic, and hopeful"; and *USA Today* "not just one of the best television movies ever made . . . [but] also a transcendent work of art."[22] The program was also syndicated on TV screens all over the world; for example, it premiered in Canada in January 2004; the United Kingdom and Ireland in February; and Australia in June. The *Ottawa Citizen* christened *Angels in America* "a multi-textured viewing experience for the ages"; the London *Independent* "a modern classic"; the Manchester *Guardian* "a thrilling and gripping piece of television"; the *Irish Times* "millennial, prophetic . . . an artistic vision of hope"; and Sydney, Australia's *Daily Telegraph* "fiercely funny, poetic, and moving."[23]

HBO reran *Angels in America* in periodic rotation through August 2004, when it strategically released the DVD version just five days before the September 19 Emmy Awards ceremony where the miniseries came out on top in a record-setting eleven different categories (surpassing *Roots'* previous high of nine statues in 1977).[24] HBO additionally achieved a new benchmark for network wins that year, with 32 Emmys out of an unparalleled 124 nominations.[25] Previously, *Angels in America* had garnered five Golden Globes including Best Miniseries or Motion Picture Made for Television on January 25, 2004. All of this critical acclaim was a boon to DVD sales, which recouped nearly 20 percent of the program's original production budget, or $12 million, by December 23, 2004.[26] HBO then made another quick $5 million by leasing the program's basic cable rights to MTV's startup gay-oriented network Logo in January 2005.[27]

In retrospect, *Angels in America* was both a bona fide television event and a critical and popular success for HBO. It signaled that bolder projects had a far greater chance of being produced on TV than ever before. "It has to do with HBO, it's as simple as that," contended Mike Nichols. "We love the freedom that there is on HBO and the economic power . . . that affords us this freedom."[28] Al Pacino, who was committed to the adaptation from the start, later "realized that everything in a sense that's in *Angels* is the province of television."[29] *Angels in America* proved to be just too long, too artsy, too political, and too gay to be funded as a theatrical motion picture. Any one of those factors alone could have probably been overcome, but this constellation of unconventional or controversial components made all of the major film studios hesitant to take the production on.

Not HBO, however. *Angels in America* is a prime example of how the country's leading subscription TV network is simply better able and more willing to assume bigger risks by pursuing a business model that is different from selling tickets to a target audience where two-thirds of the cohort is between twelve and twenty-nine years old, like the movie studios do; or carrying spot advertisements and product placements for sponsors, like the broadcast and basic cable television networks. One of the more remarkable side effects of *Angels in America* is its facilitation of a kind of "cultural mainstreaming," in which its success "contributed to the growing acceptance of gay Americans; [and] the growing acceptance, in turn, dissipated organized hostility" to the TV production and later presentations of the play. "Such a circular effect can't be quantified," admits author and stage director Terry McCabe, "but it is no less real for that."[30] "After [the terrorist attacks of September 11, 2001,] and given all that's happened in Afghanistan and Iraq and the Middle East," Colin Callender has argued, "AIDS also becomes a metaphor for those difficult, tragic things we can't control."[31]

The depth and subtlety of Tony Kushner and Mike Nichols's magic realist miniseries thus has a resonance that goes far beyond the immediate concerns of the bygone Reagan era. It penetrates, laserlike, into the heart of the American experience itself. *Angels in America*'s unflinching honesty, its brilliant insights, and its empathy and understanding for each and every one of its characters are an aesthetic, political, and even spiritual embodiment of a much freer, more generous, and increasingly tolerant version of the United States as it could and should be in the years to come.

Notes

1. Richard Stayton, "The Next Life; *Angels in America* Comes to HBO with Big Stars and Renewed Relevance," *Los Angeles Times,* 30 November 2003, E1.

2. Bruce Weber, "Angels' Angels," *New York Times,* 25 April 1993, sec. 6, 29.

3. Jack Kroll, "A Broadway Godsend: *Angels in America,* an Epic of AIDS and Homosexuality, Is a Big Ticket," *Newsweek,* 10 May 1993, 56.

4. Lou Cannon, quoted in Frank Rich, "Angels, Reagan and AIDS in America," *New York Times,* 16 November 2003, sec. 2, 1.

5. Stayton, "The Next Life," E1.

6. Dan Cox, "Fine Line Drawn for *Angels* Pix," *Daily Variety,* 12 May 1994, 12.

7. Ben Greenman, "Tony Kushner, Radical Pragmatist: The Pulitzer Prize–Winning Playwright of *Angels in America* on Queer TV and Power Politics in America," *Mother Jones,* November/December 2003, at http://www.motherjones.com/arts/qa/2003/11/ma_586_01.html.

8. Elysa Gardner, "On TV: *Angels in America,*" *USA Today,* 4 December 2003, 1A; Steven Winn, "Angels Reborn," *San Francisco Chronicle,* 30 November 2003, 12.

9. Randy Gener, "HBO's Starry Miniseries Retains the Sweep of Kushner's Epic," *American Theatre* 20:10 (December 2003): 32.

10. Gener, "HBO's Starry Miniseries Retains the Sweep of Kushner's Epic," 33.

11. Stayton, "The Next Life," E1.

12. Jean Oppenheimer, "Heaven Sent," American Cinematography 8:11 (November 2003): 44.

13. Debra Kaufman, "A Precise Palette," *American Cinematography* 8:11 (November 2003): 45; Michael Goldman, "Making Angels," *Millimeter,* 1 December 2003, 12.

14. Eric Deggans, "Transcendent *Angels,*" *St. Petersburg Times,* 7 December 2003, 1E.

15. Tom Shales, "HBO's *Angels:* Glory Be! Adaptation of Tony Kushner Play Soars with Visual, Emotional Splendor," *Washington Post,* 30 November 2003, N1.

16. Stephen Kiehl, "Winged Victory: With a Life from *Angels in America,* HBO Soars at Last Night's Emmys," *Baltimore Sun,* 20 September 2004, at http://www.baltimoresun.com/entertainment/tv/bal-to.emmys20sep20,1.5220164.story?coll+bal-tv-storyutil.

17. Tony Kushner, quoted in Gloria Goodale, "*Angels in America* Earns Its Wings the Hard Way," *Christian Science Monitor,* 5 December 2003, 18.

18. Tony Kushner, quoted in Ed Siegel, "Kushner Goes from *Angels* to Bush," *Boston Globe,* 13 February 2004, D21.

19. Gener, "HBO's Starry Miniseries·Retains the Sweep of Kushner's Epic," 31.

20. Bill Carter, "For *Angels,* High Marks, but Fair Ratings," *New York Times,* 22 December 2003, C10; Denise Martin, "HBO Sends *Angels* to Fill Holiday Sked," *Variety,* 22 December 2003, 30.

21. Carter, "For *Angels,* High Marks, but Fair Ratings," C10.

22. Rich, "Angels, Reagan and AIDS in America," sec. 2, 1; Shales, "HBO's *Angels,*" N1; Chris Jones, "*Angels* in a Strange New World; The Pulitzer Prize-Winning Play Arrives on HBO with an All-Star Cast but a New Set of Issues under Its Halo," *Chicago Tribune,* 30 November 2003, 1; James Poniewozik, "Heaven on Earth: In the Dazzling HBO Miniseries *Angels in America* the Politics and Crises of the '80s Feel Close to Home," *Time,* 8 December 2003, 82; Robert Bianco, "Believe in HBO's *Angels;* Movie Overflows with Wit, Talent and Storyline Twists," *USA Today,* 5 December 2003, E13.

23. Ed Bark, "Divine Talents at Work in *Angels in America,*" *Ottawa Citizen,* 6 December 2003, J12; David Thomson, "Film Studies: Where Hollywood Fears to Tread," *Independent,* 14 December 2003, 8; Mark Lawson, "Lawson on TV: Even Better Than the Real Thing," *Guardian,* 2 February 2004, 10; Ian Kilroy, "Where *Angels* Dare to Tread—Believe the Hype: Tony Kushner's *Angels in America* Is about Much More Than Chronicling the Effect of AIDS in the U.S.," *Irish Times,* 31 January 2004, 55; Des Partridge, "Praying for *Angels* to Fly," *Daily Telegraph,* 3 June 2004, T23.

24. John M. Higgins, "*Angels,* Emmys and DVD; Award Haul Promises to Lift HBO Miniseries' Home-Video Sales," *Broadcasting & Cable,* 27 September 2004, 12.

25. Bernard Weinraub, "HBO: The Tough Act TV Tries to Follow," *New York Times,* 25 September 2004, B11.

26. "Market Data; Top DVD Sellers," *Video Business,* 23 December 2004, 42.

27. "Logo Catches *Angels,*" *Broadcasting & Cable,* 17 January 2005, 76.

28. David Ansen and Marc Peyser, "City of Angels," *Newsweek,* 17 November 2003, 80.

29. Stayton, "The Next Life; *Angels in America* Comes to HBO with Big Stars and Renewed Relevance," E1.

30. Terry McCabe, "*Angels* in Our Midst," *Chronicle of Higher Education,* 5 December 2003, B19.

31. Gardner, "On TV: *Angels in America,*" 1A.

PART TWO

COMEDY

At Home on the Cutting Edge

Bambi Haggins and Amanda D. Lotz

HBO takes comedy very seriously. Former network chairman and CEO Chris Albrecht—a key architect of HBO's brand and identity—notably stated that HBO considers itself "a patron [and] celebrates standup," and this attitude arguably has been integrated into the network's comedy series as well.[1] Before coming to the premium cable channel in 1985, Albrecht spent years spotting and nurturing comic talent, as an agent involved in signing Jim Carrey, Keenan Ivory Wayans, Billy Crystal, and Whoopi Goldberg and as a co-owner of The Improv in New York, where he was known to do a set or two. The comedy tradition at HBO may have preceded Albrecht by a decade, but his connection to comedy—and stand-up in particular—has contributed to HBO's status as both training ground and Holy Grail for contemporary comic voices.

HBO's comedic programming encompasses two different but related strands. At the time of the network's launch, HBO's telecasts of stand-up comedy performances first provided some of its most distinctive and important programming, often becoming significant cultural events among its small early subscriber base. The network added a second component in the late 1980s with narrative comedy series that addressed comedy tastes too narrow for broadcast comedies, although these scripted series have been more mainstream than the boundary-defying content that remains characteristic of the network's stand-up and sketch programming.

HBO's scripted comedy series may bear many formal similarities to those found on broadcast and basic cable networks, but both forms of comedy indicate the distinctive competitive circumstances of the network. Changes in the nature of HBO's stand-up and comedic series also illustrate the broader industrial changes in which competition from a subscription cable network and a rapidly fracturing industrial environment have radically adjusted industry norms for all networks. HBO's particular financial model has enabled it to defy conventional narrative comedy formats, and it has defined its comedy series with distinctive stories, narrative techniques, and production values. For example, most HBO comedy series used a single-camera film style in shooting series whereas network comedies maintained the long-standing three-camera proscenium stage. Just as single-camera comedies began to dominate on broadcast networks in the mid-2000s, HBO debuted *Lucky Louie* (2006), which deliberately returned to the older three-camera, shot-in-front-of-a-studio-audience style. HBO's stand-up and series comedy embodies the distinctive and expansive narrative possibilities available to a pay cable network and the particular strategies characteristic of this industrial status.

HBO Stand-up Comedy: Now Playing on the Main Stage in Your Living Room

Before HBO, stand-up comics had few venues that could widen their appeal and help them enter mainstream American popular consciousness. From the early 1960s to the early 1990s, the comic's trek from the comedy club circuit and college tours to five-minute acts on talk/variety shows might culminate in a spot on *The Tonight Show Starring Johnny Carson* (NBC, 1962–92) and a coveted seat on the couch (Carson's implicit approval of the quality of your act). In the mid-1970s, two significant "alternative" spaces for nationwide exhibition of stand-up talent widened this path: *Saturday Night Live* (*SNL* [NBC, 1975–]) and HBO. *SNL* aired on NBC in a slot previously regarded as untenable for new programming and offered a late night sketch comedy series populated (at least initially) by improvisational comedy veterans from Chicago's Second City and Los Angeles' The Groundlings and scripted by many writers from the *Harvard Lampoon*. Over the next three decades, *SNL* mainstreamed "cutting-edge" comic stage performance while facilitating the transformation of several "Not Ready for Prime Time Players" into A-list comic actors, including John Belushi, Bill Murray, Eddie Murphy, Mike Myers, Adam Sandler, and Will Ferrell.

Also in 1975, HBO premiered its *On Location* series of comedy specials. Although the series offered a smaller market share (and during its initial outings seemed more visually akin to a concert bootleg than a concert film), HBO stand-up programming began to establish itself as an arbiter of comic taste. HBO's single-act stand-up, although no longer called *On Location,* continues to flourish in terms of both cultural and industrial cachet because, for the comic, the "Not TV" component of HBO's defiant slogan indicates substantially greater creative autonomy. HBO's approach to stand-up comedy programming exponentially widened the playing field for comic stage performance—in terms of freedom in style and content as well as national exposure. From the inaugural episode of the *On Location* series, featuring Robert Klein, HBO stand-up programming brought the comedy club experience into American living rooms. As Klein stated, "true to the name, Home Box Office, it brought to your home the performer in toto."[2] HBO's *On Location* exposed the hottest and the hippest of A-list comic talent in stand-up concert specials that spotlighted those already on the top of the comedy club marquee.

On Location allowed comedians to bring their actual stand-up act, complete with "blue" humor, expletives, and in some cases, socially and politically controversial material. These specials introduced audiences to the unadulterated comic personas of comedians that had not been or could not easily be translated for network television. The *On Location* series—as well as the string of long-format specials that followed over the next three decades—provide audiences with the next best thing to the live stand-up comedy experience. When Redd Foxx, star of NBC's *Sanford and Son* (1972–77) and veteran comedian of the nightclub and "chitlin' circuit" (as well as the decidedly adult "party record") fame, came onstage in his 1977 installment of the *On Location* series, the audience in Las Vegas—and the viewers at home—were given a taste of the deep blue comedy that was his comic fare before, during, and after the sitcom's run. In the 1970s, the *On Location* specials featured the acts of comics who had honed their craft on the club circuit and were experiencing varying degrees of success on stage or screen (big and small). Both Freddie Prinze and George Carlin had spent time on Carson's couch and garnered varied praise for their network television appearances before their first HBO specials. Yet, in his *On Location* appearance in 1976, the exuberant, culturally specific humor of newly minted sitcom star Freddie Prinze provided a more complicated vision of the Chicano condition than "Chico" could discuss with "The Man." Likewise, the well-honed act of comic veteran George Carlin offered incisive and humorous observations about language, social and political practices, and an unabashed contempt for hypocrisy from either side of the political spectrum that grew progressively more controversial. In the second of his twelve HBO specials (1978), Carlin's performance of the Federal Communications Commission–challenging "seven words you can't say on radio" routine unequivocally established HBO stand-up as a space for comics to assert their creative agency without fear of industrial repercussions.

In 1978, HBO stand-up programming augmented its "cutting-edge" comedy library with *HBO Comedy Presents,* a series of specials that introduced a new generation to veterans of the "Borscht belt" and Playboy Club circuits (the Catskills and hipster comedy venues, respectively, in the 1960s and 1970s) including Norm Crosby, George Kirby, and Shelley Berman, whose television appearances had been limited to *The Ed Sullivan Show* (CBS, 1948–71), *The Dean Martin Show* (NBC, 1965–74), and *The Tonight Show Starring Johnny Carson.*

HBO aired two distinct stand-up performances in 1983—acts that presented two different directions in American comedy style, content, and comic ethos: *Bill Cosby: Himself* and *Eddie Murphy: Delirious.* Cosby became a television icon in the 1980s as the father who knew best in a colorized American Dream, and the role of Dr. Cliff Huxtable on *The Cosby Show* (NBC, 1984–92) very directly corresponded to his stand-up persona. In the aptly titled *Bill Cosby: Himself,* possibly the quintessential example of his stand-up skills, Cosby's performance represented the fully evolved incarnation of his comedic persona—the product of two decades on stage and television.

The premiere of *Eddie Murphy: Delirious* marked a new direction for HBO stand-up specials. Murphy had garnered a young, diverse, and rabid fan base before the special as the dominant comic presence on *SNL* and had begun his move to big screen superstardom with *48 Hours* (1982) and *Trading Places* (1983). Already a bona fide star, Murphy appeared in *Delirious* "clad in the type of red and black leather suit that

Eddie Murphy does his best Bill Cosby in *Eddie Murphy Raw* (1987), directed by Robert Townsend.

he would later lampoon as Axel Foley in *Beverly Hills Cop* (1984)" and "prowled the stage . . . with all the swagger of a standup virtuoso turned sex symbol."[3] The special captured the audaciousness in Murphy's act, which was reminiscent of the irreverent blueness of Richard Pryor's material (in terms of language and sexually explicit content)—although arguably without Pryor's sociopolitical edge.

These landmark stand-up specials spotlighted two African American comics, both of whom developed comic personae that began and continue to cross over with comic constituencies that transcend boundaries of race, ethnicity, and gender. Both acts were well received despite their difference in call. Cosby offered a "sitdown" routine and talked casually to the audience from a chair with stogie in hand in a performance devoid of spectacle, whereas Murphy's special and those that followed ushered in the era of stand-up specials as event programming that relied on a level of high-octane performativity characteristic of a rock or rap show. This legacy of 60-minute stand-up specials helped to make stand-up comics like rock stars and an HBO appearance a signifier of one's place on the A-list.

From 1984 to 1986, three comics who came into their own via the theater, sketch comedy, and the sitcom performed their first HBO specials—*Billy Crystal: A Comic's Line* (1984), *Whoopi Goldberg: Direct from Broadway* (1985), and *Robin Williams: Live at the Met* (1986)—each receiving accolades from across the entertainment media spectrum. Goldberg was already the toast of Broadway when she brought her Mike Nichols–directed one-woman show to the network. The show's series of monologues not only attested to Goldberg's range as an actor— playing diverse characters from a black male junkie to a teenage white surfer chick—but revealed her affinity for those on the margins of society. In his 1984 special, *A Comic's Line,* a parody of the play *A Chorus Line* (1975), Crystal employed the impersonation skills that made his two-season tenure on *SNL* (1984–85) memorable, using the premise of auditions for a Broadway musical to play a diverse cast of characters trying out for the parts. Robin Williams already had become a sitcom star as the sweetly hyperactive alien from the planet Ork in *Mork & Mindy* (ABC, 1978–82) when *Robin Williams: Live at the Met* premiered in 1986. Williams captivated audiences with the frenetic physicality of his performance and his improvisational bravado. By the mid-1980s, Goldberg, Crystal, and Williams were firmly ensconced on comedy's A-list and used their celebrity to deal with one of the sociopolitical issues that crossed lines of race, ethnicity, and gender in Reagan America— homelessness.

By the mid-1980s, HBO had, undeniably, played a role in contributing to a stand-up renaissance that Goldberg, Crystal, and Williams, along with writer-producer Bob Zmuda, leveraged into Comic Relief, a nonprofit organization created in 1986 to raise funds and awareness of homelessness. The *Comic Relief* telethon stand-up show ran (more or less) annually from 1986 through 1998 and provided a venue for comedians from all over the sociopolitical and stylistic spectrum to engage in comic discourse on the American condition—from Henny Youngman, Steve Allen, George Carlin, Paul Rodriguez, Bobcat Goldthwait, and Dick Gregory on *Comic Relief I* to Jon Stewart, Dave Chappelle, Chris Rock, Roseanne Barr, and Dennis Miller on *Comic Relief VIII.*[4]

Comic Relief provided showcases for A-list talent (albeit for altruistic reasons), while HBO's commitment to producing stand-up series featuring up-and-coming comedy talent—those who opened the bill as well

HBO played a role in contributing to a stand-up renaissance that (left to right) Billy Crystal, Whoopi Goldberg, and Robin Williams, along with writer-producer Bob Zmuda, leveraged into Comic Relief, a nonprofit organization created in 1986 to raise both awareness of homelessness and funds to combat it.

as those in the middle—played an equally significant role in maintaining the HBO comedy brand. HBO developed an elaborate network of stand-up series that replicated the de facto apprenticeship form of the comedy club bill and helped to create and/or nurture comedy's "it" performers. These (stand-up) showcase series, which feature between three and five comics doing short sets of their best material, attract a wide spectrum of comic talent with stylistic as well as demographic diversity. As is true on the bill of many comedy clubs, the "either/or" rule of diversity (including either a woman or a person of color) often seemed to apply to the broader-aimed showcase series—although it was not unusual to see an all-white male lineup. HBO's *Annual Young Comedians* series provided an excellent opportunity for comedians to position themselves to climb the HBO comedy ladder, as illustrated by Jerry Seinfeld, Drew Carey, Ray Romano, Dave Chappelle, and Louis C.K., among many others. Conventional wisdom suggested that a spot on an HBO *Young Comedians* special was worth ten *Tonight Show* appearances in terms of selling comedy club tickets, reaffirming HBO as a stop on the road to stand-up success.[5]

Another (roughly) annual series featured Rodney Dangerfield as the headliner on his own comedy showcase programs (*It's Not Easy Bein' Me* [1986], *Nothing Goes Right* [1988], and *Opening Night at Rodney's Place* [1989]) and introduced audiences to up-and-coming comic talents who affected the tone of comedy in the late 1980s and early 1990s. These showcases introduced both "shock" comics (e.g., Sam Kinison, Andrew Dice Clay) and those whose acts emphasized lampooning and/or contesting gender roles (e.g., Roseanne Barr, Tim Allen), some of whom would translate their acts rather smoothly into sitcom fare.

These showcase series reflected changing sensibilities in American popular culture and sociocultural politics in a manner that increased attention to racial, ethnic, and gender diversity—although not usually at the same time or on the same show. The showcase served as HBO comedy basic training for many women and people of color through a "separate but (somewhat) equal" programming paradigm: most clearly illustrated by the roughly triennial *Women of the Night* (1988, 1991, 1995) and *Russell Simmons' Def Comedy Jam* (1992). *Women of the Night*— hosted by female comics Rita Rudner (1988), Sandra Bernhard (1991), and Tracey Ullman (1995), who had already carved out a niche in American comedy—provided a showcase where female comics had the option not to play nice. They were able to speak more freely about politics, gender, and sex than a five-minute spot on late night network television would allow them to. For the "Women of the Night," including Caroline Rhea, Judy Tenuta, Paula Poundstone, and Ellen DeGeneres, this show provided significant national exposure that would facilitate a move up the HBO comedy ladder. Some would move up higher and more quickly than others, but this women-centric comedy programming gave white female comedians the significant opportunity to perform on a nationally televised stage.

Russell Simmons brought black and "blue" comedy to HBO at the moment hip-hop was blowing up and into mainstream American popular culture. Condemned by some critics from the black and mainstream press as too sexually explicit and expletive-filled for even late night cable, the series launched the careers of its first host, Martin Lawrence, as well as Chris Tucker, Steve Harvey, Bernie Mac, Cedric the Entertainer, and Eddie Griffin. Also, *Def Comedy Jam* offered a comedy product apropos of television's zeitgeist in the early 1990s, as exemplified by the black block programming strategies on upstart network Fox, and later The WB and UPN. HBO's comic spaces aided the discussion of racism on the institutional as well as personal level as a staple of comic narratives after April 1992 in post-LA Uprising America. With the exception of Whoopi Goldberg's HBO specials and the fortunate few black female comics like Mo'Nique, Adele Givens, and Wanda Sykes, the means to move up the HBO comedy ladder were (and are) somewhat limited for women of color.

Additionally, promising but not yet (entirely) proven comics were given single-act, thirty-minute comedy specials on HBO on series such as *One Night Stand* (1989–82, 2005–) and *HBO Comedy Half-Hour* (1997–98). A majority of the A-list comics of the new millennium passed through the three phases of the HBO stand-up apprenticeship: (1) the opener, appearing on the showcase series; (2) the middle, doing a thirty-minute set on a single-act comedy series; and (3) the headliner, starring in an hour-long special crafted to capture, enhance, and, one might argue, "brand" the comic persona of the comedian whose name is in the title. For example, Chris Rock began with appearances on *Uptown Comedy Express* (1987), advancing to his HBO Comedy Half-Hour, *Chris Rock: Big Ass Jokes* (1994), and then to his breakthrough special, *Bring the Pain* (1996). The evolution of both the comedy content and its delivery is easily discernible through this progression as the social commentary is sharpened and the timing honed. After becoming the headliners, Rock, as well as Bill Maher and Dennis Miller—all of whom had moved off the stand-up comedy food chain at HBO—opted out of the well-trodden path to sitcom stardom and were able to create their own idiosyncratic versions of talk/sketch comedy series: *The Chris Rock*

Chris Rock is an equal-opportunity offender in his HBO special *Bring the Pain* (1996), directed by Keith Truesdell.

Show (1997–2000), *Real Time with Bill Maher* (2003–), and *Dennis Miller Live* (1994–2002). Without HBO comedy programming, Rock, Maher, and Miller would likely have become part of the comedy A-list—but their time in HBO apprenticeship arguably allowed them a space to develop their voices with minimal inhibition and certainly brought more attention to their stand-up simply because more people could see their *actual* set, undiluted, sometimes profane, often profound, and very funny.

HBO continues to seek and, to greater and lesser degrees, nurture comic talent and potential. For twelve years, the HBO Comedy Festival (formerly the U.S. Comedy Arts Festival) has been a marketplace for independent comedy and the celebration of stand-up. It offers a point of entry to HBO stand-up programming for some, while providing a site of tribute for others, including George Carlin and the members of Monty Python. HBO stand-up programming has become progressively more available to those not on the premium channel grid: in 2004, Comedy Central, which had been under the media conglomerate umbrellas of both HBO's parent company, Time Warner, and Viacom (1991–2003), purchased more than 100 titles from HBO's stand-up library. This brought the stand-up specials of some of today's most popular comics (e.g., Dave Chappelle, Jeff Foxworthy, George Carlin, Ellen DeGeneres) to a wider audience, albeit with some of the language "bleeped" if it's not playing on the "Secret Stash."[6]

As a self-proclaimed "patron" of stand-up, HBO Comedy programming is not without its faults: as previously mentioned, the process of narrowcasting is certainly driven by market share but has the by-product of exclusion—P. Diddy's *Bad Boys of Comedy* (2005–) is as much a boys' club (with an occasional white boy) as *Dane Cook's Tourgasm* (2006) is part concert film/part road trip and is bereft of women (except in the audience) and people of color. Since Comedy Central and Showtime also offer spaces for the comedy of women, people of color, and gay and lesbian comics, one would hope that stand-up comedy on HBO, which has become a required stop on the trip to the comic A-list, would embrace the multiculturally informed "Gen Y" comics (and audiences). That is, after all, the new "cutting edge" of comedy—which is where HBO has been since 1975.

HBO Comedy Series: The Mainstream of a Niche Comedy Provider

It wasn't until a decade after its launch that HBO first attempted an original series. Perhaps due to its established reputation as a source for comedy, it began with a comedic series and created a show that was unlike any other on the air. *Not Necessarily the News* debuted in September 1983 and provided an early indication of the comedic distinction available to a pay cable outlet through its edgy political satire. Formatted as a mock newscast, the show appeared as a longer version of the "Weekend Update" segment already established on *Saturday Night Live*. *Not Necessarily the News* aired on the network for four years before becoming a series of occasional one-hour specials. Although cable distribution (let alone premium cable) still had not reached 50 percent, *Not Necessarily the News* made its mark on popular culture through the introduction of "sniglets"—words that aren't in the dictionary, but should be—into American vernacular, suggesting the complicated future for HBO programming as a significant cultural influence, yet one with limited reach.

The network launched its first conventional situation comedy two years later when it introduced *1st & Ten*. The series, which explored a fictional football team, first appeared as a "limited series," no doubt as a result of the network's uncertainty about the role of original series programming on a network that had already established itself as a location for "different" television. Reviews of the series note it as part of a strategy to help premium cablecasters compete with the growing video and video rental markets. *1st & Ten* lasted until 1991; most seasons featured only thirteen episodes, with each season structured as a limited series built around a theme or event (e.g., *1st & Ten: Training Camp; 1st & Ten: The Championship*).

HBO continued to tread lightly in its comedy series development. Critics praised the network's next effort, *Tanner '88* (1988), produced and directed by Robert Altman. Despite the critical lauding (by many who had panned *1st & Ten*), *Tanner '88* did not catch on with subscribers. Like many subsequent series, *Tanner '88* offered a sophisticated blend of comedy and drama (categorized as a drama in this collection) that warrants its mention here, especially given its continuation of the political satire begun by *Not Necessarily the News*.

The network next developed a group of series that mark what might be considered an "emergent" period for HBO original series production. *Dream On* (1990–96), *The Larry Sanders Show* (1992–98), and *Arli$$* (1996–2002) enjoyed multi-year runs; but with only a few episodes per season and the network lacking other ongoing scripted hits, most of these series existed as only cult and critical favorites. The network did not truly establish itself as a formidable producer of original series until late in the decade, with the 1998 premiere of *Sex and the City* (1998–2004) and its subsequent pairing with *The Sopranos* (1999–2007).

Part of the obscurity of the networks' shows during much of this period resulted from industry conditions. In 1994, HBO had just 18 million subscribers, less than 20 percent of U.S. television households at the time.[7] In this era, HBO primarily branded and promoted itself as a provider of theatrical features and sports programming, which brought little attention to its series. Many of these shows enjoyed fanatic audiences, but few crossed over into the mainstream popular culture space as would be the case beginning in the late 1990s. Cable disbanded its CableACE awards in 1997, which pushed HBO toward the more high-profile Emmy Awards and also expanded popular awareness of its series—even though cable had been eligible for Emmys since 1987.

Many of these emergent comedies continued the emphasis on storytelling about sports or the backstage Hollywood industry narratives characteristic of the network's first comedies. *Dream On* offered six years of stories focused on Martin Tupper's search for romance after his divorce and was best known for integrating old film footage, for pushing the boundaries of sexual content, and as the network's first "hit" series with its reach of 4.3 million viewers.[8] *The Larry Sanders Show* then offered the quintessential backstage narrative, providing a vehicle for the comedy persona Garry Shandling had developed in Showtime's *It's Garry Shandling's Show* (1986–90; which also reached a broader audience through airings on Fox). HBO followed next with *Arli$$*, featuring Robert Wuhl as the title character, an unscrupulous sports agent.

All three shows placed a white male baby boomer nearing middle age in the center of the narrative. Whether behind the scenes of a talk show, in sports locker rooms, or in Tupper's Manhattan publishing environment, these characters negotiated similar worlds, and the shows telegraphed their target audience with this repeated scenario. The settings for the shows established the link to celebrity that would continue in many HBO series in which notable actors or athletes appeared as themselves, a characteristic that arguably can be traced to *1st & Ten*'s mix of "real" football players and actors (and football players turned actors such as O.J. Simpson). This blending of "real" and fictional celebrities and actors recurs consistently in HBO comedy series. The use of film clips in *Dream On* also employs this strategy, albeit in a different way.

These series also established production techniques that would remain characteristic of many HBO comedies. Nearly all of the HBO comedies have avoided the conventional broadcast network comedy production style of using three cameras and a laugh track or studio audience. Instead, these early comedies used a single camera and were shot film style, creating a distinction that marked their "quality"— particularly as the comedy format struggled across the television dial in the early 2000s. Other sophisticated production techniques—such as *Dream On*'s incorporation of film footage and *The Larry Sanders Show*'s shift between film and video for "on air" shooting—also distinguished the shows as uncommon productions.

In addition to their airing on HBO, each of these shows achieved a broader audience through subsequent distribution—internationally in the case of *The Larry Sanders Show* and *Dream On,* or through small syndication deals on cable. Both series shot extra footage to increase the syndication opportunities on outlets having more stringent language and nudity restrictions. In the most unconventional arrangement, episodes of *Dream On* originally produced for HBO aired on Fox in 1995. Fox had an option to produce original episodes of the series if HBO discontinued the show, but the series' performance was not as strong as Fox hoped (it averaged a nine share in its Sunday time slot following *Married . . . with Children* [1987–97]).[9] HBO released all three series on DVD once this became a popular form of distribution, allowing the shows to find audiences that had never seen them as a result of the limited HBO audience at the time of their original production.

The breakout success of *Sex and the City* marks an important transition for HBO comedies and audience's expectations of them. *Sex and the City* premiered just months before *The Sopranos,* the show that may be most responsible for the growth in cultural awareness of HBO as a site of original series production. Like some of the preceding shows, *Sex and the City* provided rich, character-driven comedy and defied broadcast standards in its characters' discussions and the show's depictions of their dating lives. By most other measures, however, the show differed substantially. Although the revealing and frank depiction of four attractive women enjoying their sex lives unquestionably offered voyeuristic pleasure for HBO's long-targeted male viewers, *Sex and the City* ultimately became a "girls' show," particularly as the characters evolved and the series negotiated a careful balance of exploring dramatic struggles while maintaining a comedic edge. With the success of *Sex and the City* and *The Sopranos,* the network's identity became increasingly associated with original series production. Comedies played a role in this identity, although it was primarily dramas such as *The Sopranos, Six Feet Under* (2001–5), *Deadwood* (2004–), *The Wire* (2002–), and *Rome* (2005–7) that secured the network's status as premiere outlet for uncommon and excellently executed television programming.

HBO's subsequent comedic successes returned male characters to the forefront, in both Larry David's *Curb Your Enthusiasm* (2000–) and *Entourage* (2004–). As in the case of *Sex and the City,* both shows rely

Entourage follows the HBO tradition of integrating narratives about the Hollywood social and professional scene with many guest appearances and jokes at the industry's expense. Manager Eric Murphy (Kevin Connolly, left) sometimes locks horns with high-powered agent Ari Gold (Jeremy Piven, right) over their client Vince Chase's latest career move.

on character-driven comedy—although in very different ways. *Curb Your Enthusiasm* uses David's absurdist humor and scenes at least partially improvised by the actors, whereas *Entourage* recaptures the relational comedy often key to *Sex and the City*. Both *Curb Your Enthusiasm* and *Entourage* follow the HBO tradition of integrating narratives about the Hollywood social and professional scene with many guest appearances and jokes at the industry's expense.

The character-driven comedy at the core of these shows was rarely found on broadcast networks at the time. The fact that HBO writers need not manufacture commercial breaks helped contribute to the shows' narrative distinction, as did the extra 25 percent of narrative time gained by the lack of commercials. *Sex and the City, Curb Your Enthusiasm,* and *Entourage* all premiered during the period in which broadcast networks struggled to develop new comedies, while basic cable— although successful in establishing original drama series—struggled to launch a narrative comedic success. The additional sophistication in character and plot development possible in thirty rather than twenty-two minutes advantaged the HBO shows and considerably distinguished them from advertiser-supported fare.

The other development marking *Sex and the City* as characteristic of a different era in HBO comedy series production resulted from the ample aftermarket available to the series. Not only did it achieve extensive coterminous international syndication, but the show also achieved an unanticipated deal with TBS and Tribune broadcast stations that netted the show—which was initially produced for $900,000 per episode—$450,000 for each of the ninety-four episodes from the TBS sale alone. The terms of the Tribune deal were not disclosed, but a month later HBO sold the series to a single independent San Francisco station for $10.4 million plus advertising time (Tribune owns twenty-six stations).[10] DVD sets of the show have also sold well, further profiting the network. These secondary distribution markets are important for all television series, but provided particularly important opportunities for series airing on a subscription network available in less than 30 percent of U.S. television homes. In many cases, DVD and cable syndication provided the first opportunity for many to view the series and consequently provided a significant boon to the network's bottom line, as non-subscription revenues supplied 20 percent of the network's revenues by 2004.[11] DVD distribution also allowed access to the original versions of the shows, whereas broadcast and cable syndication required a re-edited version in accord with network standards and commercial insertion.

Notably, HBO also had many quickly forgotten comedic failures in this era. Despite claims that it would be a *Sex and the City* for men, *The Mind of the Married Man* (2001–2) never delivered the critical or creative heft common to HBO series at the time and that *Entourage* subsequently offered. HBO comedy also experimented with form, with notable failures: *K Street* (2003), with its strange real and fictional blend of actors and politicians telling political stories, and *Unscripted* (2005), a similarly uncertain blend of real actors and improvised and fictionalized storytelling that featured the increasingly trademark incorporation of the Hollywood celebrity machine. *The Comeback* (2005) provided similar generic uncertainty as it seemed a fictional "reality" show meant to produce laughs, but mainly produced uncomfortable awkwardness; it, too, centered its humor in Hollywood's star culture. The 2006 comedy

Lucky Louie attempted to locate the adult humor common to HBO series in a conventional situation comedy setting and format with three-camera production, a live studio audience, and sets so staid and unremarkable that they rivaled those of *All in the Family* (CBS, 1971–83). The style of the series was jarring for viewers, as by that point even most broadcast sitcoms had adopted much of the visual style of the previous HBO hits.

With the exception of *Lucky Louie,* HBO comedies have depicted a consistently affluent and virtually uniformly white narrative world in its comedic successes and failures since the late 1990s. This is particularly inconsistent with the network's showcase of black comedians in its stand-up and clear commitment to exploring race and racism in original films (*Introducing Dorothy Dandridge* [1999], *Lumumba* [2000], *Lackawanna Blues* [2005], *Sometimes in April* [2005], *Something the Lord Made* [2004]) and dramas of that era (*The Corner* [2000], *The Wire*). The particular economics of the subscription network reward those networks that can provide diverse enough programming to induce a broad range of viewers to pay the monthly subscription fee, but the network does derive benefit from over-serving some groups, which might explain this notable inconsistency.

HBO provided an ideal industrial context for certain types of comedy series as the consequences of the end of the network era befell the industry. The last cycle of inordinately successful broadcast sitcoms emerged just as the transition from the network era transpired. A steady progression of comedies including *Cheers* (NBC, 1982–93), *The Cosby Show, The Golden Girls* (NBC, 1985–92), *Roseanne* (ABC, 1988–97), *Murphy Brown* (CBS, 1988–98), *Seinfeld* (NBC, 1990–98), *Home Improvement* (ABC, 1991–99), *Frasier* (NBC, 1993–2004), *Friends* (NBC, 1994–2004), and *Everybody Loves Raymond* (CBS, 1996–2005) provided two decades of popular and critically regarded television comedy series. But the norms of the television industry in place when *Cheers* debuted in 1982 had nearly completely eroded by the time *Everybody Loves Raymond* left the air in 2005. Although a new broadcast comedy on a par with these iconic shows could not be found in the decade following *Everybody Loves Raymond*'s premiere, this is precisely the period in which HBO sitcoms moved from niche obscurity to niche renown.

Conclusion: Serious about Funny

Since early in its programming history, HBO has consistently provided daring, original comedy programming—from the earliest *On Location* stand-up specials and the *Young Comedian* specials to the A-list stand-up superstars doing their acts on Broadway. Its series have not proven as audacious as the network's stand-up, but the scripted series have offered their own imprint by challenging and remaking narrative forms long familiar to television audiences. The innovations of HBO comedy result from play with style and form and an understanding of the evolution of contemporary comedy: it is not a stretch to see at least a spiritual kinship between the comic performances in Whoopi Goldberg's one-woman shows, in which she disappears into multiple characters, and the transformations (augmented by makeup and, sometimes, unknowing players) that take place in *Tracey Takes On* (1996–99) or *Da Ali G Show* (2003–4).

As John Moffitt, the producer of all seven iterations of *Comic Relief,* stated succinctly, "I think if you go to any comic and say freedom, they'd say HBO."[12] The words "daring" and "unconventional" float across the screen before HBO programs. There is perhaps nothing more daring than trying to rework the most familiar television genre there is, the situation comedy, not for TV but for HBO.

Appendix: HBO Comedy

Stand-up Comedy (Major Programming)

STAND-UP SPECIALS

Cedric: Taking You Higher (2006)
Dennis Miller: All In (2006)
Bill Maher: I'm Swiss (2005)
George Carlin: Life Is Worth Losing (2005)
Robert Klein: The Amorous Busboy of Decatur Avenue (2005)
Tracey Ullman: Live and Exposed (2005)
Whoopi: Back to Broadway—the 20th Anniversary (2005)
Chris Rock: Never Scared (2004)
Ellen DeGeneres: Here and Now (2003)
Ellen DeGeneres: The Beginning (2000)
Chris Rock: Bigger & Blacker (1999)
David Cross: The Pride Is Back (1999)

Jeff Foxworthy: Totally Committed (1998)
Jerry Seinfeld: "I'm Telling You for the Last Time" (1998)
Denis Leary: Lock 'N Load (1997)
Eddie Griffin: Voodoo Child (1997)
Janeane Garofalo (1997)
Chris Rock: Bring the Pain (1996)
Dennis Miller: Citizen Arcane (1996)
Paula Poundstone Goes to Harvard (1996)
Dana Carvey: Critics' Choice (1995)
Rosie O'Donnell (1995)
Billy Connolly: Pale Blue Scottish Person (1992)
John Leguizamo: Mambo Mouth (1991)
Sinbad: Brain Damaged (1990)
On Location: Share the Warmth: An Evening With Bobcat Goldthwait (1989)
On Location: The Roseanne Barr Show (1987)
Paul Rodriguez Live! I Need the Couch (1986)
Robin Williams: Live at the Met (1986)
Rodney Dangerfield: It's Not Easy Bein' Me (1986)
A Steven Wright Special (1985)
Martin Mull: The History of White People in America (1985)
Whoopi Goldberg: Direct from Broadway (1985)
Billy Crystal: A Comic's Line (1984)
Eddie Murphy: Delirious (1983)
On Location: George Carlin at Phoenix (1978)
On Location: George Carlin at USC (1977)
On Location: Redd Foxx (1977)
On Location: Freddie Prinze & Friends (1976)
On Location: Steve Martin (1976)

STAND-UP SERIES

Dane Cook's Tourgasm (2006)
P. Diddy Presents the Bad Boys of Comedy (2005–)
One Night Stand (1989–92, 2005–)
HBO Comedy Showcase (1995–97)
Russell Simmons' Def Comedy Jam (1992)
Rodney Dangerfield: Opening Night at Rodney's Place (1989)
Uptown Comedy Express (1987)

ANNUAL STAND-UP PROGRAMMING

U.S. Comedy Arts Tribute to George Carlin (2003)
U.S. Comedy Arts Festival Tribute to Monty Python (1998)
Comic Relief I–VIII (1986–98)
Annual Young Comedians series (1982–95)

Women of the Night II–IV (1987, 1991, 1995)
*The 2nd Annual HBO Young Comedians Show–14th Annual Young Comedians
  Show* (1989–92)

Comedy Series

Lucky Louie (2006)
The Comeback (2005)
Unscripted (2005)
Entourage (2004–)
Da Ali G Show (2003–4)
K Street (2003)
The Mind of the Married Man (2001–2)
Curb Your Enthusiasm (2000–)
Sex and the City (1998–2004)
Arli$$ (1996–2002)
Tracey Takes On (1996–99)
Mr. Show (1995–98)
The Larry Sanders Show (1992–98)
Dream On (1990–96)
Tanner '88 (1988)
1st & Ten (1984–91)
Not Necessarily the News (1983–90)

Notes

1. Deborah Brown, "Special Report Freeze Frame: HBO at 25," *Variety*, 3–9 November 1997, 40.

2. Brown, "Special Report Freeze Frame," 40.

3. Bambi Haggins, *Laughing Mad: The Black Comic Persona in Post-soul America* (Piscataway, N.J.: Rutgers University Press, 2007), 102.

4. By the final installment of the stand-up telethon, HBO had taken over all of Comic Relief's administrative and production costs, thus guaranteeing that pledge money raised by the telecasts went directly to twenty-five homeless projects in twenty-three cities.

5. This adage (which we personally have heard comics say in "green room" chat) was originally attributed to Jerry Seinfeld, although no documentation could be found.

6. "The Secret Stash" refers to the weekend late night programming block (starting at 1:00 a.m. on Saturday and Sunday mornings) in which Comedy Central screens unedited films and stand-up specials; a warning appears before and during the night's offering touting the program's unaltered state.

7. Cheryl Heuton, "Is There Life after Pay Cable?" *Mediaweek*, 30 May 1994, 14–16.

8. Bill Carter, "HBO Finds Hits the Networks Miss," *New York Times*, 15 July 1991, D8.

9. Jim Benson, "Cable Likely *Dream* Target," *Daily Variety*, 24 May 1995, 5.

10. John Dempsey, "HBO Sells *Sex* Reruns to TBS Net," *Daily Variety*, 30 September 2003, 6; John Dempsey and Meredith Amdur, "Tribune Spices up HBO's *Sex*," *Variety*, 10 September 2003, at http://www.variety.com/article/ VR1117892266.html?categoryid=1236&cs=1 (accessed 11 September 2003); John Dempsey, "*Sex* sells its *Sex* to KRON for $10.4 million," *Daily Variety*, 21 October 2003, 5.

11. John M. Higgins and Allison Romano, "The Family Business," *Broadcasting & Cable*, 1 March 2004, 1, 6.

12. Ray Richmond, "Aspen's Laugh Riot," *Daily Variety*, 8 March 1999, 8.

ELEVEN

Comedy Talk Shows

Jeffrey P. Jones

HBO's executives have always recognized that, as a subscription television network, its programming must be similar enough to network fare to seem familiar and inviting to audiences, yet different enough to be worth paying for. HBO's approach to comedy is no different. As Chris Albrecht, then HBO's president of original programming, noted in 1996, "there are not a lot of places like us and we have to continue to explore and expand the boundaries of comedy content-wise and form-wise" to be successful.[1] Two years earlier, HBO had embarked on its own approach to reinventing that mainstay of late night network programming—the comedy talk show. As HBO searched for ways to increase its original offerings (as well as provide fresh alternatives for weekend viewing beyond its usual lineup of movies, stand-up comedy, and erotic documentaries), the comedy talk show became a logical vehicle for such experimentation and brand differentiation.

With the introduction of *Dennis Miller Live* (1994–2002) on Friday nights, the network launched what would become a series of successful late night comedy talk shows that provided the much-desired cachet as an innovator in television programming that the network continually seeks. Beyond Miller's run of nine years, these shows have included *The Chris Rock Show* (1997–2000) and *Real Time with Bill Maher* (2003–). This limited but award-winning set of talk shows has helped define the network as a place for brash yet smart and entertaining political humor beyond the pale of typical network talk show programming.

Miller came to HBO after a five-year stint as the "Weekend Update" anchor with *Saturday Night Live* (*SNL* [NBC, 1975–]), a comedic bit he carried over to his HBO show. But it was his signature "rant," a five-minute, smartly written screed against the ills of society and foibles of pompous public people that came to define the show. Rock, also an alum of *SNL*, continued to employ *SNL*-type sketch-comedy routines on his HBO show. But Rock's unpredictable and sometimes confrontational interviews with popular African American celebrities, as well as his tendency to feature uncensored hip-hop musical guests, helped establish the show as the premier location for black talk and variety entertainment in the wake of network talk show failures by other African Americans—Arsenio Hall, Keenan Ivory Wayans, Sinbad, and Magic Johnson. Finally, Maher, too, came to HBO as a known entity, further building on the signature style of roundtable political discussion that he offered for nine years on *Politically Incorrect with Bill Maher* (on Comedy Central and ABC, 1993–2002).

Each of these HBO talk shows, therefore, has provided familiar material to viewing audiences yet also developed the genre beyond the tired formula of celebrity product pitches, scripted interactions between host and guests, and the ubiquitous house band and musical sidekick. Although each show begins with a comedic monologue and includes interviews with guests, it is there that the relationship to the Steve Allen–Johnny Carson–David Letterman brand of late night talk generally ends. With no concerns for offending advertisers about "controversial" political material and no strictures on the language allowed, each host went on to develop a successful talk show persona as an opinionated sociopolitical commentator with a no-holds-barred approach to what could or should be said about the state of the world. The result, in short, has been shows that are opinionated without being predictable, political without being boring, and entertaining without being formulaic.

Dennis Miller Live

Although HBO had never aired a late night comedy talk show prior to 1994, it had dabbled in topical political humor before. From 1983 to 1990, the network produced an American version of the British import *Not Necessarily the News,* a sketch comedy show that also included humorous slants on the news. And in 1993, HBO Downtown Productions, an affiliated production company that developed programming for Comedy Central, created *Politically Incorrect* for the comedy channel and witnessed the subsequent critical success of this new form of entertainment talk show that dealt directly with politics. HBO then contracted with Dennis Miller for a six-episode run of *Dennis Miller Live,* a thirty-minute live comedy talk show airing weekly at 11:30 P.M. (EST) on Fridays and repeating on Sundays. Miller had just come from a failed attempt at a syndicated talk show that lasted only six months (during 1992–93), but was more famously known for his work on *SNL* from 1986 to 1991. *Dennis Miller Live,* which debuted on April 22, 1994, similarly focused on Miller's strengths as a caustic and biting commentator on the day's events.

The talk show format for HBO brought Miller out from behind the news and talk show desk. Standing center stage, Miller opened the show with a monologue of comedic material largely based on headline news stories and bizarre news oddities. The lack of regulation on language gave Miller's acerbic wit an added punch as a result of his notorious potty-mouth. This format allowed him to accompany typical jokes with commentary that, although it might not be funny, would be greeted by laughter or applause nonetheless due to his articulation and amplification of his audience's feelings. For instance, after beginning the July 13, 2001, show with a few jokes about Congressman Gary Condit's role in the disappearance of former intern Chandra Levy, Miller takes the joking a step further by boldly stating, "Fuck you, Gary Condit—you're a bad guy," to which the audience erupts in cheers. The jokes, then, are blended with Miller's strong-willed and pointed commentary, usually laced with profanity, with little differentiation between the two. Johnny Carson once said, "I just don't feel Johnny Carson should become a social commentator. . . . If you're a comedian, your job is to make people laugh. You cannot be both serious and funny."[2] Miller took the opposite approach.

This is seen most clearly in the next feature of the program—the five-minute segue between the monologue and the guest interview known as the "rant." Miller would begin by saying, "Now I don't want to get off on a rant here, but . . ." and proceed to soliloquize on that evening's topic of discussion (covering over the course of the show's run topics as disparate as affirmative action, disappearing manners, fame, and civil disobedience). As the defining feature of the show, Miller established his persona as a smart and intellectually nimble social and political critic through his mix of literary and cultural references (although detractors found his persona "smug," or "smarter-than-thou"). The show won five Emmy Awards for comedy writing, largely attributable to the rants (material he also converted into four best-selling books).

After the rant, Miller would bring on a guest to discuss the topic he had just introduced. Sometimes the guest would have a connection to the topic (such as Dr. Joycelyn Elders on teen pregnancies), and sometimes not (as with Jon Stewart on bad habits). Although most of the guests were celebrities, they were not appearing to pitch their latest media projects, but rather to talk about the issue at hand. And as with the rant, there was no segregation between serious talk (like Oprah Winfrey) and entertaining talk (like Letterman). Miller's gift was the ability to be both serious and funny at the same time. The show would conclude with Miller reprising his bit from *SNL* in front of "The Big Screen," narrating photographs of politicians and famous people with what often amounted to verbal cartoon bubbles and funny captions. The feature added a lighter touch to finish off the program and ended with Miller's signature statement from *SNL*: "That's the news, I'm outta here." This part of the show, however, often seems like a return to Miller's previous comedic manifestation as the sophomoric guy in the corner of the room lobbing spitballs—amusing, but ultimately insignificant.

Dennis Miller Live ran for nine seasons and 215 episodes, finally going dark on August 30, 2002. Over those episodes, Miller (along with Bill Maher on *Politically Incorrect*) helped insert a healthy dose of politics into the genre of late night comedy talk. The program demonstrated that substantive conversations could occur in a thirty-minute show that still included comedy routines. It also showed that a comedy show could focus on a single topic of discussion with a single guest and that audiences were interested in political talk from someone other than the inside-the-beltway crowd. Perhaps most importantly, Miller proved that a talk show host didn't have to be a Carsonesque Everyman—appealing to all, offensive to none.[3] Rather, the talk show host could establish himself as a polemical and aggressive social commentator who, despite his assertiveness, was both entertaining and appealing. *Dennis Miller Live* helped HBO fill a void in its late night weekend programming while simultaneously creating the model upon which the network's next talk show would be built.

The Chris Rock Show

The idea of a talk show featuring Chris Rock arose after Rock's second stand-up special for the network, *Bring the Pain* (1996), garnered considerable critical acclaim (earning two Emmys and a CableACE award). With 22 percent of HBO's subscriber base being African American (and 42 percent of all black households in America subscribing to the network),[4] Chris Albrecht saw an opportunity to use the talented comedian to address his paying constituency at a time when other networks had been unsuccessful with black talk show hosts.[5] *The Chris Rock Show* premiered on February 7, 1997, following *Dennis Miller Live* on Friday nights. Albrecht described Rock as "one of the few guys out there who has the writing ability and the intelligence to create a point of view and the performing ability to make that point of view entertaining to watch." He "is the missing voice in late night," Albrecht said. "We think he can create a signature platform for himself similar to what Dennis [Miller] has done."[6] The network, therefore, allowed Rock to develop his own take on the genre, although the show came closer than Miller's to the traditional late night format.

Rock opened each show with a comedy monologue before introducing a taped sketch-comedy segment, then conducted a celebrity interview, and ended the program with a musical guest performance. Instead of a stage band, Rock hired Grandmaster Flash, one of the pioneers of hip-hop, as his musical director. Indeed, hip-hop was central to Rock's self-conception and stage persona. He has noted, "I'm a rap comedian, the same way Bill Cosby is a jazz comedian. But Cosby's laid back. I'm like bang, bang, bang right into it."[7] This relationship to hip-hop culture included more than the rhythm; it also included the content of the jokes themselves. Rock used material about young black artists who were too obscure for most late night talk show hosts. "On my show," Rock said, "we keep a youthful slant. We're joking about people never joked about before," such as Wu Tang Klan member Old Dirty Bastard, Lil' Kim, and Puffy (P. Diddy/Shawn Combs). "No one ever put on a suit and did a monologue and talked about these people."[8]

Central to every program are the videotaped sketch-comedy bits similar to those aired on *SNL* or *In Living Color* (Fox, 1990–94)—a show Rock joined after leaving *SNL*. Most deal directly in parody. They include fake advertisements, such as products for black professionals who want to disguise their love for watermelon; doctored photographs, such as how presidential candidates can appeal to black voters (e.g., Al Gore with gold teeth, George W. Bush drinking malt liquor); fake public service announcements, such as "How to Not Get Your Ass Kicked by the Police"; fake campaign commercials, such as "Mike Tyson for President"; and fake television programs, such as "Taxi Driver Confessions" (Rock's parody of HBO's *Taxicab Confessions* [1995–]). Here, Rock taped actual segments of himself as a New York City cab driver, but used himself as the joke (by smoking a bong, listening to dirty rap lyrics, and crying) to get reactions out of customers. Finally, Rock also employed aspects of a fake news show (preceding its later mastery on *The Daily Show* [Comedy Central, 1996–]) by cutting to faux news correspondents for updates (on location in the Middle East, for instance) or conducting news interviews with faux talking heads (such as a debate over violence in music and television).

The other form of taped comedy segments involved Rock conducting man-in-the-street interviews or surveys with citizens. More often than not, these pieces aimed to contrast the thinking, interests, or desires of black and white people. For instance, Rock ventured to Harlem to learn what African Americans thought about paying $2,500 for a ticket to see Barbra Streisand at Madison Square Garden. Conversely, he went to Howard Beach to ask white citizens to sign a petition to rename a major road in the community "Tupac Shakur Boulevard." Rock returned to his birthplace of South Carolina to survey black and white citizens' opinions about the Confederate flag flying over the state capitol dome (ending the segment by hoisting a newly designed flag over the capitol that simply substituted the stars of the Confederate flag with head-shots of the black "stars" of the WB television network). These comedy segments worked to establish an "us versus them" relationship between laughing audiences and those being ridiculed on screen, while bluntly dealing with issues such as race, racism, and poverty.

This "partisan" approach was somewhat new to late night comedy talk shows, but Rock also made it clear that he spoke either to or for African Americans. When interviewing Martin Lawrence after a hospital stay by the star, Rock asks, "Hey man, I seen you on a couple of shows, but the black people wanna know, how you feelin,' man?"

(October 20, 2000). Indeed, beyond the topical jokes in his monologues and the focus of his sketch comedy bits, he also announced his own position and that of his show with African American audiences through the selection of his celebrity guests. Most of his interviewees were black, and their selection had more to do with their stature in the black community than whether they were pitching a project. Rock's guest list included celebrities such as J. C. Watts, Johnnie Cochran, Ed Bradley, Allen Iverson, and Bernie Mac, to name a few.

But the fact that Rock held conversations with some of the leading African American figures in American culture and politics didn't mean his interviews were overly deferential (which critics argue was a limitation of Arsenio Hall). In fact, Rock often used the interview to distinguish himself as a unique interviewer, to ask a question he honestly wanted to know the answer to, or as an extension of his persistent stand-up comedian style of engagement. In his interview with Pamela Anderson, for instance, she eventually breaks from his line of questioning and says, "This is a very strange interview. You're asking me all these—," at which point Rock interrupts her with, "Because I'm trying not to sound like Jay Leno" (October 6, 2000). Rock was very deliberate in making his interviews more than the typical run-of-the-mill celebrity/host banter. "You've gotta attack an interview like a pretty woman," he argued. "You've got to realize that everybody tries to talk to her, so you've got to try to figure out the things nobody's talked to her about. If she's tall, don't mention she's tall. . . . I try to be like a funny 'Face the Nation.'"[9]

Rock's overly blunt and unpredictable questioning style can also be seen in his interview with Spike Lee. After noting Lee's successful career and his level of cultural respect, he asks, "So why are you so mad? You are the maddest black man" (September 17, 1999). Similarly, interviewing the Reverend Al Sharpton after he had barely lost the Democratic primary for New York's mayoral election, Rock explains to him, "You're like a haircut and an apology from getting the nomination. I'm saying that like in a cool way," at which point a somewhat bewildered Sharpton responds, "For you, that is a compliment" (November 21, 1997). Refusing to let go, Rock then proceeds to make a case for why Sharpton needs to change his hairstyle because only pimps wear their hair that way. Though aggressive, Rock considers such exchanges part of his job as an artist. "Somebody should always be offended," he contends. "Somebody in your life should always be like, 'Why did you have to do that?' Always. That's just being a real artist. That's the difference between Scorsese and Disney."[10]

The Chris Rock show aired live from New York and ran for five seasons, ending its run on November 3, 2000. Produced by HBO Downtown Productions, the series earned an Emmy Award for writing in a variety or musical show and was reportedly "one of HBO's highest-rated . . . series."[11] Although comedian Dave Chappelle (*Chappelle's Show,* 2003–6) would later pick up where Rock left off in offering side-splitting sketch comedy with a strong racial critique, no African American late night talk show host has emerged to fill Rock's shoes as someone capable of delivering no-holds-barred comedy *and* talk.

Real Time with Bill Maher

In the wake of the terrorist attacks of September 11, 2001, comedian and talk show host Bill Maher saw his long-running and popular round-table discussion program, *Politically Incorrect,* cancelled by ABC in the summer of 2002 as a result of remarks made on the show that some (including advertisers) saw as unpatriotic.[12] In criticisms Maher later made about the lack of accountability in the Bush administration over its role in the lead-up to September 11 he joked, "The only person who has ever been fired over 9/11 is me!" With *Dennis Miller Live* also cancelled in 2002, HBO began looking for a way to get back into political talk comedy, especially in a time of war and with a presidential election just around the corner. Nancy Geller, senior vice president of original programming at the network, noted, "We're hoping that we'll have our kind of version of a news show, a comedy news show. We did 'Not Necessarily the News' and have played around in that area . . . but to have a voice back on again is I think important in these times."[13]

In the fall of that year, HBO announced a new talk show featuring Maher doing essentially the same type of political talk show that he did with *Politically Incorrect,* but now on the subscription network. As with the network's interest in Miller and Rock, HBO executives enunci-ated their interest in having not just a comedy talk show, but rather a comedy talk show with a strong point of view. "[Maher's] really got a lot of terrific stuff to say, and it's a good time for him to say it," Geller noted. "We're interested in his opinion and his comedy and his tone. We're fans."[14]

Maher's revised version of the roundtable talk show debuted on February 21, 2003, with a rotating group of three celebrities and politicians instead of the four guests he previously hosted (some of whom were not well known or necessarily the best discussants). The format of the HBO show includes a quick comedy sketch to open the program, a comedic monologue, two interviews (often via satellite with politicians or policy makers) interspersed throughout the show, the roundtable discussion, and Maher's own version of a "rant" (à la Dennis Miller) called "New Rules." With the move to HBO, the producers have been much more successful in getting bigger-name personalities to appear as interviewees via satellite—from Noam Chomsky and Gray Davis to Dan Rather and Benjamin Netanyahu. According to co-executive producer Sheila Griffiths, most of these higher-profile people would never appear as discussants on the panel because the unfettered discourse there is "just too unprotected" for people who expect public engagements to be controlled-discourse situations.[15] The fact that public persons of this stature are willing to give serious interviews to a comedian on an entertainment talk show demonstrates just how far Maher and the genre of entertaining political talk have come since he and Dennis Miller established the credibility of the form a decade previously.[16] But it also suggests that the roundtable forum Maher hosts still retains a measure of unpredictability and an "anything goes" form of deliberation and argumentation that pundit shows like *Meet the Press* (NBC, 1947–) simply don't offer.

In the "New Rules" section of the program, Maher crafts several brief op-ed-type comedic statements to forcefully establish a rhetorical position while remaining humorous. Maher has also circulated these to various newspapers for publication *as* op-ed pieces. In a New Rule called "Bad Presidents Happen to Good People," Maher tries to explain to citizens in foreign countries that "We're not with stupid," and that ridiculing the president is his patriotic duty: "If I could explain one thing about George W. Bush to the rest of the world it's this: We don't know what the hell he's saying either! Trust me, foreigners, there's nothing lost in translation, it's just as incoherent in the original English. Yes, we voted for him—twice—but that's because we're stupid, not because we're bad" (September 8, 2006). Whereas Maher proclaimed himself a libertarian with Republican sympathies when *Politically Incorrect* first aired in 1993, by the time he started his HBO talk show, his politics were largely anti-Republican and his persona had evolved into a presidential gadfly. "Politics is so off-kilter [now]," he has argued. "In my lifetime, I've never seen it as bad as it has been. George Bush is such a polarizing figure. There is a hunger to see the people in power taken down because they are an arrogant bunch up there. The Republicans pretty much control everything." Maher, of course, realizes that his role as a comedian on an uncensored public stage gives him special license and privilege to ridicule and satirize the powerful. "When people are bloated with pomposity and religiosity and arrogance and a thirst for power," he says, "that's the perfect time for comedy."[17]

Maher's success in producing a roundtable talk show that could be both entertaining and informative was established prior to his arrival at HBO. But with no concern that his opinions would offend advertisers and knowing that his network not only tolerated a strong point of view but actually wanted it, Maher has been able to reconfirm the place of comedic political talk shows as relevant sites for an alternative form of mediated engagement with politics.

Bill Maher, Chris Rock, and Dennis Miller have all helped revive America's understanding of the important role that political satirists play as sociopolitical commentators. What they also established is a redefinition of the late night comedy talk show—one that can be entertaining and informative, playful yet also offering a point of view. The structure of a network not dependent on advertising or constrained by limitations on language has helped produce such unfettered political talk, while simultaneously branding HBO as the location where such talk can always be found on television.

Notes

1. Joe Flint, "Cable: Comedy's Land of Riches," *Daily Variety*, 9 February 1996.

2. Rodney Buxton, "The Late-Night Talk Show: Humor in Fringe Television," *Southern Speech Communication Journal* 52 (summer 1987): 377–89.

3. Although one could argue that David Letterman was the first to establish himself as an anti-Carson, that persona was much less in play as Letterman battled Leno for the title of "King of Late Night."

4. "HBO Skeds Black History Month Shows, Film Tour," *Daily Variety*, 22 January 1997, 55.

5. Although Fox had been quite successful with *The Arsenio Hall Show* (1989–94), that program had been off the air for three years.

6. Ray Richmond, "Rock Rolls to Latenight Talker on HBO in Feb.," *Daily Variety*, 14 November 1996, 3.

7. Cindy Pearlman, "He Will Rock You," *Chicago Sun-Times*, 3 September 2000, Show, 4.

8. Ibid.

9. Ed Bark, "Comedian Chris Rock Feels Restricted by Questions of Race," *Dallas Morning News*, 28 August 1998, E8.

10. Christopher John Farley, "Seriously Funny: Chris Rock is on a Roll," *Time*, 13 September 1999, at http://www.time.com/time/magazine/article/0,9171,991949,00.html.

11. Adam Sandler, "Rock Rolls with Comedy, TV and Pic Biz," *Daily Variety*, 8 March 2001, A12.

12. For a detailed account of Maher's fall from grace at ABC, see Jeffrey P. Jones, *Entertaining Politics: New Political Television and Civic Culture* (Lanham, Md.: Rowman & Littlefield, 2004), 80–87.

13. "Maher to Host New HBO Latenight Yakker," *Daily Variety*, 21 November 2002, 22.

14. Ibid.

15. Sheila Griffiths, interview by Jeffrey P. Jones, 8 January 2004.

16. See Jones, *Entertaining Politics*.

17. Betsy Boyd, "Cable is Able amid Network Laffer Lull," *Daily Variety*, 15 June 2005, A1.

TWELVE

The Larry Sanders Show

George Plasketes

Before HBO's prestigious programming proclamation, "It's Not TV . . . ";
before its Emmy Award dominance and critical acclaim; before its cast
of colorful characters, from Carrie and the city gals to Tony and the
Jersey boys to the dysfunctional Fisher funeral family; before the narcissistic entourage of Hollywood wannabes and the improvisational enthusiasm of Larry David, there was another neurotic, self-absorbed
"Larry"—Larry Sanders. *The Larry Sanders Show* lies at the forefront
of HBO's impressive string of "appointment" and "watercooler talk"
groundbreaking original series. Premiering in August 1992, and running through May 1998—a total of eighty-nine thirty-minute episodes
in HBO's efficient thirteen-installment seasons, *The Larry Sanders
Show* holds the distinction of being the first cable series to earn Emmy
nominations in the awards' major categories. (In 1988, Academy rule
changes made original cable programs eligible to compete for the same
awards as network series). Although *Sanders* routinely lost to NBC's
Frasier (1993–2004), the series was among the nominees for Best Comedy Series during each of its six seasons between 1992 and 1998.

The Larry Sanders Show features stand-up comedian Garry Shandling as generic late night talk show host Larry Sanders. The show-
business satire is a "surreality series" that blends and blurs the real and
the fictional, studio and story, on-camera and off-camera, the backstage
and behind-the-scenes machinations of television networks and the talk
show format. Intelligent, irreverent, and inventive, *The Larry Sanders
Show* loosely links the elements of the television working-group sitcom
of *The Dick Van Dyke Show* (CBS, 1961–66) with the ripple-effect
humor of more contemporary comedies such as *Seinfeld* (NBC, 1990–

98) and *Curb Your Enthusiasm* (2000–), to HBO's "dramady" and reality series *Entourage* (2004–) and the short-lived *The Comeback* (2005), to the fake news format employed by Jon Stewart on Comedy Central's *The Daily Show* (1996–). The series evokes the "let's put on a show" atmosphere of the classic Hollywood backstage musicals, though in an edgier tone closer to Robert Altman's film *The Player* (1992) and to a lesser degree Martin Scorsese's obsessive *The King of Comedy* (1983). However, the *Sanders* series' most obvious inspiration and origins in theme, structure, iconography, production elements, comic stylings, and setting lie in the late night talk realm, in particular *The Tonight Show* (NBC, 1954–).

Larry Sanders picks up where Johnny Carson leaves off. Although Shandling has downplayed the influence, insisting that Sanders's character is patterned as much after Sally Jessy Rafael as anyone, the archetypal Carson seems to hover in the shadows of the parallel television universe of the *Sanders Show.* "With Carson gone, we can pass Arsenio [Hall] and [Jay] Leno," urges Larry's producer Artie in an early episode. The Carson connections are so precise, the *Sanders* production borders on pure parody. However, the approach to the show draws extensively from Shandling's vast experience in the talk show format, which explains Larry's exact hand-in-his-suit pockets presence when emerging from the curtain into the studio spotlight to deliver a monologue. Since 1983, Shandling had been one of the regular guest hosts on *The Tonight Show* and was considered a long shot, behind Jay Leno and David Letterman, as a possible successor for the desk job in the esteemed late night lineage. (Shandling relinquished his designated "sitter" role for Carson following the first season of *It's Garry Shandling's Show* [Showtime, 1986–90]). When Leno inherited King Carson's throne in 1992, Shandling received offers to host his own late-late night (1:00 A.M.) network talk show. He declined, claiming that he was more interested in the challenges of producing "a show about a talk show," which allowed him to stretch as a writer and actor.

The origins of *The Larry Sanders Show* not only are rooted in Shandling's stand-up and talk show background, but also can be traced to the quirky comedy *It's Garry Shandling's Show.* Although comedy has always been a cornerstone of television programming, the mid-1980s signaled a prime time for comics that extended well into the 1990s. The

programming trend characterized as "stand-up sitcom" was best epitomized by Bill Cosby's *The Cosby Show* (NBC), which debuted in 1984.
Other stand-up comedians also made the successful transition to small-
screen situation comedy on the broadcast networks. Among those in the
comic current were Roseanne Barr (*Roseanne* [ABC, 1988–97]), Richard Lewis (*Anything but Love* [ABC, 1989–92]), Jerry Seinfeld (*Seinfeld*
[NBC, 1990–98]), Tim Allen (*Home Improvement* [ABC, 1991–99]),
Paul Reiser (*Mad about You* [NBC, 1992–99]), Tom Arnold (*The Jackie
Thomas Show* [ABC, 1992–93]), Brett Butler (*Grace Under Fire* [ABC,
1993–98]), Ellen DeGeneres (*Ellen/These Friends of Mine* [ABC, 1994–
98]), and Drew Carey (*The Drew Carey Show* [ABC, 1995–2004]).
Garry Shandling was also part of the movement, although he was located
on the fringes, where he pursued a different comic route.

Between 1986 and 1990, *It's Garry Shandling's Show* aired on the
cable network Showtime. Beginning in 1987, it also crossed over to the
fledgling Fox network's Sunday-night lineup, which included *Married
. . . with Children* (1987–97) and *The Tracey Ullman Show* (1987–90;
featuring Matt Groening's animated shorts that evolved into *The Simp-
sons* [1989–]). Created by Shandling and former *Saturday Night Live*
writer Alan Zweibel, and inspired to some degree by *The George Burns
and Gracie Allen Show* of the 1950s, *It's Garry Shandling's Show* introduced a fresh alternative to the traditional TV comic presentations. The
show features a monologue; a silly, whistling theme song composed and
performed by Randy Newman; and a structure and technique that routinely and playfully manipulates reality. Shandling plays himself, a
stand-up comic and star of a television show, which is telecast from his
fictional Sherman Oaks, California, condominium. The unusual approach foreshadows *The Larry Sanders Show* (as well as *Seinfeld* and
its co-creator Larry David's adaptation in *Curb Your Enthusiasm*), with
Shandling surrounded by an ensemble of fictional characters as his
friends and family, and stars routinely appearing as themselves. Among
the notable guest cameos on *Shandling's Show* are Red Buttons, Gilda
Radner (in one of her last television appearances in April 1988), and
rock musician Tom Petty. Petty is cast as Shandling's next door neighbor who frequently drops by, whether to return Garry's hedge clippers
that he borrowed or to serenade a woman in the late stages of her pregnancy with a living room acoustic version of "The Waiting."

The Larry Sanders Show features stand-up comedian Garry Shandling (right) in the title role as a generic late night talk show host who is surrounded by an offbeat cast of characters including his talentless sidekick Hank Kingsley (left), played brilliantly by Jeffrey Tambor.

Shandling's Show borrows the Burns technique of breaking the "fourth wall," with Shandling addressing the studio and home audience with plot and character commentary, one-liners, and jokes. Shandling pushes the gag further by encouraging the studio audience to contribute ideas to unfolding story lines. In one episode, he even tells the audience to feel free to use his apartment (the set) while he goes to a baseball game. The television evolution of Shandling's "surreal" shtick and production preferences can be traced slightly further back to former Monkee Michael Nesmith's *Television Parts* (NBC, 1985), in a sketch that features Shandling providing on-camera narration of his date with Miss Maryland.

It's Gary Shandling's Show represents a building block for *The Larry Sanders Show*. Both shows implement Shandling's nasal, sometimes whiny, comic persona and rhythm. The unorthodox style and some of the core elements are interchangeable, with "Garry Sanders" and "Larry Shandling" as shape-shifting comic cousins. Yet, the behind-the-scenes basis of the *The Larry Sanders Show* is inherently more revealing and a shade darker, with an undercurrent of desperation and divisiveness. The studio and stage constitute an angst-ridden sanctuary for Larry and his staff, where they can temporarily escape from personal crises and problems, which nevertheless tend to resurface off camera and backstage.

Shandling's Sanders is surrounded by a quietly complex cast of characters that generates continuous comic chemistry, conniving conflict, and occasional awkward affection. Most mask their emotions and struggle to communicate. Larry himself has a difficult time praising his staff and sustaining a meaningful relationship. Over a number of seasons, his arc recycles marriage, divorce, and dating. His tantrums, addictions, and isolation deepen and darken each season, to the point that Larry is the stereotypical prima donna who never quite grows up. Hank Kingsley (Jeffrey Tambor) is Larry's talentless sidekick and pitchman fashioned in the Ed McMahon mold. Hank replaces McMahon's trademark "Hi-yo" with his own signature catchphrase, "Hey now!"— a phrase that matches Larry's "No flipping" command to the audience when going to commercial break. Over the opening titles, Hank can be heard warming up the audience, joking that the flashing sign in the studio reads "applause" not "apple sauce," and that "the better you are, the better Larry is."

Artie (Rip Torn) is the savvy executive producer who cleans up Larry's messes, soothes wounds, and navigates the delicate dynamic between the show's star, the disgruntled staff, network executives, and narcissistic guests. "I swear I killed her in the war," he says about a forceful female network programming executive. Larry's wife, Jeannie Sanders (Megan Gallagher), leaves Larry after the first season, cuing the return of his ex-wife Francine (Kathryn Harrold). Others on Sanders's staff are Paula (Janeane Garofalo), a detailed talent coordinator and booking agent; Hank's assistant Darlene (Linda Doucett); head writer Jerry (Jeremy Piven); and apprentice Phil (Walter Langham). Larry's dependable assistant Beverly (Penny Johnson) is one of the few grounded characters on the staff.

Although many of the familiar workplace situations and relationship dynamics are evident, the comedy, themes, story lines, and reference points presented in *The Larry Sanders Show* are framed by the circumstances and routines, the protagonists and antagonists, of the entertainment industry as they relate to the talk show production process. There are creative differences, memo leaks and rumors, contract negotiations, focus groups, ratings competition, and tabloid coverage. Scheduling conflicts, cancellations, and complications are common. When musical guest Janet Jackson's plane is unable to land, Larry is forced to pad the show, extending a segment with a dog therapist before sinking further into desperate rescue mode with Hank sharing idiotic personal anecdotes. Meddling network executives abound, whether insisting that Larry do on-air commercials for the Garden Weasel or tweaking the show in hopes of a ratings rise.

The show's unconventional reality-warp structure relies extensively on Larry's guest stars. Each episode features celebrities who appear as themselves within the fictional world of the Sanders show. The array of stars represents a cross section of eras and all walks of Hollywood life, including Carol Burnett, Robin Williams, Dana Carvey, Dana Delaney, Peter Falk, Mimi Rogers, Billy Crystal, Catherine O'Hara, Richard Simmons, Courteney Cox, David Letterman, Henry Winkler, Rob Reiner, Bob Saget, David Spade, Chris Farley, Sharon Stone, Danny DeVito, Roseanne Barr, Jon Lovitz, and Elvis Costello. The guests are a primary source of comic conflict. Triangulated with Larry and his staff, they trigger tensions, ignite egos, and expose insecurities on and off stage, professional and personal. When Dana Carvey is substitute host, Larry can't resist watching the show from home where he sits in the dark, looking for reinforcement from his amused wife. Larry is so threatened by Carvey's successful stint he returns early from a planned vacation. Billy Crystal, expecting to plug his new movie, gets annoyed when Larry dominates their discussion with his own material. David Spade's last minute appearance on rival Jay Leno's show the night before he is booked for Larry's show leads to scheming among all the stars. And Larry's wife grows increasingly jealous because she thinks Mimi Rogers is overly flirtatious with Larry.

Other situations align between the absurd and the peculiar. Hank nods off during a show in his sidekick spot on the set. Carol Burnett worries that Larry's testicles are exposed beneath the Tarzan costume he is wearing for a sketch. David Duchovny, star of *The X-Files* (Fox, 1993–2002), parodies Sharon Stone's "flashing" scene from *Basic*

Instinct (1992) and implies that, though straight, he is strongly attracted to Larry. Chevy Chase wanders around backstage in a corridor assuring everyone that he has recovered from his disastrous talk show. "It's been 18 months now," he proclaims.

One of the most distinguishing characteristics of *The Larry Sanders Show* lies in its clever production values and pseudo-verité visual style that intermingles on-camera, in-studio segments with backstage, behind-the-scenes components. The ambitious approach uses a seven-camera setup (four video and three film), including handheld cameras. The show's iconography—lighting, stage, set design, and details—is talk show precise, beginning with the title and graphics with power pop music accompaniment to the curtain and spotlight. Shots reveal an occasional boom microphone intrusion top-screen; cameras and monitors; Larry's desk with coffee mug, microphone, and pencils for tapping; the guest chair and couch; tropical potted plants; and Hollywood hills backdrop. The backstage settings—hallways, offices, conference and dressing rooms—may be even more critical to the show's creative and comic aims and its character arcs; and Larry's home is a secondary location.

The show's in-studio segments use the conventional talk show production method, shot on videotape with multiple cameras before a live audience. After the first season, only select episodes were taped before a live audience, and a laugh track was added. Shandling felt the process, especially scheduling a studio audience, was too time-consuming and complicated. In contrast, the off-stage scenes, even if a cutaway to a producer's point of view from within the studio, are often shot with a single handheld camera. The documentary method creates the illusion of an all-access pass, a "looking in" perspective. The feeling is that of "insider," as the camera reveals the before and after of *The Larry Sanders Show*. The portrayals capture the professional and personal dynamics of Sanders and his staff, the pervasive bunker mentality, the fragile egos, meddling and manipulation, insecurities and insincerities, petty jealousies, panic, paranoia and power plays, and conversations in code. Ken Kwapis helped establish the visual approach while directing much of the series' initial season. He later employed the "mockumentary" film style in the network adaptation of the BBC series *The Office* (NBC, 2005–) and in *Malcolm in the Middle* (Fox, 2000–2006), and it is also used by producer Ron Howard in another offbeat comedy, *Arrested*

Development (Fox, 2003–6). Shandling did not want to get too heavy-handed with the documentary technique to avoid having the visuals and camera movement distract from the writing and characters.

The transitions—from set to story, studio to backstage, on-camera to off-camera—are not choppy; they are clearly defined by the distinct looks of the video and film modes, as well as the camera angles. Shifts commonly occur during predictable moments within the show—the end of Larry's monologue, a commercial break, or after Larry wraps up the show they are taping. The typical episode structure includes opening *Sanders* titles and a monologue snippet, with Larry delivering topical jokes befitting the era, from Dan Quayle's misspelling to Ice T's "Cop Killer." From there, the show's direction varies, sometimes lingering backstage in meetings, hallways and telephone conversations, then cutting to in-studio interviews or a brief domestic diversion. There is no consistent pattern to the proportionality between studio and backstage for each episode, although the backstage scenes tend to be more prevalent.

Cutting, brisk dialogue complements the production elements. Shandling's droll, observational stand-up comic persona is commonly channeled through alter ego Sanders, accented with entertainment industry vernacular. Larry describes an abbreviated romance in television terms, saying it lasted "from the Emmys to the People's Choice Awards." On the O.J. Simpson murder case, he reasons, "If he had just admitted he was guilty from the get-go, he'd be out by now." Straight-man sidekick Hank, defending his former neighbor Simpson, counters that "the real victims of this crime are my property values."

Comments routinely reinforce the Access Hollywood, "insider info" climate. When briefed by his wife Jeannie that actress Barbara Hershey will be his first guest, Larry can't resist a collagen dig: "Will she be with or without lips?" "Well that's what I wanted to talk to you about," says Larry's assistant Beverly. "One is still thin and the other one is fat. It's kinda funky, so don't bring it up." Lines also contain wisdom from lessons learned along the industry way. "It's one of the cardinal rules; never get sick in showbiz so they can't shove a knife in your back," cautions executive producer Artie upon returning from an illness early because he suspects the new producer of trying to hijack the show with new ideas.

Another notable trait of the writing is the use of expletives, including the "f-word," which flows freely in the snappy, nuanced dialogue. The writers took advantage of cable's looser content standards. However, such language is not used gratuitously; rather it fits the characters and provides emotional insights as they respond to various personal and professional situations within their environment. The writing for *The Larry Sanders Show* can be viewed as a profuse profanity precursor for the cable network, as it established an impressive cursing quota. Profanity and "language" have become an undeniable dimension of the HBO brand, manifest in the scripts and characters of original series such as *Oz* (1997–2003), *The Sopranos* (1999–2007), and *Deadwood* (2004–), which followed in *Larry Sanders*'s footsteps.

Garry Shandling chose to end *The Larry Sanders Show* in 1998 after its sixth season. *Sanders*'s run ended in typical fun-house-mirror fashion true to the television business. With the show mired in low ratings, there is network pressure to make changes. When Jon Stewart sits in for Larry, the ratings spike. Larry and partner Hank realize that they are powerless and replaceable. After much soul searching, Larry announces he will not sign a new contract. The *Sanders* staff is left scrambling; Artie cries alone in the costume room. And in Johnny Carson farewell fashion, a parade of celebrities visits Larry's final show.

Despite its critical and comic acclaim and award-winning status, encores of *The Larry Sanders Show* in the multimedia marketplace are surprisingly sparse. The complete first season was released on DVD in 2002; these remain the only episodes currently available in the United States. (The volume features an insightful interview with Shandling by Pulitzer Prize–winning television critic Tom Shales.) A "Best of" compilation of the first two seasons has been distributed in the United Kingdom, and a syndicated package of episodes had a limited run on the arts and entertainment Bravo cable network. In 1999, Shandling, in character as his alter ego Sanders, wrote *Confessions of a Late Night Talk Show Host: The Autobiography of Larry Sanders*.

Beyond its unconventional convergence of comic and visual styles, *The Larry Sanders Show* represents a pioneering presentation that previewed possibilities for the creation of original series on cable, in particular comedies with a show-business premise. A steady stream of "backstage" series that provided satirical looks at the entertainment industry and celebrity culture bear the *Sanders* imprint, though with considerably less success and critical kudos. Among these comedian-centered shows were Bravo's comedy-writing contest *Situation: Comedy* (2005); Comedy Central's *My Life on the D-List* (2005) with Kathy Griffin, Howie Mandel's *Hidden Howie* (2005), and David Spade's *The Show Biz Show* (2005); and TBS's *Minding the Store* (2005) with Pauly Shore.

Broadcast networks took a similar cue, with programming fare such as Fox's *Action* (1999–2000) with Jay Mohr. The *Sanders* template extended into the 2006 fall lineup, with NBC's workplace comedy *30 Rock* and ABC's *Studio 60 on the Sunset Strip*. The Larry Sanders legacy within HBO lies not only in comic and creative influences, but in network programming philosophy. The show's production values and visual style have been adapted in various HBO productions, from the political verité of *K Street* (2003) to the reality warp of *Unscripted* (2005) to the Hollywood showbiz backdrops of *Entourage* and *The Comeback*. Arguably, Larry David's contentious *Curb Your Enthusiasm* owes as much to *Sanders* as it does to *Seinfeld*.

The conception and subsequent success of *The Larry Sanders Show* suggests several emerging qualities in HBO and its approach to cable programming in the early 1990s. In contrast to the broadcast networks' common modes of operation, HBO's programming executives demonstrated a willingness to take risks with concepts, content, and characters, and an interest in providing a creative environment with limited constraints for writers and producers. Rather than requiring Shandling to submit the standard pilot for his high-concept, talk show satire, HBO ordered thirteen episodes. The number was striking in comparison with the broadcast network's standard twenty-two- to twenty-six-episode season for its series. *The Larry Sanders Show*'s six seasons provide early evidence of HBO's commitment to quality and creative freedom. In the process, *The Larry Sanders Show* helped to establish HBO's credibility and vision. This inventive, surreal showbiz satire marks a significant stepping stone for other innovative comedies that subsequently followed on the network during the 1990s and 2000s.

THIRTEEN

Sex and the City

Ron Simon

From its debut in June 1998, *Sex and the City* became a comic epicenter of vigorous debate on such issues as gender, lifestyle, materialism, and orgasms. Unlike previous landmark situation comedies, many of which seemed retrograde in either form or content, this HBO series engaged the contemporary world wholeheartedly, infusing the mise-en-scène and narrative with an up-to-the-minute trendiness. *Sex and the City* not only satirized social mores, but also engendered a framework to understand postmodern romantic predicaments. As the *New York Times* noted in 2004, its comedy "so perfectly captures the mood of a culture that it becomes more than a hit: it becomes a sociological event."[1] Like its network, which promised something beyond TV, *Sex and the City* evolved into a weekly forum on American dating rituals and sexual semiotics, energizing the network's upscale demographic into heated conversation at the water cooler and in the bedroom.

From Print to HBO

The genesis of *Sex and the City* parallels the earliest days of radio, when women's magazine articles often served as the basis of programming. Candace Bushnell's weekly newspaper columns for the *New York Observer,* anthologized in a 1996 book, *Sex and the City,* attracted the attention of producer Darren Star. Bushnell used her alter ego, Carrie Bradshaw, to provide "an unsentimental examination of relationships and mating habits."[2] Star, who had rejuvenated the prime-time soap opera with such youthful hits as *Beverly Hills 90210* (Fox, 1990–2000) and *Melrose Place* (Fox, 1992–99), was interested in producing a sex comedy from a single woman's perspective. He took the idea to ABC, which had pioneered the single-woman-in-the-city genre with *That Girl* in the late sixties. By the nineties, ABC was having success with such traditional sitcoms as *Home Improvement* (1991–99) and *The Drew Carey Show* (1995–2004), and the commercial network was troubled by the adult sexuality of Star's idea.

As Star was given the funding by HBO to produce a pilot, the defining comedy on television, *Seinfeld* (NBC, 1990–98), was winding down. Star had originally conceived of an anthology comedy with different guest stars each week, very much in the spirit of the column, but realized the comic serial was a much more engaging form. By the time the pilot was created in 1997, the proposed series bore many structural similarities to *Seinfeld*: four strongly contrasted lead characters totally absorbed by the minutiae of metropolitan existence. But whereas *Seinfeld* occasionally broached such sexual taboos as masturbation and shrinkage on commercial television, Star's series would be consumed with a frank, sometimes shocking, discussion of sexuality every episode, devoted exclusively to the female viewpoint. Perhaps, this in-your-face sex talk was the closest thematic connection with the HBO ethos of the mid-nineties. From the seventies on, HBO programming philosophy was oriented to the masculine: the dominant locales of HBO specials, boxing rings and stand-up clubs, were aggressively male. The successful comedies—*Dream On* (1990–96), *The Larry Sanders Show* (1992–98), and *Arli$$* (1996–2002)—were psychiatric journeys into the tortured male ego. Maybe Star was initially given the green light by HBO not to extend its very male-centric comedy tradition but to build on its reality sex programming, most notably exemplified by *Real Sex* (1990–) and *Taxicab Confessions* (1995–). In fact, the first season of *Sex and the City* integrated sexual testimonials from real-life people into the plots, a device that made the show more a comic take on urban anthropology.

What distinguished *Sex and the City* visually was Star's insistence that his series be shot on film. Foregoing four video cameras and a live studio audience, he explicitly stated that he wanted "to bridge the gap between a television series and a movie,"[3] affirming HBO's premium subscription model. Star also eschewed the laugh track, demonstrating conclusively that verbal comedies do not require artificial support; in the process he laid the groundwork for such commercial no-laughs series as *Malcolm in the Middle* (Fox, 2000–2006) and *My Name Is Earl* (NBC, 2005–). For the pilot, he hired director Susan Seidelman to enliven the production with the independent spirit of her groundbreaking 1985 film *Desperately Seeking Susan*. HBO eventually committed close to $1 million an episode, ensuring that the production was both edgy and tasteful. Even if the talk was raunchy and dirty, *Sex and the City* always had high-gloss production values of exquisite chic.

The Postfeminist Quartet

The first HBO press release promoted *Sex and the City* as a designer series, "Darren Star's New Comedy," but it was his characters that stole the show. Unlike a slew of network comedies of the early nineties, including *Murphy Brown* (CBS, 1988–98), *Roseanne* (ABC, 1988–97), *Cybill* (CBS, 1995–98), and *Ellen* (ABC, 1994–98), whose feminist concerns are expressed through a dominant lead character, *Sex and the City* orchestrates four individualized voices grappling with the choices and opportunities available to women as the millennium approached. This gang of four is more than a commercial construct; individually, they do not have the galvanizing goofy appeal of an Ally McBeal or Bridget Jones, throwbacks to a fifties conception of single-hood. As Astrid Henry has noted in her essay "Orgasms and Empowerment," each woman embodies an archetypal option of sexual and cultural behavior of third-wave feminism.[4] The audience seemed to concur, as exemplified by a 1999 quote from a twenty-something software consultant in the *New York Times* Sunday Styles: "I felt like they are saying the things that we're all thinking."[5]

The *Sex and the City* women are not children of the sixties, but were children in the sixties, growing up in an era after feminism had taken root. We can imagine each of the characters having been exposed in some way to Betty Friedan and Helen Gurley Brown, Gloria Steinem and Mary Richards. Choices and identities significantly increased for all women of the postfeminist generation, and this is implicit in the women's unstated back stories. Sarah Jessica Parker noted how feminism informed both the actors and their roles: "These characters, and the actresses playing them, reap enormous benefits from the women's movement. The characters have sexual freedom, opportunity, and the ability to be successful."[6]

195

The svelte blonde Carrie Bradshaw (Sarah Jessica Parker) is the social anthropologist of the group. A columnist for a New York newspaper (bus advertising trumpets "She Knows Good Sex"), Carrie uses her friends for research in writing her dating and relationship advice. Her quandaries on appropriate behavior in a blurry era (e.g., Does gender really exist? Are we 34 going on 13?) serve as the motif for individual episodes. Carrie is a cutting intellect wrapped in old-fashioned expectations, with her Manolo-shod feet solidly placed in the prefeminist and postfeminist eras. Two of her friends grabbed aspects of women's newly gained freedom, but still struggle for wholeness. Samantha Jones (Kim Cattrall), who manages her own public relations firm, is pure comic id. She exults in her sexual conquests, having no desire for monogamy or children. Samantha exemplifies total experimentation in fulfilling her sexual desires, a character unthinkable without the women's movement. Miranda Hobbes (Cynthia Nixon) is the group's cynic, a successful lawyer searching for a personal life. She has realized autonomy in the workplace, becoming part of the second generation empowered by the Equal Employment Opportunity Commission's enforcement of Title VII of the Civil Rights Act of 1964; but no law can ensure an emotional center. Charlotte York (Kristin Davis) brings to the quartet an idealistic spirit reminiscent of their mother's generation. Although an employee at an art gallery, she is still beholden to dreams of a perfect marriage and mate, images straight out of a fifties women's magazine.

New York, USA

But as Sarah Jessica Parker revealed in a Museum of Television & Radio seminar, there is another starring role, in fact one implied in the show's title—New York City, "the greatest character ever written."[7] New York has typified many things in the media, from violent crime to extravagant luxury, but *Sex and the City* underlines a startling reality of the nineties and beyond: Manhattan is a mecca of single living. Unmarried New Yorkers head more than 48 percent of households in the city, and in this respect the Five Boroughs are not atypical of the rest of the country. The mythic household of the married couple, dominant at the beginning of the postwar era, is quickly achieving minority status; married couples accounted for 50.7 percent of households in 2002, down from 80 percent in 1950.[8] So Carrie and crew symbolize demographic trends in the twenty-first century far more than do the family comedies of the commercial networks, epitomized especially by the domestic *Everybody Loves Raymond* (CBS, 1996–2005).

In many ways, the lead characters represent the homogeneity of small-town America more than the diversity of New York. Although individualized, the four are very much cut from the same quality fabric: white, upper-middle class, stable, with challenging jobs and values informed by postindustrial capitalism. The clash of diverse cultures, racial and ethnic, that make Manhattan unique, vital, and frustrating is largely absent from this HBO city. The juxtaposition of radically different economic groups, rich and poor living cheek by jowl, confronts every New Yorker every day, but almost never the women of *Sex*.

But the series did expand upon Woody Allen's East Side provincialism of the seventies and eighties. Not drenched in George Gershwin–style nostalgia for the past, Carrie and crew are frenetic, seeking the hottest new clubs and restaurants downtown. Their metropolis is up-to-the-second, very much on the cutting edge of style and fashion. Unlike such network comedies as *Seinfeld* (NBC, 1990–98) and *Friends* (NBC, 1994–2004), produced entirely in Los Angeles, *Sex and the City* was shot in Manhattan studios and on its streets. Approximately 40 percent of every show consists of the women interacting with the city, networking in such newly revitalized areas as Union Square and the meatpacking district. *Sex and the City* helped to establish verisimilitude as a prime value of an HBO series. A vivid and unpredictable sense of place became the network's calling card, revealing unseen layers in Baltimore (*The Wire* [2002–]), New Jersey (*The Sopranos* [1999–2007]), and *Sex*'s Big Apple.

Viewers around the country did not tune in just for mise-en-scène, however. The writers of *Sex and the City* borrowed a page from the earliest serials on television and emphasized not only the quartet's negotiation with the city, but their innermost thoughts on these adventures. The most revealing moments on *Sex* come when the women just sit down at a café and riff on their romance—pretty much what soap characters have been doing since the invention of the genre. This series, with an adult advisory, was able to combine the frankest talk about sex in a comfortable setting, only this time the kitchen has been transformed to an eatery. The diner has generally been a masculine arena where men debate girls and sports, as in such movies as *Marty* (1955) and Barry Levinson's aptly titled *Diner* (1982). The gals of *Sex* remade the locale, where talk is now of funky spunk, post-it breakups, and guys who are good on paper. The women revel in one other's company, building third-wave friendships based on intimate sharing and raucous laughter.

The Creative Team

Like most situation comedies, *Sex and the City* has not been studied as a creative work, composed by a team to express a singular take on the world. Numerous articles have critiqued sociological underpinnings of the series, and many essays have psychoanalyzed the characters, but the show has been treated much differently than a successful HBO drama. Critical appraisals of the dramas begin with the motivating vision of the creator, generally a middle-aged man using a specific genre to comment upon tensions in the contemporary world. David Chase's mob story *The Sopranos*, David Milch's western *Deadwood*, and Tom Fontana's prison tale *Oz* all transcend their generic restrictions and are seen as artistic explorations of the American empire. The creators of *Sex and the City* have not risen to the auteur level, and their work is rarely approached as serious commentary on twentieth-century culture. If the sitcom can be analyzed as personal expression, however, perhaps one of HBO's defining series provides some clues in deciphering comedy as art.

For the show's first three seasons (June–August 1998, June–October 1999, June–October 2000), creator Darren Star organized the production team. His responsibilities extended from shaping the stories to supervising casting and editing. Producer Michael Patrick King, former writer of *Murphy Brown* and *Will & Grace* (NBC, 1998–2006), assisted him, and individually they were responsible for writing the majority of episodes during the first season. Star left to create new series after the third season, and Patrick assumed the role of executive producer. For most of the run, a team of six women—Cindy Chupak, Jenny Bicks, Julie Rottenberg, Elisa Zuritsky, Amy B. Harris, and Liz Tuccillo—contributed scripts, stripping their personal lives for ideas and incidents. In interviews over the years, the members of the writing room have been remarkably candid and articulate on how the series grew organically, conscious that each season they strove for material that was more mature and complex. King has described the evolution of the characters and situations in terms of budding romance, from first date to a committed relationship over four seasons.

The fourth season (in two parts: June–August 2001, January–February 2002) proved particularly pivotal for the writers and the emotional development of the characters. What began as a sex farce in 1998 advanced to a series that could seamlessly integrate such weighty issues as abortion ("Coulda, Woulda, Shoulda"), testicular cancer ("Belles of the Balls"), and death ("My Motherboard, My Self"). This was not a rash decision to become Norman Lear relevant, but a progression in which, according to writer and eventual executive producer Chupak, the characters were now rounded "to the point where they can handle weighty topics with humor and grace."[9] Unlike most network series, the writers were not required to churn out approximately twenty-two scripts annually; *Sex* was produced irregularly, ranging from eight to twenty shows a season. The smaller number of annual episodes ironically yielded greater dimensionality to the characters. The final episode of the fourth season, "I Heart New York," is downright autumnal, as Carrie is forced to confront the idea that love and her city are forever in flux. Few works in any media that year prophetically anticipated the emotional devastation of post–September 11 America.

If *Sex and the City* did not have a dominant auteur like much of HBO programming, the creative dialogue between the gay sensibilities of the male executive producers and the multitudinous real-life experiences of the female writing team gave the series its unique voice. From peeing politicians ("Politically Erect") to power lesbians ("The Learning Curve"), the series is an investigation into the sheer fluidity of gender and sexual proclivity. Different critics have read the same characters and situations through gay and heterosexual prisms, thus demonstrating how the queer/straight creative team subverted stereotypical depictions of desire. Alan Frutkin pointed out in the *New York Times* that anytime *Sex and the City* tackles "a gay story line, the writers seem to be able to make it accessible to all audiences, handling it with dexterity and humor," unlike almost all network and cable series.[10] The only character that has generated a representational debate is Carrie's friend Stanford Blatch (Willie Garson), a classic archetype of the thirties—the plain gay confidante who is sexually nonthreatening. An irritating stereotype to some, an all-too-human portrait to others, Stanford, like the

The creative dialogue between the gay sensibilities of the male executive producers, creator Darren Star and Michael Patrick King, and the female writing team gave *Sex and the City* its unique voice and distinctive cast of characters, including (left to right) Willie Garson as Carrie's gay confidante Stanford Blatch, Sarah Jessica Parker as Carrie Bradshaw, Kristin Davis as Charlotte York, Kim Cattrall as Samantha Jones, and Cynthia Nixon as Miranda Hobbes.

other regular gay role, Charlotte's adviser Anthony Marentino (Mario Cantone), underline for Frutkin that *Sex* "follows no agenda but its own" in portraying lifestyle.

The Romance of the Narrative

On the August 28, 2000, cover of *Time* magazine, *Sex*'s characters were used to probe the question of why many women were seemingly embracing the single life. They were symbols of a growing number of women who were forsaking marriage and flying solo. By the time of the fifth (July–September 2002) and sixth (in two parts: June–September 2003, January–March 2004) seasons, the characters have been wounded by their choices and forced to confront their innermost demons. Charlotte's perfect white Anglo-Saxon protestant marriage to upper-crust Trey

Sex and the City chronicles the up-and-down relationship between Mr. Big (Chris Noth, left) and columnist Carrie Bradshaw (Sarah Jessica Parker, right), encouraging its audience to reflect upon such interrelated issues as sex, career, and marriage.

MacDougal (Kyle MacLachlan) crumbled during the third season, and she now grapples with alternatives outside the rules of romance she had constructed: marrying a short, hairy, Jewish attorney (Evan Handler) and considering adoption as a viable alternative for children. Defining herself by an alluring body image, Samantha first struggles with breast cancer and then the possibility that her radical independence is not curtailed by commitment to a younger man (Jason Lewis). Miranda's desire for corporate success is interrupted when she conceives an out-of-wedlock child and is transformed by her role as parent, leading to her proposal to Steve Brady (David Eigenberg), her working-class boyfriend. Each week viewers entered the mind of Carrie, overhearing her thoughts and confusions on millennial love. In the end, she tackles the most traditional choice in romantic fiction, whom to love: the older, sophisticated artist Aleksander Petrovksy (Mikhail Baryshnikov), or her dream match, the recurring heartbreaker Mr. Big (Chris Noth), who inspires and frustrates Carrie throughout the series. As the final seasons grew reflective in tone, *Sex and the City* was still able to walk the tightrope between realism and fantasy, encouraging its audience to ponder issues of sex, career, and marriage.

The constant throughout the varying seasonal moods of *Sex and the City* is its televisual look as conveyed by fashion. A major contributor to the success of the series was designer Patricia Fields, who communicated the aspirations and contradictions of the characters through clothes. Luxury items by designers such as Jimmy Choo, Fendi, Manolo Blahnick, and Bulgari, sprinkled in every episode, became not only objects of desire for upscale HBO viewers, but also linchpins for the railings against the show's supposed endorsement of conspicuous consumption. But few characters in the history of television have been defined as sartorially as Carrie, whose psyche was on display each week via her dresses, shoes, and accessories. If Carrie is lucid and articulate in her voice-overs, her wacky clash of designer couture and vintage chic betray an often-divided self. As Stella Bruzzi and Pamela Church Gibson have emphasized, her clothes are very much about independence, not manipulation by the garment industry: "Carrie's behaviour and clothes are not circumscribed by either social or professional constraints; fashion for her is a means of personal expression."[11]

Awards and Afterlife

Ninety-four episodes of *Sex and the City* were produced over six years (1998–2004), and the show engaged an audience of almost 6.5 million households on a regular basis, a strong showing for a premium cable channel. Its impact was even greater, as the series helped to establish HBO as a dominant force in the industry. In 2001, *Sex and the City* received the Emmy Award for Outstanding Comedy Series, making it the first cable program to win the Academy of Television & Sciences' major prize in comedy or drama. Illustrating the show's international appeal, the Hollywood Foreign Press Association awarded it the Golden Globe for Best Television Series: Musical or Comedy for three consecutive years (2000–2002).

Sex and the City has had a profitable afterlife since its initial run on HBO. The series has been packaged creatively on DVD, including a limited edition collector's gift set and such individual discs as *Best of Lust* and *Best of Breakups*. Although considered soft-core pornography by some conservative groups that threaten to boycott screenings on "free" television, the series has performed remarkably well in syndication. HBO, the copyright owner, edited out some sexually provocative material and provided an alternative audio track that softens some offensive language. *Sex and the City* has played with little controversy in numerous countries around the world. Although originally banned in Shanghai, the American version eventually aired, as did a knock-off version entitled *Hot Ladies*. In the end, *Sex and the City* proved to be television's most daring and provocative comedy, exulting in sexuality and sensual pleasure like no series before it. During the run, the women had 101 sexual encounters, with such men as Gay Straight Man, Tuchus Lingus, and Denial Guy. What began as an exclusive comedy on premium cable was relished the world over for its sexual exploration among women and willingness to confront subterranean emotions.

Notes

1. Dinitia Smith, "Real-Life Questions in an Upscale Fantasy," *New York Times,* February 1, 2004, Television, 4.

2. Candace Bushnell, *Sex and the City* (New York: Warner Books, 2001), ix.

3. Amy Sohn, Sex and the City: *Kiss and Tell* (New York: Pocket Books, 2004), 14.

4. Astrid Henry, "Orgasms and Empowerment: *Sex and the City* and Third Wave Feminism," in Kim Akass and Janet McCabe, eds., *Reading* Sex and the City (London: I. B. Tauris, 2004), 65–82.

5. Nancy Hass, "'Sex' Sells, in the City and Elsewhere," *New York Times,* July 11, 1999, Sunday Styles, 1.

6. Sohn, Sex and the City, 24.

7. Sarah Jessica Parker talking at a seminar hosted by the Museum of Television & Radio, October 1, 2003.

8. Elaine Maag, "Taxes and Marriage for Cohabiting Parents," Urban Institute, 2005, at http://www.urban.org/publications/1000788.html.

9. Sohn, Sex and the City, 38.

10. Alan Frutkin, "The Return of the Show That Gets Gay Life Right," *New York Times,* January 6, 2002, sec. 2, 33.

11. Stella Bruzzi and Pamela Church Gibson, "'Fashion is the Fifth Character': Fashion, Costume, and Character in *Sex and the City,*" in Akass and McCabe, eds., *Reading* Sex and the City, 117.

FOURTEEN

Curb Your Enthusiasm

David Lavery

"We'll go to ABC. I don't have to be at HBO. 'It's not TV?' It's TV. What do they think people are watching? You watch it on TV don't you? You don't go to the movies to watch it."
—Larry David in *Curb Your Enthusiasm* ("The Shrimp Incident," 2:4)

When *Curb Your Enthusiasm* debuted on HBO in October 2000, HBO was in its halcyon days. The first two seasons of its flagship series *The Sopranos* (1999–2007) had aired (season three would begin the following March); *Sex and the City* (1998–2004) was ending season three that same night; *Oz* (1997–2003) was on hiatus in the middle of its fourth season; and *Six Feet Under*, debuting in June 2001, was still months away. It was not the first sitcom on HBO (*Dream On* [1990–96], for example, had preceded it), nor the last (*Lucky Louie* debuted in 2006). *Curb* was, however, the first to follow the formula for success that generated such HBO dramas as *The Sopranos, Six Feet Under,* and *Deadwood* (2004–), each of which had been the creation of an individual who, after forging a reputation elsewhere—in network television (*The Sopranos'* David Chase, *Deadwood's* David Milch) or the movies (*Six Feet Under's* Alan Ball)—accepted an invitation and welcomed the opportunity to experiment with making "Not TV."[1]

Curb would offer Larry David, co-creator of NBC's *Seinfeld* (the smash, "must-see" comedy running from 1990 through 1998 ranked by *TV Guide* as television's all-time greatest show), the chance to take the gloves off. *Seinfeld*, of course, had already succeeded in presenting, even within the limitations of American network television, outrageous, politically incorrect, ribald humor. One episode famously deals with a contest to see who can go the longest without masturbating; in another, Elaine (Julia Louis-Dreyfus) interviews possible lovers before sex in order to determine whether they are worthy enough for her to use one of her now-limited supply of contraceptive sponges. *Seinfeld* even got away with "murder": the insistence of George (Jason Alexander) on cheap wedding invitations kills his envelope-licking fiancée Susan. *Seinfeld's* George, the quintessential schlemiel,[2] was based on David himself, but his on-screen presence on the show was limited to a few cameos and some voice work (he ventriloquized New York Yankees owner George Steinbrenner).[3] On *Curb*, however, the author steps forward from behind the curtain.

When *Curb* became an ongoing series, David imported *Seinfeld's* successful and innovative formula: an obsession with the trivial details of modern urban existence—with "nothing," as it would be called in *Seinfeldiana*—and a reliance on a "domino effect plot structure."[4] In an interview with HBO's *The Buzz* just before *Curb's* fifth season, Robert Weide, the show's executive producer and director of twenty-six of its fifty episodes, pretended to "spoil" the season about to air: "I will tell you all about Season Five, and don't let Larry know I told you this. Larry's going to say things that are going to upset people. They are going to get very mad at him, and there will be a big misunderstanding. He'll try to clear it up, things will get worse, they'll snowball, and it will all blow up in his face at the end of every episode. That's just for you. Nobody else should know that." The joke here is that this supposed inside scoop tells us nothing we don't already know if we have seen even one episode of this "cringe comedy."[5]

Unlike the scripted *Seinfeld*, however, *Curb*, like the original HBO mockumentary *Larry David: Curb Your Enthusiasm* (1999) that was its foundation,[6] relies heavily on improvisation. Working from a detailed outline, actors and actresses, both regulars and guest performers, often not yet aware of future developments in the story, invent in real time their often profane and frequently sacrilegious dialogue over multiple takes and with minimal direction.[7] For example, in "Krazee-Eyez Killa" (3:8), when the eponymous rapper (played by Chris Williams) reads Larry the obscene lyrics to "I'm Coming to Get Ya," David was hearing them for the first time on the set the day of filming, and his response—

his identification of a Rice Krispies allusion, his suggested substitution of "bitch" for one of the "mother fuckers"—was improvised.[8] Scenes are captured following the basic conventions of documentary filmmaking—for example *Curb* customarily uses only a single, handheld camera.[9] The final cut of each episode is presented with no laugh track, a major difference from *Seinfeld,* and minimal musical scoring, almost always variations on the show's Felliniesque theme music.[10]

Borrowing a schtick from earlier HBO series like *The Larry Sanders Show, Curb* is set in the world of show business and features "real" personalities[11]; David plays himself, or rather a fictionalized version of himself,[12] the now unemployed but fabulously wealthy co-creator of *Seinfeld,*[13] a disgruntled, crass, disingenuous, prevaricating, egomaniacal, misanthropic, opinionated, perpetually kvetching equal-opportunity offender. David's "deadpan portrait of a guy who has achieved legendary status in the TV industry, but who remains an unhappy, insecure jerk"[14] has earned him several Emmy nominations (for Outstanding Lead Actor in a Comedy Series).

Cheryl Hines plays David's unimaginably forgiving and long-suffering shiksa (non-Jewish) wife, Cheryl; Jeff Garlin appears as "his portly Sancho-esque manager and foil"[15] Jeff Greene; Susie Essman is Jeff's ultra-foul-mouthed wife Susie; and legendary stand-up comic Shelley Berman plays David's dad. Among the show's many "as himself/herself" guests are the neurotic comedian and actor Richard Lewis and the African American comic Wanda Sykes (both in recurring roles as friends of Larry and Cheryl, respectively), and such actors, athletes, musicians, directors, and celebrities as Ted Danson, Mary Steenburgen, Julia Louis-Dreyfus, Jason Alexander, Rob Reiner, Shaquille O'Neal, Michael York, Alanis Morissette, Paul Reiser, Martin Short, Martin Scorsese, Mel Brooks, Ben Stiller, David Schwimmer, Anne Bancroft, Nathan Lane, Rosie O'Donnell, Gary Player, and Hugh Hefner.

Except for the first, seasons of *Curb* also exhibit multiple-episode story arcs. In season two, Larry tries (unsuccessfully) to find a network home for a new sitcom vehicle for Jason Alexander and Julia Louis-Dreyfus. In season three, a new restaurant, in which Larry is investing, prepares to open. In season four, Larry stars in a meant-to-fail new version of Mel Brooks's *The Producers* and seeks to have a promised tenth anniversary extramarital affair. And in season five, Larry tries to find

In *Curb Your Enthusiasm,* creator Larry David (left) plays himself as a disgruntled, crass, disingenuous, prevaricating, egomaniacal, misanthropic, opinionated, perpetually kvetching equal-opportunity offender, while Cheryl Hines (right) portrays David's unimaginably forgiving and long-suffering shiksa (non-Jewish) wife, Cheryl. Photograph by Larry Watson.

HBO's *Curb Your Enthusiasm* features Larry David (right) as a curmudgeon whose tone deafness to even the most basic forms of civility gets him into one difficult situation after another, while Jeff Garlin (left) appears as "his portly Sancho-esque manager and foil" Jeff Greene. Photograph by Larry Watson.

Among *Curb Your Enthusiasm*'s many "as himself/herself" guests are such actors, athletes, musicians, directors, and celebrities as Martin Short (to the right with Larry David), Ted Danson, Mary Steenburgen, Julia Louis-Dreyfus, Jason Alexander, Shaquille O'Neal, Alanis Morissette, Martin Scorsese, and Mel Brooks. Photograph by Ron Batzdorff.

his real parents after learning he might be adopted, and agrees to donate a kidney to Richard Lewis.

Like *Seinfeld, Curb* has a devoted (though smaller, given its limited premium cable audience), cultish fan following who revel in water-cooler discussion of its outrageous moments. *Curb* is not without its critics, however. In a caustic indictment of *Curb* in the *New Republic,* Lee Siegel finds the series almost as annoying as most of the characters in the *Curb*verse Larry finds himself in. "Rather than taking as his targets the Stuffed Shirt, the Self-Absorbed Sucker, and the Bully," as classical film and stand-up comedy traditionally did, Larry David, in Siegel's judgment, "sets his sights on the little guy, the perennial target of the Stuffed Shirt, the Self-Absorbed Sucker, and the Bully." David's nemesis, according to Siegel, "is usually just the service industry and all the people who work in it" (although "what really drives David into fits of animadversion," he observes, "are people who impede his desire for instant gratification"). "David almost never picks on someone his own size." Whereas the comic tradition, going back to its classical origins, "set the spiritual order right by turning the social order upside down," *Curb* "return[s] the social order to its upright position by standing comedy on its head," Siegel suggests. "For perhaps the first time in the history of the genre," he concludes, David "has put comedy on the side of the big guy."[16]

Like those of most critics with an axe to grind, Siegel's complaints are not terribly precise. It is patently untrue, for example, that David never picks on anyone his own size on *Curb*. The network executives (at HBO, ABC, CBS, and NBC), physicians, and lawyers with whom he locks horns are certainly formidable, as are the stars (Stiller, Schwimmer, O'Donnell, Danson, Alexander, Louis-Dreyfus) and producers and directors (Brooks, Scorsese). Surely Siegel would not argue that the 7 foot 1 inch, 325 pound National Basketball Association star Shaquille O'Neal (accidentally tripped by Larry when he stretches his legs in Jeff's courtside seats ["Shaq," 2:8]) is not David's size. As longtime collaborator Larry Charles has noted, it is easy to overlook the "egalitarian" nature of David's cantankerous character.[17]

Siegel's assessment of *Curb* contrasts sharply with TV critic Joyce Millman's cogent observation that although Larry may well be "a sarcastic, immature, abrasive asshole . . . the people whom he's offended often turn out to be the bigger assholes."[18] Is Larry guilty as charged of racism because he doesn't hire the African American actress for a part in *Sour Grapes* ("Affirmative Action," 1:9)?[19] Does Larry really deserve to be attacked by the waiter in "The Acupuncturist" (2:6) for dowsing his arm with water when it accidentally catches fire at his table? Is that horrible typo ("Beloved Aunt") in the obituary David volunteers to write for Cheryl's aunt Larry's fault? (1:8) Is Larry a bad man because he plays along, exchanging finger-gun fire, with the kids in the back seat of a professional wrestler's car ("Thor," 2:2)? Does he really deserve to be upbraided for commenting on Wanda Sykes's tush ("Thor")?[20] Is the toilet-papering of his house warranted, just because he refuses to give a treat to two obnoxious, blasé teens who aren't wearing costumes on Halloween ("Trick or Treat," 2:3)? Does Larry really deserve to have the police sicced on him (not to mention a boyfriend attack him in a restaurant) because he is annoyed by an intrusive clerk in a clothing store ("Club Soda and Salt," 3:3)?

If put on trial for his "crimes" (as are the "New York Four" in the final episode of *Seinfeld*[21]), Larry would certainly be found guilty by any jury in the world. But guilty of what? Of breaking up a full-immersion baptism (which he mistakes for a drowning) and then accepting the out-of-place praise of his fellow Jews for stopping a conversion ("The Baptism," 2:9)? Of missing his mother's funeral and then repeatedly exploiting her death for his own gain ("The Special Section," 3:6)? Of lusting after the Virgin Mary and then coughing up a pubic hair ("Mary, Joseph, and Larry," 3:9)? Of stabbing Ben Stiller in the eye with a skewer ("Ben's Birthday Party," 4:2)? Of stealing a gold club from a coffin ("The 5 Wood," 4:5)? Of hiring a prostitute so he can drive in the high-occupancy vehicle lane ("The Car Pool Lane," 4:6)? Of buying *Girls Gone Wild, College Edition* ("Wandering Bear," 4.8)? Of feigning racism to avoid jury duty ("The Car Pool Lane"), a handicap to jump the line in a restroom ("The Bowtie," 5:2), and a heart condition to escape a tire-iron-wielding thug ("The Surrogate," 4:7)? Of driving Yoshi to suicide with his jests concerning his failed kamikaze father ("The Kamikaze Bingo," 5:4)? Of inviting a child molester to a Seder ("The Seder," 5:7)? Of pretending to be an orthodox Jew in order to suck up to the head of the kidney consortium in a scheme to get out of donating the organ he has promised Lewis, offering the man's very hungry, ultra-religious daughter a pair of edible panties to eat, and accusing a woman of hiding Mickey Mantle's five-hundredth home-run ball in her "unusually large vagina" ("The Ski Lift," 5:9)? To the delight of viewers, the list could go on and on.

Asked in an interview to explain the philosophy behind *Curb*, David explains simply that, "We're split down the middle, between good and evil, and good isn't funny."[22] As Weide reveals, "Our slogan for the show, we used to say, [was] no good or bad deed goes unpunished."[23]

Having run for five seasons, *Curb*'s future was in doubt. The title of the season five finale, "The End," an episode in which Larry, reluctantly donating a kidney to Lewis, dies on the operating table, goes to heaven, and is sent back after proving, as usual, to be insufferable, certainly suggests closure. But in the summer of 2006, HBO announced that

David had agreed to a presumed-to-be-final sixth season, which ran in the fall of 2007.

Larry David the character, biting the hand that feeds the real Larry David, may dismiss HBO's brand-establishing insistence that it is "Not TV."[24] *Curb* remains, nonetheless, a quintessential HBO show. Like *Larry Sanders* before, and *Entourage* (2004–), *The Comeback* (2005), and *Extras* (2005–6) after, it continued the HBO tradition of shows dealing with the entertainment industry, and its mix of reality and fiction would prove contagious, replicated in HBO shows like *K Street* (2003) and *Unscripted* (2005). Larry David the creator of *Curb* has delivered a series that more than satisfies the reigning mission statement. There may never be a season seven of *Curb,* but as David has made patently clear, one thing is certain: he and his outrageous humor will never return to network television.[25]

Notes

1. Other examples exist, of course. *Tanner '88* (1988; created by film director Robert Altman), *Band of Brothers* (2001; produced by director Steven Spielberg and actor Tom Hanks), and *Oz* (1997–2003; the brainchild of *Homicide*'s Tom Fontana) also followed this formula.

2. See Carla Johnson, "Lost in New York: The Schlemiel and the Schlimazel in *Seinfeld*," *Journal of Popular Film and Television* 22:3 (1994): 116–24.

3. *Seinfeld* is a constant presence on *Curb*. See Joyce Millman, "By George," *Salon,* 9 October 2000, at http://archive.salon.com/ent/col/mill/2000/10/09/larry_david/index.html, and David Lavery and Marc Leverette, "Afterword: Rereading *Seinfeld* after *Curb Your Enthusiasm*," in David Lavery and Sara Lewis Dunne, eds., Seinfeld, *Master of Its Domain: Revisiting TV's Greatest Sitcom* (New York: Continuum, 2006), 204–6.

4. Millman, "By George." With *Curb*, Millman observes, in the show's first season "David brazenly recycles—OK, steals—his old show's nothing-and-everything premise and domino-effect plot structure. But, look, it was a *great* premise and plot structure, and he seems to have more than enough funny stuff to do it justice here, so I'm inclined to let the grand-theft-sitcom charges slide."

5. Dana Stevens, "Excruci-fiction: HBO's Sunday Night Cringe-Comedy Lineup," *Slate,* 23 September 2005, at http://www.slate.com/id/2126840/. When HBO ran a season five marathon on New Year's Eve 2005, ads for the event invited viewers to "cringe in the New Year" with *Curb*.

6. This followed David's post-*Seinfeld* bicoastal effort to restart his stand-up career. For more on David's stand-up career, see Marc Leverette, "Deconstructing Larry, 'The Last Man': Larry David, *Seinfeld, Curb Your Enthusiasm,* and

Comedies of the Self," *Studies in Popular Culture* 27:1 (2004): 1–17. The original *Curb* ends with Larry telling HBO executives he is quitting the project due to the death of his stepfather (David, of course, has no stepfather), but in the fashion of Federico Fellini's *8½* (1963), the film he fails to make is the film we are watching. *Curb Your Enthusiasm* the documentary, directed by Robert Weide, is available on the season one *Curb* DVD set.

7. Contemplating where to pitch a sitcom idea, *Seinfeld* alum Louis-Dreyfus suggests HBO: "I want to be able to say 'fuck,'" she admits to Larry ("The Shrimp Incident," 2:4). David nevertheless insists that he often toned down the use of four-letter words ("A Stop and Chat with *Curb Your Enthusiasm*," Curb Your Enthusiasm: *The Complete Third Season* [DVD], [New York: HBO Home Video, 2005]).

8. Bob Costas, "Interview with Larry David," Curb Your Enthusiasm: *The Complete First Season* [DVD], (New York: HBO Home Video, 2004).

9. In an interview, Robert Weide provided many insights into the show's documentary feel. Weide had made several documentaries, including films on comedians Mort Sahl and Lenny Bruce, prior to his work on *Curb*. *Sound of Young America,* 8 October 2005, at http://libsyn.com/media/tsoya/tsoya100805 .mp3.

10. David had heard Luciano Michelini's "Frolic" years before on a local television bank commercial and chose it for the show because he sensed (correctly) that it would mollify viewers as they encountered *Curb*'s frequently over-the-top subject matter (Costas, "Interview with Larry David").

11. For example, on *Larry Sanders* the star of *The X-Files* plays a David Duchovny homoerotically obsessed with Larry (Garry Shandling), the series' eponymous TV talk show host, and Jon Stewart appears, as himself, as Larry's substitute host, who is plotting to make the show permanently his.

12. As David explained on *60 Minutes,* "I love the character. At first I didn't realize it was gonna be a character. I just thought I was gonna be doing me. And eventually as I kept writing it, something emerged that was not quite me but a version of me" ("Larry David: *Curb Your Enthusiasm*," Interview by Bob Simon, *60 Minutes II, CBS News,* 11 August 2004, at http://www.cbsnews .com/stories/2004/01/19/60II/main593983.shtml.

13. In "The Shrimp Incident" (2:4), an HBO executive, angry over Larry's charge of shrimp theft from a Chinese take-out order, tells Larry what he can do with his "$475 million."

14. Millman, "By George."

15. Lee Siegel, "The Little Things: The Insignificance of Larry David," *New Republic,* 13 January 2003, at http://www.tnr.com/doc.mhtml?i=20030113&s= siegel011303.

16. Lee Siegel, "The Little Things."

17. "A Stop and Chat with *Curb Your Enthusiasm*."

18. Joyce Millman, "As Nasty As They Wanna Be: The Squirm Appeal of *Curb Your Enthusiasm* and *Airline*," *Boston Phoenix*, 16–22 January 2004, at http://www.thebostonphoenix.com/boston/arts/tv/documents/03516006.asp.

19. For more on the charge of racism sometimes levelled against *Seinfeld*, see Lavery and Leverette, "Afterword: Rereading *Seinfeld* after *Curb Your Enthusiasm*," 212–15.

20. Larry's actual remark when he sees Sykes jogging ("I'd know that tush anywhere") becomes a reference to her "fat ass" when she reports it to Cheryl.

21. The infamous *Seinfeld* finale was written by Larry David, who returned for the finale after having left the show at the end of season seven. For more on *Seinfeld*'s last episode, see Joanne Morreale, "Sitcoms Say Goodbye: The Cultural Spectacle of *Seinfeld*'s Last Episode," in Joanne Morreale, ed., *Critiquing the Sitcom: A Reader*, The Television Series (Syracuse: Syracuse University Press, 2003), 274–85, and Albert Auster, "Much Ado about Nothing: Some Final Thoughts on *Seinfeld*," in David Lavery, ed., *Seinfeld, Master of Its Domain: Revisiting TV's Greatest Sitcom* (New York: Continuum, 2006), 13–22.

22. "Crowds Can Barely Curb Enthusiasm for Larry David," Interview with Larry David on WCBS-TV, New York, 12 January 2006, at http://wcbstv.com/entertainment/local_story_012114244.html.

23. "A Stop and Chat with *Curb Your Enthusiasm*."

24. For more on the development of the HBO brand and its influence on programming, see Mark C. Rogers, Michael Epstein, and Jimmie Reeves, "*The Sopranos* as HBO Brand Equity: The Art of Commerce in the Age of Digital Reproduction," in David Lavery, ed., *This Thing of Ours: Investigating* The Sopranos (New York: Columbia University Press, 2002), 42–57; Michael M. Epstein, Jimmie L. Reeves, and Mark C. Rogers, "Surviving the Hit: Will *The Sopranos* Still Sing for HBO?" in David Lavery, ed., *Reading* The Sopranos: *Hit TV from HBO* (London: I. B. Tauris, 2006), 15–25.

25. Costas, "Interview with Larry David."

PART THREE

SPORTS

OVERVIEW

It Isn't TV, It's the
"Real King of the Ring"

Toby Miller and Linda J. Kim

Sport has always been at the core of HBO.[1] A National Hockey League (NHL) fixture was among its first programming at the time of the channel's launch in Pennsylvania in 1972. By 1974, HBO typically showed two films each evening, or a film and a sporting event, often live from Madison Square Garden.[2] Movies, then as now a key programming component, initially proved a somewhat unreliable means of capturing and retaining viewers, because they were replayed so regularly. During the 1970s, HBO took a catholic attitude to sport, featuring gymnastics, boxing, college hoops, figure skating, surfing and so on alongside the National Basketball Association (NBA), the American Basketball Association (ABA), and the NHL.[3] Sport became an important means of establishing the station's difference, its distinct profile, in that complex interplay of repetition (to standardize and cut costs) and innovation (to differentiate and draw viewers) that characterizes the culture industries. Since that time, sport has been a routine—and sometimes a featured—presence on the station (the masculinist gossip program *Inside the NFL* [1978–] is the longest-running series on U.S. cable).

In some ways, HBO represents a fascinating residue from the idea of a more comprehensive network than that of the niche, genre-driven nature of cable television today. For when it began, the station was rather like half of a conventional comprehensive TV service, minus extensive news and current affairs. Sport is the programming feature that lingers on from that period, a residual reminder of the universalism of the old networks, where sport, weather, news, lifestyle, and drama had a comfortable and appropriate frottage, in a way that would be inconceivable on today's movie channels or lifestyle networks, those highly centralized

217

but profoundly targeted consumer stations that fetishize lifestyle and consumption over a blend of purchase and politics, of fun and foreign policy.

Sport on HBO has won six Peabody Awards, sixty-four Emmy Awards, and a duPont–Columbia University Broadcast Journalism Award; so it has been important in a significatory sense, as part of establishing and maintaining the association of the network with quality TV that is somehow distinct from ordinary fare. And sport rates ahead of films on the network, provides 6–7 percent of video on demand, and is prominent through Web sites and archival sales online, so it has also been important in an economic sense.[4] Today, the station sees itself as having "created our own niche in sports television as storytellers, journalists and boxing programmers."[5] Sport and HBO go together in peer recognition and private revenue.

But if you look for references to HBO in academia and the bourgeois press, the network's drama and comedy offerings predominate. Sport is normally absent. In the world of TV scholarship, sport is generally a poor cousin, despite work on it by a stream of gifted researchers.[6] This lacuna in turn reflects the low standing of kinesiology, sport history, and sport sociology within the academy. In the world of press engagement with TV, sport is usually relegated to issues of access; reviews of content are largely restricted to fiction, apart from the occasional critiques of prominent commentators. The mainstream media generally address HBO via the quality discourse of high-end drama; very occasionally, sports columnists interrogate its managerial conflicts of interest. It is symptomatic that this book dedicates entire chapters to particular fiction programs—but the field of sports is allocated just one.

In the space available here, we consider the interlocking relations of the media and sport; the specific history of HBO and sport; and the most important part of that story—boxing. Our aim is to provide some contextualization of the network in terms of the wider world of sport and the media, to touch briefly on its overall sports programming, and to engage its movement into administering as well as covering "the sweet science." In the process, we hope to tease out certain tensions and differences between HBO's conception of itself and wider questions that both complicate and explain how athletes, fans, and audiences are located in the station's policies and programs.

In some ways, HBO represents the disorganized, decentralized, flexible post-Fordism of contemporary cultural capitalism. It relies on a wide variety of workers, many of whom do not have tenure and benefits, who are employed by small companies even when they sell their labor to the giant corporation of Time Warner that is the network's parent organization (you can register your desire to join the production *précariat* at HBO via its Web site). At the same time, it also represents the organized, centralized, inflexible post-Fordism of contemporary cultural capitalism, because it is part of a huge conglomerate's vertical integration through basic cable, premium cable, and pay-per-view, for all the world cloned from a movie studio of the classical Hollywood era.

In the contemporary moment, HBO sport, and the network more generally, work like the model for cable stations: very old-fashioned top-40 radio with high rotation of a tiny amount of programming. The network is a lot like radio in other ways, for it was transformed from a local service, in the spirit of *early*-1970s cable, to a national network, in the spirit of *late*-1970s cable—the shift from democratic localism to centralized monopoly capital that characterized the change in how U.S. TV was regulated as the neoliberal era ushered in corporate power.[7] Both the free-cable, free-video social movements of the 1960s and 1970s, and the neoclassical, deregulatory intellectual movements of the 1970s and 1980s, saw a people's technology allegedly emerging from the wasteland of broadcast television. Portapak equipment, localism, and unrestrained markets would supposedly provide an alternative to numbing nationwide commercialism. The social-movement vision saw this occurring overnight. The technocratic vision imagined it in the "long run." One began with folksy culturalism, the other with technophilic futurism. Each claimed it in the name of diversity, and they even merged in the depoliticized "Californian ideology" of community media, which quickly embraced market forms.[8] Neither formation started with economic reality. Together, however, they established the preconditions for unsettling a cozy, patriarchal, and quite competent television system that had combined, as TV should, what was good for you and what made you feel good, all on the one set of stations—i.e., a comprehensive service. Hence the supposed diversity of U.S. TV today. The outcome is summed up in one of Brian Winston's characteristically acerbic remarks: for all the bizarre, pumped-up, jumped-up claims about diversity made to justify neoliberal deregulation, cable and satellite television "have almost totally failed to alter the established genres and forms of television broadcasting in any significant way, never mind add to them," due to the elemental barriers to entry created by the costs of the corporate system.[9] HBO transformed itself from a neo-network to a niche station driven by genre.

Time Warner zealously protects its copyrighted material and information about its operations. Widespread rumors of unrest among employees are difficult to confirm or deny. But they are warning signs, along with what we *can* glean about HBO, that direct us to a more skeptical approach than do the celebrations of the network that we often read. The conclusions we draw from the political economy of HBO and its parent take us some distance from the kind of television studies that celebrates TV systems, networks, and texts, for all the world as if it were the academic wing of publicity departments or award ceremonies.

Sport and the Media

Modern sport and the media developed simultaneously and symbiotically, supplying each other with capital, labor, audiences, promotion, and content. From its appearance in the mid-nineteenth century, the telegraph carried round-by-round information on boxing bouts, which led to huge audiences milling around telegraph offices[10]—and the first imaginings of television-centered sport. In 1879, a *Punch* cartoon imagined a wife and husband seated in front of a domestic wide screen showing mixed tennis. Fifty years later, a premonitory article about TV for the *Encyclopedia Britannica* illustrated the medium's possibilities by referring to athletics coverage. Film theorist Rudolf Arnheim's 1935 "Forecast of Television" predicted that the new device would offer viewers simultaneous global experiences, exemplified by boxing.[11] When TV was briefly introduced before the interruption of war, it began with sport. Berliners with sets saw the 1936 Olympics, London cricket fans could watch the 1938 Ashes Test from Kennington Oval, and New York broadcasts a year later featured wrestling, football, and baseball. The first live coverage of a disaster (a New York fire) was possible because cameras were at a nearby swimming pool.[12]

Just as we might associate shifts in capitalism with new technology (early nineteenth-century national capital and steam, late nineteenth-century imperialism and electricity, and late twentieth-century multinational capital and electronics), so we could venture a history of sport connected to technology—wire reports and the radio enabling descriptions of play across the world from the 1930s, and television carrying cricket, association football (known to 4 percent of the world's population as "soccer"), and the Olympics since the 1960s. The satellite and digital era is erasing and rewriting relations of time and space in sport once more.

Technological developments made sport increasingly manageable and indeed spectacular on TV. At first there were no monitors for outdoor broadcast teams, who often had just one camera to cover vast spaces. The initial model of a view from a grandstand seat was refined over half a century via such innovations as parabolic reflector microphones, mobile cameras, color, video recording and editing, caption generators, computer-aided design, video amplifiers, international switching grids, chalkboards, and cameras up close and personal. Accompanying these developments in the positioning of spectators was a new political economy of audiences. In the 1950s, the U.S. networks discovered that their westerns and situation comedies were attracting many viewers who lacked significant disposable incomes. A new target was selected: the young adult male with a maturing income and consumer preferences; hence the hegemony of sports. And as the idea of a universal service that provided broad coverage of news and drama was displaced by all-entertainment networks via the deregulation that began in the 1980s, sport turned into a cheap source of TV time that appealed to the fraternity.[13]

These days, at the truly expensive top end (the summer Olympics and the Super Bowl), TV sport attracts the last remnants of a national audience, drawing revenue from major advertisers and enticing viewers to make the monetary and technological shift to new forms of television, such as color, cable, satellite, and digital. This last is where HBO has been so successful. Its sporting offerings have been very popular since becoming part of digital on-demand services in 2006 as Time Warner seeks to restrain any audience gallop to satellite.[14]

But whereas the United States was once a television innovator in sport, it has recently run into difficulties. Why is this? *Time* magazine's European business correspondent acknowledges the world-historical extent of cultural protectionism here.[15] U.S. sport is underwritten through socialism-by-stealth: a draft for faux students who have been trained for free in directly and indirectly state-subsidized universities; limits on salaries; mandated revenue sharing; privately owned grounds paid for through taxation; exemptions for businesses from antitrust legislation; cross-subsidies galore; legislated support for televising college football; no true market dynamics as per a system of relegation; and limits on cable competition.[16] This is a planned, command economy by any other name, one that works with the recognition that sporting firms need opponents to survive. Competition is an end rather than a means, as in other forms of capitalism. But the system has entered a crisis because of overproduction. Moves to obtain cheap labor from poor countries (most notably, baseball players from Latin America) have helped to decrease the cost of production, but U.S. sports have failed the second task that overproduction requires—securing affluent consumers elsewhere. And networks, cable companies, and municipal governments have begun to question the vast subsidies they offer to the four major professional sports of hockey, baseball, basketball, and football in the self-anointed land of laissez-faire.

Most research on the political economy of U.S. television, other than via publicly available data, is proprietary—the real ways and means of the sector are known to subscribers to business reports, consultancy services, financial analyses, and so on. Occasionally, some of this material falls into the public domain. Very little indeed is available about HBO itself. But we do have access to some information about trends in the overall relationship between sport and the media. For example, Morgan Stanley predicted that the major TV networks would lose $1.3 billion on sports between 2002 and 2006. And it is widely reported that the NFL's fortunes are in decline, with a decrease in TV ratings of 13 percent in the five seasons to 2002; symptomatically, Disney dispatched *Monday Night Football* from ABC to ESPN in 2006 due to falling audience numbers. This has led to an expected $3 billion write-down in the value of rights to TV sport paid by U.S. media companies.[17] Having exclusivity can attract advertisers and/or fans to a communications technology like broadcast or premium cable (in the case of HBO), but it can also commit networks to immensely costly long-term contracts.

Sport on HBO

HBO learned this lesson before the bourgeoisie of Yanqui TV did. At first, it put on up to 250 events annually, from dog shows to gymnastics, but soon ran into financial difficulties with rights payments, and virtually shuttered the sports department in 1978. A reprieve was granted via what it named the "less is more" strategy of "three distinct demographics": boxing, tennis, and football, two of which remain today.[18] Because in the 1970s the networks covered the All-England Championships from Wimbledon only on the weekends, there was room for a new presence, and HBO set a precedent for nonstop coverage.[19] But the station's ongoing success in sport derived from its realization that bidding wars for rights would lead to oversupply. So it withdrew from such contests—hence the end to its coverage of Wimbledon tennis in 2000 after a quarter of a century of solid ratings (between 1 and 2 ratings points).[20] In accordance with its status as "quality television," the network also pioneered various technological and stylistic norms for presenting sport, such as the delightfully named Punchstat (which provides a count of the number of blows boxers land on each other), microphones near management, Spanish translations, and cameras above the action.[21]

In place of expensive events, cheap sporting gossip programs proliferate on HBO. They are euphemized for fragile male watchers as "sports documentary shows"—a splendidly Orwellian move that only a Time Warner could manage. Such programs feature the likes of Bob Costas and Bryant Gumbel—TV stars who were not significant athletes, but whose stature is constructed around an almost old-fashioned notion of journalism.[22] HBO's longest-running gossip show, *Inside the NFL*, has been on the air for three decades, while the quasi-investigative *Real Sports with Bryant Gumbel* (1995–) has garnered seventeen Emmy Awards in eleven years. The format of such programs fits Umberto Eco's concept of "sport cubed," or sports chatter, where sport is multiplied first by TV coverage and then by TV talk, putting us at one further remove from the supposed origin—and enabling material to be recycled.[23] University tests suggest an inverse relationship between the time sporting programs devote to live sporting activity and their ratings. Spectator numbers and interest may increase with stoppages, discussion, replay,

In place of expensive events, cheap sporting gossip programs proliferate on HBO. Its longest-running gossip show, *Inside the NFL*, has been on the air for three decades, while the quasi-investigative *Real Sports with Bryant Gumbel* (pictured) has garnered seventeen Emmy Awards in eleven years.

advertisement, and diversion.[24] Talking about sport is often phatic, an empty space bridged between people. The talk shows point to the masculinist discourse that characterizes sport, leavened and induced by video replay.

Costas Now (2005–) features quarterly reports on major events and controversies. HBO asserts that it delivers "issue-oriented sports pieces that had been swept under the rug." But the program does not effectively problematize the essence of U.S. sport—its degenerative impact on the intellectual mission of universities; its brutal misuse of player's bodies and minds; its intense political conservatism; its constitutive racism, homophobia, and sexism; its ties to social Darwinism; its nativist terror in the face of international difference; and its mythification, above all, of violence and nationalism. HBO's "stories" are not about socialism-by-stealth underwritten by the state. They concentrate on trivialities around the margins of a powerful system from which the network and its corporate parent benefit.[25] The Costas method is generally to individuate issues, as per the banalities of U.S. journalism schools and editorial desks, where tyros are required to pick out families or people to personalize broader issues. This is in keeping with the star system of sport itself, and the way that much U.S. coverage has sought to retain

Costas Now features quarterly reports on major events and controversies. HBO asserts that it delivers "issue-oriented sports pieces that had been swept under the rug," but the Costas method is more in keeping with the star system of sport itself, and the way that much U.S. coverage has sought to retain and broaden audiences.

and broaden audiences.[26] The program offers little space for cultural, sociological, economic, and scientific understanding, because so much is resumed to individual conduct. So NFL commissioner Paul Tagliabue is described as "beyond reproach" in an affectionate 2006 farewell segment about his seventeen years of service—this of a man presiding over a league where the average life expectancy for retired players is fifty-four. Does that make an industry regulator "beyond reproach"?

Of course, the weight of a story, or the people working on it, sometimes overdetermines this personalization ethos. A notable instance was *Real Sports'* coverage of the environmental despoliation encouraged by the Republican Party and its horrendous impact on young athletes. A 2006 segment entitled "The Air We Breathe" may have gone no further or deeper than the conventions of a competent environmental beat, but that made it infinitely better than average network fare on sport, the environment, or any major policy issue, and led to plaudits from the *Columbia Journalism Review Daily.*[27] And some of the documentaries produced, such as *Billie Jean King: Portrait of a Pioneer* (2006), are frank—in this case about the class, gender, and sexuality of King's subjectivity (though not her Native American ancestry or her taste for Ayn Rand and astrology).

The president of HBO Sports, Ross Greenburg, claims that Costas, Gumbel, and the documentaries "penetrate the American mind" and "sociologically look at our country through the eyes of sports," inspired by civil rights, social equality, and the movement against the American War in Vietnam—supposedly exemplified in imperialist paeans such as nostalgia for the victory of the U.S. ice hockey team against the Soviet Union in 1980![28] This sociology lite matches the overall branding of the network. It cultivates a corporate social responsibility (CSR) ethos, even as it claims to be driven by consumer desire. Such rhetoric is now virtually universal in the annual reports and executive suites of major multinationals, alongside the mantra of growth and profit. CSR is said to generate new markets, massage labor, deliver positive public relations, and heighten recognition. So 2006 visitors to HBO's Web site encountered a section entitled "COMMUNITY," inviting readers to participate in polls, subscribe to a newsletter, and express views on bulletin boards. Of course, this "COMMUNITY" was also and equally a system of surveillance, permitting the network to monitor viewers for ideas without paying them for their intellectual property, in keeping with corporate policing of what should be fan rights.[29] And the network links safely banal, third-sector subscribers to sports' wonder and the legitimacy of competition and capitalism, alongside advertisements for such programs as *Dare to Dream: The Story of the U.S. Women's Soccer Team* (2005), a lachrymose nationalist reverie about association football.

Boxing and Boys

The transparent nature of these CSR falsehoods is exposed by the network's adherence to male violence, exemplified in boxing, where its executives paint themselves to Congress and the media as benevolent figures in a maelstrom of corruption.[30] In many ways, boxing typifies the way TV narrates sport in general. Training in commentary emphasizes personal, gladiatorial aspects. In place of the thick description offered by radio, the thinness of television commentary individuates, seeking out personal difference, "character," history, and conflict.[31] Embellishing sport with drama is integral to the narrative.[32] Broadcasters are instructed: "Create a feeling that the competitors don't like each other. . . . Studies have shown that fans react better, and are more emotionally involved, if aggressive hostility is present. . . . Work the audience at the emotional level."[33]

Boxing used to be a staple of network television, and in this sense, HBO's famous slogan is accurate—HBO *is* more like the mythical world of one-shot live 1950s television than twenty-first-century television— i.e., lots of cheap boxing, gossip, studio-based original drama, and films recycled from theaters![34] Greenburg boasts "we'll always have our mainstay of boxing that continues to drive massive ratings for the network." Proprietary research, which is kept secret from public scrutiny, is said to have "confirmed that sports remains a very potent vehicle for HBO." This led the network to place additional boxing on pay-per-view services, which averaged more than $24 million per screening in the first six months of 2006.[35] Its narrowcast of a championship bout that year out-rated the Stanley Cup hockey finals on free-to-air by half a million people.[36]

How did this come to pass, when boxing is discredited as corrupt, and its TV demographic (the genre draws old white men and Latinos) is different from that of the rest of HBO's programming? Because, like the decision by RCA to make boxing its first sporting broadcast on radio in 1921, the activity offers a cheap route to new audiences without losing fans of "quality" television. Boxing has a dirty little secret—illegal betting—that is at the core of its popularity. It seems safe to assume that much of the audience is being enabled by HBO to participate in this activity; that gambling encouraged them to subscribe in the first place. No wonder Greenburg told the U.S. Senate in 2003, "we are deeply committed to boxing, both on an emotional and business level." He did so to justify exemption from regulation, even as the network wanted practically everyone else involved in the sport subject to it.[37] This "emotional and business" commitment has an interesting archaeology.

At the time of HBO's formation, the networks had deserted boxing, which mostly circulated through closed-circuit arena screenings. The station approached the leading promoters and offered to pay a fee to co-screen events, arguing that the station posed no threat to the existing model because of its tiny size. The telecast via satellite of the world heavyweight boxing bout between Joe Frazier and Muhammad Ali in Manila in 1975 established HBO as a household acronym. Its average monthly increase of 15,000 subscribers quickly doubled. By the end of the year, 300,000 homes had signed up through hundreds of small cable companies; the network could boost a system's subscriber rolls by as much as 20 percent. A 1981 survey disclosed that the Marvin Hagler–Mustafa Hansho and Mike Weaver–James Tillis fights outrated commercial network shows.[38]

This increase in subscriptions inspired senior management to "claim some ownership in the sport," in Greenburg's words, building up likely contenders as stars, then signing them to long-term contracts.[39] HBO spent tens of millions of dollars marketing Mike Tyson during his heyday. Corporate parent Time Warner fetishistically referred to him as "a walking billboard for HBO." In 1991, boxing became the most successful pay-per-view genre, with 1.5 million sales for a contest between George Foreman and Evander Holyfield, in an era when pay-per-view was available in 15 million homes, and the decision to buy necessitated a physical visit to rent a converter box—all for an event that the network itself helped to organize. Today, boxing is the second or third reason customers give for subscribing.[40]

HBO progressively turned into a virtual boxing monopsonist from 1978. It became responsible for many details of the bouts it produced, rather than simply competing for the rights to television coverage, a scenario where competitive bidding could become prohibitive. HBO says boxing is "a sport that we can basically call our own." It has broken down the barriers between sporting administration, journalism, and coverage. This is a major conflict of interest, given the assumption that the media have some operational independence from the public activities that they cover. When the media promote and own what they report on, there is room for major malfeasance. The (in)famous promoters Don King and Bob Arum are excoriating about the network on this score. In King's words, HBO executives are "promoters without portfolio," dodging legal standards. Other critics call this "acting as unlicensed promoters . . . in a virtually unregulated sport." Although such testimony is far from disinterested, press coverage indicates widespread concern about the probity of HBO policies. For concerned journalists, it is a "mogul . . . signing fighters to contracts, setting up bouts and giving million-dollar paydays without the necessary promoters license, fees or federal regulations." It eludes the Muhammad Ali Safety Act, which mandates disclosure of boxing contracts, because it presents itself to Congress as simply covering bouts rather than creating and managing them.[41] But *SecondsOut.com* recognizes that the sport's "primary power rests with television," with HBO "the money tree," a "leader in determining what fights matter most."[42] *SportsBusiness Journal* says that "through its economic clout," the network is "boxing's economic engine" and "reigns as de facto custodian of the fight game."[43] Journalist Anwar S. Richardson argues that "while most people believe promoters or boxers rule the sport, boxing is secretly being run by the network responsible for *The Sopranos, Sex and the City, Deadwood* and *Carnivale.*" He calls HBO "The Real King of the Ring."[44]

Boxers under contract to HBO often fight what are known colloquially as "bums"—easy beats, or as a rival Showtime executive put it, "mailmen and cops."[45] Audiences became restive in the early part of the twenty-first century as the bums were trotted out on regular HBO, with leading talent either protected from potential humiliation or reserved for pay-per-view, thus adding to fans' financial burden on top of subscribing to a premium channel ($40 to $50 per fight in addition to the $10 to $12 monthly fees).[46] *Maxboxing.com* noted that "the best fighters are on HBO; too bad that they're never in real fights." It accused the network of a descent from being "'the Heart and Soul' of boxing" to "a tired old man in desperate need of a quadruple bypass."[47] To repel critics and mollify fans, Greenburg claimed no bums would fight the network's contracted stars from 2006. He even coined one of the embarrassing masculinist-managerial neologisms that private-sector bureaucrats favor, stating that the network would be "stiff in our opponent approval in the coming years."[48] Fresh from $126 million in pay-per-view receipts the previous year, the network advised in 2006 that its boxing centerpiece was "as big as any commitment that we've ever made . . . the anchor and foundation of our efforts."[49]

Of course, this is all very gendered and racialized. Sport has always licensed men to watch and dissect other men's bodies in fetishistic detail, creating a legitimate space to gaze on the male form.[50] Even the male caress is generally accepted by sports commentators, because it is associated with friendship and struggle—almost part of the game. Paradoxically, the fact that such contact is so openly looked at renders it a privileged space. It also allows HBO to activate bloodcurdling masculinist rituals that induct viewers into violence (and aberrant spelling). Visitors to the Web site http://www.hbo.com/boxing/features in July 2006 found the network proclaiming, for instance, that "Arturo Gatti and Micky Ward became blood brothers the hard way. They bled on each other to do it. Theirs was not a slicing of thumbs and co-mingling of plasma around a campfire. They became blood brothers in a way unique to a sport as elemental as boxing. They pummeled each other into it."

This represents the contradictory valorization of men's bodies: at once cherished symbols of manhood, yet infinitely dispensable. The literature on the medical impact of boxing is chilling.[51] And HBO colludes in the terrible price paid by its "talent" in return for their labor. Consider Sugar Ray Leonard's 1984 fight against Kevin Howard (an HBO exclusive). Leonard had recently undergone eye surgery, and questions arose over whether he should participate. Seth Abraham, HBO Sports vice president, insisted Leonard was sensible and financially secure and would not fight if it might endanger his vision.[52] Right. Now go forward two decades: Oscar De La Hoya brought $43.8 million to HBO in a 2006 contest on pay-per-view. Afterward, he was depicted cuddling Greenburg, who bragged that a further fight might sell more than a million subscriptions, even as De La Hoya advised that he had just fought with a torn rotator cuff that had not permitted him to raise his arm during training camp.[53] The extraordinary irresponsibility of the network and the sport in permitting mammon to overdetermine health is nowhere better exemplified.

At the same time, it has to be said that boxing's racialized world of masculinity has an important class component. Away from expensive ringside seats colonized by actors and CEOs, the sport continues to be an aspirational milieu. It has been important to generations of poor ethnic minorities, from eastern and central European Jews to African Americans and Latinos. These aspirations course not only through pumped-up fighters, but viewers and filmmakers as well.[54] For example, the wildly popular Web site YouTube, with its free access, simple technology, and publicly available data, has featured unauthorized uploads of the network's bouts.[55] A few hours after Fernando Vargas was knocked out by Shane Moley in the summer of 2006, footage of the last thirty-three seconds of the fight as narrowcast by HBO on pay-per-view was available at the site. Within less than a week, 180,000 watchers had seen it, compared with 350,000 HBO subscribers who had paid close to $50 each for live access. The network was exasperated, not the least because this compromised its plans for a replay.[56] It remains to be seen what will happen to such transgressive copyright activity with the arrival of Google as owner of the site.[57] Meanwhile, HBO lobbies to restrict what its subscribers may do with what they have paid for, arguing before the Federal Communications Commission that its programs should not be subject to the same reuse rights as free-to-air material. Many critics worry that it wants to criminalize copying programming— a "pure and simple money grab" rather than, as is claimed, a necessity if the service is to remain afloat. This is a question of monetarizing new forms of content and delivery, not of surviving.[58]

One thing is likely to remain constant in the world of HBO. It will continue to be a loyal wing of a clinical, cynical, secretive multinational corporation, even as it bizarrely identifies itself with quality and progressive politics though CSR rhetoric. At the same time, it will worship, promulgate, and profit from hidebound, cruel conventions of becoming a man, and reach out to "underserved" audiences to do so, in best neoliberal style. Step aside, *Sex and the City*. In order to stand for the network and emboss it as "quality television," you need to transcend thirty years of brutalized bodies down for the count, with no end in Sugar Ray's sight.

Notes

Thanks to Bill Grantham, John McMurria, Jim McKay, Rick Maxwell, Dave Andrews, and the editors for their comments. Bill's expertise as a major entertainment lawyer, John's as a pioneering historian of cable, Jim's and Dave's as two of the leading sociologists of sport, and Rick's as an eminent media-studies person were invaluable, while the editors provided extremely cogent and detailed feedback.

1. The network is aired in seventy nations and sells programming to eighty more via HBO and Cinemax. We focus here on its Yanqui incarnation.

2. Timothy Hollins, *Beyond Broadcasting: Into the Cable Age* (London: BFI Publishing, 1984).

3. Tom Umstead and Ross Greenburg, Interview, Cable Center Oral History Collection, May 2003.

4. "Thought Equity Announces the HBO Archives now Available, at www .thoughtequity.com," *Business Wire*, 27 February 2006; R. Thomas Umstead, "A Powerful Franchise," *Multichannel News*, 4 November 2002, 12A.

5. R. Thomas Umstead, "Five Questions for: Ross Greenburg," *Multichannel News*, 19 June 2006, 21.

6. For examples and summaries of this valuable but oft-neglected literature, much of which has informed our work here, see David L. Andrews, *Sport—Commerce—Culture: Essays on Sport in Late Capitalist America* (New York: Peter Lang, 2006); Steven Barnett, *Games and Sets: The Changing Face of Sport on Television* (London: British Film Institute, 1990); Alina Bernstein and Neil Blain, "Sport and the Media: The Emergence of a Major Research Field," *Culture, Sport, Society* 5:3 (2002): 1–30; Raymond Boyle and Richard Haynes, *Power Play: Sport, the Media and Popular Culture* (London: Longman, 2000); Raymond Boyle and Richard Haynes, *Football in the New Media Age* (London: Routledge, 2004); Rod Brookes, *Representing Sport* (London: Arnold, 2002); David Rowe, *Sport, Culture and the Media: The Unruly Trinity*, 2nd ed. (Buckingham: Open University Press, 2005); Lawrence A. Wenner, ed., *MediaSport* (New York: Routledge, 1998); Garry Whannel, *Fields in Vision: Television Sport and Cultural Transformation* (New York: Routledge, 1992); Jorge Mariscal, "Chicanos and Latinos in the Jungle of Sports Talk Radio," *Journal of Sport & Social Issues* 23:1 (1999): 111–17.

7. William M. Kuntz, *Culture Conglomerates: Consolidation in the Motion Picture and Television Industries* (Lanham: Rowman & Littlefield, 2007).

8. Megan Mullen, "The Fall and Rise of Cable Narrowcasting," *Convergence* 8:1 (2002): 62–83; Richard Barbrook and Andy Cameron, "The Californian Ideology," *Science as Culture* 6 (1996): 44–72.

9. Brian Winston, *Media Technology and Society: A History: From the Telegraph to the Internet* (London: Routledge, 1998), 318.

10. Janet Lever and Stanton Wheeler, "Mass Media and the Experience of Sport," *Communication Research* 20:1 (1993): 125–43.

11. Irving Settel and William Laas, *A Pictorial History of Television* (New York: Grosset and Dunlap, 1969), 10, 35; Rudolf Arnheim, *Film as Art* (London: Faber and Faber, 1969), 160–63.

12. Garry Whannel, "Television Spectacle and the Internationalization of Sport," *Journal of Communication Inquiry* 9:2 (1985): 62; Jean-Pierre Geurens, "The Brainbusters: The Upside Down World of Television Wrestling," *Spectator* 9:2 (1989): 57; Settel and Laas, *A Pictorial History of Television*, 43; Richard Harmond, "Sugar Daddy or Ogre? The Impact of Commercial Television on Professional Sports," in Frank J. Coppa, ed., *Screen and Society: The Impact upon Aspects of Contemporary Civilization* (Chicago: Nelson-Hall, 1979), 82–83.

13. Whannel, *Fields in Vision*, 64–66; Donald Parente, "The Interdependence of Sports and Television," *Journal of Communication* 26:3 (1977): 128–32.

14. John Ourand, "On-Demand Demand: Dedicated HBO Sports Category Scoring with Viewers, Network Says," *SportsBusiness Journal*, 9 October 2006, 13.

15. J. Ledbetter, "The Culture Blockade," *Nation*, 4 November 2002.

16. P. Ford, "In Business of Sport, U.S. One of Less-Free Markets," *Christian Science Monitor*, 19 June 2002.

17. Toby Miller, David Rowe, Jim McKay, and Geoffrey Lawrence, "The Over-Production of U.S. Sports and the New International Division of Cultural Labor," *International Review for the Sociology of Sport* 38:4 (2003): 427–40; Michael Hiestand, "Colts-Steelers Likely to be Last Good 'MNF' Game," *USA Today*, 28 November 2005, 2C.

18. Bruce Bebb, "Sports Tackle Real Issues, Pay-Per-View," *Variety*, 3 November 1997, 50–52.

19. Umstead and Greenburg, Interview, May 2003.

20. Thomas R. Umstead, "HBO Bids Adieu to Wimbledon," *Multichannel News*, 5 July 1999, 6, and "Five Questions for: Ross Greenburg."

21. Umstead and Greenburg, Interview, May 2003; Melanie M. Clarke, "More Than a Game," *Broadcasting & Cable*, 25 April 2005.

22. Walter Metz, "Home Box Office," in Horace Newcomb, ed., *Museum of Broadcast Communications Encyclopedia of Television*, 2nd ed. (New York: Fitzroy Dearborn, 2004), 1113–15.

23. Umberto Eco, *Travels in Hyperreality*, trans. William Weaver (London: Picador, 1987), 162–64.

24. Klaus V. Meier, "Much Ado about Nothing: The Television Broadcast Packaging of Team Sport Championship Games," *Sociology of Sport Journal* 1:3 (1984): 263–79.

25. Umstead, "Five Questions for: Ross Greenburg"; Bebb, "Sports Tackle Real Issues, Pay-Per-View."

26. Thomas Hauser, "The State of Boxing," *SecondsOut.com*, 2002, at http://www.secondsout.com/usa/colhauser.cfm?ccs=208&cs=3933.

27. Felix Gillette, "HBO's *Real Sports* Shows the Way," *Columbia Journalism Review Daily*, 13 July 2006.

28. Umstead and Greenburg, Interview, May 2003.

29. This is achieved through the customary corporate policy of intellectual enclosure:

> In accessing this website or certain of the resources on the website, you may be asked to provide registration details. It is a condition of use of this website that all the details you provide will be correct, current, and complete. If HBO believes the details are not correct, current, or complete, we have the right to refuse you access to the website or any of its resources. Subject to the provisions of any Additional Terms, by posting or uploading any content to this website and/or providing any communication or material to HBO ("User Content"), you automatically and irrevocably:
>
> (i) grant and assign to HBO any and all rights in the User Content throughout the world including, without limitation, all copyright, together with all consents (if any) necessary to enable its reproduction, distribution, modification, publishing and/or other exploitation by HBO and/or by any person authorized by HBO, by any means and in all media now known or hereafter devised, in whole or in part, without payment or other reference to you or any other person, and to advertise and promote such exploitation, for the full period of all such rights (together with any extensions and renewals) and insofar as possible in perpetuity;
>
> (ii) waive all moral rights in the User Content which may be available to you in any part of the world and confirm that no such rights have been asserted;
>
> (iii) appoint HBO as your agent with full power to enter into any document and/or do any act HBO may consider appropriate to confirm the grant and assignment, consent and waiver set out above;
>
> (iv) warrant that you are the owner of the User Content and entitled to enter into this Agreement;
>
> (v) confirm that no such User Content will be subject to any obligation, of confidence or otherwise, to you or any other person and that HBO shall not be liable for any use or disclosure of such User Content.

30. Consider the alternately self-regarding and unctuous exchanges on this topic in Umstead and Greenburg, Interview, May 2003, and Ross Greenburg's "Written Testimony" to the Senate Committee on Commerce, Science and Transportation, 5 February 2003.

31. Barbra Morris and Joel Nydahl, "Sports Spectacle as Drama: Image, Language and Technology," *Journal of Popular Culture* 18:4 (1985): 105.

32. Jennings Bryant, Paul Comisky, and Dolf Zillmann, "Drama in Sports Commentary," *Journal of Communication* 26:3 (1977): 140–49.

33. John R. Hitchcock, *Sportscasting* (Boston: Focal Press, 1991), 75–76.

34. Anna McCarthy, "'Like an Earthquake': Theater Television, Boxing, and the Black Public Sphere," *Quarterly Review of Film and Video* 16:3–4 (1999): 307–23.

35. Umstead, "Five Questions for: Ross Greenburg."

36. Keith Idec, "The Final Bell," *Herald News*, 23 June 2006, C9.

37. Greenburg, "Written Testimony."

38. George Mair, *Inside HBO: The Billion Dollar War between HBO, Hollywood, and the Home Video Revolution* (New York: Dodd, Mead, 1988).

39. Umstead and Greenburg, Interview, May 2003; Nat Gottlieb, "MORE HATS IN THE RING: OLN to Launch Series with Ex-HBO Exec's Help," *TigerBoxing*, 27 June 2006, at http://tigerboxing.com/articles/index.php?aid =1001235653; Umstead and Greensburg, Interview, May 2003.

40. Jerry Magee, "HBO: Boxing Not at All on the Ropes," *San Diego Union-Tribune*, 11 December 2005, C18; Joel Millman, "The Harder They Fall," *Forbes*, 26 November 1990, 14–16; Metz, "Home Box Office," 1113; Mark Robichaux, *Cable Cowboy: John Malone and the Rise of the Modern Cable Business* (Hoboken: John Wiley & Sons, 2002); Winston, *Media Technology and Society*; Bebb, "Sports Tackle Real Issues, Pay-Per-View"; Keith Idec, "Pay-Per-View Marksman," *Herald News*, 6 April 2006, B1.

41. Tim Smith, "King, Arum Whack HBO," *Daily News*, 19 March 2006, 61; Keith Idec, "Shaw Abruptly Cut Loose by Wright," *Herald News*, 8 February 2006, D1; Anwar S. Richardson, "The Real King of the Ring," *Tampa Tribune*, 20 January 2006, 1; Greenburg, "Written Testimony."

42. Hauser, "The State of Boxing."

43. Bill King, "From Russia with Glove: Who Will Step Up?" *SportsBusiness Journal*, 9 October 2006, 22.

44. Richardson, "The Real King of the Ring."

45. Umstead, "Five Questions for: Ross Greenburg"; Idec, "Pay-Per-View Marksman"; Richardson, "The Real King of the Ring"; Jay Larkin of Showtime quoted in Hauser, "The State of Boxing."

46. Dan Rafael, "HBO Plans to Ramp Up Championship, *After Dark* Cards," *Insider*, 22 December 2005, at http://proxy.espn.go.com/sports/boxing/columns/ story?id=2269069; Kevin Iole, "HBO Pursues Better Matches," *Las Vegas Review-Journal*, 4 December 2005, 4C.

47. Steve Kim, "No Longer 'The Heart and Soul' of Boxing," *MaxBoxing .com*, 21 November 2005, at http://www.maxboxing.com/Kim/Kim112105. asp; Allan Scotto, "Jones is Out! Is Greenburg Next?" *MaxBoxing.com*, 28 January 2006, at http://www.maxboxing.com/news/scott0012806.asp.

48. John C. Cote, "HBO Wants Improved Fight Slate," *St. Petersburg Times*, 11 December 2005, 11C.

49. Thomas R. Umstead, "HBO Plans Knockout Year," *Multichannel News*, 6 March 2006, 30.

50. Toby Miller, *SportSex* (Philadelphia: Temple University Press, 2001).

51. For a small sample, see G. Rodriguez, P. Vitali, and F. Nobili, "Long-Term Effects of Boxing and Judo-Choking Techniques on Brain Function," *Italian Journal of Neurological Science* 19:6 (1998): 367–72; M. Otto, S. Holthausen, E. Bahm, N. Sobuchen, J. Wiltfang, R. Geese, M. Fischer, and C. D. Reimers, "Boxing and Running Leads to a Rise in Serum Levels of S-100B Protein," *International Journal of Sports Medicine* 21:8 (2000): 551–55; W. Goldsmith, "The State of Head Injury Biomechanics: Past, Present, and Future: Part 1," *Critical Review of Biomedical Engineering* 29:5–6 (2001): 441–600; S. Leclerc and C. D. Herrera, "Sport Medicine and the Ethics of Boxing," *British Journal of Sports Medicine* 33:6 (1999): 426–29; Antoinette Vacca, "Boxing: Why It Should Be Down for the Count," *Sports Lawyers Journal* 13 (2006).

52. Mair, *Inside HBO*.

53. Iole, "HBO Pursues Better Matches"; for background on De La Hoya and his symbolic and financial stature, see Fernando Delgado, "Golden but not Brown: Oscar De La Hoya and the Complications of Culture, Manhood, and Boxing," *International Journal of the History of Sport* 22:2 (2005): 196–211.

54. Kath Woodward, "Rumbles in the Jungle: Boxing, Racialization and the Performance of Masculinity," *Leisure Studies* 23:1 (2004): 5–17; Michelle A. Holling, "*El Simpatico* Boxer: Underpinning Chicano Masculinity with a Rhetoric of *Familia* in *Resurrection Blvd.*," *Western Journal of Communication* 70:2 (2006): 91–114; Peter Stanfield, "A Monarch for the Millions: Jewish Filmmakers, Social Commentary and the Postwar Cycle of Boxing Films," *Film Studies* 7 (2005): 66–82.

55. They have attracted a significant audience, albeit not one that is broken down demographically. At least this information is not proprietary—HBO is notorious for refusing to disclose what it pays for fights. Network fees for sports are openly available, by contrast. We do know that the boxing budget for the station was at least $40 million in 2005. See Hauser, "The State of Boxing"; Rafael, "HBO Plans to Ramp Up Championship, *After Dark* Cards."

56. John Ourand and Eric Fisher, "YouTube: Love It or Fight It?" *SportsBusiness Journal*, 24 July 2006, 1.

57. We are aware of how utopic but finally reactionary ideas of an online "community" can be, as per HBO's use of the concept. For an excoriating account of YouTube, see John McMurria, "The YouTube Community," *Flow: A Critical Forum on Television and Media Culture* 5:2 (2006), at http:///flowtv .org/?p=48.

58. Eric Bangeman, "HBO Wants Its Programming to Be Off-Limits for DVRs," *ArsTechnica*, 9 February 2006.

PART FOUR

DOCUMENTARIES

OVERVIEW

Form and Function

Thomas A. Mascaro

HBO paid little attention to documentaries in the network's early days. But beginning in the late 1970s, HBO executives began to look to documentary programming to expand its schedule. Slowly, HBO became a destination for both documentary viewers seeking original works from different producers and a valued collaborator for documentary filmmakers. Seasoned pioneers and emerging novices have found a nurturing environment as well as ample funding for documentary expressions at HBO. Thanks to this eclectic cadre of creative talent, HBO viewers enjoy diverse nonfiction offerings. And documentary aficionados have an entirely new body of works available for viewing, purchase, and future study. In short, HBO has made a substantial contribution to the catalog of American television documentaries.

The person most responsible for developing documentaries at HBO is Sheila Nevins, president of HBO documentary and family programming. Nevins's imprint on HBO documentary programming is akin to others who have become synonymous with their network brands. The PBS series *Frontline* (1983–), for instance, has adopted a style, journalistic standard, and investigative approach inseparable from executive producer David Fanning. Documentary series produced from a black perspective, such as *Eyes on the Prize* (PBS, 1987), bear the distinctive mark of Henry Hampton. *ABC Close-Up!* (1960–) is respected in the documentary field because of the creativity of Pamela Hill and the journalism of Richard Richter. Just as the history of television documentaries is indivisible from these figures, the history of HBO documentaries is intimately linked with Sheila Nevins.

Understanding Nevins's influence, however, requires a more macro

The person most responsible for developing
documentaries at HBO is Sheila Nevins, president of
HBO documentary and family programming. Her style
at the network is noted for its eccentricity, sexuality,
ominous shadows, and bright probing light.

view of HBO documentary programming. She paints with a palette
knife, not a fine brush, and is unafraid of eccentricity, sexuality, ominous
shadows, and bright probing light. "I have respect for people who take
a freer attitude toward life, who enjoy sex, who laugh, who aren't
cerebral," said Nevins. "There's a balance going on. We're all divided
somewhere between our brains and our groins." She gravitates toward
extremes and a shooting style created in the early 1960s by Robert Drew,
Ricky Leacock, and David and Albert Maysles. "I love all that in-your-
face stuff," said Nevins. "It still influences what I do today."[1]

Nevins was born on the Lower East Side of Manhattan in 1939. Her
mother suffered from a serious illness resulting in the loss of several
limbs but worked various jobs to help the family survive. Her father was
a postal worker who moonlighted as a bookie. Not surprisingly, Nevins's
programming reflects the challenges of surviving a difficult world and a

tolerance for people who break rules. "We film people in their reality," Nevins said. "Being born with a disability, that puts people in crises and races of their own." This clearly sums up the range of HBO documentary programming produced under Nevins's supervision, which she describes as "the profound and the profane."[2]

Nevins was a bookish, curious child who lingered in the Museum of Natural History exploring dinosaurs and who developed an appreciation for film, theater, and dance. Nevins's mother disdained the new medium of television out of concern about its negative impact on her daughter's studies. Sheila Nevins credits family discipline for her love of intellectual pursuits, and as a result of her formative experience, she adopted characteristics well suited to documentary sensibilities. Documentaries produced on Nevins's watch are eclectic and reflect her wide-ranging interests, tolerance, and appreciation for others' experiences. Like the writer Paddy Chayefsky, who honored "the marvelous world of the ordinary," Nevins is interested in average people struggling with mundane life. She is fascinated by stories of those striving to counter life's unfairness, as commonly seen on *The Oprah Winfrey Show* (1986–). And like the talk show host David Susskind, Nevins has an insatiable curiosity for life's complexities.[3] HBO documentaries produced by Nevins exhibit, therefore, various shades of these creative traits.

After graduating from Barnard College in 1960 with a bachelor's degree in English, Nevins went to Yale and earned a Master of Fine Arts degree in the School of Drama, one of just two women in the directing program. Theater became the benchmark for her view of television: "[In the] theatre you have a captive audience. They've paid and they're in the dark, and they have only one place to look. When you do television you really are in a sort of whirling dervish business. You have to stop it, stop the turning dial, stop the surfing."[4]

Nevins sees television as a stage with lots of competition, so she stresses the performance of real people as actors in their own lives. "I'm most moved," she said, "by people who play the part of their life with bravado—negative, positive, heroic, dangerous, sexual. . . . The people that go to the theatre in the main [are] the top percentage of people, or people on holiday. Television is everyday. It's like cereal and milk, and you have to make that everyday occurrence spectacular, and yet at the same time you have to keep that humanity going."[5] When today's HBO viewers see documentaries in which average people, not always well spoken, relate their experiences spanning from the nightmare of Hurricane Katrina and its aftermath to kinky sexual fetishes, they are seeing the cumulative effects of Nevins's career in television production and her creative signature. "I don't have a feeling that my audience has dinner parties," said Nevins. "I think they have more beer and pretzels."[6]

After Yale, Nevins moved to Washington, D.C., and landed a job at the United States Information Agency (USIA). Attracted to a want ad for a film researcher, she went for an interview but was sidetracked by a sign announcing "auditions." Nevins was hired to host the television series *Adventures in English* (1964–69), designed to teach vocabulary in foreign countries. Nevins's childhood appreciation for teaching and learning proved a good fit with the documentary genre.[7] She later moved behind the camera, apprenticing with director Don Mischer and producer Bob Squire. This was the start of Nevins's documentary career, and a formative experience for her HBO documentary programming. She went to Mexico to make a film then decided to leave the USIA and return to Manhattan. Mischer put her in touch with documentary producer Al Perlmutter at Channel 13. It was an experimental period for the channel, which was producing the observational film of the renowned Loud family, *An American Family* (1973), as well as Perlmutter's *The Great American Dream Machine* (1971–72).[8] Working with Perlmutter, Nevins was in her element, canvassing New York streets with cinema verité pioneers Albert and David Maysles.

Nevins and the Maysles brothers filmed interviews with ordinary people explaining what they thought about the American Dream. It was a professional collaboration that Nevins would rely on later as an executive producer for HBO. But the involvement with people on the street also left a mark that would form the basis for the kinds of documentaries she would commission. "Everybody has a story and everybody has a struggle," explains Nevins, "and life is very, very difficult, even for people who laugh all the time." The challenge is making the audience interested in the person next door. "Once he starts telling the truth about what he's had to live through," says Nevins, "or what he's lost or gained, or laughed at or cried at, you can hook somebody. But that's the thing—getting them in there, getting them to watch it."[9]

As Nevins was enhancing her credentials and gaining experience through brief stints as a field producer for ABC's *20/20* (1978–), a writer on Children's Television Workshop's *3-2-1-Contact* (1980–88), and a producer for Don Hewitt at CBS News on the profile series *Who's Who* (1977–), cable television was on the rise. HBO decided to increase its offerings from eight to twelve hours daily. Meanwhile, *Who's Who* had ended at CBS. Nevins turned down Hewitt's offer to join *60 Minutes* (1968–) and instead interviewed with HBO vice president Michael Fuchs. Fuchs offered Nevins the position of director of documentary programming at a time when the network was ready to get serious about documentaries.[10] Nevins was disappointed that she would not be *directing* programs but instead supervising others who would produce forty documentaries by the end of 1979. But her broad interest in the subject matter and her ability to collaborate resulted in a series of relationships with documentary film and television producers that translated into the panoply of documentary programs now seen on HBO.

Development of HBO Documentary Programming

The emergence of the documentary genre on HBO mirrors the experiences of previous television networks in some respects, notably the availability of time on the schedule and financial resources to support production costs. The form and function of HBO documentaries, however, differ substantially from HBO's broadcast progenitors. This distinction coincides with significant changes in visual media in the latter part of the twentieth century, including more personalized, on-demand program-ming; more format variety; and a shift from complex social issues to the intricacies of individuals. The HBO documentary experience also illustrates a willingness by new networks to collaborate with, rather than ban, outside producers.

When cable television began to catch on, documentaries represented a value-added feature for basic-cable subscribers and a magnet for advertisers trying to reach upscale viewers.[11] A&E, The History Channel, and The Discovery Channel networks offered "buyers" a sense that their investment was money well spent on educational programs. In this sense, documentary channels provided the same kind of public-service counterbalance to the cable entertainment mix that existed in the broadcast model. Documentaries appeared sporadically in the early years of HBO, and then HBO turned to documentary programming to help fill the program schedule. By striving to offer "home" access to "theatrical" programs, HBO cultivated the documentary as a complement to uninterrupted features and sporting events and to broaden its subscriber base.

HBO was also freed from the licensing and public-service requirements tied to early broadcast documentaries. Because broadcasters are licensed by the Federal Communications Commission (FCC), they depended for decades on using documentaries as a means of offering public-affairs programming to fulfill that requirement for renewal of a license. As a pay cable service, HBO has no licensing requirement or need to project educational wholesomeness. Neither is HBO dependent on documentaries for prestige, although there is an expectation that HBO documentaries will attract a large audience or garner awards. Still, the acclaim wrought by entertainment series such as *Angels in America* (2003), *Band of Brothers* (2001), *Sex and the City* (1998–2004), *The Sopranos* (1999–2007), and *The Wire* (2002–) relieves documentary programming from showcasing nonfiction quality to justify profitable entertainment shows. Even though HBO strives for documentary recognition, it is not dependent on documentaries for limelight or licensing.[12]

The function of HBO documentaries is to give premium-cable subscribers another retail choice when shopping for commercial-free programming. Because the function is different, form follows. HBO documentaries are less restricted than basic cable channels and especially broadcasters in terms of language and visual content. This has led HBO to explore eccentric or sensational topics, candid treatments of sexuality, and quirky and controversial subjects, and to serve neglected audiences. HBO documentaries are distinguished less by their intellectual arguments, common to PBS and traditional network news documentaries, and more by their visceral examinations of human culture. Nevins explained, "Our job is a little different than that of most documentary makers. This is pay-TV, so the stuff we do sure as hell better be vivacious. It has to fly and get some numbers."[13]

From the beginning of Nevins's involvement with HBO documentary programming, we can see the influence of the experiences of her youth. One of Nevins's first projects was a six-part historical series entitled

Time Was (1979), a retrospective on American history hosted by Dick Cavett. Other family-oriented and nature documentaries also made it into the early programming schedule, such as *Lefty the Dingaling Lynx* in April 1982. Additional early documentaries include a 1981 Australian program about a family with twenty handicapped children, *Stepping Out: The DeBolts Grow Up. Coupling: Other Choices* (1980), by Harry Wiland, contrasted traditional relationships with "commercial sex clubs, 'happily unfaithful' swingers [and] polygamists."[14]

History is a staple of documentary programming, and this is true for HBO, which produced programs on General George S. Patton; Field General Erwin Rommel; the famous fires at Boston's Coconut Grove and on the cruise ship *Morro Castle*; *Hitler's Master Race: The Mad Dream of the SS* (1989); and the 1966 Chicago nurse slayings in *Real Detectives: The Speck Cases* (1982). It was *She's Nobody's Baby: A History of American Women in the 20th Century* that earned HBO's (and cable television's) first Peabody Award, in 1981.[15] This program was coproduced with *Ms. Magazine* and profiled notable figures like Shirley Temple and Eleanor Roosevelt.

When Nevins temporarily left HBO to care for her child in 1980, she produced two independent projects for the network, both turning points for HBO as well as Nevins. *Eros America* (1985) was a multipart documentary intended for HBO's companion channel Cinemax. Cinemax emerged as a variation in the HBO product line and an outlet for risqué programming that could attract HBO viewers without tarnishing the HBO name. The most salacious documentary topics would appear on Cinemax, not HBO.[16] Nevins urged Michael Fuchs to approve *Eros America* and was retained as producer. Because the FCC does not regulate cable content, broadcast decency standards do not apply to cable programmers. In fact, one of the attractions for early subscribers to cable was access to sexually explicit programs, such as those available on the Playboy Channel.

Eros America was Time Inc.'s foray into what the *New York Times* referred to as "Testing the Limits of Explicitness." The project "proceeded quietly, in part because the show represents a significant step into potentially controversial territory." Nevins defended *Eros America,* saying, "I don't think a show about sex and love in America is a problem.

It is not explicit sex and we are careful." Although *Eros America* appeared on Cinemax, the experiment paved the way for HBO's venture into similar treatments and evolved into the uninhibited HBO reality series *Real Sex* (1990), which led to *G-String Divas* (2000), *Shock Video* (1993–), and *Private Dicks* (1999). Despite concern from some that even soft pornography is harmful to women, Nevins is unapologetic: "We never go farther than the R-rated movies we present. But our viewers are in essence paying admission . . . we've got to give them what they're paying for. I would argue that our films show much less violence and are much more sexual in terms of pressing the limits. And I've learned over the years that sex is harmless."[17]

The other program Nevins produced while away from the network was *Braingames* (1984), which featured animation and instructional vignettes pitched to young viewers. It was neither a documentary nor enthusiastically received. But Nevins championed the series; she submitted it on her own to the Peabody Awards for the 1985 season and won. When Fuchs called to congratulate Nevins, she implored him to rehire her, and Nevins returned to run documentary and family programming. Having proved that she could deliver popularity and acclaim, Nevins settled on production goals for HBO documentaries—to attract viewers and/or win awards. "The truth is," explains Nevins, "that documentaries aren't the bread and butter of HBO. They are more like the dessert or appetizer, but we're not the main course, so consequently we don't have people judging us all the time."[18]

Documentaries now enjoy a secure place at HBO, which for many years exceeded the broadcast networks' commitment and rivaled PBS as the prize venue for documentary viewers and producers. Each year, HBO offers approximately one hundred hours of documentary programming, including specials produced specifically for television, theatrical documentaries, and a loosely organized group of documentaries under the series title *America Undercover*. *America Undercover* appeared as an umbrella heading in 1983. By 1995, the series owned a weekly time slot on the HBO schedule. This marked a departure in programming strategy from the occasional documentaries that appeared within the "home box office" open framework. Five years later, HBO was able to improve the lead-in to documentaries and raise their ratings by 15 percent—from 2.3

million to 4.7 million viewers—by scheduling a regular time slot following the popular Sunday-night entertainment series *The Sopranos.* This move, however, also signals a subtle shift in pressure on HBO documentaries to achieve predictable ratings.[19]

The title *America Undercover* calls to mind subjects that are off the broadcast network or mainstream radar—what some refer to as the underbelly of American culture. This seems to be a scheduling or branding tactic rather than a theme. However, numerous documentary subjects do conform to the "undercover" promise in the series label. Titles appearing under the *America Undercover* brand—usually one-hour programs—include racy installments from *Taxicab Confessions* (1995–), in which late-night passengers are prodded to discuss sexual habits, prostitution, sex-change operations, and body piercing. In one story on *Taxicab Confessions,* a police officer describes the condition of a body crushed in a subway train accident. This episode inspired a dramatic episode on the NBC crime drama series *Homicide: Life on the Street* (1993–99), and, ironically, a PBS documentary on *The Making of "The Subway Episode"* (1998). As occasional reviews in the *New York Times* show, *America Undercover* topics include the drug Ecstasy; the terrorist attacks of September 11 and their painful aftermath; the outing of gays at work; depression; suicide; congenital heart defects in children; immigrants; guns and death; homeless "skid row" vagrants; the inner damage caused by rape; the criminally insane; and abortion.

Another offbeat documentary series coming out of HBO has a different logo—*Cinemax Reel Life.* This series also reflects the artistic sensibility of Sheila Nevins: no time limits, no regular time slots, no rules. *Reel Life* began from HBO's documentary cast-offs with programs too long, too short, too artsy, or just too strange to justify HBO's big-budget treatment. A single example explains much: filmmaker Michael Negroponte had befriended a middle-aged homeless woman who believed she was the wife of the god Jupiter. Over time, he deciphered her cryptic speech and was able to document her middle-class past. Although this Central Park bag lady was not a suitable topic for HBO, Nevins nevertheless could not bear to let it go. Using her executive influence, Nevins was able to get a budget for the production by convincing her bosses, "This is an award topper; let's not lose it."

Jupiter's Wife (1995) won a special jury prize at Sundance and Cinemax's first Emmy.[20]

One media observer praised *Reel Life* as a boon to independent filmmakers and the art-house crowd. But its awards have also brought the network respectability and prestige. *Breathing Lessons: The Life and Work of Mark O'Brien,* about a poet journalist who survived forty years in an iron lung, won the Academy Award for Best Documentary (Short Subject) in 1996. *The Diving Bell and the Butterfly* (2007) profiles a French man who suffered a stroke and communicates only by fluttering his eyelid. *The Dying Rooms* (1995), about the genocide of baby girls in China, won a Peabody, a CableACE Award, and an Emmy. Nevins explains, "The beauty of 'Reel Life' is it's a workshop to develop things that have a right to be seen but don't fit mainstream TV."[21]

A New Business Model for Documentaries

When HBO first promoted *Time Was,* vice president Michael Fuchs publicized the series as "docutainment," a variation on the pejorative "infotainment." Fuchs's idiom foreshadowed a trend that blossomed in the 1980s in the form of syndicated tabloid journalism shows like *Hard Copy* (1989–99) and *A Current Affair* (1986–96). These topical programs eschewed edification in favor of sensationalism and titillation. Critics sensed entertainment values were displacing journalistic values and adopted "infotainment" to represent the genre and the degradation of journalism. Although some HBO documentaries are infotainment, others are in the classic network news documentary mold. Still, Sheila Nevins is the first to admit that instead of "journalists" she prefers "storytellers."[22]

There were also sociopolitical trends occurring when HBO was launched that forced television companies to alter their business models. These changes are reflected in HBO's documentary programming. HBO began, for instance, during a time when presidential administrations sought to deregulate communications markets. An initiative begun during the Carter administration came to fruition during the Reagan era, when the FCC rescinded much of the regulatory structure that had existed throughout broadcast history. Instead of having the government reward stations with licenses because of their public service, the standard adopted during the Reagan years was based primarily on helping companies serve individual tastes and needs.

The genesis of HBO coincided with these trends, which again are reflected in its documentary programming. Instead of white-paper treatises on complex social problems and foreign affairs—the staple of the 1950s and 1960s—there was a shift toward more-individual narratives. That does not mean HBO ignores social issues. But its documentary treatments are more likely to use the individual as the *focal point* of the program, instead of the traditional network device of using the individual to *represent* society. This also corresponds to Sheila Nevins's view that ordinary citizens have interesting stories to tell: "We are interested in the depths of the human psyche. Not social issues, but personal experiences or suffering: a child handling abuse at the hands of priests, a policeman going mad from the job. I have a serious view of the human condition."[23]

Finally, there is a difference in the economic purposes of documentary or infotainment *broadcast* programs and those at HBO. The economic purpose of commercial broadcast programming is to attract viewers and deliver "eyeballs" to advertisers. The economic purpose of HBO programming is to sell premium-cable subscriptions. As American culture evolved from the era in which first radio and then television broadcasting provided a communal bond or "social glue," HBO emerged in an era of individualism in which subscribers would purchase programs they wanted to consume—not because they were good for society, but because they appealed to the subscriber. The home box office model of HBO documentaries is a good fit for this business model.[24]

This model requires that the overall product lineup attract a large audience of individual buyers with varying tastes. HBO buyers who desire sexuality can choose *Pornucopia* (2004), *Real Sex, Thinking XXX* (2004), *Cathouse* (2002), or *G-String Divas*. History buffs can view *4 Little Girls* (1998), about the 1963 Birmingham church bombing; *Balseros* (2002), about Cuban refugees in Miami; *Mighty Times: The Legacy of Rosa Parks* (2002); and *In Memoriam: New York City, 9/11/01* (2002). Crime fans have *The Iceman and the Psychiatrist* (2002), the story of a hit man; *Juvies* (2004), youth offenders tried as adults; *Gang War: Bangin' in Little Rock* (1994); or *Rape in a Small Town: The Florence Holway Story* (2004), about a seventy-five-year-old New Hampshire woman. Political junkies can select *Journeys with George* (2002), inside the Bush campaign 2000; *Diary of a Political Tourist*

Produced and directed by Spike Lee, *4 Little Girls* recounts
the people and events surrounding the 1963 bombing of the
Sixteenth Street Baptist Church in Birmingham, Alabama, in
which four young African American girls lost their lives.

(2004), Democrats on the campaign trail; *Indian Point: Imagining the
Unimaginable* (2004), the post-September 11 nuclear threat near New
York City; and *Left of the Dial* (2005), a portrait of Air America
radio.[25]

Another way HBO documentary programming entertains is through
creative variety. Network documentaries, most PBS programs, and cable
series typically adopt conventions. PBS's *P.O.V.* (1988–) offers experimentation; and Henry Hampton (*Eyes on the Prize*), Ken Burns (*The

Civil War [1990]), and others have innovated shooting, interview, or storytelling techniques. Although there has been no lack of creative vision throughout much of TV documentary history, many programs adopt a quality recognizable as "network."[26] Even offerings on basic "documentary" channels tend to be formulaic, especially the timing of segments to commercial breaks and "up-next" appeals. But although cable networks have developed several outstanding documentaries—for instance, a series on Watergate by The Discovery Channel, the Cold War on CNN, many National Geographic explorations, and others—their programming structure is still bound by the commercial-break format of the network. Not so with HBO.[27]

"It has to look like it's on HBO," said Nevins, "so if you're surfing, you'll say, 'This must be HBO.'" HBO documentaries also adopt a cinematic style. In Spike Lee's *4 Little Girls,* the constantly moving camera, frequently cutting off part of the subject's face, contributes to the uneasiness demanded of the viewer to appreciate the pain of losing a loved one in a hate crime. Alexandra Pelosi's handheld mini digital video camera in *Journeys with George* conveys the feeling of being a rider, not a distant observer, on Bush's campaign bus. In Jacqueline Glover's *Unchained Memories: Readings from the Slave Narratives* (2003), actors bring to life interviews conducted in the 1930s with slavery survivors. This technique is also used in *Dear America: Letters Home from Vietnam* (1987), by Bill Couturié.[28]

Fans of social explorations, especially those that challenge society to right wrongs or empathize with cultural minorities, are also well served by HBO. Filmmaker Rory Kennedy has produced documentaries on how social and educational systems affected a seven-year-old Mississippian in *A Boy's Life* (2003), the AIDS crisis in *Pandemic: Facings AIDS* (2003), and Appalachian poverty in *American Hollow* (1999). Maryann DeLeo returned to the site of the Chernobyl nuclear disaster to reveal the devastation evident in abandoned villages, asylums, and orphanages. Gerardine Wurzburg followed a student with Down Syndrome from sixth grade through high school in *Graduating Peter* (2001). *LaLee's Kin* (2001), directed by Deborah Dickson and Susan Frömke, with cinematography by Albert Maysles, profiles three generations of African American cotton pickers mired in Mississippi poverty. After Hurricane Katrina in 2005, Sheila Nevins wanted a

In Spike Lee's *4 Little Girls,* the constantly moving camera, frequently cutting off part of the subject's face, contributes to the uneasiness demanded of the viewer to appreciate the pain of losing a loved one in a hate crime.

Alexandra Pelosi's handheld mini digital video camera in *Journeys with George* conveys the feeling of being a rider, not a distant observer, on Bush's campaign bus in 2000.

Produced and directed by Bill Couturié, *Dear America: Letters Home from Vietnam* uses well-known actors such as Robert DeNiro, Kathleen Turner, and Martin Sheen to read the words of soldiers written to their loved ones back at home at the time of the war.

Dear America: Letters Home from Vietnam features actual footage filmed during the Vietnam War, including some shots taken by the soldiers themselves.

documentary that would stand apart from other projects then in the works. She again collaborated with Spike Lee and Sam Pollard on *When the Levees Broke: A Requiem in Four Acts* (2006).[29]

Analyzing the content and quality of these programs challenges researchers to separate individual documentaries from the HBO "monolith," and also to distinguish HBO theatricals from television projects. What emerges is the realization that HBO offers more of a *distribution* brand than a one-size-fits-all *creative* brand. Whether any HBO documentary is paradigmatic in the network tradition is doubtful, given the makeup of the HBO audience and the differences in HBO's premium pay cable delivery as compared with network television's free, collective delivery. But to classify or dismiss HBO documentaries as "docutainment," as though all are equal or as if HBO offerings differ from other long-form television documentaries, pigeonholes the programming without allowing for normal variations in the information-entertainment mix.

The nonfiction programming formula at HBO has unmistakably enhanced the documentary field with distinction. HBO's programs have won an impressive collection of awards for documentary excellence, including the Emmy, the Academy Award, the Alfred I. DuPont-Columbia University Award and the George Foster Peabody Award. Overall, HBO and Cinemax documentaries have won forty-seven Emmy Awards, twelve Academy Awards, and seventeen George Foster Peabody Awards.[30]

"They Never Make You Feel Like You're Workin' for 'The Man'"

One of the notable characteristics of HBO documentary programming stems from the community cultivated by Sheila Nevins. HBO has become a hub for producers who appreciate HBO financing but also the moral and collegial support offered by Nevins & Company. Of course, hopeful producers are unlikely to voice criticism about a potential partner. But the chorus of opinions from several documentary makers suggests mutual appreciation between filmmakers and HBO. Again, this reflects industry changes and a difference between network news broadcast documentaries and cable television, especially premium pay cable.

HBO distributes documentaries developed by outside production companies. As a rule, the broadcast networks will not. Because broadcast documentaries are generally classified as journalism and are almost exclusively produced within news divisions, each program bears the network's imprint. The only way any organization can stand behind its journalism—and protect its brand—is to control the newsgathering and production. The person responsible for ensuring that broadcast news upholds the expectations of network executives is the news division president. These news presidents, exclusively men, represent the ultimate authority over the networks' news reports. So, documentary producers broadcasting under the imprint of ABC, CBS, or NBC News report to a *man*, figuratively and literally. There have been women executives leading news documentary units or particular news operations—Marlene Sanders and Pamela Hill at ABC News, and Linda Mason at CBS News. But anyone who wanted to produce a documentary for broadcast news ultimately had to deal with *a* man who represented *the* man.

Not at HBO. First, by executive decree and personal philosophy, Sheila Nevins doesn't do journalism—she does stories. Second, Nevins is certainly the boss, but she's not the traditional "suit." Documentary producer Alexandra Pelosi remarked, "It's the only place where I've worked with so many women." Nevins and her staff, including Lisa Heller and Sara Bernard, nurture documentary projects. "You never feel rushed or hurried. It's like talking with a friend," said Pelosi, characterizing her experiences as a producer. "They never make you feel like you're working for 'the man.'"[31]

Pelosi found little enthusiasm at the networks for *Journeys with George,* but the project caught Nevins's attention. She gave Pelosi a slot on HBO. Pelosi's reaction is not surprising: "HBO is the greatest thing that ever happened to me." One reason is financing. "They don't worry about the check," Pelosi said. The budget for an individual documentary at HBO ranges from $600,000 to $1.5 million, compared with $50,000 to $250,000 at other cable networks. "Very few places respond to documentaries as HBO does," said Pelosi. "They push it to make sure people see your stuff. They promote documentaries with the same intensity as other programming. They throw parties for premieres like they do for entertainment programs."[32]

Rory Kennedy has directed five documentaries for HBO and worked on other HBO projects. Of the two kinds of HBO documentaries—sensational (dealing with sex, crime, and drugs), and those seeking critical attention—Kennedy's interests lie in the latter. Here, too, she explains, HBO is "willing to push the envelope and offer treatments that are provocative and controversial. They do things that can't be done or said in other places." *Indian Point,* for example, took the nuclear power industry to task to highlight lapses in national security. And after *Pandemic: Facing AIDS* was shown on Capitol Hill, Congressional representatives said to Kennedy, "I didn't know it was that bad," and then appropriated more money. "HBO is expanding how people see that issue and respond to it," Kennedy said. "They want a more compassionate society and to represent the more marginal people in society."[33]

Nevins's executive clout also helps. She can say yes or no on the spot, as she did for Kennedy's film on poverty in Appalachian eastern Kentucky. Kennedy had finished *American Hollow* as a one-hour program and sent it to HBO for final notes. When Nevins called and asked Kennedy if she was "sitting down," the producer suspected her time slot had been lost. Instead Nevins said that the story deserved ninety minutes and HBO would pay for the expansion. Kennedy attributes HBO's editorial freedom to the freedom from advertising. Advertisers are leery of associating their brands with controversial material, salty language, or risqué subject matter, Kennedy explains, so viewers of commercial television "have a skewed view of the world not based on facts." HBO's economic structure protects documentary projects, producers, and viewers.[34]

Documentary legends also recognize HBO's contributions. Albert Maysles noted, "I'm at my best working for HBO." HBO usually pitches ideas to Maysles rather than the other way around. After legislation changed national welfare laws, HBO asked Maysles to look for a story. He found LaLee Wallace, great grandmother to three generations of cotton pickers in the Mississippi Delta. *LaLee's Kin* was nominated for an Academy Award in 2001 for Best Documentary Feature. Maysles collaborated with Susan Frömke and Deborah Dickson to produce the HBO film *Abortion: Desperate Choices,* in 1992. *Abortion* reported opinions from pro-life and pro-choice mothers and won wide critical acclaim. The same threesome documented death and dying in 1996 with *Letting Go, A Hospice Journey.*[35]

D. A. Pennebaker—like Maysles an originator of cinema verité—took longer to come to terms with HBO, but eventually was engaged to do a spontaneous, behind-the-scenes shoot on Broadway legend Elaine Stritch. He and partners Chris Hegedus and Nick Doob used multiple cameras to capture Stritch's stage performance and backstage persona (the kind of intimate profile Pennebaker used with Bob Dylan in *Don't Look Back* [1967]). HBO also offers instant visibility at a low per-minute cost, said Pennebaker. They don't need 12,000 film prints: "HBO opens nationally—Bang!"[36]

This relationship between producers and the HBO network marks a change in documentary history and reflects part of the media-economic climate in America since the 1980s. Documentary producers once had to choose between earning a network paycheck without receiving residuals, or raising money independently to get a slot on PBS. PBS has long collaborated with documentary makers on production and distribution, but without the deep pockets of HBO. The HBO arrangement gives the producer editorial freedom, access to HBO audiences, and leverage in the financial negotiations for the film's ultimate exhibition and distribution.

Conclusion

Documentaries fulfill the most basic individual needs of producers seeking to express their visions to audiences who strive to understand their own worlds. In this sense, HBO's emergence in the documentary field is like earlier networks and eras. HBO has become a welcome outlet for producers of theatrical release documentaries and specific programs that seek to evoke a cinematic feel. And the network sustains a production environment for documentaries more like the Hollywood independent model than the broadcast television model. Sheila Nevins refers to her producer associates as her "repertory company," a loosely affiliated creative group that enjoys individual recognition and can share the profits from after-market sales. "We cast docs like we cast a feature," she said. "Eighty percent of the time we come up with the concept. We develop it into something correct for HBO. The filmmakers work with the concept until it's their own."[37]

On broadcast and most cable television networks, viewers see documentaries for free, whereas HBO charges a monthly fee. Prior to the 1980s, most documentaries were mostly ephemeral; in contrast, today's viewers can now own reproductions of these programs. On many networks, documentaries adopt a signature appearance, whereas on HBO the filmmaker's individualism emerges in the way that an auteur's might on the silver screen. In the case of HBO, moreover, viewers can see treatments and topics that would never come to light on broadcast television and only rarely on PBS or basic cable.

The appearance of the documentary at HBO resembles the experience of other emerging networks—commercial broadcast, PBS, and basic cable—because HBO has "the luxury of time."[38] Each of these outlets has contributed a worthy collection to the documentary field. The trajectory for HBO documentaries will depend on the level of corporate micromanagement as the network continues to mature, along with the impact of corporate sales or mergers, and the tenor of the professional and financial relationships between the network and its filmmakers. Furthermore, changes in political climate, viewer tastes, and competition from other distribution services such as the Internet or digital movie delivery may affect HBO documentaries. For now, however, HBO and its companion *Cinemax Reel Life* serve a critical role in producing documentary programming. Even if the quality varies or offends the tastes of some critics, HBO has made a substantial commitment to use television to expand the perspective of American viewers, to give attention to grave matters of public interest, and to permit audiences to encounter the underbelly of the human experience—if they decide to subscribe and tune in.

Notes

1. James Rutenberg, "Seamy or Serious, It's Now Center Stage," *New York Times,* 21 March 2001, E1. Chris Grove, "Nevins Makes HBO Docus a Cut Above," *Daily Variety,* 17 November 1998, A4.

2. Museum of Television & Radio (MTR), "She Made It," a program to honor the contributions of women in television and radio, at http://www .shemadeit.org/meet/biography.aspx?m=44 (accessed 17 July 2006). Sheila Nevins, interview with Steve Nelson, Cable Center Oral History Project, July 2000, 17 July 2006, at http://www.cablecenter.org/education/library/oralHistoryDetails. cfm?id=153#transcript (accessed 17 July 2006), 2–3. Mike Reynolds, "Passionate Programmer; From Strippers to Sept. 11, HBO's Sheila Nevins Tells It Like It Is," *Multichannel News,* 28 January 2002, 18W. Daniel S. Moore, "Docus Find Welcoming Forum," *Daily Variety,* 29 April 1996.

3. On Chayefsky, see Mary Ann Watson, *Defining Visions: Television and the American Experience since 1945* (Fort Worth, Tex.: Harcourt Brace, 1998), 15–19. P. David Marshall, "Winfrey, Oprah (1954–)," *Encyclopedia of Television*, vol. 4, 2nd ed. (New York: Fitzroy Dearborn, 2004), 2558–60. On Susskind, see Mary Ann Watson, "Open End, A Mirror of the 1960s," *Film and History* 21:2–3 (May/September 1991): 70–76.

4. MTR, "She Made It." Nevins, interview with Steve Nelson, 1.

5. Nevins, interview with Steve Nelson, 1.

6. Sheila Nevins, "A Conversation with Sheila Nevins," *Kodak on Film*, undated Web article, at http://www.kodak.com/US/en/motion/forum/onFilm/nevinsQA.shtml (accessed 17 July 2006), 21.

7. Ibid., 3–4. MTR, "She Made It." Nevins, interview with Steve Nelson, 4.

8. Nevins, interview with Steve Nelson, 4–5. Eleanor Blau, "Museum Show Honors 25 Years of Channel 13," *New York Times*, 11 February 1988, C34.

9. Nevins, interview with Steve Nelson, 6.

10. Ibid., 6–9. MTR, "She Made It." On *Who's Who*, see Daniel Einstein, *Special Edition: A Guide to Documentary Series and Special News Reports, 1955–1979* (Metuchen, N.J.: Scarecrow, 1987), 714–15.

11. Kara Swisher, "Voyages of Discovery," *Washington Post*, 17 June 1991, Business, 1. Wayne Walley, "Discovery Seeks Bold New Worlds," *Electronic Media*, 22 April 1991, 1.

12. Nevins, interview with Steve Nelson, 3.

13. Grove, "Nevins Makes HBO Docus a Cut Above."

14. Peter Funt, "Tomorrow—'A Video Supermarket,'" *New York Times*, 22 July 1979, D1. John J. O'Connor, "TV View," *New York Times*, 4 May 1980, D37.

15. Nadine Brozan, "Party Marks the 10th Anniversary for *Ms. Magazine*," *New York Times*, 24 June 1982, C6.

16. Nevins, interview with Steve Nelson, 13–15. John J. O'Connor, "Testing the Limits of Explicitness," *New York Times*, 20 November 1983, H36.

17. O'Connor, "Testing the Limits of Explicitness," H36. Sally Bedell, "NBC Fights to Save 'St. Elsewhere,'" *New York Times*, 8 March 1983, C15. Nevins, interview with Steve Nelson, 13–15. Ray Richmond, "Hard-Hitting Docus Rack Up Awards," *Variety*, 3 November 1997, 42.

18. John J. O'Connor, "'Wonderworks' and 'Braingames,'" *New York Times*, 5 November 1984, C17. Nevins, interview with Steve Nelson, 13–14. Rory Kennedy, interview with the author, 27 June 2006. Al Maysles, interview with the author, 18 July 2006. Nevins, "A Conversation with Sheila Nevins," 3.

19. Julie Salamon, "Nevins Rules," *New York Times Magazine*, 3 March 2002, 66–68. Stephen Farber, "HBO Documentaries Fill 3 Networks' Breach," *New York Times*, 27 June 1984, C26.

20. Gini Sikes, "Cinemax Bites Reality and Tastes Respect," *New York Times*, 25 January 1998, Arts & Leisure, 33.

21. Ibid.

22. Funt, "Tomorrow—'A Video Supermarket.'" John J. O'Connor, "Fluff Is Clouding Cable's Future," *New York Times,* 25 July 1982, H21.

23. Daniel S. Moore, "Docus Find Welcoming Forum," *Daily Variety,* 29 April 1996.

24. On "social glue," see Watson, *Defining Visions,* 3.

25. "About HBO Documentaries," at http://www.hbo.com/docs/about/ (accessed 28 July 2006).

26. "*POV* Garners Six News and Documentary Emmy Nominations, A Record for the PBS Series," at http://www.pbs.org/pov/utils/pressroom/2006/index.html (accessed 28 July 2006). Tom Mascaro, "Pioneer Profile: Henry Hampton," *Television Quarterly* 32:2–3 (summer/fall 2001): 54–58. Gary R. Edgerton, *Ken Burns's America* (New York: Palgrave, 2001).

27. Todd Gitlin, "Through a Lens, Starkly," *American Prospect* 14:10 (November 2003): 59+. Diane Werts, "Illuminating Our Times: 'It's a Mad War' Comes Front and Center in a Festival Saluting the Search for Meaning in News Events," *Newsday,* 20 April 2003, D14. James Collins, "The Cold War: From Twilight to Dawn," *Time,* 21 September 1998, 94.

28. Janet Maslin, "Still Reeling from a Day of Death," *New York Times,* 9 July 1997, C11. Caryn James, "Food, Jokes and Few Issues on the Bush Campaign 2000," *New York Times,* 5 November 2002, E1. Henry Louis Gates Jr., "Not Gone with the Wind: Voices of Slavery," *New York Times,* 9 February 2002, AR1. Samuel G. Freedman, "Vietnam Echoes: 'We Are All Afraid To Die,'" *New York Times,* 3 April 1988, 86. Virginia Rohan, "HBO Documentary Is Still Evolving," *Record* [Bergen County, N.J.], 4 May 2001, Lifestyle, 47.

29. Rebecca Traister, "A Harrowing, Inspiring 'Boy's Life,'" 24 March 2004, at http://www.salon.com (accessed 31 July 2006). Nancy Ramsey, "Daughter of Privilege Films Lives of Pain," *New York Times,* 25 June 2003, E1. Stephen Holden, "A Film United By Home and Want," *New York Times,* 26 May 1999, E5. *Chernobyl Heart,* 2004, at http://www.chernobylheart.com/ (accessed 28 July 2006). Gerardine Wurzburg, *Graduating Peter,* "A Film by Gerardine Wurzburg," HBO, 21 January 2003, at http://www.graduatingpeter.com/ (accessed 31 July 2006). A. O. Scott, "Pride, Hope and Hardship in the Land of Cotton," *New York Times,* 22 June 2001, E12. Chuleenan Svetvilas, "Bamboozled on the Bayou, Spike Lee Profiles Katrina Survivors," *Documentary* 25:5 (August 2006): 14–15.

30. "About HBO Documentaries," at http://www.hbo.com/docs/about/ (accessed 12 November 2006).

31. Alexandra Pelosi, interview with the author, 14 June 2006.

32. Pelosi, interview. James Sterngold, "HBO Programmer Likes to Kindle Both Heat and Light," *New York Times,* 15 April 1998, E2.

33. Kennedy, interview.

34. Ibid.

35. Maysles, interview.

36. D. A. Pennebaker, interview with the author, 18 July 2006.

37. Nevins, interview with Steve Nelson, 22. Moore, "Docus Find Welcoming Forum."

38. Reuven Frank, interview with the author, 20 October 1993. Perry Wolff, interview with the author, 12 April 1994.

FIFTEEN

America Undercover

Susan Murray

HBO's documentary series *America Undercover* has been on the air since 1983; in that time it has not only showcased the work of some of the finest documentarians in the world, but has also come under some critical fire for its tendency to focus on the sensational and the titillating. Most documentaries made for and shown on HBO come under the *America Undercover* heading, with the exception of a few special presentations and those films that have already had a theatrical release, so the identity of the series really represents the identity of HBO documentaries writ large. With documentaries such as Nick Broomfield's *Aileen: Life and Death of a Serial Killer* (2003), Joe Berlinger and Bruce Sinofsky's *Paradise Lost: The Child Murders at Robin Hood Hills* (1996), Shari Cookson and Linda Otto's *Living Dolls* (2001), and Fenton Bailey and Randy Barbato's *Monica in Black and White* (2002), and late night programming such as *Real Sex* (1990–), *G-String Divas* (2000), *Autopsy* (1994–), *Cathouse* (2002), and *Taxicab Confessions* (1995–), the anthology series has, throughout most of its history, trod the line between traditional, independent documentaries with a point of view, and the showcasing of subjects that verge on exploitation.

Reporters have described both the series and the documentaries contained within it as "balancing the crass with the crusading," "an odd mix of sensationalistic fare and social crusading," and a coming together of "prestige and sizzle."[1] Sundance festival director Geoffrey Gilmore uses the term "docutainment" to describe the tenor of HBO nonfiction programming, by which he means "transgressive, or at least sensational, subject matter given sober, respectful treatment."[2] Sheila Nevins, president of documentary and family programming at HBO, claims that although she isn't on the lookout for one particular type of documentary, she does tend to be attracted to those that are "uplifting, violent or vulgar" and believes that her audience feels the same way. She says that *America Undercover* is "more emotive and visceral than intellectual. We don't ever forget who our audience is and what it wants from us."[3]

The reasons behind HBO's decision to market *America Undercover* in such a way may have to do with the history of HBO's nonfiction programming division, which developed largely in response to the content limitations of its competitors. When she first came to the cable network in 1979 after working at Children's Television Workshop and as a producer for CBS's *Who's Who* (1977–), Nevins had little experience with the types of documentaries that now make up *America Undercover*. Believing both that documentaries had to be about "serious subjects like Winston Churchill or WWII" and that the network had hired her to help expand in a cost-effective manner their daily programming schedule from eight to twelve hours, for the first few years Nevins produced primarily traditional historical documentaries and a series that she created in conjunction with *Consumer Reports*.[4] However, she soon noticed that the most successful movies on cable were R-rated and came up with the idea of doing singular nonfiction programming. After experimenting with the idea through the series *Eros America*, which she created for HBO's sister channel Cinemax in the early 1980s, Nevins produced similar R-rated reality shows for *America Undercover*. She also sought out documentaries for the series that had a related element of titillation or sensation to them—even if they were not explicitly about sex. At the same time, she began to cultivate relationships with some of the top independent filmmakers in the country, including Albert Maysles, Jon Alpert, Barbara Kopple, Lee Grant, and Alan and Susan Raymond (*An American Family* [1973]), as well as supporting up-and-coming independent filmmakers. Gradually, she and HBO garnered a reputation among those in the documentary community as a trusted and prestigious outlet for their material. In fact, by 1998 the network was producing or acquiring forty hours of documentaries annually, and more and more filmmakers were willing to give up the idea of a theatrical run altogether just for the chance to work with Nevins and HBO.

The early to mid-1990s saw a significant shift in the market for television documentaries, because the culture wars over arts funding and increasing competition from cable outlets left PBS (the primary outlet for television documentaries up until that point) in a state of crisis. As a result of the close scrutiny that the network was receiving, it became increasingly difficult for it not only to fund documentaries, but also to air work that was explicit or controversial. It is exactly this type of content that HBO excelled at. The very nature of HBO's premium-channel payment structure allows the network to escape the cultural vilification and calls for censorship that plague broadcast and some basic cable stations. This, coupled with an audience that wishes to see itself as more capable, responsible, and mature than the average television viewer, creates an ideal setting for the presentation of "tasteful" but possibly lurid nonfiction programming. Over time, whereas PBS has become best known in the documentary community for its *P.O.V* series, which has been on the air since 1988 and is marketed as "putting a human face on social issues,"[5] HBO became a major funder and supporter of a slightly different type of independent documentary. When asked if Nevins would ever want to do a documentary for HBO with Ken Burns, she replied, "We could, but I'd worry about the audience. What would I give them that they wouldn't get for free? I think he's established a fit in what he does [for PBS], free television for the 1% of the population that's intellectual. But would my audience pay for *The Civil War* or *Baseball?* If they saw a whole bunch of stills, would they not think they were paying for PBS?"[6]

Trying to avoid what she considers to be "boring" documentaries has worked for Nevins and *America Undercover.* The critical praise and industry accolades that the programs have acquired over the years (*America Undercover* has won forty-seven Emmys, twelve Oscars, seventeen Peabody Awards, and the Alfred I. DuPont-Columbia University Award, as well as many others) have helped HBO in its effort to brand itself as *the* quality cable network. *Dear America: Letters Home from Vietnam* (1987), which offers a gripping look at the experiences of soldiers told in their own words from actual letters written home from Southeast Asia, was the first *America Undercover* documentary to win an Emmy. The first documentary in the series to win an Oscar was Lee Grant's 1986 *Down and Out in America,* which chronicles the human

The first *America Undercover* documentary to win an Emmy was *Dear America: Letters Home from Vietnam* (1987), which offers a gripping look at the experiences of soldiers told in their own words from actual letters written home from Southeast Asia.

toll that Reaganomics and the ensuing economic recession had on poor Americans. It has a strong point of view and a passion for the topic, and is told through the personal stories of its subjects.

Although often focusing on issues that are socially relevant, many of the documentaries that followed *Down and Out* have born a similarly intimate and emotionally evocative tone. In part, this is due to the personalities of those that are the subjects of these productions. These people are usually representative of both a social problem and their surrounding circumstances while remaining, as characters, uniquely their own—whether it is the exceptionally gifted and interesting autistic young boy in *George* (2000), the emotionally stunted divorced dad who goes to raves and does drugs with his kids in *Small Town Ecstasy* (2002), or the woman who has adopted and raised eleven special-needs children on her own in *My Flesh and Blood* (2003). Moreover, the manner and style in which they are filmed typically brings the viewer closer to them, because the majority of the films under the *America Under-*

The first *America Undercover* documentary to win an Oscar was *Down and Out in America,* which chronicles the human toll that Reaganomics and the ensuing economic recession had on poor Americans, such as the urban unemployed. Photograph by Mariette Pathy Allen.

Directed and narrated by Lee Grant, *Down and Out in America* focuses on the plight of the estimated 34 million Americans living in poverty, including tens of thousands of dispossessed farmers. Photograph by Mariette Pathy Allen.

Down and Out in America has a strong point of view and a passion for its topic, and is told through the personal stories of such subjects as this impoverished family. Photograph by Mariette Pathy Allen.

cover rubric have been filmed in a relatively loose verité style. As Ann Marsh writes in her review of *Soldiers,* a 2001 documentary on those who actively and often violently oppose abortion, "as often is the case with HBO documentaries, there is no narration, no comforting voice of authority to pass judgment on the hair-raising twists of logic laid out by the film's real-life protagonists."[7]

Over the past decade, HBO has aggressively marketed itself as a quality network for the (paying) television connoisseur. Through its original programming, such as *The Sopranos* (1999–2007), *Six Feet Under* (2001–5), and *Sex and the City* (1998–2004), the cable network has refashioned liberal notions of "quality" television to include "adult" content. Consequently, viewers come to programs such as the nonfiction anthology series *America Undercover* with the expectation that what they are about to see is above and beyond the usual network fare. In

March 2001, *America Undercover* was moved into one of HBO's prime program slots. After being shown on a rather sporadic monthly basis, *America Undercover* garnered the coveted 10:00 P.M. (EST) slot on Sunday nights in the spring and summer of that year, which meant that the program followed *Six Feet Under* and *The Sopranos,* and which gave the show not only increased visibility but also a higher level of prestige. At that point, the network invested more in its promotion of the show, even taking out two-page full-color ads in highbrow venues such as the *New Yorker.* Consequently, Nevins claimed, what was once a "weak umbrella" of a series had managed to find a stronger identity with viewers.[8]

One of the stated reasons for giving the series such a coveted time slot was the growing popularity of reality programming on network TV. According to the *New York Times*, Chris Albrecht, HBO's president of original programming at that time, "gave Ms. Nevins' documentaries the slot because he thought the wider television audience was ready for her provocative style, given the taste for voyeuristic shows like CBS's *Survivor* and Fox's *Temptation Island.*" The same article notes that some people in the documentary field were beginning to question Nevins's focus on films that seemed to verge on the territory covered by reality and tabloid television. This was particularly troubling to those who noted that *America Undercover*'s $20 million annual budget (a figure virtually unheard of in documentary television) meant that Nevins has the power to give any documentary she selects an unprecedented level of visibility in a commercial-free setting. Nevins's response to such criticism is that the production and inclusion of programs such as *G-String Divas* in the *America Undercover* series is really about an exchange of sorts: they help her reach the expectations for ratings that HBO executives have for the program, which will buy her the room to show "very serious and award-winning documentaries." However, she notes that virtually all the documentaries she's commissioned "have always been marked by a sort of extreme emotion: sobbing and feeling and touching. I'm an extreme person: I believe in extremes. I've never been polite and our documentaries are not polite. Whether it's about violence or child abuse or sex, it's in your face and why not? Life is in your face."[9]

It is just this quality of showcasing "extreme emotion" or carrying

"visceral appeal," as it is described on the HBO Web site, that has provided *America Undercover* with a unifying quality or theme.[10] While
almost every documentary that shows on the cable network is included
in this series, the majority of them, whether political or personal, bear
this marker. This "loose umbrella" that Nevins describes is really held
together by a blend of nonfiction genres and formats that all contain
varying degrees of the serious and the sensational, and the series is marketed in such a way as to intentionally blur the boundaries between
reality programming and documentary. Alternating between works that
engage in the "discourse of sobriety," covering topics such as labor
struggles, racial profiling, terrorism, and the death penalty, and the
regular round of sex-based programming, *America Undercover* strad-
dles traditional formats and viewing positions.[11] As Nevins herself
states, she and her staff "try to balance programs that nudge the world
and programs that are more titillating and fanciful" in order to temper
or contain the reception of its risqué episodes and to help sensationalize
more staid subject matter.

Outlining the way in which she negotiates the often conflicting
desires of her audience, Nevins told the *Los Angeles Times* that "if you
could see it on A&E, if an advertiser would sponsor it, then I don't want
to put it on HBO, because people are paying to see something a little
spicier. But if it's ugly like Playboy, if it's lowbrow sexuality, then it's not
what I like to call 'erotic eros,' and I don't want it."[13] Nevins has also
asserted that the unifying element of the nonfiction programs that air
on *America Undercover* is their ability to fully represent "the real,"
even as she has tried to distance her programming from the type of reality found on network television. She has stated that, although the popularity of reality has helped *America Undercover* in many ways, shows
like *Survivor* (CBS, 2000–) would never appear on HBO: "We don't
offer prizes; we don't put people in a room or on an island."[14] Back in
1998, she told *Realscreen* that "the concept of our unexpurgated [pro-
grams] began to mean a certain kind of license to push reality to where
it would naturally go without any censorship. There was no need to
curtail what was happening. That's when reality began to be as interesting to me as theater, because it meant people could realize their stories
to their full extent and where they could take them, whether the stories
were happy or sad or violent or tragic or sexual."[15]

Nevins is making a claim here for all her nonfiction programming that equates lack of mediation or censorship from higher authorities with the ability of these programs not only to make truth claims, but to move beyond realism and into the area of unfiltered reality. In doing so, she is touching on arguments that are made by both reality television and documentary producers and marketers. However, texts that are placed in the documentary genre tend to make an additional claim—that of social and historical relevance, or, in the language of television, public service. Nevins's statement is trying to shift the discourse to incorporate her presentation of sexual and other kinds of controversial content as a public service in itself.[16] Or, at least that sensational/sexual and educational/informational content is not mutually exclusive.

With *America Undercover,* HBO has been able to successfully incorporate popular pleasure into a discourse of quality. Nevins and her team reworked the discourse around their program to not only suit their network's brand image, but also redefine the terms on which it was understood and classified. Certainly *America Undercover*'s anthology format contributed to the success of their strategy, but it was also a result of an audience who, through their prior experience with HBO and their conception of themselves as a unique and select audience, were willing to accept a dismantling of the bifurcations that separated traditional definitions of documentary and reality television. Some of this willingness can be attributed to HBO's championing of the first amendment, which Nevins says provided HBO with "a comfort zone. If you had a Richard Pryor special, you could do a show called *Eros America*; if you showed an [unedited] R-rated movie, you could push your exposure of a crack house to the full extent of what was going on inside. It was the mandate of the network, because that's what people were paying for."[17]

In the fall of 2003, Nevins added a regular series with continuing characters and plotlines to *America Undercover,* telling the press, "We're trying to reinvent ourselves. We've always been more like an anthology, but now we're trying to have continuing characters going through continuing stories."[18] It was also one more step for the network into the realm of reality television. *Family Bonds* (2004), which follows the business and family life of a bail bondsman and bounty hunter in Queens, New York, has many characteristics of a reality program but was still often described by HBO executives as a "multi-hour documentary franchise" or a "documentary soap opera." The series soon broke away from the *America Undercover* umbrella, however, becoming its own weekly series airing on Sunday nights through 2005. At the same time, *America Undercover* lost its weekly time slot and went back to appearing more irregularly and infrequently (roughly twelve times a year).

Although not airing as frequently as it did a few years ago, *America Undercover* is still producing its unique blend of the sensational and the high-minded. It also continues to work on a regular basis with well-known directors such as Barbara Kopple, Nick Broomfield, and Rory Kennedy. Kennedy has focused on the personal effects of poverty, class, and race in America in documentaries such as *American Hollow* (1999), which explores the effects of welfare on the culture and economy of the rural south through the story of one disenfranchised Kentucky family; *The Execution of Wanda Jean* (2002), the complicated issues, character, and personal narrative of the first African American woman executed in modern times, which was produced by Kennedy and directed by Liz Garbus; and *A Boy's Life* (2003), the story of a troubled seven-year-old from Mississippi. Most recently, Kennedy expanded her reach internationally focusing on the effects of AIDS on individuals living in different parts of the world in the five-part documentary *Pandemic: Facing AIDS* (2003).

In the summer of 2006, the series showcased *Baghdad ER* by Jon Alpert, a provocative and well-respected investigative journalist and documentarian and founder of Downtown Community Television, who has produced a number of documentaries for *America Undercover* over the years, including *One Year in a Life of Crime* (1989) and *Rape: Cries from the Heartland* (1992). The series also continues to keep up with topics usually reserved for reality television, with documentaries such as *Plastic Disasters* (2006), which focuses on "plastic surgeries gone wrong," and *The Virtual Corpse* (2003), which covers the dissection of the body of a former killer in the name of science. And in a rather surprising but telling turn, A&E announced in February 2006 that it would be re-broadcasting seventeen episodes of *America Undercover,* including *Skinheads USA: Soldiers of the Race War* (1993) and *The Execution of Wanda Jean.*

Sheila Nevins had once singled out this particular network as a venue where her documentaries were too "spicy" to air. It would seem that over the years, more and more cable channels and broadcast networks are starting to follow HBO's lead in trying to present nonfiction television with an edge. Yet, very few of them contain the socially progressive or investigative bent that has characterized HBO's longstanding approach to documentaries. As a result, *America Undercover* remains a unique yet highly influential television series that both contributes to the branding of HBO as a quality network and helps determine the direction of American independent documentary production.

Notes

Sections of this essay have appeared in "'I Think We Need a New Name for It': The Meeting of Documentary and Reality Television," in Susan Murray and Laurie Ouellette, eds., *Reality Television: Remaking Television Culture* (New York: NYU Press, 2005), 40–56.

1. Paul Lieberman, "Confessions of an HBO Original," *Los Angeles Times,* 28 May 2000, C3; Lieberman, "Confessions of an HBO Original," C3; John Clark, "Calendar," *Los Angeles Times,* 4 February 2001, C2.

2. Clark, "Calendar," C2.

3. Ed Kirchdoerffer, "Flash, Cash and the Ratings Dash: HBO's Sheila Nevins," *Realscreen,* 1 September 1998, 33.

4. Diane Werts, "It's not Just about Sex: Sheila Nevins' Original Programming for HBO Goes to Extremes," *Newsday,* 11 March 2001, D11.

5. *P.O.V.* Web site, at http://www.pbs.org/pov/utils/aboutpov.html.

6. Lieberman, "Confessions of an HBO Original," C3.

7. Ann Marsh, "*Soldiers* Follows Violent Opponents of Abortion," *Los Angeles Times,* 31 March 2001, F12.

8. Jim Rutenberg, "Seamy or Serious, It's Now Center Stage," *New York Times,* 21 March 2001, E1.

9. Rutenberg, "Seamy or Serious, It's Now Center Stage," E1.

10. "About HBO Documentaries," on the HBO Web site, at http://www.hbo.com/docs/about/.

11. "Undercover Wins Spotlight," *Boston Globe,* 9 March 2001, C4.

12. "Undercover Wins Spotlight," C4.

13. Lieberman, "Confessions of an HBO Original," C3.

14. Mike Reynolds, "Passionate Programmer; From Strippers to Sept. 11, HBO's Sheila Nevins Tells It Like It Is," *Multichannel News,* 28 January 2002, 18W.

15. Kirchdoerffer, "Flash, Cash and the Ratings Dash," 33.

16. Brian Winston decries this sort of thinking, considering this willingness

to investigate sexuality and nudity—which he calls "docu-glitz"—cable's "'un-public service' contribution to the documentary form." Brian Winston, *Lies, Damn Lies and Documentaries* (London: BFI, 2000), 48.

17. Kirchdoerffer, "Flash, Cash and the Ratings Dash," 33.

18. Andrew Willenstein, "HBO Docu Unit Mulling Series; Focus on Continuing Characters," *Hollywood Reporter,* 30 October 2003, 4.

SIXTEEN

Erotica

Jeffrey P. Jones

From HBO's early days as a nascent satellite channel to its current status as the most profitable network in television history, the one form of programming that has seemingly fulfilled the promise inherent in the network's popular branding campaign, "It's Not TV, It's HBO," is erotica. As a subscription channel, HBO has taken advantage of its ability to show nudity and sexual situations without fear of censorship. Initially airing uncut R-rated Hollywood movies but quickly offering spicier fare, the network has routinely banked on sexually oriented programming as an inexpensive yet enormously popular form of programming that contributes to the brand's distinctiveness. Through its erotic offerings, HBO has indeed supplied content that cannot be found on network television.

Yet in many ways, its erotic fare—from early usage of soft-core "B" movie imports to the more recent reliance on sex-centered documentary specials and reality series—*is* very much TV. Although critics want to point to HBO's erotica as a crass form of titillation, exploitation, sensationalism, or outright pornography that panders to its subscriber base, a cursory look across television programming suggests that HBO has no monopoly in these regards (see, for instance, Fox's *The Howard Stern Show* [1987–], MTV's *Undressed* [1999–2002], *Flavor of Love* [VH1, 2006], the FX network, music videos, *Real TV* [1997–2001], or the soundtrack to the poorly scrambled Playboy Channel appearing on an empty cable channel near you). Although HBO can be more overt in its use of language or displays of nudity than other channels, the forms of erotic programming it has offered over the last thirty years are perhaps best seen as a fun-house mirror, reflecting what has also appeared elsewhere on television.

In the late 1970s and early 1980s, for instance, the airing of soft-core imports such as *Emmanuelle* (1974) and *Lady Chatterley's Lover* (1981) positioned the network somewhere between the edited R-rated movies shown on superstations TBS and WGN and the overt pornographic material shown on the competing subscription network, the Playboy Channel.[1] As the network began changing its emphasis from movie channel to original programmer in the early 1990s, it shifted these movies—originally packaged as "HBO After Dark"—to Cinemax. In the process, the move earned HBO's sister network the popular moniker "Skinemax." When reality television began finding its footing in an expanded cable TV universe in the early 1990s with shows such as *Cops* (1989–) and *The Real World* (1992), HBO offered its own reality specials in the form of *Real Sex* (1990–) and *Taxicab Confessions* (1995–), resulting in two of the network's longest running series.

The success of uncut feature films on HBO and its subscription-only competitors, as well as the popularity of such material on home video, had paved the way for the social acceptance of sexual programming as televisual fare.[2] Finally, when unscripted reality programming consumed network television at the turn of the century with the likes of *Big Brother* (2000–) and *Temptation Island* (2001–3), HBO took voyeurism one step further with its more bona fide peek into locations of naughtiness—*G-String Divas* (2000; a strip club) and *Cathouse: The Series* (2005; a brothel).[3] In short, although HBO is widely known for its erotic fare, this programming has never been too far removed from other television offerings. Network executives position the programming as normal and "respectable" material that "curious" viewers can enjoy (or at worst, put up with). Like other television programming, then, it is fit for the living room (though probably after the kids are ushered off to bed).

Or at least that has been the philosophy of the person most singularly responsible for producing HBO's erotic programming over the last twenty years—Sheila Nevins, president of HBO documentary and family programming.[4] As the network transformed itself from a movie channel to an original programmer, it was Nevins who financed and executive produced erotic documentaries (as detailed in this volume in the overview of part 4 and in chapter 15). Beginning with *Real Sex* in 1990, Nevins has provided a stream of erotic documentary programming that has included *Taxicab Confessions, Sex Bytes* (1997–), *G-String Divas, Cathouse* (2002), *Cathouse 2: Back in the Saddle* (2003), *Cathouse: The Series, Pornucopia: Going Down in the Valley* (2004), *Thinking XXX* (2004), *Shock Video* (1993–), *Hookers at the Point* (2002), and *The Sex Inspectors* (2004). "When HBO started," she notes, "R-rated movies were the reason people watched HBO. So I thought, why can't there be R-rated reality?"[5] She also justified this move toward sexual programming as one of the network's distinctive markers of original programming by noting, "At HBO we knew we could push [the] limits of comedy. There was no reason not to push the form of 'reality' [as] far as we could, into a certain kind of sexual explicitness that was legitimate and safe and funny."[6]

Yet Nevins vehemently resists charges by critics that her inclusion of sex in the spectrum of reality programming amounts to exploitation or pandering to audiences. "It seems very false to say we have a license to do this, and that's why we do it. We do it with grace, with taste, with dignity."[7] For Nevins, portrayals of sex are not a "dirty" endeavor. "I don't think we've ever been vulgar in our programming," she contends, "other than maybe when we're showing man's inhumanity to man [in the more serious documentaries the network airs]. We may have been energetic when it came to depicting sex, but not in a way that was ever harmful."[8] Showing sex provides a balance to HBO's documentary programming because life itself, she argues, requires balance. "I'm Chekhovian. I believe it's dark and rainy outside almost all the time and that sex is a big laugh and we're too serious about what's fun and we're not honest enough about what's sad."[9] Similarly, she notes that "I have respect for people who take a freer attitude toward life, who enjoy sex, who laugh, who aren't cerebral. . . . There's a balance going on. We're all divided somewhere between our brains and our groins."[10]

That balance, though, is as much about business as it is a view of life. HBO's profane programming also provides a balance with those documentary offerings that are more serious and profound. "I watch 10 hours of someone taking drugs or something like that, I need to watch 'Taxicab Confessions,'" she says. "This is a business, and it's successful as long as we have a balance. As long as that balance works, I'll do the sex stuff." But she also quickly adds the second important reason for balance: "It's money-efficient."[11] The efficiencies come into play because shows such as *Real Sex* and *Taxicab Confessions* are often cheaper to produce (averaging $500,000 per one-hour episode) than some of the more serious documentaries (which can cost as much as $1.5 million per hour), yet tend to garner much higher ratings than the programs that win awards. Spike Lee's documentary about the 1963 church bombing in Birmingham, Alabama, *4 Little Girls,* for instance, brought in 874,000 viewers during its premiere in February 1998, while *Shock Video 2* garnered 1.45 million viewers and *Real Sex 19* was seen by 2.3 million people during the same month.[12] Erotic fare is inexpensive to produce, requires no promotion, and appears in a late night time slot. Nevertheless, it can garner stronger ratings than some of the network's more expensive dramatic and comedic series (*Pornucopia,* for instance, averaged 1.6 million viewers per episode, whereas *Entourage* [2004–] garnered 1.3 million in 2005).[13] Furthermore, it is this imbalance between cost and popularity that also contributes to Nevins's emphasis on providing distinctive programming that viewers believe is worth paying for and that can't be found anywhere else on television. As she notes, "Extremes are interesting. Extremes are what my audience is paying for."[14]

But HBO's erotic offerings, as a special genre of documentary, also assist in the network's efforts to craft its "look" or special appeal. Nevins admits that "there's an HBO spin, though I can't define it." Instead, erotica meets her informal test for what should constitute HBO programming. "I ask, 'Could I see this on free TV? Is it something unexpected? Is there something surprising? Does it have legs?'"[15] Erotica, of course, fits the bill nicely with its unexpected subject matter, which surprises viewers with "activities" that are openly portrayed on HBO but only alluded to elsewhere on television. Furthermore, such programming "has legs." In industry lingo, erotic programming is "evergreen." It never gets old and can be repeated in numerous venues without seeming dated, while always drawing big audience numbers.[16] In short, erotic programming fits within the network's mandate, which has led Nevins to take chances and experiment with this form of programming.

Such experimentation began in 1990 with the program *Real Sex.* Each program is shot as an individual, stand-alone documentary that is shown numerous times throughout the year (with three new releases per year). Produced and directed by Patti Kaplan, a former professor of art at the City University of New York, the hour-long program (which Chris Albrecht described as a "nude magazine" show) is composed of five segments that depict the often bizarre yet humorous ways in which people explore sex and sexual practices.[17] Sample segments include a visit to a vibrator workshop; the Miss Nude World contest; Penis Puppeteers in New York; a sex circus in New Orleans; London's annual Sex Maniacs' Ball; a couple who sell custom-designed whips; another couple who engage in bondage and discipline games; a female nude-wrestling competition; a visit with Germany's "Sex Shop Granny"; a factory that produces male sex dolls; and Annie Sprinkle's one-woman sex show. Between each segment are street interviews with pedestrians explaining their own experiences or attitudes toward sexual activities. Overall, the programs display little in the way of explicit sex (no intercourse or erections), but offer what one commentator described as a "healthy curiosity combined with a jaunty pluralism."[18] That is, they typically provide a peek into the diversity of sexual activities and sex-related businesses that people engage in throughout the United States and around the world, with an emphasis that ranges from the unusual to the bizarre.

Both Nevins and Kaplan situate the origins of the series in the late 1980s and early 1990s, describing its intentions as a response to the AIDS crisis. "When we did the first 'Eros in America,'" Nevins notes (referring to her first sexually oriented documentary for Cinemax in 1985), "there was no AIDS, and it was a different kind of exploration. Now the need to be funny and to have a good time with sex, and to be free . . . is much more important because of all the terror that surrounds it."[19] Kaplan agrees, saying, "I think a lot of the eccentricity that's available in sexual activities today—the kinds of workshops, the kinds of sex, the kind of no-contact sex—have been spawned in this era of AIDS. Whether it's masturbation workshops or peep shows or telephone sex or computers, there are more ways for people to get turned on than by promiscuity. That eccentricity is part of what makes it funny."[20]

Kaplan and Nevins also characterize what they document as a form of expression, and they both embrace the freedoms associated with that expression—through sex or simply the ability to display it uncensored on television. "This kind of freedom of expression," Kaplan contends, "is as important as any other freedom of expression. And it has to be treated respectfully."[21] Likewise, Nevins argues, "These are real people who are making livings but are enjoying themselves with their sexual freedom. There is a whole subculture in this country of escapees from Puritanism who want to tell their stories."[22] And telling stories, especially about people or subjects that have traditionally been relegated to the margins of television, is central to Nevins's conception of the freedom *she* has as a television programmer to facilitate such storytelling. The lack of censorship in subscription TV, she notes, has meant that "people could realize their stories to their full extent and where they could take them, whether the stories were happy or sad or violent or tragic or sexual."[23] And it is this unrestricted continuum of life's stories that shapes her approach to offering both the profound and the profane as different yet related forms of documentary programming.

Yet the manifestation of these stories as documentary narratives has often resulted in an alternative kind of nonfictional narrative.[24] Kaplan's intentions are less to expose or explain sexual practices (and the people who engage in them) as much as to allow a performative space for their display. *Real Sex* takes viewers into subcultures they may never have known existed. Indeed, there is an element of "sexual tourism," bordering on voyeurism, in the films of the *Real Sex* series. Viewers may be bounced between subjective positions of fascination, amusement, and disbelief ("Are people really aroused by doing *this* with *that?*"). The films rarely interrogate their subjects, who are ultimately of less interest than the creative or "forbidden" sexual enterprises that they are engaging in. The result, therefore, is what Bill Nichols calls the "scopophilic" pleasure, or pleasure in looking (a form of spectatorship more typical of fiction film, as opposed to documentary's tendency toward "epistephilic" pleasure, or pleasure in knowing).[25] Nevertheless, the films are not pornographic, for they are not intended for viewer arousal (and rarely take this kind of approach).[26] Instead, the defining aspect of the show is a window into a world of sexual experience and expressions typically beyond the realm of viewer practices.

Yet, as quoted above, Sheila Nevins sees these films as a means for the people in them to tell their stories. The one HBO series in this subgenre that best fulfills that function is the Emmy Award–winning *Taxicab Confessions*. Based on the surreptitious filming of unsuspecting cab patrons, *Taxicab Confessions* provides a unique forum for the intimate first-person narratives of ordinary people's lives. The director-producer

Taxicab Confessions reveals the innermost thoughts and secrets of actual taxicab passengers using lipstick-size cameras hidden throughout the moving vehicle. Photograph by Will Hart.

brothers Joe and Harry Gantz created the long-running series in 1995 by embedding five lipstick-sized cameras and recording equipment in several New York City taxicabs, then watching as late night riders bared their hearts, souls, and (at times) their bodies to the sympathetic drivers. The result is what many critics have claimed are "unexpectedly deep and poetic and moving" stories about ordinary people in their own words.[27]

First filmed in New York for three seasons, the show moved to Las Vegas for seven seasons after the New York Taxi and Limousine Commission under Mayor Rudolph Giuliani proclaimed the show "unsafe" and denied the producers a permit. After Giuliani left office, however, the show returned to New York in 2003, where it continues to be filmed. Each hour-long episode typically includes nine cab rides, the best of the approximately five hundred rides recorded in a given season.[28] Perhaps most surprising is that between 65 and 75 percent of the people recorded agree to let their stories air. Nevins surmises that "the people who really let their heart out tend to be the ones who willingly sign the release because they want someone to know their story."[29] Harry Gantz believes that "most people really want to tell their stories. The cab has turned out to be the perfect place to capture this."[30] He is correct in this regard, whether because of the intimacy of the small space, the limited eye contact with the driver, a sympathetic driver/listener, or simply that it is late at night and the tired riders let down their guard as they get in "off the cold streets into a warm cab or off the warm streets into a cool cab."[31]

Whatever the reasons for their telling, the stories can be bizarre, painful, tragic, sad, hilarious, uplifting, and compelling (so much so that Nevins contends the program "is possibly the most spiritual and the most sensual show on television"[32]). Viewers have witnessed a woman describing how her boyfriend with bipolar disorder died in her lap from an overdose of cocaine while the police looked on; a woman who performs solo-sex acts on the Internet but rarely sleeps with her fiancé; a lonely thirty-five-year-old virgin who describes giving oral sex to a man while on vacation but not knowing whether he achieved orgasm, despite seeing white stains on her sweater; a hooker who reveals that her partner is a burn victim but doesn't want to marry him for fear of breaking his heart; a trio of women describing toe sucking and anal sex, including one who claims her G-spot is in her anus; a man who tells of how his father murdered his mother; a woman who propositions the female cab driver; and a young pimp and his friends who describe how to recruit hookers. In the eleventh episode of *Taxicab Confessions* (2005), the last ride consists of two young women and a man who take off their tops and sing "I Will Survive." As one commentator noted about this scene, "It's no 'Girls Gone Wild' moment, or even remotely sexual, but just a sudden bit of Eden in the New York night." Nevins extends the observation by noting the beauty of this scene as an especially joyous slice of life that is the forté of the documentary: "You just want to cry for their happiness. I mean, that doesn't happen, couldn't happen, in a movie, could it? And they love each other, and they like the driver and they like New York. It's so full of life, it's so invigorating in such a depressing world. We have so little to believe in, people are constantly betraying us—so to see simple people you can . . . revere on some level, it's worth it."[33]

Whereas the documentary movement known as cinema verité maintains that observational documentary catches "life unawares," the known presence of the camera is still an influential factor in the subjects' performances.[34] In *Taxicab Confessions,* however, people are truly unaware of the camera, even though their recorded behavior results in a particular version of what Bill Nichols calls the "performative" mode of documentary. According to Nichols, such films portray knowledge and understanding of the world as "concrete and embodied, based on the specificities of personal experience."[35] There is a rawness and honesty to these confessional monologues that is particularly appealing, regardless of whether the sometimes unbelievable stories are actually true. As one critic put it, "It doesn't matter whether the story is 'true,' only that it's true for the person telling it. If he or she puts up a front, it's only the everyday sort of front we all use with one another—in other words, an authentic front. Under these terms, even those who lie, lie honestly."[36]

The embodied experience of the confessors who unsuspectingly share their stories with the driver—and ultimately the viewing audience—is central to the appeal of these programs. We meet these characters briefly, but are left wanting more. As one critic has asserted, "the profane becomes profound as face-value assumptions are continually confounded by unexpected depth."[37] It is perhaps indicative of such filmic encounters that these films, as Nichols argues about performative documentaries in general, "generate a feeling of tension between the film as a representation and the world that stands beyond it. . . . Film represents the world in ways that always leave more unsaid than said, that confess to a failure to exhaust a topic through the mere act of representing it. The world is of a greater order of magnitude than any representation, but a representation can heighten our sense of this discrepancy. Experience does not boil down to explanations. It always exceeds them."[38] And it is here that *Taxicab Confessions* offers so much more than shock, titillation, or voyeuristic pleasure. Each episode of the series provides a particularly arresting view of humanity, and as with most intimate encounters (however brief they may be), allows the viewer to contemplate such humanity long after that view escapes our eyes.

Perhaps a different view of humanity has emerged in the stories HBO tells with its erotic programming of late. The network has extended one of its documentary brands by transforming it into a reality series. *Cathouse* debuted as an *America Undercover* documentary film that featured the Moonlite Bunny Ranch, a legal brothel outside of Reno, Nevada. Produced by Patti Kaplan (the creator of *Real Sex* and *G-String Divas*), the documentary had a sequel, *Cathouse 2: Back in the Saddle.* But in 2005, HBO transformed the concept into a reality series, *Cathouse: The Series.* As Nevins explained, "We're trying to reinvent ourselves. We've always been more like an anthology, but now we're trying to have continuing characters going through continuing stories."[39]

Aside from the unusual location for a reality show, *Cathouse: The Series* adopts many of the techniques that have become standard in the genre. The show features a regular cast of characters, including the ranch's male owner, the madam of the house, and a crew of "working girls." And as with most reality programming, the central feature of the show is talk (more than sex). The show examines the relationships between these characters—the owner and the girls, the owner and the madam, the girls and their clients, and so on—by observing casual interactions as well as incorporating edited interviews with each of them (including the clients). And every week, the show demonstrates some new aspect of life at the ranch. In one episode, for instance, we meet prostitute twins who are just "dying" to have sex with the owner. Another week we watch a porn star train the girls in the best way to perform oral sex. Other episodes include a girl demonstrating her shaving techniques, another girl demonstrating how to use sex toys on men, and yet another showing how to fulfill fantasy fetishes.

The series differs from its earlier manifestation as a documentary, however, by taking the viewers into the bedrooms to watch the sex (albeit in almost cartoonish ways by fast-forwarding through much of the "action" so as not to resemble pornography). The show is also replete with (fake) boobs, butts, and bleached-blond hair, all of which ultimately become rather banal (if not grotesque) after extended viewing. Although the viewer is transported to a place that he or she will likely never visit, the viewer also leaves without caring too much for the people encountered there. Perhaps due to the presence of the camera, the residents offer a decidedly romantic view of life at the ranch. Much of the "narrative" the working girls and owner weave couches the interactions there through the familiar and normalizing framework of "girlfriends," "dating," "jealousy," and even "marriage" (as opposed to having a job, working hard, making money, experiencing boredom, and exhibiting disdain for the management, as is the more common narrative in other employment situations). We really don't hear much about the unerotic nature of having sex with fat, slovenly men either (to name just one unattractive aspect of life there).

The series has included eleven thirty-minute episodes, and as with the network's other sexually oriented programming, continues to draw large audiences (for example, 1.5 million viewers for the show's finale). As with several other sex-related shows that have appeared as "best of" compilations, moreover, the series is also primed to enter the lucrative aftermarket of DVD retail sales through HBO Home Video.[40] With *Cathouse: The Series,* HBO has wholeheartedly embraced the genre of reality programming that has preoccupied much of contemporary television. The question, however, is whether HBO, in providing viewers exposure to the "reality" of the world's oldest profession, is offering programming that is truly distinctive and "groundbreaking" (as the latest branding line suggests) or simply something far more routine and predictable.

In summary, the airing of erotica on HBO—from uncensored movies to documentaries and reality series—will continue to be a lucrative business strategy for the network, primarily because of low production costs, the enormous popularity of this genre, and the brand distinctiveness it offers the network. It also plays a role in tempering reactions to overtly erotic depictions appearing elsewhere on the network—namely original dramatic programming such as *Sex and the City* (1998–2004) and *Tell Me You Love Me* (2007–). Erotica will also continue to have a place in HBO's documentary output as long as Sheila Nevins is in charge. As we have seen, she believes that erotic documentaries provide a welcome antidote to both the seriousness and sadness the world has to offer, while also believing that HBO should play a leading role in providing these lighthearted and frivolous narratives to television viewers. HBO's erotic programming ranges from poignant to pathetic with each and every stop in between. In the end, the network offers its viewers an array of stories including sexual activities and nonsexual intimate encounters that are appealingly different from programming found elsewhere on television. And in this regard, especially, erotica is and has been a defining feature of HBO.

Notes

1. As with the diffusion of other new communication technologies—most notably the VCR and the Internet—access to pornography in the privacy of one's home was a significant factor for some early adopters of cable television. See Jonathan Coopersmith, "Pornography, Videotape, and the Internet," *IEEE Technology and Society Magazine* (spring 2000): 27–34. Although the Playboy Channel provided such access for households where pornography wasn't a moral issue, HBO's movies could be seen as a more "respectable" means of obtaining racy yet unobjectionable programming in discerning households. One should also remember the historical context of satellite television's entry into the market. Movies such as *Deep Throat* (1972) and *The Story of O* (1975) had actually appeared in mainstream movie theaters by the mid-1970s, as American audiences briefly flirted with a move away from Puritanism in its visual arts.

2. Chris Albrecht, HBO senior vice president of original programming at that time, put it best when he said, "I think uncut feature films appearing on cable and home video have broadened what people consider acceptable on the small screen. There's nothing new about people's interest in sex. But there's more availability now, and more tolerance." Mark Lorando, "The Blue Tube," *Times-Picayune* [New Orleans], 22 June 1995, E1.

3. Nevins admits, "*G-String Divas* was our *Temptation Island*, except we shot real people working in a real situation." Mike Reynolds, "Passionate Programmer; From Strippers to Sept. 11, HBO's Sheila Nevins Tells It Like It Is," *Multichannel News*, 28 January 2002, 18W.

4. Nevins recognizes this when she distinguishes between the different documentary forms she produces and where they are placed in the marketplace. "Some things need spectacle and some things need living rooms and some survive in both. I'm not going to put *Real Sex* or *Autopsy* [in cinemas]." Reynolds, "Passionate Programmer," 18W.

5. Pat Saperstein, "Brothels to Bush, Docs Cover Wide Span," *Variety*, 4 November 2002, A14.

6. Scott Williams, "HBO's 'Real Sex' . . . Now THAT's 'Reality' Programming," *Associated Press*, 16 March 1994, PM Cycle, at http://www.lexis-nexis.com (accessed September 4, 2006).

7. James Sterngold, "HBO Programmer Likes to Kindle Both Heat and Light," *New York Times*, 15 April 1998, E2.

8. Ray Richmond, "Hard-Hitting Docus Rack Up Awards," *Variety,* 3 November 1997, 42.

9. Jim Rutenberg, "Seamy or Serious, It's Now Center Stage," *New York Times,* 21 March 2001, E1.

10. Sterngold, "HBO Programmer," E2.

11. Ibid.

12. Ibid.

13. These audience figures, compiled by Nielsen Media Research and reported in the trade press, reflect season-to-date averages for both series. See James Hibberd, "'Cathouse' Not a Secret to Viewers," *Television Week,* 11 July 2005, 6.

14. Julie Salamon, "Nevins Rules," *New York Times Magazine,* 3 March 2002, sec. 6, 66.

15. Saperstein, "Brothels to Bush," A14.

16. For instance, referring to the *G-String Divas* series, Nevins notes, "They play as well in replay as they did during their premieres." Reynolds, "Passionate Programmer," 18W.

17. Lorando, "The Blue Tube," E1, 8.

18. John Koch, "HBO's Shameless 'Real Sex' and Cheesecake," *Boston Globe,* 13 February 1993, Living, 32.

19. Williams, "HBO's 'Real Sex.'"

20. Ibid.

21. Ibid.

22. Rutenberg, "Seamy or Serious," E1.

23. Ed Kirchdoerffer, "Flash, Cash and the Ratings Dash: HBO's Sheila Nevins," *Realscreen,* 1 September 1998, 33.

24. See, for instance, the review of the program in John Koch, "HBO's Shameless 'Real Sex,'" 32.

25. Bill Nichols, *Representing Reality* (Bloomington: Indiana University Press, 1991), 178.

26. I agree with Bill Nichols that arousal is a defining feature of pornography, where "the basic unit is a situation or event exemplifying sexual engagement between actors/characters, organized and photographed from the perspective of an ideal spectator." Nichols, *Representing Reality,* 214. Patti Kaplan also distinguishes the function of these films, noting in reference to another sex-related documentary series she produced for HBO, "That is not to say that 'G-String Divas' is a show to whack off to. It's more of an educational-titillating-docu-soap." Christina Oxenberg, "Hellfire and Khakis," *Salon.com,* 23 August 2000, at http://archive.salon.com/sex/feature/2000/08/23/hellfire/index1.html.

27. Robert Lloyd, "Fares of the Heart," *Los Angeles Times,* 30 January 2005, E28.

28. The producers tape five hundred rides, then ask three hundred riders to sign permission release forms. Around two hundred typically agree, with half of those conversations being good enough for consideration. Twenty-five are then

edited for airing, and roughly nine make the cut. Alan Bash, "How Cab 'Confessions' Gets Intimate Fare," *USA Today,* 5 December 1995, 3D.

29. Robert Lloyd, "Fares of the Heart," E28.

30. Bash, "How Cab 'Confessions' Gets Intimate Fare," 3D.

31. Harry Gantz, quoted in Lloyd, "Fares of the Heart," E28.

32. Lloyd, "Fares of the Heart," E28.

33. Ibid.

34. It is hard to argue that the camera has had little to no effect on the "performances" of main "characters" such as Bob Dylan in *Don't Look Back* (1967), James Carville in *The War Room* (1993), or Little Edie in *Grey Gardens* (1975).

35. Bill Nichols, *Introduction to Documentary* (Bloomington: Indiana University Press, 2001), 131.

36. Lloyd, "Fares of the Heart," E28.

37. Matt Roush, "'Taxicab Confessions' Takes a Right Turn to Gritty Reality," *USA Today,* 13 January 1995, 3D.

38. Nichols, *Introduction to Documentary,* 158.

39. Andrew Wallenstein, "HBO Docu Unit Mulling Series, Focus on Continuing Characters," *Hollywood Reporter,* 30 October 2003, at http://www.lexis-nexis.com (accessed September 4, 2006).

40. Anne Sherber, "Cable Shows Corner the Vid Market; A&E, HBO Building on Success at Retail," *Billboard,* 12 April 1997, at http://www.lexis-nexis.com (accessed May 28, 2005).

SEVENTEEN

Theatricals

Carolyn Anderson

HBO's branding slogan—"It's Not TV, It's HBO"—is never more fulfilled than through its production and distribution of documentary and
narrative films exhibited on big screens nationwide. Building on a general environment of robust independent feature production, a developed
network of high-profile festivals that serve as launching pads for indie
films and filmmakers, an unparalleled resurgence of interest in feature-
length documentaries, and a concomitant increase in recent commercial
possibilities for theatrical distribution of documentaries, HBO has
extended its already impressive reach across media types into theatrical
film production and distribution. Because it need not operate under the
censorship restraints of advertiser-supported networks yet has the secure
exhibition base of cablecast, HBO occupies an enviable position in its
ability to produce theatrical films with risky content or nontraditional
form. It can simultaneously use the influence of its brand to nurture the
work of both first-time filmmakers and experienced directors moving
into new types of filmmaking. HBO thus repurposes these feature-
length documentary and narrative films in a number of ways. It first
introduces them at prestigious film festivals in the United States and
abroad. It next distributes them outside the television industry through
HBO Films Theatrical Releasing. Then it telecasts them on one or more
of the HBO-affiliated networks. Subsequently, it syndicates them internationally, before finally releasing them worldwide through HBO DVD
and Video.[1] At each stage, HBO primes the audience for the ensuing
step in the distribution process. The rotation begins at the highest-pres-
tige point (festival screenings) and ends at the site of the greatest profit
potential (the DVD and video markets).

HBO's first venture into theatrical distribution began in 2002 and was centered on documentary features, most of which were produced or coproduced by HBO. This extension into theatrical distribution of documentaries bolstered HBO's already substantial reputation for outstanding documentary programming, a reputation that continues to grow. In 2004, Anne Thompson expressed an opinion shared by many in the film industry: "Over the last twenty-five years, few people have done more to propel documentaries to popularity than Sheila Nevins, [then] executive vice-president of HBO and Cinemax for original programming, documentaries, and family."[2] Hired as HBO's director of documentary programming in 1979, Nevins was named president of HBO documentary and family programming in 2005. By 2006, she had supervised or assigned seventeen short and feature documentary projects that earned Academy Awards. In addition, she received the Lifetime Achievement Award from the International Documentary Association in 1998 for her imaginative leadership in supporting original documentary productions. "Widely regarded as the most powerful executive in television documentary," Nevins responds to projects that provoke a "skipped heartbeat," and reveal a surprise contained within the ordinary. She looks for programs that demonstrate the remarkable dialogue of real people interacting. The executive producer compares HBO's association with Cinemax to "a little art house . . . [and a] mini–New Line studio for documentaries" that provides "consistent financing for low-budget docs or co-productions."[3]

Most of the documentaries produced or distributed theatrically by HBO address contemporary topics, and the stories are typically set in the United States. Two memorable exceptions to this pattern are *The Agronomist* (2003), directed by Academy Award–winning Hollywood veteran Jonathan Demme, and *Favela Rising* (2005), codirected by relative newcomers Jeff Zimbalist and Matt Mochary. In both films, political issues and social inequities are explored through the personal stories of charismatic figures. Demme, a progressive activist himself, has long been a supporter of land reform in Haiti, and he knew and greatly admired Haitian radio owner Jean Dominique and his wife, the journalist and fellow activist Michele Montas. *The Agronomist* is Demme's third documentary project set in Haiti and clearly a labor of love, with footage compiled from hundreds of hours of conversation with the ebullient Dominique, photographed over a decade, including footage shot when the exiled couple resided in New York City in the early 1990s.

Jean Dominque, an upper-class, light-skinned Creole, was educated in France as an agronomist and formed his attachment to peasant culture through his early professional work. Later, he devoted himself to the nurturing of free speech, the peasant Left, and the use of Creole as the broadcast language on Dominique's Radio Haiti-Inter. Demme documents these noble and eventually fatal attachments in a compelling piece that is unflinching in its condemnation of the role of the United States in Haitian politics. The film ends with the unstoppable Montas rebroadcasting one of her husband's most moving speeches after Dominique's assassination in 2000. Not widely seen theatrically, but telecast on HBO and distributed on DVD, *The Agronomist* brings to its varied audiences a glimpse into the horrors of Haitian politics, a vivid portrait of two admirable activists, and an opportunity to enjoy the pulsating music of the popular Haitian composer Wyclef Jean.

Whereas world music exists as an important background presence in *The Agronomist, Favela Rising* (distributed, but not produced, by HBO) foregrounds indigenous music, focusing on those who create it and its powerful impact on the lives of the dispossessed. An interest in documenting successful grass-roots movements in Latin America led coproducers/directors Zimbalist and Mochary to the slums of Rio de Janeiro and to Anderson Sa, a former drug-trafficker who had joined the "mastermind" Jose Junior in starting a community movement in Vigario Geral, a dangerous squatter settlement on the outskirts of the Brazilian metropolis.[4] Seeking an alternative to crime for himself and others, Sa operated as the man on the mean streets, mobilizing disaffected, and often hopeless, young favela residents through the musical collective AfroReggae and its inspired and politically successful use of Afro-Brazilian dance, theater, and bands. The documentary features interviews with the dynamic Sa, his fiancée, and other favela residents, supported by direct cinema footage of musical workshops and performances and shocking archival footage of the violence residents endure from both the drug gangs and the brutal military police. Among the most memorable scenes of life in the streets are those shot by favela youngsters who had been given digital cinematography instruction by the documentarians. *Favela*

Rising presents glimmers of hope amidst desperate circumstances, functioning as both a general investigation into the successful AfroReggae movement and a biographical portrait of a remarkable man. In mid-production, Sa was paralyzed from the neck down in a surfing accident, a seeming tragedy that prompted the filmmakers to shift focus to the activist's personal struggle. Sustained by support from his community, Sa experienced what to some was a miraculous recovery that enabled him to continue his performance and leadership work.

Favela Rising was an immediate success, earning deserved cheers from the Tribeca Film Festival audience at its world premiere, at which Zimbalist and Mochary were named best emerging documentary filmmakers. Other awards followed, most notably the 2006 International Documentary Achievement Award. *Favela Rising*'s move into the rarefied world of theatrical distribution is probably typical of how independently produced documentaries attract and negotiate an HBO connection. Several theatrical and broadcast distributors showed interest in *Favela Rising,* but HBO was especially attractive to the filmmakers because of its reputation and audience reach.[5] The downside of such an alliance was HBO's insistence on a TV premiere *before* a theatrical release. HBO executive Sheila Nevins played the lead role in these negotiations. She supported the film and the larger interests of the filmmakers, was kind and helpful, and was strongly committed to her vision of what was best for HBO. A "day and date" agreement was forged in which publicity and advertising were combined for the broadcast and theatrical releases of the film. All reviews mentioned both the HBO/ Cinemax broadcast date and the Think Film theatrical debut. These influential brands worked together to get *Favela Rising* short-listed for the Best Feature Documentary Academy Award. By the summer of 2006, *Favela Rising* was made available to multiple audiences: it aired as part of the *Reel Life* series on Cinemax; was exhibited in movie theaters, museums, and other venues internationally; and was released on HBO DVD and video.

For generations, documentary filmmakers have grappled with the challenge of filming "the other" without the taint of exploitation or condescension. Concern for this dilemma has accelerated in recent decades, resulting in a growing shift toward reflexive filmmaking, the embrace of various strategies of engagement, and the formation of multiple types of "first person" approaches. Executive producer Shelia Nevins's "respect for people telling their own stories" is reflected in many HBO-funded documentaries, including several successful projects that demonstrate a range of "first person" strategies.[6]

Alan Berliner's fifth documentary, *Wide Awake* (2006), continues the decidedly autobiographical approach of his earlier films. Berliner's nonfiction films are notable for their inventive editing and for their sense of humor, a rare quality in a genre distinguished by its seriousness. In *Wide Awake,* the fifty-year-old filmmaker confronts his lifelong insomnia, now rethought and intensified as he awaits the birth of his first child. Bringing his characteristic obsessiveness and self-deprecation to the topic of sleep deprivation, Berliner once again creates a charming meditation on the intricacies, frustrations, and pleasures of family life.

A far more somber look at the complications of family propels *Heir to an Execution: A Granddaughter's Story* (2003), in which Amy Meeropol attempts to discover what her paternal grandparents—Julius and Ethel Rosenberg—"were like as people." Structured as both a literal and a figurative journey, the film shows Meeropol talking with family members and finding many relatives still unwilling to talk about Julius and Ethel. She interviews elderly fellow travelers and friends of her grandparents and visits sites that demonize or honor the infamous couple. After the execution of Julius and Ethel for espionage, Meeropol's father and his younger brother were adopted by a leftist couple who raised them to believe that their birth parents were innocent victims of the Red Scare that poisoned post–World War II American political life. In her quest to know the personal story of her grandparents, Meeropol predictably re-examines their political lives. Surprises ensue, largely resulting from the release of long-withheld government documents that confirm Julius Rosenberg's involvement with the Soviet Union. These revelations are confirmed by frank comments made by Julius's close friends and fellow Communist Party members. Other documentaries have examined the hysteria surrounding the arrest, trial, conviction, and execution of the Rosenbergs, arguably with more historical and political insight, but this documentary succeeds in putting a human face on the couple. *Heir to an Execution* shows the sacrifices and consequences of Ethel Rosenberg's unflappable decision to stand by her husband, even if it meant dying in the electric chair. The film makes visible the pride the Rosenbergs' orphaned sons take in their parents' convictions, despite the traumas that the boys suffered.

Family secrets, the elusive nature of truth, and the consequences of parental decisions on their children's lives also lie at the center of *Capturing the Friedmans* (2004). Written and directed by newcomer Andrew Jarecki, the documentary depends on home movies and video shot by various members of the Friedman family before, during, and after the arrest and conviction of retired schoolteacher Arnold Friedman and his son Jesse on charges of sexual assault on boys who took computer classes in the Friedman home. Although the charges against the Friedmans were of a completely different nature than those against the Rosenbergs, once again we see an atmosphere of hysteria taking hold. In this film, a less-than-expert legal counsel for the defendants and unreliable witnesses are similarly manipulated by the prosecution. What results are situations in which a person *probably* guilty of some offenses is convicted of crimes he *probably* didn't commit. Even more unjustly, another family member—Friedman's son—is also found guilty, even though he is *probably* innocent of all charges.

Jarecki's integration of the Friedmans' extensive archive of home footage into *Capturing the Friedmans* makes family history and current family dynamics visible and presents most of the family as complicit in the documentary enterprise. David, the oldest of three sons, is deeply involved in self-documentation. At the time of Jarecki's filming, he is a middle-aged man working as a clown for children's parties. His intimate "diary" footage—which he says should not be seen by anyone except him—is included in the film, a decision that elicits concern—and perhaps doubt—regarding the web of motives that shape this (or any) documentary film.

Like *Wide Awake* and *Heir to an Execution, Born into Brothels: Calcutta's Red Light Kids* (2004) adopts the common reflexive technique of the filmmaker's voice-over narration. *Brothels* charts the efforts, frustrations, and successes of a London-born photographer—Zana Briski—who changes the lives of eight children born into the brothels of Calcutta by teaching them photography and becoming a champion of their work (later featured on an Amnesty International calendar). Because of a lack of access and out of a sense of respect for the families, the horrors of the brothel are more often described by the children than pictured by Briski and her codirector Ross Kauffman. We get to know the children by observing them in a variety of situations, by hearing their interview comments, and by seeing the photographs they take. The enthusiasm, charm, and genuine talent of the children infuses the film with hope, albeit a hopefulness tempered by the realities of how much effort, skill, and determination it takes to make even the slightest changes in the lives of children born into such systemic and oppressive desperation.

All six of these documentaries premiered at prestigious film festivals (*Born into Brothels, Capturing the Friedmans, Heir to an Execution,* and *Wide Awake* at Sundance; *The Agronomist* at Venice; *Favela Rising* at Tribeca). All were also well received by critics and won impressive recognitions (*Capturing the Friedmans* was an Academy Award nominee; *Born into Brothels* an Oscar winner). Moreover, they all had limited commercial releases in theaters, were screened in numerous other venues, and enjoyed modest financial success.[7] None approached the tremendous profit of Michael Moore's polemical *Fahrenheit 9/11* (2004) or of the whimsical French nature documentary *March of the Penguins/ La Marche de l'empereur* (2005).[8] And none introduced stylistic or conceptual changes in the documentary form to the extent of Errol Morris's groundbreaking *The Thin Blue Line* (1988) or Jonathan Caouette's surprising *Tarnation* (2003). However, each of these documentaries added to the prestige of the HBO brand, clearly demonstrating that HBO could operate successfully in theaters as well as TV.

Once HBO's ability to launch and distribute feature documentaries had been established, the next logical step in solidifying its position as a player in the international film world was to add narrative features to its production and distribution roster. In the summer of 2003, Dennis O'Connor, formerly vice president of marketing at United Artists, became head of the newly formed HBO Films Theatrical Releasing. This division entered into "an innovative distribution arrangement" with another Time Warner subsidiary, Fine Line Features, the specialty film arm of New Line.[9] The first release of the new outfit was the HBO-produced *American Splendor* (2003), an offbeat comedy inspired by a comic book of the same name, which is the autobiographical rendering of the mundane, frustrating life of its author, Harvey Pekar. In the 1970s, the success of the cranky *American Splendor* helped introduce a new subgenre of American comics for sophisticated readers. After being a cult antihero for almost three decades, Harvey Pekar was introduced to a wider audience in a biopic as unconventional as its subject.

Written and directed by the wife-and-husband team Shari Spring Berman and Robert Pulcini, *American Splendor* presents three Harveys: a cartoon version of Harvey in the film's animated sequences; a barely alive Harvey played by talented character actor Paul Giamatti; and "the real Harvey," the comic creator who appears in various sequences shot for the film and also in archival clips of hilarious visits to *Late Night with David Letterman*. A collection of fine actors portrays important figures in Harvey's banal life, most significantly Hope Davis, who plays author Joyce Brabner, Harvey's third wife; and Judah Friedlander as Pekar's file-room buddy at a Cleveland Veterans Affairs hospital. Amid the many jokes, *American Splendor* questions the distasteful tendencies of either ignoring the unattractive or turning them into ironic icons.

Fresh and creative, *American Splendor* charmed the film festival circuit, winning a prize for originality at Cannes, the Grand Jury Prize at Sundance, and a new directors' award from the New York and Toronto Film Critics associations. The film's screenplay and lead actor Paul Giamatti were also widely honored. Nevertheless, the quirky biopic grossed only $6 million in limited release, although its theatrical exposure paved the way for its TV debut, its subsequent syndication at home and abroad, and most significantly, the lucrative DVD market.

HBO Films Theatrical Releasing's second feature, *Elephant* (2003), alludes to the shocking killings at a Columbine, Colorado, high school and features a cast of nonprofessional teen actors. The title—never explained within the film—recalls a 1989 TV film by Alan Clarke "about Northern Ireland and the unmentionable, ubiquitous violence that is the 'elephant in the living room.'"[10] American critics were sharply divided in their responses. Many were angered when *Elephant* took Cannes by storm, winning the director's award, the Palme d'Or, and perhaps most controversially, the Cinema Prize of the French National Education System. Written, directed, and edited by Gus Van Sant with great daring and restraint, *Elephant* was brilliantly photographed by Harris Savides at a high school in Portland, Oregon. Favoring the hand-held camera and the observational long shots of direct cinema, the film has a documentary feel as it calmly tracks the movements of a cluster of students on what seems to be an ordinary high school day.

However, unlike Fred Wiseman's direct cinema classic, *High School* (1968), *Elephant* was not bound to filming in "real time." It enjoyed the elasticity of fiction, and in his edit, therefore, Van Sant could return to a previously shown scene for a second and sometimes a third time to follow the actions of a different student. The result of this stylistic strategy is to deepen and broaden the perspective and underscore the theme of chance. *Elephant* also emphasizes how arbitrary are the placements of students who will be shot by two classmates who have ordered an arsenal of firearms from the Internet. One of the two shooters is shown being taunted by another boy; the two are presented as lovers—a controversial decision by a gay director—but the boys are not decidedly "different." Some of the other teenagers we meet seem similarly lonely and misunderstood. Part of the horror in watching *Elephant* for the first time is the sense that any number of students presented might turn out to be a killer. *Elephant* is a subtle, disturbing, and important film. It would never have been made in a studio system. *Elephant* had a limited release in the United States and remains better known and appreciated by film enthusiasts than by the American mainstream movie audience.

Another thoughtful HBO narrative is *Maria Full of Grace* (2004), the heart-wrenching story of a pregnant teenager who works as a "mule" carrying drugs from her native Colombia to the United States. With an unknown actor, Catalina Sandino Moreno, playing the demanding lead role of the strong-willed Maria, writer and director Joshua Marston had difficulty in obtaining funding when he insisted the film be shot in Spanish. The project was fortunately rescued by the "famously far-sighted HBO."[11] Marston, a film school graduate who workshopped the screenplay for his first feature at Sundance, devoted himself to the project for five years, finally shooting much of the film in Ecuador because of unsafe conditions in Colombia. After presenting a harrowing airline journey taken by Maria and three other Colombian women who have also ingested drugs, the last act takes place in New Jersey and New York, where one woman is arrested and another dies from the ingested drugs. With many difficulties, Maria and another young Colombian woman find their way to the temporary safety of "Little Colombia" in Queens. The film ends with Maria not joining her friend for the return flight to

Bogotá. Although momentarily safe, the hopeful teen mother-to-be now faces an uncertain future as an illegal immigrant. *Maria Full of Grace* was the first-ever Spanish-language film in competition at Sundance, winning the Audience Award and a nomination for the Grand Jury Prize. Joshua Marston won or was nominated for dozens of other awards. Even more accolades, including an Academy Award nomination for Best Actress, went to the luminous Catalina Sandino Moreno. The film screened theatrically in the United States, Latin America, and Western Europe.

Real Women Have Curves (2002) likewise features the travails of an independent teenage girl, but the conventions of comedy shape its narrative and promise the pleasures of a happy ending. Introducing America Ferrera as Ana and featuring the irrepressible Lupe Ontiveros as Ana's mother, the film pits the ambitions and dreams of a bright, self-directed young woman against the traditional values of Mexican immigrant parents who wish to keep her close to their East Los Angeles neighborhood. Directed by Colombian Patricia Cardoso, this engaging, "feminist lite" comedy (which featured women in all the key production positions) charmed the Sundance crowd, garnering the Audience Award, a Special Jury Prize, and the Humanitas Prize. *Real Women Have Curves* speaks most directly to the greatly underrepresented audience of Latina and Chicana women and girls in the United States, but also has a decidedly broader appeal, demonstrated when it screened at Cannes in 2003 and won an Independent Spirit Award for its producer, Effie Brown. The comedy had a successful theatrical run in the United States, Spain, and Italy in which it nearly doubled its production costs before moving to DVD.

No other HBO theatrical has approached the amazing commercial success of its 2002 romantic comedy *My Big Fat Greek Wedding,* which grossed $241 million in worldwide theatrical rentals.[12] But astounding profits from theatrical rentals are not required for HBO to have good reasons to keep its "little art house" open, since this newest dimension of its production and distribution repertoire extends its product well beyond its subscriber base into other audience and profit possibilities. Between 2002 and 2006, HBO vigorously entered the world of theatrical film and demonstrated, with more than a dozen features, a successful method of supporting modestly budgeted, nontraditional documentary and narrative features. This method depends upon executives who are able to recognize and sustain talented independent filmmakers and worthy projects. HBO and its partners have provided such executive insight, as well as the requisite corporate structure that assures an expanded pattern of distribution from festival openings to theatrical screenings to national and international telecasts to DVD and video availability. Whenever its features shine at Cannes and Sundance, HBO enhances its already stellar reputation and reinforces the reach and value of its corporate brand.

Notes

1. HBO Video returned to the 1990s pattern of "indie pick-ups" in 2006. See John Dempsey, "Can Discs Fill Tills for HBO?" 25 June 2006, at http://www.variety.com/article/VR1117945899?categoryid=18&cs=1&nid=2562.

2. Anne Thompson, "Made for TV, but Shown First in a Theater," *New York Times,* 10 May 2004, C7.

3. Amy Taubin, "Documenting Women," *Ms. Magazine,* summer 2004, at http://www.msmagazine.com/summer2004/womenonfilm.asp; Sheila Nevins, "A Conversation with Sheila Nevins," *Kodak on Film,* undated Web article, at http://www.kodak.com/US/en/motion/forum/onFilm/nevinsQA.shtml.

4. Comments regarding the filmmakers' intentions and results are from a question-and-answer session following a public screening of *Favela Rising* at the Pleasant Street Theater, Northampton, Massachusetts, 17 August 2006.

5. Comments on negotiations and arrangements with HBO are from a telephone interview by the author with Jeff Zimbalist, 27 August 2006. See an interview with Zimbalist by David Tamés at http://www.nefilm.com/news/archives/05september/zimbalist.htm.

6. Nevins, quoted in Taubin, "Documenting Women."

7. Some HBO-produced documentaries that premiered at Sundance (such as *Protocols of Zion* [2005], a film about anti-Semitism directed by Marc Levin) were exhibited only in a handful of theaters. Others, most noticeably *Comandante* (2003), had no U.S. theatrical release. This admiring portrait of Fidel Castro, directed by Oliver Stone, played theatrically only in Spain, despite opening at Sundance, screening at numerous international festivals, and participating in the Cannes film market.

8. The Internet Movie Database (http://www.imdb.com) lists the estimated budget of *Fahrenheit 9/11* as $6 million, and its theatrical gross as of October 2004 as exceeding $119 million. The budget estimate for *March of the Penguins* is $8 million; its box office take by November 2005 (before its Oscar) exceeded $77 million.

9. As quoted in Eugene Hernandez, "HBO Launches Theatrical Division with Fine Line," *Indie Wire,* at http://www.indiewire.com/biz/biz_030725hbo .html.

10. Peter Bradshaw, "Elephant," *Guardian,* 30 January 2004, at http://film .guardian.co.uk/News_Story/Critic_Review/Guardian_review/0,,1134158,00 .html.

11. Zoe Williams, "Passage to 42nd Street," *Guardian,* 26 February 2005, at http://www.guardian.co.uk/print/0,,5135283-103425,00.html.

12. See http://www.imdb.com on *My Big Fat Greek Wedding.* The extraordinarily popular comedy, made on an estimated budget of only $5 million, did not play on the festival circuit but won many audience awards and was nominated for an Oscar for Best Original Screenplay. It also spawned a short-lived television series, *My Big Fat Greek Life* (CBS, 2003).

PART FIVE

REFLECTIONS

EIGHTEEN

What Has HBO Ever Done for Women?

Janet McCabe and Kim Akass

Carmela Soprano (Edie Falco), Ruth Fisher (Frances Conroy), Brenda Chenowith (Rachel Griffiths), Carrie Bradshaw (Sarah Jessica Parker), Alma Garrett (Molly Parker), Barbara Dutton Henrickson (Jeanne Tripplehorn), Nicolette Grant (Chloë Sevigny), and Atia of the Julii (Polly Walker) are some of the most compelling women on our television screens—and they all come courtesy of HBO. Strong, complex women have, of course, long been part of the television landscape, from Lucille Ball to Roseanne, from Christine Cagney (Sharon Gless) and Mary Beth Lacey (Tyne Daly) to Alexis Carrington (Joan Collins). But this recent crop of truly troubling yet always mesmerizing women has left audiences and critics sensing that HBO is doing something with gender and sexuality not seen elsewhere. Are these female characters really breaking new ground, contributing to a vibrant conversation on the state of contemporary feminism, changing female identities, and the dilemmas facing modern womanhood in a postfeminist age? Or are they merely recycling old stereotypes under new guises?

HBO Women, (Post)Feminism, and the Rhetoric of Choice

Only weeks after *Sex and the City* (1998–2004) debuted on June 6, 1998, *Time* magazine asked, "Is Feminism Dead?"[1] The front cover traced American feminism through the images of four women: Susan B. Anthony, Betty Friedan, Gloria Steinem, and TV lawyer Ally McBeal (Calista Flockhart). What we were meant to conclude was that if Generation X had nothing more to offer than a highly neurotic, anorexic-looking TV character—professionally accomplished and financially independent but miserable and boy-obsessed—then feminism was dead.[2] Yet *Time* proclaiming (once again) feminism's demise coincided with a new moment in the history of feminism. It was being redefined by a generation who had always lived with the idea of female liberation, but had a decidedly different perspective on feminist politics, sexuality, and lifestyle choices than previously. Whereas few at HBO, either as executives or as producers, often mention the "f-word," the network's shows, from *Sex and the City* to *Big Love* (2006–), nonetheless tackle similar concerns and themes preoccupying those struggling to come to terms with the feminist inheritance at a time when we are told we have unlimited opportunities and no need for feminist politics.

When HBO's new sex comedy about thirty-something single women navigating relationships in Manhattan premiered it prompted the latest round of hand-wringing over constructions of women's lifestyle choices. Media commentators were deeply divided over Carrie Bradshaw and her chums. The quartet were attacked for being too feminist or not feminist enough[3]; lauded for being smart, sassy, and financially independent yet condemned as dreadfully old-fashioned in their quest for Mr. Right; pilloried for appropriating the language of feminist empowerment only to bitch about men[4]; applauded for talking candidly about sex while damned as sluts.

Critics may have been unsure of what to make of it all, but viewers (particularly women) loved *Sex and the City* and it became an instant hit, surprising even some executives at HBO. "Never before in an American film or TV series has sophisticated girl talk been more explicit, with every kink and sexual twitch of the urban mating game noted and wittily dissected," wrote Stephen Holden.[5] From bad dates to broken heels, Carrie Bradshaw and her girlfriends—Samantha Jones (Kim Cattrall), Charlotte York (Kristin Davis), and Miranda Hobbes (Cynthia Nixon)—became icons for today's women, "trying to figure out why trying to have it all seems to add up to nothing."[6]

Few television series have had such an impact on female culture as *Sex and the City*. It even made the cover of *Time* magazine in 2000, when the four girls were paraded as encapsulating women's changing attitudes toward marriage and career. Under the headline "Who Needs a Husband?" Carrie, Samantha, Charlotte, and Miranda became the face of a generation of "women who had more independence, options

When HBO's *Sex and the City* premiered, it prompted the latest round of hand-wringing over constructions of women's lifestyle choices. Media commentators were deeply divided over Carrie Bradshaw and her chums. (Left to right) Kim Cattrall as Samantha Jones, Cynthia Nixon as Miranda Hobbes, Kristin Davis as Charlotte York, and Sarah Jessica Parker as Carrie.

and sexual freedoms"[7] than ever before, and who chose to remain single. Furthermore the series contributed to current thinking on feminine style and fashion trends,[8] discussions on female sexuality, dating etiquette and sex,[9] as well as debates about modern femininity and the single woman.[10] Without being explicitly feminist, *Sex and the City* has initiated the discussion,[11] but subsequent HBO original series like *Six Feet Under* (2001–5), *The Sopranos* (1999–2007), and more recently *Big Love* and *Lucky Louie* (2006) continue to talk out the lived messiness of contemporary female lives.

Contradictory definitions of and differences within what we mean by contemporary femininity and female experience have been profoundly guided by the struggle between various feminisms (second-wave, liberal, post, third-wave), as well as by the media-produced, conservative, antifeminist backlash starting in the 1980s. HBO women epitomize this postfeminist paradox—a paradox that Rachel Moseley and Jacinda Read describe as the "experience of being female, feminist, and feminine in the late-twentieth and early-twenty-first centuries."[12] No woman is a simple archetype. She instead embodies the experiences of "being female, feminist, and feminine" that more often than not involve uneasy choices and irreconcilable compromises.

For example, social-climbing Mafia housewife Carmela Soprano lives comfortably in her leafy New Jersey suburb, partly paid for by prostitution, wanting for nothing; while daughter Meadow (Jamie-Lynn Sigler) sneers at her mother's choices and berates her for not thinking "beyond being dependent on some man" and yet, at the same time, remains financially reliant on Daddy. Charlotte York gives up a career she adores for marriage and possible motherhood, appropriating a liberal feminist rhetoric to validate that choice: "The women's movement is supposed to be about choice and if I choose to quit my job, *that* is my choice. . . . It's my life and my choice . . . I chose my choice! I chose my choice!" (*Sex and the City,* "Time and Punishment," 4:7). Yet, she doth protest too much, constantly justifying her decision and even phoning Miranda to (once again) defend her choice, repeatedly shouting, "I chose my choice!" Beth Montemurro argues that Charlotte betrays her "insecurities about her decision and her concerns regarding how she would be judged" about not working, as well as how much she has internalized the message that somehow women compromise their identities if they reorient themselves around husbands and family.[13]

Carmela and Ruth Fisher have chosen to live the scripted ideal of American womanhood—mother, wife, homemaker—that the media works so hard to promote.[14] Both women nevertheless struggle to take control of their lives as their marriages wane, with options closed down, and without a defined role. As Carmela tells her daughter, "You have options, I have a lawyer." Then there is the disaffected teenager Claire Fisher (Lauren Ambrose), who may turn her counselling sessions into an analysis of the restrictive norms governing appropriate feminine behaviors,[15] but who slips effortlessly into the selfless role of a Harlequin romance novel heroine when she tries to help her deeply troubled boyfriend. Similarly, Brenda Chenowith, the highly intelligent girlfriend (and later wife) of Nate Fisher (Peter Krause), attempts to reclaim her identity after being the subject of the best-selling book *Charlotte Light and Dark*. Never quite able to decide what she wants, or even who she really is, she compulsively sabotages her relationships with men and indulges in sex with strangers. And let us not forget mother of three Barbara Dutton Henrickson, who adores her husband, but after being diagnosed with cancer followed by a radical hysterectomy, chooses to allow him to take two other wives.

Contradiction is inherent in the uneasy choices that these women must make. It is also in their perplexing decision making, in their complicated morality, in their competing desires, and in their holding fast to scripted fantasies of the heterosexual romance that feminism warns us about. Furthermore, contradiction exists in their being aroused by politically incorrect erotic pleasures, in their *reproducing* sexism and sexist stereotypes, as well as sometimes in their colluding and complex emotional investment in those who oppress other women.

Such representational paradoxes are *only* possible because HBO offers an alternative to the master narrative of mainstream television culture. Does it in fact meet the requirements of what Bonnie J. Dow describes as a site of "prime-time feminism," which traces discernable shifts in how the "liberated" woman is portrayed and functions as "an important ideological forum for public discourse about social issues and social change"?[16] Maybe so. But in taking up such feminist cultural work this cable network does make visible female representations that complicate rather than clarify female identities and experience in this age of troubled liberation.

HBO and the Politics of Representation

HBO has long made a virtue out of its autonomy from the constraints and restrictions limiting network television. Doing different, setting itself against what is prohibited elsewhere on mainstream broadcasting channels, emerges as a crucial institutional strategy. Arguably, then, the complex women starring in its original programs are produced in and through an institutional discourse that works hard to tell us how HBO defies, resists, and scandalizes. But let us be cautious. For, as Tania Modleski eloquently puts it, "we exist inside ideology . . . we are all victims, down to the very depths of our psyches, of political and cultural domination."[17] HBO does not function outside our culture; it is in fact always "inside" cultural discourse and subject to its rules, prohibitions, and controls governing norms of gender and sexuality. Dow says it best when she writes, "We need to appreciate media for what it can do in giving us images of strong women; yet, at the same time, we need to maintain a very keen sense of the limitations of media logic."[18]

From the libidinal fantasies of Dr. Jennifer Melfi (Lorraine Bracco) involving boorish mob boss Tony Soprano (James Gandolfini), to Brenda Chenowith's sexual peccadilloes with two twenty-something stoners, from self-confessed feminist Janice Soprano (Aida Turturro) letting fiancé Richie Aprile (David Proval) hold a gun to her head during sex, to Carrie Bradshaw beginning her season three adulterous affair with Mr. Big (Chris Noth), female sexuality and erotic desire has rarely been represented in such complex ways. Across different series, and within episodes, images of women and sex participate in feminism's "sex wars," concerned with both sexual pleasure and sexual danger.[19] Navigating a new sexual politics finds these women making visible ambivalence. Carrie never reconciles her guilt over her sexual addiction to Big; Janice may get an erotic charge from her own sexual degradation, but when Richie hits her in the mouth one night over dinner, she calmly shoots him dead. And Brenda feels nothing, despite her addiction to feeling thrillingly powerful and dangerous, as she transgresses sexual limits. Even while these women are exhilarated at pursuing their desires, and indeed "take for granted a range of options for their sexual behaviour,"[20] they more often than not end up hesitant, sometimes shamed, and always troubled by their sexual bravado. Indeed, such frustrations echo complaints from third-wave feminists that feminism has yet to establish a vocabulary "for understanding what we—as women, as feminists—*like* about sex."[21]

Options for talking about sexual freedoms and choice are only possible for a privileged few. Although Samantha Jones may aggressively celebrate sexual gratification as her fundamental right, such debates hold little relevance for other HBO women, like *Deadwood* whore Trixie (Paula Malcomson) or pregnant Bada Bing! exotic dancer Tracee (Ariel Kiley), who are simply struggling to survive. Each belongs to a rigid patriarchal hierarchy and is subject to its strict codes—and God help the woman who transgresses. Vengeance is swift and chillingly cruel. The thirteen lethal blows Tracee takes from psychotic mobster Ralph Cifaretto (Joe Pantoliano) are in exchange for her denigration of his manhood in front of his crew. Likewise, Cy Tolliver's savage beating of young Flora on the streets of Deadwood is in retribution for her thieving ways. But there is more to these vicious assaults than simple misogyny.[22]

In *Rome*, Atia of the Julii (Polly Walker) assembles a formidable network of alliances within a culture in which her gender has no official authority with the men absent for years on military campaigns.

From Tracee daring to entertain fantasies of domestic bliss with Ralph to Trixie taking an opium overdose at the thought of leaving the abusive Al Swearengen (Ian McShane), these women have complex motivations. Neither is simply a victim nor victimized, but instead offers a complex critique of women who have few options, deeply enmeshed in the ideology of family values, for example, while having no experience of what that actually means. Tracee gets into trouble (and loses her life), as do Gloria Trillo (Annabella Sciorra) and Adriana La Cerva (Drea de Matteo), for daring to believe it could be any different. The aching potency of Adriana as she is driven to her execution for ratting on the mob (but, really, what choice did she have?) lingers long in our minds.

At first glance those women at the other end of the social spectrum—the wives, mothers, homemakers—fare little better, entirely dependent on male patronage and mired in compromise. From the noble women of ancient Rome and the widow of a Deadwood prospector to the latter day Mafioso wife and the sister-wives of a polygamist, each confirms the work of feminist historians like Susan Stanford Friedman who identify ways in which women have over time negotiated an uncompromising social power constraining them.[23] Atia of the Julii, for example, has assembled a formidable network of alliances within a culture in which her gender has no official authority with the men absent for years on military campaigns. Using daughter Octavia (Kerry Condon) to further her political ambitions, manipulating her friendship with aristocrat Servilia of the Junii (Lindsay Duncan), and trading sex for power, she ruthlessly emerges as a powerful woman acting as one of the unseen rulers of Rome.

Centuries later, Alma Garrett struggles for agency. Marrying Brom Garrett to help solve her father's insolvency, she accompanies her husband out West as he prospects for gold, a difficult situation alleviated with liberal doses of laudanum. After Brom is murdered, learning that a gold strike on her land is perhaps the most lucrative in town, she decides to stay and work the claim. Not without difficulty, however. Holed up in the Grand Central Hotel for two seasons and requiring help from Wild Bill Hickok, Seth Bullock, and the prospector Ellsworth to fend off those (including her ne'er-do-well father) who would take advantage of her, she demonstrates considerable fortitude as she tries to reinvent herself in the frontier town.

And still later, the Mafioso wife is no longer a hapless casualty of male (generic) violence. Carmela Soprano possesses a tremendous sense of agency from within the institutions that seek to disenfranchise and even oppress her. She is saturated in the nostalgic language of the media antifeminist backlash, seducing us with the promise of simpler times when women knew their place and life was less complicated. Her husband may say, "[Out] there it's the 1990s; in this house, it's 1954" ("Nobody Knows Anything" 1:11), but it is Carmela who compels us to think in these terms. In the patriarchal world par excellence of the Mafia, where women matter little, Carmela operates inside meticulous codes of marriage sanctified by the Catholic Church; of motherhood extolled by popular media rhetoric; of family valorized by the Mafia and its generic laws. But she is a lesson in unseen power whereby the legitimate wife and mother quite literally lays down the law. She is privileged, she is privilege. Her steely silences and

The Mafioso wife is no longer a hapless casualty of male violence. Carmela Soprano (Edie Falco), pictured here with her husband, Tony (James Gandolfini), exerts a tremendous sense of agency from within the institutions that seek to disenfranchise and even oppress her.

reproachful looks often speak louder than her words. One stern look can stop Tony dead in his tracks. Yet she pays a high price for her preeminent narrative position. This is a woman who understands the collateral damage that must be sustained in the turf war with her obstinate gangster husband and the intransigence of patriarchal law.

Where the Real Women Are

We revel in the ways that the *Sex and the City* girls talk dirty; we relish those no-nonsense rebukes Carmela serves up with coffee; we delight in the emotional complexity of these women. But we are also perplexed to see women living with so much compromise, and stirred by those whose options are closing down or are nonexistent. HBO may be offering new forms of female subjectivity, new opportunities for transforming how women are represented on television, but it cannot avoid the broader cultural ambivalence toward women, female identities, and feminism. Only certain women are liberated enough to take control. Others make choices many of us find hard to fathom. "Even if we ultimately decide that shows like *The Sopranos, Six Feet Under, Sex and the City,* and other popular original series are *not* feminist," writes Lisa Johnson, "the narrative arcs and visual rhetoric of these texts provoke rich, energetic conversations *about* feminism."[24] In this sense, HBO gives representation to our complex age of troubled emancipation—and may in fact offer more realistic female characters—fallible, inconsistent, complicated, virtuous, troublesome, and both emotionally strong and fragile. Steering clear of feminist agendas, but valuing individuality, these women have much to tell us about the contradictions we all live with each and every day.

Notes

1. "Is Feminism Dead?" *Time,* 29 June 1998, front cover.

2. Kristyn Gorton provides an important corrective by asking why women enjoy a character like Ally McBeal. Her answer is that "programmes such as *Ally McBeal* become pleasurable insofar as they offer play with some of the conflicting inheritances of feminism: desire for both independence and companionship" (161). Kristyn Gorton, "(Un)fashionable Feminists: The Media and *Ally McBeal*," in Stacy Gillis, Gillian Howe, and Rebecca Munsford, eds., *Third Wave Feminism: A Critical Exploration* (New York: Palgrave, 2004), 154–63.

3. Wendy Shalit, "Sex, Sadness, and the City," *Urbanites,* autumn 1999, at http://www.city-journal.org/html/9_4_a4.html.

4. Charlotte Raven, "All Men Are Bastards . . . Discuss," *Guardian,* 9 February 1999, 5.

5. Stephen Holden, "Tickets to Fantasies of Urban Desires," *New York Times,* 20 July 1999, E2.

6. Diane Werts, "Even Better Sex and the Single Girls," *NewsDay,* 1 June 2001, B39.

7. Astrid Henry, "Orgasms and Empowerment: *Sex and the City* and the Third Wave Feminism," in Kim Akass and Janet McCabe, eds., *Reading* Sex and the City (London: I. B. Tauris, 2004), 82.

8. Emine Saner, "Guess What? Carrie's Gone Shopping," *Evening Standard,* 2 April 2003, 26.

9. Lee Siegel, "Relationshipism: Who Is Carrie Bradshaw Really Dating," *New Republic,* 18 November 2002, 30–33; Shalit, "Sex, Sadness, and the City."

10. Nancy Franklin, "Sex and the Single Girl," *New Yorker,* 6 July 1998, 74–76, 77.

11. Akass and McCabe, eds., *Reading* Sex and the City.

12. Rachel Moseley and Jacinda Read, "'Having it *Ally*': Popular Television (Post-) Feminism," *Feminist Media Studies* 2:2 (2002): 240.

13. Beth Montemurro, "Charlotte Chooses Her Choice: Liberal Feminism on *Sex and the City,*" *Scholar and Feminist Online* 3:1 (fall 2004), at http://www.barnard.edu/sfonline/hbo/montemurro_01.htm.

14. Janet McCabe and Kim Akass, "What Has Carmela Ever Done for Feminism? Carmela Soprano and the Post-feminist Dilemma," in David Lavery, ed., *Reading* The Sopranos: *Hit TV from HBO* (London: I. B Tauris, 2006), 39–55; Kim Akass, "Mother Knows Best: Ruth and Representations of Mothering in *Six Feet Under,*" in Kim Akass and Janet McCabe, eds., *Reading* Six Feet Under: *TV to Die For* (London: I. B. Tauris, 2005): 110–20.

15. Janet McCabe, "Claire Fisher on the Couch: Discourses of Female Subjectivity, Desire, and Teenage Angst in *Six Feet Under,*" *Scholar and Feminist Online* 2:1 (fall 2004), at http://www.barnard.edu/sfonline/hbo/mccabe_01.htm.

16. Bonnie J. Dow, *Prime-Time Feminism: Television, Media Culture, and the Women's Movement since 1970* (Philadelphia: University of Pennsylvania Press, 1994), xi.

17. Tania Modleski, *Feminism without Women: Culture and Criticism in a 'Postfeminist' Age* (New York: Routledge, 1991), 45.

18. Bonnie J. Dow, *Prime-Time Feminism,* 214.

19. Lee Damsky, ed., *Sex and Single Girls: Straight and Queer Women on Sexuality* (Seattle: Seal Press, 2000); Merri Lisa Johnson, ed., *Jane Sexes It Up: True Confessions of Feminist Desire* (New York: Four Walls Eight Windows, 2002); Astrid Henry, "Taking Feminism to Bed: The Third Wave Does the Sex Wars," in *Not My Mother's Sister: Generational Conflict and Third-Wave Feminism* (Bloomington: Indiana University Press, 2004), 88–114.

20. Lee Damsky, "Introduction," in Damsky, ed., *Sex and Single Girls,* xiii.

21. Merri Lisa Johnson, "Jane Hocus, Jane Focus," in Johnson, ed., *Jane Sexes It Up,* 7; also see Naomi Wolf, *Fire with Fire: The New Female Power and How It Will Change the 21st Century* (New York: Random House, 1993), 184.

22. Lisa Johnson reads Tracee as "a site of struggle over what can be said or not said, and under what circumstances, a struggle over what is 'obvious'—an

ideological struggle—from the question of misogyny on *The Sopranos* (is the show *obviously* sexist or not?) to the problem of objectification in feminism (is stripping *obviously* oppressive or not?) to the element of commerce in all heterosexual relationships (is money merely a less *obvious* exchange in marriage than in lap dances?)." Lisa Johnson, "The Stripper as Resisting Reader: Stripper Iconography and Sex Worker Feminism on *The Sopranos*," *Scholar and Feminist Online* 3:1 (fall 2004), at http://www.barnard.edu/sfonline/hbo/johnson_01.htm.

23. Susan Stanford Friedman, "Making History: Reflections on Feminism, Narrative and Desire," in Diane Elam and Robyn Wiegman, eds., *Feminism beside Itself* (New York: Routledge, 1995), 11–54.

24. Lisa Johnson, "Way More Than a Tag Line: HBO, Feminism, and the Question of Difference in Pop Culture," *Scholar and Feminist Online* 3:1 (fall 2004), at http://www.barnard.edu/sfonline/hbo/intro.htm.

NINETEEN

HBO's Ongoing Legacy

Gary R. Edgerton and Jeffrey P. Jones

The expectations game is an essential part of how television works. Each new season brings a fresh batch of original programs that are tested by networks, handicapped by critics, and sampled by audiences. Viewers are bombarded with a seemingly endless stream of promos and ads that are all intended to get them to watch what is supposedly the next sure-fire hit. Most of these shows fall rapidly by the wayside: an estimated three-quarters never make it beyond their first seasons. Still, breakout series do occasionally transform a few select networks into the hottest destinations on TV. Given their longevity, NBC, CBS, and ABC have all climbed to the top of the broadcast television world more than once over the past half-century. In the cable and satellite TV sector, HBO was the first service to break away from the pack by adding satellite to cable distribution in 1975, causing its subscriber base to skyrocket from a mere 287,199 at the close of that year to 14.6 million a decade later.[1]

By the end of 1994, however, HBO was stalled at around 19.2 million subscribers.[2] During the next decade, "the HBO leadership team decided to 'jump fully off this cliff,'" recalls Jeffrey Bewkes, then the newly appointed chairman and CEO of the network, referring to his staff's total commitment to "produce bold, really distinctive television."[3] In turn, HBO set itself apart from the competition for the second time in its short history by deciding to emphasize innovative, original programming above all else, increasing its number of subscribers by more than 50 percent between 1995 and 2007. More importantly, HBO also emerged in the late 1990s as the most talked about, widely celebrated, and profitable network in all of television.

Jeffrey Bewkes is largely credited with initiating and nurturing the still-thriving conditions at HBO where creative people are welcomed and encouraged to do their best work. Time Warner's then-president Gerald Levin replaced Michael Fuchs with Bewkes as head of HBO in November 1995. After eleven years at the helm, Fuchs's controlling, top-down managerial style proved inhibiting for his colleagues, as did his longstanding belief that "HBO has to offer subscribers a wide range of programming they couldn't see anywhere else" with a continuing emphasis on movies. Fuchs's stated preference was for "commercial rather than artistic" program development.[4] In contrast, Jeffrey Bewkes brought a more collaborative, bottom-up way of doing business to the company, unleashing a great deal of creative energy and a new era at HBO.[5]

The tipping point for HBO was the unprecedented success of *The Sopranos* (1999–2007). In July 1997, *Oz* (1997–2003) had enjoyed a promising debut with 2.6 million viewers; *Sex and the City* (1998–2004) garnered 2.75 million in June 1998; and *The Sopranos* 7.5 million in January 1999.[6] To be sure, these were robust numbers for any cable and satellite network at the time. For HBO, though, these audience figures were even more striking when seen in the context of a subscriber base that then totaled slightly more than one-quarter of all of the television households in America. Furthermore, HBO's latest spike in popularity and prestige was just beginning. By the start of its third season in March 2001, *The Sopranos* attracted 11.3 million viewers, and the premiere of the edgy, idiosyncratic *Six Feet Under* (2001–5) followed up three months later with 4.8 million.[7]

HBO was certifiably white hot in September 2002 when *The Sopranos* opened its fourth season to an audience of 13.4 million, which not only won its time slot, but placed "sixth for the entire week against all other prime-time programs, cable and broadcast," despite HBO's "built-in numerical disadvantage." Even though HBO was based on an entirely different economic model than most of the rest of the U.S. TV industry, it had beaten all of the advertiser-supported networks at their own game. More significantly, it was also asserting once and for all that "the underlying assumptions that had driven television for six decades were no longer in effect."[8] The momentum in the industry had shifted unmistakably and irrevocably away from the traditional broadcast networks and more toward the cable and satellite sector of the business, with HBO leading the way.

Along with HBO's newfound ascendancy, "cable-and-satellite delivery systems were now entrenched, with generations of viewers knowing, and expecting, a wide range of channels. They would even pay outright for a handful of favorites."[9] For its part, HBO boasted 29 million subscribers during the first quarter of 2007—approximately twice the number of its nearest rival, Showtime, at 14.5 million.[10] Back on September 19, 2004, moreover, HBO had made TV history by winning a staggering 32 Emmy Awards after receiving a record-setting 124 nominations. "This will never happen again," admitted HBO's newest chairman and CEO Chris Albrecht, who had replaced Jeffrey Bewkes in July 2002 when the latter was promoted to president and chief operating officer of Time Warner because of what he had just accomplished at HBO.[11]

HBO was no longer benefiting as it had a decade earlier from the expectations game because most industry watchers now assumed that the network would just keep producing more popular and critically acclaimed programming. In the mid- to late 1990s, no one other than HBO insiders expected the network to emerge as the gold standard for original programming in all of television. By 2005, however, TV professionals and critics alike were expecting HBO to create one breakout hit after another. That year, journalists nationwide first began referring to an apparent drop-off in "high-quality programming" from the "once-invincible HBO."[12] A mild undercurrent of HBO fatigue was clearly surfacing.

As one representative reviewer observed at the time, "there's an ebb and flow to what's hot and what's not on television. A personality, a show, even a whole network or cable channel can be the talk of the water cooler one moment and yesterday's hot topic the next." According to this line of reasoning, HBO was now in decline because "its newer original series didn't generate the buzz of past programming."[13] Many other TV critics took HBO to task for the perceived hypocrisy of its branding line—"It's Not TV, It's HBO." Aaron Barnhart of the *Kansas City Star,* for example, pointed out that "it is TV, in that HBO is susceptible to the same laws of hit-making as any other network."[14] In response, Carolyn Strauss, HBO's president of entertainment, explained: "We're in a very competitive environment right now. We always need a hit, but everybody does."[15]

In the face of such growing skepticism, HBO continued to outperform the rest of network television from both a commercial perspective and in terms of winning more top institutional awards than any other service. Throughout the mid- to late 2000s, HBO was trapped in a game of ever-higher expectations. For instance, FX's Emmy-nominated flagship series *The Shield* (2002–) was widely praised in the popular press for achieving its largest audiences ever by averaging 2.8 million for its eleven-episode fifth season between January and March 2006.[16] In contrast, the 4.6 million garnered by HBO's *Big Love* for its thirteen-episode first season run between March and June 2006 was viewed as somewhat of a disappointment because it was merely "holding onto about half of its *Sopranos* lead-in," even though FX reaches 60 million more television households than HBO.[17]

In the short-term, at least, the unusual success of *The Sopranos* and other breakout series such as *Sex and the City* clouded the ongoing legacy of HBO. The extraordinary success of these two programs in particular led to the mistaken assumption that other HBO shows were underperforming when in fact many were still artistically challenging and were averaging more viewers per episode than just about any other cable and satellite series on TV. Instead of overemphasizing the importance of a few high-profile programs in the more-than-thirty-year history and development of HBO, therefore, a broader historical critical perspective suggests at least seven distinguishing features that characterize the legacy and continuing relevance of HBO.

1. *The full measure of HBO's historical importance is best delineated by taking into account all four main programming groups where it has broken new ground—comedy, documentary, sports, and drama—and the ways in which television has changed as a result of the innovations that the network has made in each of these areas.* In every instance, HBO has become the premier location for creative talent as well as the place where audiences can turn for quality viewing. HBO Comedy, for example, has replaced *The Tonight Show* (NBC, 1954–) as the launching pad for up-and-coming stand-up comics. It is also the primary showplace for established comedians. With its $20 million

annual budget, HBO Documentary, too, has surpassed public television as the principal outlet for cutting-edge social documentaries while employing some of the most respected producer-directors working in this programming genre.

HBO Sports has not only replaced ABC Sports as the premier showcase for boxing, but has been at the forefront of producing intelligent talk and investigative exposes into the inner workings of professional and amateur athletics. Last but not least, HBO Drama has transformed the creative landscape of television since the mid-1990s with its potent range of innovative series that have both captured the zeitgeist, as with *The Sopranos* and *Sex and the City,* as well as broken new ground with consistently well-drawn characters and finely crafted narratives. The highly acclaimed *The Wire* (2002–) is a prime example of these latter sorts of shows, having taken top honors among a poll of sixty-seven critics across the country as the "Best Overall Program" on television in 2006. Ellen Gray of the *Philadelphia Daily News,* for instance, explained her vote by asserting that "*The Wire* lives in a world that broadcast networks can't even find on the map, much less afford to visit."[18] In addition, HBO's dominance of the Emmys since the mid-1990s, and the numerous Golden Globes, Oscars, and Peabody Awards that it garners on a near-annual basis, demonstrates the extent to which HBO achieves a level of "excellence" across four very different television genres.

2. *HBO's dramatic series in particular have provoked an "aftereffect" in the industry, which raises the bar and influences the kind of original programming that all of its various competitors across subscription, cable and satellite, and broadcast TV produce.* As is discussed in this book's introduction, HBO's original series have inspired some of the most innovative shows of the 2000s that have appeared on Showtime, FX, the USA Network, TNT, Fox, and ABC, among other networks. In particular, Miller Tabek & Company media analyst David Joyce reports that "Showtime is reinventing itself following the HBO mold by generating more proprietary content."[19] Moreover, HBO's creative influence has been as widespread over the last decade as CBS's was in the early 1970s, ABC's in the mid- to late 1970s, and NBC's in the early to mid-1980s. In short, HBO continues to inform shows as widely diverse as Showtime's *Weeds* (2005–), TNT's *The Closer* (2005–), and ABC's *Desperate Housewives* (2004–), to name just a few, with such

HBO's ability to attract the entertainment industry's top creative people is currently unmatched by any other broadcast, cable, or pay-television network. For example, *Seinfeld*'s creator, Larry David, the producer and star of *Curb Your Enthusiasm* (right, with former HBO chairman and CEO Chris Albrecht), brought this project to HBO.

stylistic signatures as the use of innovative and unconventional narrative pacing, characterization, dialogue, subject matter, music, wit, and irony. HBO's aftereffect permeates the full range of contemporary television, from its pay-TV rivals to basic cable and satellite channels to the traditional broadcast networks as well.[20]

 3. *HBO's legacy is also characterized by an unusually supportive relationship between the network's programming executives and the creative talent they nurture and work with time and again.* Chris Albrecht

credits this mutually beneficial arrangement to "the philosophy of HBO." He explains that HBO is "a place where creative people can come and do their best work. We are the patrons of these terrifically talented people."[21] Similarly, Sheila Nevins, president of HBO documentary and family programming, refers to her division as "a repertory company" where her personal involvement and backing attracts many of the leading nonfiction filmmakers in America, including Jon Alpert, Barbara Kopple, and Spike Lee.[22] Entertainment chief Carolyn Strauss has likewise cultivated close personal multi-project relationships with many HBO veterans, including David Chase, Terrence Winter, and James Gandolfini of *The Sopranos;* Michael Patrick King and Sarah Jessica Parker of *Sex and the City;* David Milch of *Deadwood;* and Doug Ellin of *Entourage,* among others.

Following the August 2005 finale of *Six Feet Under,* for example, Strauss was "surprised and grateful" that she was able to once again lure creator Alan Ball away from the movies and "back to the network with yet another passion project." By October of that year, Ball was already adapting Charlaine Harris's *Southern Vampire* books into a one-hour continuing series entitled, *True Blood.* "I wouldn't consider doing this program with just any network," he explains. "Ultimately I have a great relationship with HBO."[23] Original series such as *Six Feet Under* and *The Sopranos* have also helped HBO Films attract Hollywood's most distinguished talents. As recently as the late 1990s, "there's no way Al Pacino and Meryl Streep would have considered doing a movie there," explains co-executive producer Cary Brokaw of *Angels in America* (2003), "but their consistently good shows made it possible."[24]

Colin Callender, president of HBO Films, has subsequently nurtured relationships with other Hollywood A-list actors, such as Edward Norton and Brad Pitt, who are now co-executive producing and costarring in a ten-part miniseries based on Stephen Ambrose's historical bestseller, *Undaunted Courage: Meriwether Lewis, Thomas Jefferson, and the Opening of the American West.* Norton claimed that he and Pitt are "ecstatic that HBO wanted to take it on with us."[25] Chris Albrecht concludes that he and his executive staff never forget "what makes us different from other networks—and the reason why others are trying to emulate us—is that we support the creative talent. We don't steer them."[26]

4. *HBO is more than just a cable and satellite network and a production studio. It is also an internationally diversified entertainment corporation and a high-profile global brand.* The multifaceted nature of HBO Inc. is an important measure of its current position within the entertainment industry. HBO means several different things depending on the context, but first and foremost it is a foundational network that has generated a whole host of related spin-off channels from Cinemax to HBO Family to HBO Latino. Moreover, HBO the studio produces series, miniseries, made-for-pay-TV movies, documentaries, theatrical releases, and all sorts of related online and wireless content for its corporate Web site (www.hbo.com), its newly launched broadband video service, and HBO Mobile.[27] Most importantly, HBO is a diversified multinational corporation with longstanding ties throughout the Americas and overseas to the cable, television, home entertainment, and movie industries.

From a business perspective, therefore, HBO is best understood as an evolving work-in-progress that has aggressively expanded its worldwide presence from forty countries in 1999 to fifty in 2004 to seventy in 2007.[28] Instead of just syndicating its programming to other international television services, HBO has recently launched one branded channel after another in Britain, Germany, France, Spain, Italy, and Japan, to go along with its subscription services in eighteen different Latin American countries and six separate Central European nations, as well as HBO Asia and HBO India.[29] More than ever before, HBO is a global brand that is stamped onto an array of distinctive and generously funded series and specials that reinforce and strengthen its name recognition and reputation all around the world. HBO is thus a unique corporate entity where all of the various aspects of its commercial identity as a network, a production studio, a diverse multinational business enterprise, and a global brand work closely together to enhance one another.

5. *In a medium that is often characterized as being overwhelmingly feminine in orientation, HBO has carefully carved out a niche for itself that is strongly masculine in its programming appeals.* HBO's male identification strategies are easily recognizable across many of its most popular genres, including boxing, sports talk, stand-up comedy, and erotica (*Real Sex* [1990], *Cathouse* [2005], *Shock Video* [1993–]). Even

Hit series such as *Sex and the City* have already helped HBO
become a global brand; it now operates channels in Central
America, Britain, France, Germany, Spain, Italy, and Japan.
Its programming is now syndicated in seventy countries
around the world. (Left to right) Cynthia Nixon as Miranda
Hobbes, Kim Cattrall as Samantha Jones, Kristin Davis as
Charlotte York, and Sarah Jessica Parker as Carrie Bradshaw.

HBO's latest comedic successes have returned male characters to the forefront with such series as *Entourage*. Eric Murphy (Kevin Connolly, left) acts as manager to his lifelong friend, breakout star Vince Chase (Adrian Grenier, right), keeping him focused both personally and professionally.

HBO's dramas and documentaries regularly feature violence (*The Wire, Rome* [2005–7], *Baghdad ER* [2006]), coarse language (*Oz, Deadwood* [2004–], *Dane Cook's Tourgasm* [2006]), male narcissism (*Curb Your Enthusiasm* [2000–], *Entourage* [2004–], *A Father . . . A Son . . . Once Upon a Time in Hollywood* [2005]), and traditional male professions (*From the Earth to the Moon* [1998], *Autopsy* [1994–], *My Architect* [2003]). Ironically, all of HBO's male-oriented original series and documentaries are developed and supervised by three powerful women executives—studio head Carolyn Strauss, senior vice president for original programming Anne Thomopoulos, and documentary chief Sheila Nevins. As a result, HBO's masculinist tendencies are frequently mitigated by its numerous representations of strong women and the stories they enliven and enrich (as described in chapter 18 of this volume), providing audiences with a view of gender and sexuality that is as complex and revealing as any on television.[30]

6. *Profanity, nudity, and graphic violence are more than simple forms of titillation, shock, or brand differentiation for HBO. They are important by-products in its ongoing reformulation of standardized television genres from the gangster to the situation comedy to the western and the documentary, among many others.* HBO dramas and comedies are not for the faint of heart. From the beginning, the earthy depictions of *The Sopranos*, the frank conversations on *Sex and the City*, and the poetic brutality of *Deadwood*, each in their own way pushed the generic boundaries of their respective story forms well beyond anything that had appeared on TV before. When *The Sopranos* first aired in 1999, for example, its down-and-dirty underworld clashed brilliantly with Tony Soprano and his wife Carmela's nouveau riche suburbanite aspirations, but the conventional wisdom held that the series had limited syndication potential because of all the swearing, nude dancers, and slow-motion blood and gore. When the series finally debuted on A&E during January 2007, however, it "drew 4.3 million total viewers, making it the most-watched off-network series premiere in cable history and prompting a sigh of relief from A&E executives who dropped a record $2.55 million an episode for it in January 2005."[31]

TBS's experience was similar to A&E's when it syndicated *Sex and the City* for $750,000 per episode and began telecasting it in June 2004. The series quickly became "the No. 1 comedy in ad-supported cable among adults 18 to 34 and 18 to 49," smoothing its way into the local broadcast syndication market in September 2005.[32] The randy antics of the *Sex and the City* quartet were somewhat cleaned up in their subsequent ad-supported depictions, just as "alternative takes of the Bada-Bing girls in lingerie" and the f-word's change to "freakin'" were the sorts of mild alterations made to *The Sopranos* in its move to basic cable.[33] Overall, then, A&E found that "only about 30 seconds of the running time per episode of *The Sopranos* needed to be cut." Likewise, plans are already under way to adapt the profane and violent aesthetics of *Deadwood* to "basic-cable standards and practices" by producing "alternative shots and voice loops from HBO" to be used when the time comes to make that program available for syndication.[34] Over the last decade, in fact, the network's aftereffect has spawned so many imitators on other pay-TV, cable and satellite, and broadcast channels that the way has already been paved to a large extent for all of HBO's originals. With *The Sopranos,* specifically, A&E executive vice president and general manager Bob DeBitetto admits that "there was little need to edit" given the increasingly explicit nature of today's sexual and violent portrayals on TV.[35]

In the case of HBO's documentary programming, moreover, *Real Sex* is much more than just soft pornography. Instead, it provides a nonfictional framing and treatment of the bizarre yet all too "normal" locations of American sexuality. Similarly, *Taxicab Confessions* (1995–) is more than voyeurism or exploitative reality television. It is a window into the hearts and minds of poignant and enigmatic storytellers who tell audiences their intimate stories and experiences without realizing it. Yet even documentaries such as Spike Lee's *When the Levees Broke: A Requiem in Four Acts* (2006) bring us closer to its subject through the unadorned and intimate depictions of death and tragedy. Swearing and nudity can be the bells and whistles of unfettered and uncensored television programming. In works such as *When the Levees Broke,* however, viewers see and hear the emotional undressing of its subjects and are thereby brought much closer to the raw and unnerving realities of the street—something that the more-traditional broadcast and cable and satellite networks have always shied away from as being outside their taken-for-granted bounds of propriety (and thus deemed wholly inappropriate for their target audiences).

7. *In this way, HBO has also been at the forefront of fundamentally changing the viewing expectations of contemporary television audiences.* More so than even PBS, HBO has made TV advertisements both an unnecessary distraction and commercially obsolete with its subscriber-based business model. It has long featured weekly and monthly repeat telecasts of its film premieres as well as its original programming. It has also enhanced program availability by encouraging on-demand viewing; real-time viewing choices through multiplexing; and "appointment viewing" of its many original dramas, comedies, documentaries, and continuing sports series and specials. HBO, too, attracts the most-coveted audience cohort in television—eighteen- to fifty-four-year-olds—by the flexibility, convenience, and control it affords them in finding ways to incorporate its many viewing options into their busy

schedules. During its first incarnation prior to the 1990s, HBO became a household name by distributing uncut, uninterrupted movies by satellite to American subscribers from coast to coast. In the 2000s, HBO has expanded well beyond this initial objective of operating first and foremost as a movie service, where it currently gives many of the top studios in Hollywood a run for their money in producing groundbreaking innovative programs for television that regularly outperform and overshadow the theatrical films that it still carries.

"I think a lot of people have given up on the movies," concedes film critic David Thomson. "The truth is television, if you pick and choose, is a lot more grown-up and satisfying these days, beginning with HBO."[36] In the late 2000s, nearly 75 million viewers all around the world subscribe to its many TV and online services. Hundreds of millions more are familiar with the HBO brand.[37] The five-second prelude that precedes all of HBO's original programming is as singularly identifiable as any curtain raiser on television or the Internet. It begins with a loud hissing sound over an ordinary blackened frame. Suddenly the screen splits apart at the middle as white noise spills forth from top to bottom throughout the empty space. All at once, the hiss on the soundtrack transforms into a synthetic, choirlike chord. As if at the moment of creation, the HBO logo emerges triumphantly from the static. This opening fanfare perfectly captures the excitement and hubris of a network that has successfully reinvented itself into a diversified multinational media corporation. HBO's place in television history was already a given. Now its present and future role as a creative change agent that seamlessly operates among and between all the various segments of the global entertainment industry is also firmly established for many years to come.

Notes

1. George Mair, *Inside HBO: The Billion Dollar War between HBO, Hollywood, and the Home Video Revolution* (New York: Dodd, Mead & Company, 1988), 26, 158.

2. Elizabeth Lesly Stevens, "Call It Home Buzz Office: HBO's Challenge—To Keep the High-Profile Programs Coming," *BusinessWeek*, 8 December 1997, 77.

3. Polly LaBarre, "Hit Man: Chris Albrecht (Part 1)," *Fast Company*, September 2002, 90.

4. Mair, *Inside HBO,* 106.

5. "Jeffrey L. Bewkes: Home Box Office," *BusinessWeek,* 14 January 2002, 62.

6. "Six Feet Above (HBO Program Ratings)," *Variety,* 10 September 2001, 62.

7. Lisa de Moraes, "Sorry, 'Sopranos': 'Housewives' Still Rule the Roost," *Washington Post,* 15 March 2006, C7; "Six Feet Above (HBO Program Ratings)," 62.

8. Harry Castleman and Walter J. Podrazik, *Watching TV: Six Decades of American Television,* 2nd ed. (Syracuse, N.Y.: Syracuse University Press, 2003), 419.

9. Ibid.

10. George Vernadakis, "No Time Like Showtime: Putting a Premium on Originals," *Multichannel News,* 26 June 2006, at http://www.multichannel .com/index.asp?layout=articlePrint&articleid=CA6346382; Anne Becker, "HBO's Digital Strategy?" *Broadcasting & Cable,* 20 November 2006, at http://www.broadcastingcable.com/index.asp?layout=articlePrint&articleID=CA639 3268; Anne Becker, "A&E's *Sopranos*: A Hit," *Broadcasting & Cable,* 12 January 2007, at http://www.broadcastingcable.com/index.asp?layout=article Print&articleID=CA6407034.

11. David Bauder, "HBO Still Gold, but Slipping a Little," *azcentral.com* (Associated Press), 19 June 2005, at http://www.azcentral.com/ent/tv/articles/ 0619hbo.html.

12. Charlie McCollum, "Once-Invincible HBO Wavers; Buzz Shifting to Upstart FX," *San Jose Mercury News,* 19 July 2005.

13. McCollum, "Once-Invincible HBO Wavers."

14. Bauder, "HBO Still Gold, but Slipping a Little."

15. Marc Peyser, "HBO's Next Empire: All Roads Lead to 'Rome,'" *Time,* 22 August 2005, 67.

16. Mike Reynolds, "FX Ending *Shield,* Digging Up *Dirt,*" *Multichannel News,* 5 August 2006, at http://www.multichannel.com/index.asp?layout=artic lePrint&articleid=CA6341254.

17. These comparative averages—2.8 million viewers for *The Shield* as opposed to 4.6 million for *Big Love*—were calculated solely on the basis of ratings achieved by each premiere episode throughout the seasonal runs of these two series. This pattern nevertheless holds true for weekly cumes (cumulative ratings) as well: *The Shield* attracted an average of 5.65 million unduplicated viewers for four repeat telecasts each week, whereas *Big Love* garnered 7.1 million. Anne Becker, "HBO Shows *Big Love* Some Love," *Broadcasting & Cable,* 20 April 2006, at http://www.broadcastingcable.com/index.asp?layout= articlePrint&articleID=CA6326591.

18. Michael Malone, "Critic's Poll," *Broadcasting & Cable,* 18 December

2006, at http://www.broadcastingcable.com/index.asp?layout=articlePrint&articleID=CA6400557.

19. Vernadakis, "No Time Like Showtime."

20. HBO's aftereffect is widely admitted in industry circles by such television executives as Robert Greenblatt of Showtime, John Landgraf of FX, and Doug Herzog of Comedy Central. Herzog, for example, admitted that *Arrested Development* (Fox, 2003–6) is "more of an HBO show than a network show" and suggested that *Nip/Tuck* (FX, 2003), *The Shield*, and *Rescue Me* (FX, 2004) "kind of stole the HBO playbook a little, too." See Bernard Weinraub, "HBO: The Tough Act TV Tries to Follow," *New York Times*, 25 September 2004, B11.

21. "Expanding the Franchise: An Interview with HBO CEO Chris Albrecht," *Broadcasting & Cable*, 4 November 2002, 16A.

22. Virginia Rohan, "HBO Documentary Is Still Evolving," *Record* [Bergen County, N.J.], 4 May 2001, 47.

23. Denise Martin, "Ball Back in HBO's Court: Cabler Calls on *Six Feet Under* Creator for New Vamp Skein," *Variety*, 27 October 2005, at http://www.variety.com/index.asp?layout=print_story&articleid=VR1117931816&categoryid=14.

24. John Horn, "HBO Emerges as a Mecca for Maverick Filmmakers," *Los Angeles Times*, 19 September 2004, A1.

25. Michael Fleming, "HBO Will Blaze Trail with Mini: Pitt, Norton Join Cabler, NatGeo for 'Courage,'" *Variety*, 9 October 2005, at http://www.variety.com/article/VR1117930424.html?categoryid=14&cs=1.

26. "Expanding the Franchise: An Interview with HBO CEO Chris Albrecht."

27. R. Thomas Umstead, "HBO Plans Broadband Launch in '07," *Multichannel News*, 11 December 2006, at http://www.multichannel.com/article/CA6398584.html?display=Breaking+News; Karen Brown, "Sharpening the Moving Picture," *Multichannel News*, 3 April 2006, at http://www.multichannel.com/index.asp?layout=articlePrint&articleid=CA6321230.

28. Pravin Kumar, "Get the Best on HBO," *Times of India*, 10 December 1999, at http://www.lexis-nexis.com; Carla Power, "Art of the Tube; Market This: HBO Has Put America ahead of Britain as the Leader in Quality TV, and It's Rolling in Profits to Boot," *Newsweek International*, 1 December 2004, 77; Steve Clarke, "HBO Channels Its Presence O'Seas," *Daily Variety*, 20 January 2006, 10; Jeanne McDowell, "Media: The American Way," *Time Bonus Section*, November 2006, G25–G26.

29. Clarke, "HBO Channels Its Presence O'Seas." In Latin America, HBO has channels in Argentina, Bolivia, the Caribbean Islands, Chile, Colombia, Costa Rica, Curacao, Ecuador, El Salvador, Guatemala, Honduras, Mexico, Nicaragua, Panama, Paraguay, Peru, Suriname, and Venezuela. In Central

Europe, the network has services in Bulgaria, the Czech Republic, Hungary, Poland, Romania, and Slovakia.

30. Denise Martin, "HBO Promotes Top Programming Execs," *Daily Variety,* 5 February 2004, 7.

31. Becker, "A&E's *Sopranos:* A Hit."

32. Linda Moss, "Original Shows Add Fuel to Cable's Syndie Fire," *Multichannel News,* 29 May 2006, at http://www.multichannel.com/index.asp?layout=articlePrint&articleid=CA6338676.

33. "A&E Treads Lightly on *Sopranos* Violence," *Broadcasting & Cable,* 11 December 2006, at http://www.broadcastingcable.com/index.asp?layout=articlePrint&articleID=CA6398436.

34. Moss, "Original Shows Add Fuel to Cable's Syndie Fire."

35. "A&E Treads Lightly on *Sopranos* Violence."

36. Rob Nelson, "Hollywood's Phantom Menace: Why Are Movies So Bad? A Search for Answers with David Thomson," *City Pages* [Minneapolis St. Paul, Minn.], 29 June 2005, at http://citypages.com/databank/26/1282/article13454.asp.

37. Becker, "HBO's Digital Strategy?"; Umstead, "HBO Plans Broadband Launch in '07"; Linda Moss, "HBO Launches New Podcasts," *Multichannel News,* 14 June 2006, at http://www.multichannel.com/index.asp?layout=articlePrint&articleid=CA6343986.

CONTRIBUTORS

Kim Akass has coedited and contributed to *Reading* Sex and the City (I. B. Tauris, 2004), *Reading* Six Feet Under: *TV to Die For* (I. B. Tauris, 2005), *Reading* The L Word: *Outing Contemporary Television* (I. B. Tauris, 2006), and *Reading* Desperate Housewives: *Beyond the White Picket Fences* (I. B. Tauris, 2006). She is currently researching the representation of motherhood on American TV and is coeditor of the new journal *Critical Studies in Television,* as well as (with Janet McCabe) series coeditor for the Reading Contemporary Television book series from I. B. Tauris.

Michael Allen is lecturer in film and electronic media at Birkbeck College, University of London. His previous publications have included the books *Family Secrets: The Feature Films of D.W. Griffith* (British Film Institute, 2000) and *Contemporary U.S. Cinema* (Longman, 2002), as well as several articles on the history of media technologies and digital aesthetics. He has been a space enthusiast since he was ten years old.

Carolyn Anderson is professor in the Department of Communication at the University of Massachusetts. She has published dozens of articles and book chapters on film and television topics. With Tom Benson, she coauthored *Reality Fictions: The Films of Frederick Wiseman* (2nd ed., 2001) and *Documentary Dilemmas: Frederick Wiseman's "Titicut Follies"* (1991). A sabbatical year in Rome inspired a current book-in-progress, *Unpacking Travel Discourse: A Century of Roman Holidays.*

Christopher Anderson teaches in the Department of Communication and Culture at Indiana University and is the author of *Hollywood TV: The Studio System in the Fifties* (1994).

Gary R. Edgerton is professor and chair of the Department of Communication and Theatre Arts at Old Dominion University. He has published eight books (including *Thinking Outside the Box: A Contemporary Television Genre Reader* and *Television Histories: Shaping Collective Memory in the Media Age* for the University Press of Kentucky) and more than seventy book chapters and journal articles on a wide assortment of media and culture topics, and is coeditor of the *Journal of Popular Film and Television*.

Bambi Haggins is director of Graduate Studies and assistant professor in screen arts and culture at the University of Michigan. Her first book, *Laughing Mad: The Black Comic Persona in Post-soul America* (Rutgers, 2007), examines the place of black comedy as comedic social discourse in American popular consciousness.

Dana Heller is professor of English and director of the Humanities Institute at Old Dominion University. She is the author of *Family Plots: The De-Oedipalization of Popular Culture* (1995) and *The Feminization of Quest-Romance: Radical Departures* (1990), and the editor of *Cross Purposes: Lesbians, Feminists, and the Limits of Alliance* (1997), *The Selling of 9/11: How a National Tragedy Became a Commodity* (2005), and *The Great American Makeover: Television, History, Nation* (2006).

Jeffrey P. Jones is associate professor in the Department of Communication and Theatre Arts at Old Dominion University, where he teaches television studies, documentary film, and political communication. He is the author of *Entertaining Politics: New Political Television and Civic Culture* (Rowman & Littlefield, 2005), of numerous articles and chapters on the television talk show and the intersection of popular culture and politics, and is coeditor of *Satire TV: Politics and Comedy in the Post-Network Era* (New York University Press, forthcoming).

Linda J. Kim is a doctoral student in the Department of Sociology at the

University of California, Riverside, where she is undertaking a dissertation that utilizes a political, economic, and feminist analysis of *Sex and the City*. Her previous work has covered issues related to inequality in sport and transnational social movements.

David Lavery is chair in film and television at Brunel University, London. He is the author of numerous essays on literature and film, and the author/editor/coeditor of six books: *Late for the Sky: The Mentality of the Space Age* (Southern Illinois University Press, 1992), *Full of Secrets: Critical Approaches to* Twin Peaks (Wayne State University Press, 1994), *'Deny All Knowledge': Reading* The X-Files (Syracuse University Press, 1996), *Teleparody: Predicting/Preventing the TV Discourse of Tomorrow* (Wallflower Press, 2002), *This Thing of Ours: Investigating* The Sopranos (Columbia University Press, 2002), and *Fighting the Forces: What's at Stake in* Buffy the Vampire Slayer (Rowman and Littlefield, 2002). He is currently editing *Reading* Deadwood: *Realising the Western* (for I. B. Tauris) and *Master of Its Domain: Revisiting* Seinfeld, *TV's Greatest Show* (for Continuum).

Amanda D. Lotz is assistant professor of communication studies at the University of Michigan. She has published articles in *Critical Studies in Media Communication, Feminist Media Studies, Communication Theory, Journal of Broadcasting and Electronic Media, Television & New Media, Screen,* and *Women and Language*. She is the author of *Redesigning Women: Female-Centered Television after the Network Era* (University of Illinois Press, 2006) and *The Television Will Be Revolutionized* (New York University Press, 2007).

Michele Malach is associate professor of English/communications and gender/women's studies at Ft. Lewis College. She teaches classes in mass media theory and practice, publishes on television programming such as *The X-Files,* and is a member of the editorial advisory board of the *Velvet Light Trap*. She presented the paper "Behind Bars: Guilt, Redemption, and *Oz* Fans," at the 2003 MiT3: Television in Transition Conference. Her Catholic upbringing has given her an interest in all things dark, difficult, and naked.

Thomas A. Mascaro is associate professor in the School of Communication Studies at Bowling Green State University. He is a documentary historian whose research extends to social issues portrayed in fictional television adopting a documentary style. He also specializes in historical-critical analysis of specific documentary programs, producers, and the contexts and consequences of documentaries, and is researching a book on the NBC Washington documentary unit. His research has appeared in the *Journal of Popular Film and Television, Journalism History, Popular Culture Review, Television Quarterly,* and the *Encyclopedia of Television.*

Janet McCabe is research fellow (TV drama) at Manchester Metropolitan University. She is author of *Feminist Film Studies* (Wallflower, 2004) and coeditor of *Reading* Sex and the City (I. B. Tauris 2004), *Reading* Six Feet Under: *TV to Die For* (I. B. Tauris, 2005), *Reading* The L Word: *Outing Contemporary Television* (I. B. Tauris, 2006), and *Reading* Desperate Housewives: *Beyond the White Picket Fences* (I. B. Tauris, 2006). She is managing editor of the new journal *Critical Studies in Television,* as well as (with Kim Akass) series coeditor for the Reading Contemporary Television Book Series from I. B. Tauris.

Toby Miller is professor of English, sociology, and women's studies at the University of California, Riverside. He is the author of more than twenty books, the most recent of which is *Global Hollywood 2* (BFI, 2005). He is the editor of *Television & New Media* and coeditor of *Social Identities.*

Joanne Morreale is associate professor of communication studies at Northeastern University. She is the author of *A New Beginning: A Rhetorical Frame Analysis of the Presidential Campaign Film* (SUNY Press, 1991) and *Critical History of the Presidential Campaign Film* (Praegar Press, 1993). She is also the editor of *Critiquing the Sitcom* (Syracuse University Press, 2003), and has published several book chapters and journal articles on television and political film criticism.

Susan Murray is associate professor in the Department of Culture and Communication at New York University. She is the author of *Hitch*

Your Antenna to the Stars: Early Television and Broadcast Stardom (Routledge, 2005) and coeditor of *Reality TV: Remaking Television Culture* (NYU Press, 2004) with Laurie Ouellette. Her work has appeared in journals such as *Television and New Media* and *Cinema Journal,* as well as in numerous anthologies.

Horace Newcomb holds the Lambdin Kay Chair for the Peabody Awards and is professor of telecommunications at the University of Georgia, where he is also the director of the George Foster Peabody Awards Programs. He is the author of numerous works about television and is editor of the *Museum of Broadcast Communications Encyclopedia of Television.*

George Plasketes is professor of radio-television-film in the Department of Communication and Journalism at Auburn University. He is author of *Images of Elvis Presley in American Culture, 1977–1997: The Mystery Terrain* (Haworth, 1997) and coeditor of *True Disbelievers: The Elvis Contagion* (Transaction, 1995). He has published other articles on music, television, film, and popular culture, and is a member of the editorial board and discography editor for *Popular Music and Society.* He was never booked as a guest on *The Larry Sanders Show.*

Brian G. Rose is the editor of *TV Genres* (1985), author of *Television and the Performing Arts* (1992), *Televising the Performing Arts* (1996), and *Directing for Television* (1999), and coeditor of *Thinking Outside the Box: A Contemporary Television Genre Reader* (2005). He is professor in the Department of Communication and Media Studies at Fordham University.

Thomas Schatz is Warner Regents Professor (and former chairman) of the Radio-Television-Film Department at the University of Texas, where he has been on the faculty since 1976. He has written four books about Hollywood films and filmmaking and edited a recent four-volume collection on Hollywood for Routledge. His writing on film has also appeared in numerous magazines, newspapers, and academic journals, including the *New York Times,* the *Los Angeles Times, Premiere, The Nation, Film Comment, Film Quarterly,* and *Cineaste.* Schatz is also the founder and executive director of the newly created University of Texas Film Institute.

Ron Simon has been curator of television at the Museum of Television & Radio since the early eighties. Among the numerous exhibitions he has curated are The Television of Dennis Potter, Witness to History, Jack Benny: The Television and Radio Work, and Worlds without End: The Art and History of the Soap Opera, all of which featured screenings and a catalog. Simon is associate adjunct professor at Columbia University and New York University, where he teaches courses in the history of the media. He has written for many publications, including *The Encyclopedia of Television* and *The Encyclopedia of New York State,* as well as serving as host and creative consultant of the CD-Rom *Total Television.* He is a member of the editorial board of *Television Quarterly* and has lectured at museums and educational institutions throughout the country.

David Thorburn is professor of literature and comparative media at the Massachusetts Institute of Technology (MIT) and director of the MIT Communications Forum. His most recent books (coedited with Henry Jenkins) are *Democracy and New Media* and *Rethinking Media Change,* the launch volumes in the MIT Press series Media in Transition, of which he is editor in chief. Other writings include *Conrad's Romanticism* and many essays and reviews on literature and media in such publications as *Partisan Review, Commentary,* the *New York Times,* and the *American Prospect,* as well as in scholarly journals. His essays on television, written in the late 1970s and early 1980s, and his course, "American Television: A Cultural History," were among the first in the country to examine the medium in a humanistic context.

Television and Film Index

Italicized page numbers refer to illustrations.

General Index

Italicized page numbers refer to illustrations.